MW00780387

BACKCOUNTRY REVOLUTIONARY

James Williams (1740-1780)
with source documents

William T. Graves

Introduction by
Dr. Bobby Gilmer Moss

Published by
Woodward Corporation
doing business as
Southern Campaigns of the American Revolution Press
Lugoff, South Carolina

Published by
Southern Campaigns of the American Revolution Press
Woodward Corporation
Lugoff, South Carolina
http://www.southerncampaigns.org

First Edition
Printed in the USA

All Rights Reserved © 2012 by William T. Graves
Introduction © 2012 Bobby Gilmer Moss
"Patriots" © 2010 Dan Nance. Original in the collection of
author

No part of this book may be reproduced or transmitted
in any form or by any means, graphic, electronic, or
mechanical, including photocopying, recording, taping, or
by any information storage retrieval system, without written
permission signed by the author.

ISBN 978-0-9859999-0-2

1. United States–History–Revolution, 1775-1783–Battlefields–East (U.S.);
2. East (U.S.)–United States–History–Military–18th Century

Cover design by Sarah D. Phillips

dedicated to:

Charles B. Baxley and *David P. Reuwer*, valued friends and major forces for nurturing the expansion of scholarship relating to the American Revolution through their organization and sponsorship of numerous symposia, their tireless support of those seeking to learn more about our Revolutionary heritage and, in particular, their creating and editing of the online magazine, *Southern Campaigns of the American Revolution* posted at: http://www.southerncampaigns.org

C. Leon Harris, a valued friend and collaborator with the author in the celebration of the contributions of the soldiers who served in the Southern Campaigns of the American Revolution by creating an online database of the transcriptions of the pension applications filed by the veterans and their widows. The database is posted at http://revwarapps.org

To the memory of *Joseph C. M. Goldsmith*, one of the most unreservedly vocal advocates for the reinstatement of James Williams to his rightful place in our nation's history and an organizer of the General James Williams Chapter of the Sons of the American Revolution, Clinton, South Carolina.

Table of Contents

Maps and Photos

Maps

Photos

Epigraphs

I am, by the care of Providence, in the field in defense of my country. When I reflect on the matter, I feel myself distracted on both hands by this thought, that in my old age I should be obliged to take the field in defense of my rights and liberties, and that of my children. God only knows that it is not of choice, but of necessity, and from the consideration that I had rather suffer anything than lose my birthright, and that of my children.

James Williams to his son, Daniel, in a letter
dated June 12, 1779 (See Appendix 3)

I am informed that Colonel Williams with part of Sumpter's corps marched yesterday from Kerrel's Ford [Sherrill's Ford], giving out that they were going against you. My informant saw only 150, but the enemy told him they had 400 more—that is not good authority. Sumpter has had a quarrel with Williams about command and is gone to Hillsborough to refer it to Gates.

Charles, Lord Cornwallis to Patrick Ferguson
October 1, 1780[1]

---

[1] Ian Saberton, Arranger and Editor, *The Cornwallis Papers: the Campaigns of 1780 and 1781 in the Southern Theater of the American Revolutionary War,* 6 vols. (Uckfield, East Sussex, England: The Naval & Military Press Ltd. 2010) Vol 2, 158.

The General has the pleasure to congratulate the army on an important advantage lately obtained in North Carolina[2] over a corps of 1400 men, British troops and new Levies, commanded by Col. Ferguson. The militia of the neighbouring country under Colonels Williams, Shelby and others having assembled to the amount of 3000 men detached 1600 of their number on horseback to fall in with Ferguson's party on its march to Charlotte; they came up with them at a place called King's mountain, advantageously posted, and gave them a total defeat, in which Colonel Ferguson with 150 of his men were killed — 800 made prisoners, and 1500 stand of arms taken. On our part the loss was inconsiderable. We have only to regret that the brave Col. Williams was mortally wounded.

This advantage will in all probability have a very happy influence upon the Successive operations in that quarter. It is a proof of the Spirit and resources of the country.

General Order promulgated by General
George Washington, October 27, 1780, from his
Headquarters at Totowa.[3]

Among those who fell [at King's Mountain] was Colonel James Williams of Ninety Six, a man of an exalted character, of a career brief but glorious. An ungenerous enemy revenged themselves for his virtues by nearly extirpating his family; they could not take away his right to be remembered by his country with honor and affection to the latest time.

George Bancroft, historian[4]

---

[2] *Sic*, South Carolina.

[3] George Washington Papers, Letterbook 5, Image 204 of 411, posted by the Library of Congress at http://lcweb4.loc.gov/cgi-bin/query/P?mgw:8:./temp/~ammem_6LM8 (viewed 9/9/12).

[4] George Bancroft, *History of the United States of America* (New York: Little, Brown, 1875), 10: 339.

Acknowledgments

The resources available at the South Carolina Archives in Columbia, South Carolina; the North Carolina Archives in Raleigh, North Carolina; the South Caroliniana Library at the University of South Carolina; and the Robinson-Spangler Carolina Room at the Mecklenburg Public Library, Charlotte, North Carolina, were liberally used in researching this book. I especially acknowledge with much gratitude the able and resourceful assistance of Robert H. Mackintosh, Jr., now retired from the South Carolina Department of Archives and History, and Sam Fore, then at the South Caroliniana Library, now sharing his talents and insights as the curator of a private collection in Texas.

Many thanks for the passionate support of Lawrence Young and the late Joe Goldsmith, two tireless enthusiasts from Laurens County, South Carolina, who generously shared their time and efforts to educate me about James Williams' home county, its history and the many other residents of that area who fought valiantly in the Revolution. We were often joined in our explorations by Williams' descendant, Pierce Stockman of Greenwood County, whose encouragement has been invaluable.

A huge debt of gratitude is owed to the Clinton (South Carolina) High School Junior ROTC, and its commander, Lt. Col. Joel Rexford (U.S.A., Ret.), for their contributions to the reclamation and preservation of the memory of Williams, the regiment he led and the men who served with him. In honor of their heroes, the JROTC renamed itself the "Little River Regiment." In addition to maintaining the Williams family cemetery in Laurens County, the JROTC located what is believed to be the foundation and mill race of Williams' former under-shot mill on the Little River in Laurens County.

Ranger Brian Robson and former ranger Frank Stovall of the Musgrove Mill State Historic Site in South Carolina have been wonderful in the support they have given me in researching the many heroes who fought on both sides of that battle.

Dr. William L. Williamson, formerly the Nicholas Murray Butler Librarian at Columbia University (1954-1964), and now retired from the University of Wisconsin, Madison, is appreciated for his "random act of kindness" in deciphering some of the nearly illegible portions of the Draper Manuscripts.

A heart-felt "huzza" to Charles B. Baxley, the publisher and editor of the online magazine, *Southern Campaigns of the American Revolution (SCAR)*, and to David P. Reuwer, a major contributor to SCAR and now the editor of the magazine of the American Revolution Association—two very good friends and supporters of all who share an interest in the American Revolution. Their work can be enjoyed at www.southerncampaigns.org and in *American Revolution* magazine. Special thanks to Charles for taking the time to read and offer comments and suggestions for this edition of this book. Our fellow explorer, John Allison, has added immeasurably by locating and identifying the sites where many of the battles and skirmishes of the Revolution occurred in the Carolina backcountry.

All who study the role of South Carolina and its citizens in the American Revolution owe a debt to Dr. Bobby Gilmer Moss which is well beyond anyone's ability to repay. Through his tireless efforts, the identities and contributions of literally thousands of men and women of various ethnic backgrounds have been rescued from the anonymity to which time and indifference might otherwise have consigned them.

I acknowledge with much gratitude the wonderful aid given by John A. Robertson in preparing some of the maps used in this book. Without these maps (which appear on pages 84 and 127), the story told here would be much less informative. John is an indefatigable and selfless cartographer and expounder of the Revolution. His willingness to share his knowledge and expertise has benefited all who have availed themselves of his generosity. Not the least of his many contributions is the posting of resources relating to the Southern Campaign to be found at http://lib.jrshelby.com.

Sarah D. Phillips formatted the book and designed the cover using Dan Nance's wonderful painting *Patriots*. Thanks to both of them for their contributions.

Lastly, a huge thank you to my wife Sally for all her patient help and assistance in guiding me through the formatting and indexing of the book.

Notwithstanding the support and assistance of others, the opinions expressed, observations made, and the conclusions reached in this book are solely my own, and any errors in them are my responsibility.

Preface to Second Edition

The first version of what has now become this book was published in 2002 under the title, *James Williams: An American Patriot in the Carolina Backcountry.* Since that time, my interest in Williams and his family has not waned. I hoped that the admittedly premature publication of that book would lead to contact with members of the Williams family and others who had additional letters and other documents shedding further light on the life and times of this fascinating warrior in America's fight for independence from Great Britain. Unfortunately, although I have made contact with some wonderful descendants of Williams, none have had any such documentation.

Further research, however, has yielded some additional documents relating to Williams and his family. The information gleaned from them is reflected in this book. I chose to rename the book to emphasize the broader scope of this edition. The first edition was largely a defense of Williams against the accusations made by South Carolina Patriot militia Colonel William Hill in his memoirs. While I continue to build upon that defense, the reader will find discussion of the influences that bore on Williams' determined commitment to the Whig fight for independence; Williams' library; and his activities as a frontier miller, merchant, distiller and planter, all in an effort to give a fuller, more informative view of Williams and his time. In addition, the chapter on Musgrove Mill has been totally rewritten to reflect what I now believe to be a much more accurate description of that important engagement. Finally, several documents have come to light that significantly bolster the arguments against the validity of Hill's accusations. Based on those documents and my earlier research, I have come to the conclusion that Hill's accusations against Williams are totally baseless. That viewpoint is much more vigorously argued in this edition.

One reviewer of the first edition criticized it as falling far short of being a biography of Williams and much more like a lawyerly defense of him against Hill's allegations. I did not claim for that edition, nor do I for this one, that it is a biography of Williams. Unfortunately for those of us who are intrigued by Williams, he left too few "footprints in the sands of time" to allow a full portrait of his life. Dying as he did at the age of 39 in the midst of his country's struggle for independence, the opportunity for him to build on his legacy was denied. Glimpses into his foreshortened life are all we have.

Some have asked me why I have such interest in Williams. In addition to an abiding interest in our American history in general, part of the answer lies in family legend. My father's name was Thomas Williams Graves. His father's name was William Williams Graves. My grandfather's grandfather, born in 1801, was the first Thomas Williams Graves. In addition, a brother, uncle and several cousins all bear "Williams" as part of their name. Family lore held that our pride in the Williams name sprang from our being descendants of William Williams, one of the signers of the Declaration of Independence. Cursory research, however, quickly dispelled this lore since that William Williams was the consummate "Connecticut Yankee." He was unlikely to have descendants residing in North Carolina in the early 1800s. Knowing that family lore is often grounded on a tainted recollection of connections to past significant people or events, research uncovered that our family was descended from Henry Williams (1734-1785), the great grandfather of the original Thomas Williams Graves. In doing research on Henry Williams, I found that he had served as the executor of the estate of his brother Colonel James Williams, who at one time was celebrated as "the hero of King's Mountain." Mystery solved! The perpetuation of the Williams name in our family was a way of celebrating our tie to this significant participant in the American Revolution.

It is my hope, however, that this tie to Williams has not colored this presentation. In this as well as the earlier edition, I have tried to interpret the facts objectively. Readers are encouraged to draw their own conclusions as to the contributions Williams made not only to winning America's independence from Great Britain, but to the spread of Eurocentric culture to what were the wilds of the American West as it existed shortly before the Revolutionary War. To aid the reader, appendices are included which contain the entire text of Hill's memoirs as well as other important documents written by and about Williams. If in pressing my conclusions as to the accusations made by Hill against Williams, it strikes some readers that I have been overly adversarial in favor of Williams, I urge those readers to weigh that advocacy against the heretofore unchallenged acceptance of Hill's memoirs as a fair statement of history. As I have found invariably to be the case, there are always at least two sides to every story. In this book, I have attempted to tell Williams' story.

William T. Love

[One editorial note about the formatting of this book: Readers will observe that I have chosen to place the references at the bottom of the page instead of using the now customary practice of placing them either at the end of chapters or at the end of the book. I hope readers will indulge a personal pet peeve of mine: I dislike having to spend time flipping back and forth locating references. Footnotes (as opposed to endnotes) were used in my college days, and I continue to have a very strong preference for their use. The only exception to that approach is found in Appendix 13 where formatting constraints dictated the use of endnotes.]

Introduction

William T. Graves, with an open mind and clear eyes, has examined primary records and, through interpretation of them, laid out the true story of the life of Colonel James Williams. I feel safe in saying that few Americans have ever heard of or know anything about Williams, one of the true heroes of the American Revolution. What little they may know is no doubt tainted by the attacks on his character made long after his death by one of his rivals. In this book, Graves persuasively tells us why Williams deserves to be remembered as a very significant player in America's winning its independence from Great Britain. Graves has conclusively dealt with the confusion and misunderstandings that has tainted his name.

Reared in North Carolina, Williams moved his young family to what was then the wilds of the South Carolina Backcountry just prior to the Revolutionary War. Williams sought to create a new life for him and his family settling near the line between what was then the frontier settlements and the lands long controlled by the Cherokee Indians and other Native American tribes. There he played a prominent role in politics while establishing himself as a planter owning over 3,500 acres, a merchant and mill owner. When clouds formed heralding the onset of war between England and its American colonies, Williams played a significant role in organizing and leading the Whig (Patriot) militia in what was from the start a bloody civil war in the Carolina Backcountry.

The Revolution in frontier South Carolina pitted neighbor against neighbor, sons against fathers, brothers against brothers, even wives against husbands, etc. as strongly held beliefs on both sides found violent expression in forces almost equally divided between those who thought America's future lay in remaining loyal to Great Britain and those who thought that America must break its ties with the King and Parliament.

From the first shots fired at Ninety Six in late 1775 between opposing Whig and Loyalist militias to his death at age 39 from wounds suffered at the pivotal victory at

King's Mountain in early October 1780, Williams remained steadfastly dedicated to the cause of American liberty from England. After the British regained control of Georgia and Charleston fell in May of 1780, such noted South Carolinians as Andrew Williamson, Andrew Pickens and Leroy Hammond lost hope in the American cause and took parole from the British. Williams remained steadfast in his determination to drive the British out of the American colonies. After briefly serving with Thomas Sumter in the summer of 1780, Williams organized and led a refugee force of South Carolinians who continued the struggle in engagements fought at Musgrove Mill and Kings Mountain.

The role that Williams and the men he led as well as the men under Sumter's Lieutenants Edward Lacey and James Hawthorn played in the Whig victory at Kings Mountain has long been unappreciated and largely unacknowledged by historians. While the Overmountain men of western North Carolina (now Tennessee) and Virginia have been celebrated in America's history for their role at Kings Mountain, very little has been said about South Carolina's role in that battle. Graves' account of Williams' forces there highlights the fact that South Carolinians played a major part in securing that victory.

The story of Williams and his family's contribution to America's freedom does not end with his death. His family suffered unimaginable losses when his home was occupied and burned, his wife and family dispossessed not once but twice by the Loyalists and British during the summer of 1780, and his two oldest sons brutally murdered by a former neighbor in late 1781. Williams' obscurity is to a large degree attributable to an attack on him by Colonel William Hill, one of Thomas Sumter's lieutenants and trusted friends. Hill wrote his memoirs of the Revolution late in his life when, by his own family's admission, his memory was compromised by old age. Because his memoirs, however, are one of the few first hand recollections of the war as fought in South Carolina, many historians have been led to ascribe to them unquestioned validity, especially those portions of it in which

Hill viciously attacks Williams. Graves' book is a detailed examination of Hill's accusations against Williams and a well-deserved vindication of Williams.

Williams played a very significant role in the bloody civil war that was the American Revolution as fought in the Carolina Backcountry. His leadership in the engagements at Musgrove Mill and Kings Mountain helped secure America's freedom from Great Britain.

Some of history's most interesting characters are those who left too few footprints in the sands of time to spawn a full-blown biography. James Williams is one of those characters. In the 39 years he lived he interacted with too few people and wrote too few letters marking the events of his life for us to ever develop a full understanding of him and his accomplishments. None of his contemporaries left accounts of his life. Yet it is through the study of what we can glean about the lives and activities of men such as Williams that some of history's most memorable events are best told and understood. Graves has told Williams' story for all to enjoy, and it is a story that all who are interested in the founding of the United States should know.

Bobby Gilmer Moss, PhD
History Professor Emeritus and
Author of numerous books on the Revolutionary War

Chapter One
Prologue

James Williams died from wounds suffered at the Battle of King's Mountain fought October 7, 1780. He was one of the heroes of the American Revolution, yet few people have ever heard of him. The battle at King's Mountain pitted roughly equal numbers of American Patriots against American Loyalists. It highlights the civil war that was the American Revolution as fought in the South. Few Americans today know anything about the battle, and far fewer have ever heard of Williams. In part, the obscurity of both the battle and the men who fought it is due to a pervasive lack of interest in the battles fought to secure America's freedom from Great Britain, particularly those battles fought in the South. Until the recent publication of works countering this trend, historians have tended to focus most of their attention on engagements in the northern and middle colonies with military operations in the war culminating – as if by some inexplicable happenstance, if not miracle – with the surrender of the British at Yorktown in Virginia in the fall of 1781.[5] Far from being either inexplicable or a miracle, the British demise at Yorktown was the direct result of the many battles and skirmishes fought in the Carolinas and Georgia, not the least of which was the Battle of King's Mountain fought in upstate South Carolina.

In addition to the general lack of knowledge about the Southern Campaign, Williams' obscurity has been assured by fellow Patriot militia officer Colonel William Hill (1741-1816). In his old age in 1814, Hill dictated his memoirs

---

[5] Some of the more recent books examining the war as fought in the South include: John Buchanan, *The Road to Guilford Courthouse: The American Revolution in the Carolinas* (New York: John Wiley & Sons, Inc., 1997); Dan L. Morrill, *Southern Campaigns of the American Revolution* (Mt. Pleasant, SC: The Nautical & Aviation Publishing Co. of America, 1993); David K. Wilson, *The Southern Strategy: Britain's Conquest of South Carolina and Georgia, 1775-1780* (Columbia: University of South Carolina Press, 2005); Terry Golway, *Washington's General: Nathanael Greene and the Triumph of the American Revolution* (New York: Henry Holt and Co., 2005).

of the Revolution as fought in the South. One of Hill's self-avowed motivations for writing those memoirs was to present his view of the reasons why Thomas Sumter (1734-1832), Hill's mentor, was not present at the pivotal Battle of King's Mountain. Hill lays the blame for Sumter's absence squarely at the feet of James Williams, leveling against him accusations of usurpation and abuse of power arising from Williams' attempt to assume command of the South Carolina backcountry militia.

Starved for eyewitness accounts of events during the Revolution, historians have latched onto Hill's memoirs as the one and only version of the events related by Hill. Hill's attack has had a pervasively pernicious effect on Williams' treatment by subsequent historians and authors, including, most recently, his portrayal by former President Jimmy Carter in his historical novel about the Revolution, *The Hornet's Nest.*[6] Prior to a defense of Williams written by this writer in 2002,[7] no one, however, had critically examined the validity of Hill's accusations against Williams. From such an examination, tempered by the facts contemporary documents yield about him, a picture of Williams emerges as one of America's many heroes in its fight for independence from Great Britain, a legacy which should not be tarnished by Hill's accusations.

The outcome of the battle for independence waged by the fledgling United States against Great Britain was uncertain in October 1780. After reaching a military stalemate with the Whigs in the North and Middle states, the new British strategy was to raise her flag in the South, recruit loyal locals to fight their kinsmen, and divert red-coated regular troops to other strategic spots in the widening global war. To test this strategy, the British easily re-captured Georgia in 1778 and 1779. In the spring of 1780, British Commander-in-Chief of the British Army in North America, Sir Henry Clinton (1730-1795), successfully laid siege to Charleston, then the fourth largest city in the United States and a key port

[6] Jimmy Carter, *The Hornet's Nest: A Novel of the Revolutionary War* New York: Simon & Schuster, 2003).

[7] William T. Graves, *James Williams: An American Patriot in the Carolina Backcountry* (San Jose: Writers Club Press, 2002).

for establishing a sustainable base for supplying the forces deployed in the South. The capture of Charleston was the first step in a strategy to win the war of rebellion by dividing the southern states from their northern compatriots. Having taken Charleston, the English quickly planted enclaves throughout the South Carolina backcountry to pacify the population and encourage enlistment in Loyalist militia units, with which the British expected to swell their ranks with more than enough men to assure the success of their southern strategy. Deeming the first phase of the strategy successfully implemented, Clinton turned over command of the British army in the South to his second in command, Charles (second Earl and first Marquis) Cornwallis (1738-1805). Clinton returned to New York intent on engaging George Washington's army in the North while Cornwallis reestablished the Crown's sovereignty in the South.

On August 16, 1780, Cornwallis soundly routed the Southern Department of the Continental Army under General Horatio Gates (1728-1806) at Camden, South Carolina. Two days later, British dragoons and light infantry under the command of Lt. Col. Banastre Tarleton (1754-1833) surprised Col. Thomas Sumter[8] and his forces[9] at Fishing Creek, South Carolina, effectively putting to flight the largest militia unit in the Carolina backcountry. As a result of British and Tory successes at these two engagements, there was no organized American military force capable of opposing Cornwallis' army in the South. By late September, 1780, Cornwallis had marched out of South Carolina and occupied Charlotte, North Carolina, to prepare for the next step in the invasion of the South. It fell to a ragtag collection of Patriot militia units from the Carolinas, Georgia, and Virginia to thwart Cornwallis' plans.

[8] In the absence of any governmental authority to bestow command, following the fall of Charleston on May 12, 1780, some of the refugee Whig militiamen from South Carolina elected Sumter as their 'general.' That rank, however, was not officially bestowed on Sumter until his meeting with South Carolina's Whig governor in exile, John Rutledge, in Hillsborough, North Carolina, on October 6, 1780.

[9] Sumter's forces consisted largely of refugee militiamen from South Carolina, but he also had in his camp 100 Maryland Continental infantry and artillery, and 300 North Carolina militia which Gates had detached to Sumter's camp.

At the Battle of King's Mountain, this hurriedly collected band of Patriot (or Whig) militia units annihilated the right wing of Cornwallis' army which he had sent into the western frontier of North and South Carolina to recruit Loyalists to join his army and to suppress the Whigs of that region. This wing of Cornwallis' army consisted of approximately 1,100 Loyalists (or Tories) under the command of Major Patrick Ferguson (1744-1780).[10] The Whig units opposing Ferguson consisted of roughly the same number of men. The Patriot victory at King's Mountain, coupled with staunch Patriot resistance and over extended supply lines, forced Cornwallis to retreat from Charlotte to Winnsborough, South Carolina, to rebuild and re-supply his army. His rebuilding task was made much more difficult by the increased reluctance of the backcountry Loyalists to openly support the British army in the face of the success enjoyed by their Patriot neighbors at King's Mountain.

Cornwallis' three-month encampment at Winnsborough bought valuable time for Gates to begin to rebuild the Continental Army in the South, and for General Nathanael Greene (1742-1786) to replace Gates as commander of the southern Department of the Continental Army. Greene assumed that command in Charlotte on December 2, 1780, and immediately began planning the strategy for the confrontations with Cornwallis which would play a determinative role in the sequence of events that would ultimately lead to Cornwallis' surrender at Yorktown in the fall of 1781.

The group of eight or nine militia colonels and other officers from the Carolinas, Georgia, and Virginia led

[10] Ferguson of Edinburgh, Scotland, was simultaneously a major in the 71st Regiment of Foot of the British Army while holding the rank of lieutenant colonel in the Loyalist militia as well as Inspector of Militia, a post to which he had been appointed by Sir Henry Clinton prior to his departure from South Carolina in June 1780. In the contemporary documents relating to Ferguson, he is referred to by both ranks. Ferguson was noted as making patented improvements to an innovative breach-loading rifle which now bears his name. He is buried on King's Mountain in a grave marked by the traditional Scottish cairn. M. M. Gilchrist, *Patrick Ferguson: "A Man of Some Genius,"*(Edinburgh: National Museums of Scotland, 2003).

the American Whig units that fought at King's Mountain. Williams was one of those officers. From the beginning of the American Revolutionary War, Williams took an active and unwavering role as a Patriot politician and militia officer. Residing in the backcountry of South Carolina at the time the war broke out, Williams lived in the heart of the area that experienced a vicious civil war between loosely organized militia units supporting the Tories and similar units supporting the Whigs. As a captain commanding a small company of Patriots, Williams served in the first Battle of Ninety Six District in November 1775, the first engagement of the Revolution in which shots were fired in the Carolina backcountry. As the war progressed, he was promoted to lieutenant colonel and then to colonel in command of his own militia regiment. Williams fought in a large number of significant battles and skirmishes throughout the South. None of those engagements, however, was as important as the Battle of King's Mountain, the battle in which he sustained wounds from which he would subsequently die.

Some believe that at the time of his death Williams had risen to the rank of brigadier general in the South Carolina militia, though to date, no definitive proof of such a promotion has been found. The story of his rise to high rank within the South Carolina militia presents an opportunity to study the civil war fought in the backcountry areas of South Carolina after the fall of Charleston in May of 1780, and the resulting breakdown of civil government. That story also provides an opportunity to study the competition between Williams and Thomas Sumter, the "Fighting Gamecock," for control of the Whig militia in western South Carolina. Some understanding of that rivalry helps put into context the attack on Williams' character and motives later leveled by Hill in his memoirs.

Hill portrays Williams as a self-interested plunderer who misled South Carolina's governor, John Rutledge (1739-1800), regarding his role in a small but significant battle that occurred on August 19, 1780 at Musgrove Mill on the Enoree River in South Carolina. Hill claims Williams' motive for making exaggerated claims to Rutledge was to gain promotion to brigadier general of the South Carolina militia, a position to which Sumter's men had previously unofficially elected Sumter. Further, Hill accuses Williams of having tried unsuccessfully to divert to his home district a sizable portion of the Patriot militia, the so-called "overmountain" men, marching from western North Carolina and Virginia to engage Ferguson's Loyalist militia. According to Hill, Williams was more interested in protecting his private interests than in confronting the Tories under Ferguson at King's Mountain. Hill goes so far as to state without qualification that Williams' death at King's Mountain was the result of shots fired by Patriots unhappy with Williams' attempt to usurp command of the South Carolina militia from Sumter.

Close examination of contemporary events and documents, however, provides a different view of Williams and calls into serious question the validity of Hill's accusations. Neither Hill nor Sumter was present at the Battle of King's Mountain. Missing this battle must have been extremely disappointing to Sumter. By his own admission, Hill wrote his memoir to explain Sumter's absence from the battle, a battle that was one of the most significant battles fought in the South solely by opposing militia groups. During the lifetimes of Hill and Sumter, the battle came to be appreciated as one of the pivotal engagements fought in the South. Hill's preoccupation with explaining Sumter's absence from that battle, and the fact that no other contemporary sources support Hill's accusations against Williams, should cause historians to be skeptical of those allegations. Unfortunately for Williams' reputation, Hill's view of events has been repeated by subsequent generations of historians including, most notably, Lyman C. Draper, the historian and document collector who, in 1881, wrote the history of the battle still considered by many to be the definitive work on the battle.

Hill's accusations, and the many unquestioning repetitions of them, have so damaged Williams' reputation that the National Park Service, as custodian of the National

Battleground at Kings Mountain,[11] used to present visitors with apologetic references to Williams' role in the battle. Up until 2003, when the Park Service replaced all of the placards in the Park, one of the interpretive markers located along the trail leading up to the battleground informed visitors that Williams' death in the battle redeemed him in the eyes of his fellow commanding officers, while noting that Williams was killed after the surrender of the Loyalists by "an unidentified gun."[12] The obvious inference to be drawn from these statements was that the National Park Service ascribed validity to Hill's accusations not only that Williams' behavior prior to the battle required redemption, but also that his death occurred in a manner that at least suggests that Williams was killed by the Patriots, not the Loyalists. Even today, after rewriting their placards and installing a new interactive display at the Park, there is only passing (and erroneous) reference to Williams as the commander of a group of "30 North Carolina" militiamen at the Battle of King's Mountain. That such scant acknowledgment of Williams' role is demonstrably wrong can be readily seen from a cursory review of the pension applications and other contemporary accounts given by the men who proudly fought in that battle under Williams.

Contrary to the too-often repeated portrayal of Williams given by Hill, Williams was an ardent and uncompromising Patriot. His steadfast commitment to the Patriot cause exacted the severest sacrifices from him and his family. That commitment and those sacrifices entitle him to much better

[11] The National Park Service refers to King's Mountain as "Kings Mountain." Except when referring to the National Battleground, the location will be referred to as "King's Mountain" the form of the name preferred by General William Moultrie. In his memoirs, Moultrie states that the name of the location was derived from its ownership by a family named "King." William Moultrie, *Memoirs of the American Revolution, so Far as it Related to the States of North and South Carolina, and Georgia,* (New York: David Longworth, 1802), 1:243 fn.

[12] The text of the marker read as follows:
"Colonel James Williams of South Carolina, poorly esteemed by his fellow commanders, redeemed himself in their eyes by his heroic action at King's Mountain. Ironically, he lost his life after the surrender struck by a ball from an unidentified gun."

treatment than he has enjoyed at the hands of historians. Rather than a legacy as a self-interested usurper to which Hill and most historians have consigned him, Williams deserves and is entitled to be remembered and hailed as one of America's true heroes in its war for independence.[13]

Throughout the Revolution, many conflicts in command arose among the Revolutionaries, some of which were only resolved by duels between the differing claimants unwilling or unable to put aside their own egos. Different autonomous strata of Continental, state troops, and militia organizations mixed in with issues arising from dates of rank, resulted in multiple squabbles as to who outranked whom in this complex pecking order. With virtually no functioning government, the normal civilian resolution of these disputes bogged down. This was certainly the case in South Carolina after the fall of Charleston, when its provincial legislature ceased to function and its Governor was forced to flee the state altogether. Although the legislature invested Governor John Rutledge with virtual dictatorial powers prior to the fall of Charleston, he was in exile from his state and possessed no means by which to enforce any edicts he might issue. There was no authority handy to define areas of command or to replace the militia system's hierarchy after the surrender of Gen. Andrew Williamson, the South Carolina backcountry's militia commander.

Complicating the relations between Sumter and Williams are the underlying duties of an area militia regimental commander. Sumter, a former Continental officer who resigned his commission and position in 1778, had no particular military assignment and is not known to have held any official militia rank in South Carolina in the summer

---

[13] Attacking the credibility of Hill's account, however, should not be read as an attempt to take away or diminish any of the credit to which both Sumter and Hill are rightfully entitled. They both played significant roles in winning the war. Indeed, there can be no doubt that the role played by Sumter was far more important than that played by Williams, if for no other reason than that Sumter lived to command the backcountry militia in engagements subsequent to King's Mountain and to serve his state in the United States Congress, both as a Representative and as a Senator.

of 1780 when he returned to active service following the British raid on his plantation in an unsuccessful attempt to capture him immediately after the fall of Charleston. On the other hand, Williams was the duly commissioned chief militia officer in a specific geographic area of western South Carolina. He was responsible for protecting this area from Indians, quieting the local Tories, and expelling the British forces which invaded his area after the fall of Charleston, forces which were largely comprised of provincials from the New England and middle states, at least until the local Tories had time to steel their nerve to join the invading forces. Both commanders had their families, personal plantations, mills, and wealth threatened in different areas of South Carolina, and it is easy to see why they held starkly differing views of their immediate responsibilities and strategy. Sumter, although clearly a charismatic and experienced military leader, had never been Williams' superior officer, and whatever association they had in the summer of 1780 was clearly voluntary.

Chapter Two
Personal Background

Williams was born November 10, 1740, in Hanover County, Virginia.[14] He was the fourth child (third son) of Daniel Williams (1710-1759) and Ursula Henderson.[15] Sometime prior to 1759, Daniel and Ursula Williams moved their family to Granville County, North Carolina, located in the upper piedmont region of that state just south of the Virginia line.[16] Daniel Williams' will is dated November 15, 1759, and was probated December 18, 1759, in Granville County. In his will, Daniel divides his estate among his wife, Ursula, and his seven children, including sons James, Joseph, John, Daniel, and Henry Williams and daughters, Marya Goodman and Mary Mitchell.[17]

Little is known about Williams' education other than that he learned to read and write, at least in some rudimentary

---

[14] Lewis Shore Brumfield, *The Williamses and The Hendersons¬ Descendants of John "The Wealthy Welshman" Williams* (Yadkinville, NC: n.p., 1991), 284 found in the Mecklenburg Public Library, Charlotte, North Carolina. J. D. Bailey, *Commanders at King's Mountain* (Spartanburg, SC: Band & White, 1924, reprint with index added Greenville, SC: A Press, 1980), 250, gives Williams' year of birth as 1737, but this was the year of the birth of Williams' older brother, John Williams, who also resided in the backcountry of South Carolina.

[15] Brumfield, *Williamses*, 284.

[16] Granville County was founded in 1746 from Edgecombe County. At its formation, it was the northwestern most county and had no boundary to its west. Orange County was founded, in part, from the western most portion of Granville in 1752 and the land that later became Caswell, Person, Chatham and Alamance Counties were subsequently formed from Orange. Parts of Granville were later incorporated into parts of Person, Northampton, Franklin, Warren and Vance Counties. David L. Corbett, *The Formation of the North Carolina Counties 1663-1943*, (Raleigh: State Department of Archives and History, 1950)

[17] Thomas McAdory Owen, *History and Genealogies of Old Granville County, North Carolina 1746-1800* (Greenville, SC: Southern Historical Press, 1993), 70-71. Daniel Williams' will, dated November 15, 1759, was probated December 18, 1759. In his will, Daniel names his wife, Ursula, and his seven children, Marya Goodman, Henry Williams, John Williams, James Williams, Joseph Williams, Mary Mitchell, and Daniel Williams, Jr. and his son-in-law, Benjamin Goodman. Daniel named his wife and his sons, John and James, as his executors. His estate included 18 books, 26 Negroes, 59 head of cattle, 11 sheep, 7 horses and mares, 53 tame hogs, and an unknown number of wild hogs.

fashion. The documents known to have been written by him show that he had some appreciation for spelling and grammar. However, almost all 18th century backcountry residents, including Williams, displayed a remarkably imaginative ingenuity in their practical application of these conventions. As will be explored in more detail in Chapter 5, he collected a library that included not only the theological tracts to be expected in a library of this period, but also literary works, dictionaries, and practical instruction manuals on accounting, farming, husbandry, and other skills that a backcountry gentleman would need to employ in the everyday life of his family.

Williams is believed to have married Mary Wallace in 1762.[18] No evidence of this marriage has been found other than in secondary sources that do not list supporting documentation. Since Williams and his family had moved from Hanover County, Virginia, to Granville County, North Carolina, by 1762, it seems likely that Mary was a native of that latter region, although it is possible that he met Mary when working the farm his father left him in Halifax County, Virginia, or when traveling in other parts of the South.

In physical appearance, Williams is described as having been five feet, nine inches tall, and corpulent. His complexion was dark, his hair and eyes were black. He had a large nose with nostrils so large when distended as to provide one of his militiamen with a coarse jest of an excuse for absence from muster. The man explained that he and "... the boys had been hunting and had treed a possum in the Colonel's nose."[19] There are no known drawings or paintings of Williams.

When he died in 1759, Williams' father left him an 800-acre farm in Halifax County, Virginia. Williams sold this land in 1774 and there is no evidence that he or his family actually ever took up residence on that farm. Williams apparently continued to live in Granville County, North Carolina, until about November 1773 when he and his wife Mary sold land there to his brother Joseph. In his will dated November

---

[18] Bailey, *Commanders*, 250.
[19] *Ibid.*, 315.

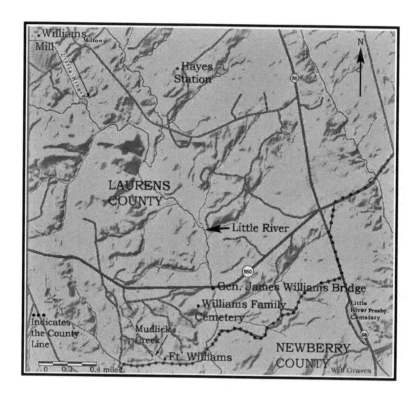

This map depicts the area of Laurens and Newberry Counties in which Williams acquired approximately 3,600 acres of land. There he built his home, a blockhouse (Ft. Williams), a mill and operated a store. The location of Williams' mill is shown where John Black later operated his mill, believed to have been acquired by Black from Williams' heirs. Williams probably operated his store at or near the mill.

1773, Joseph refers to the land on Great Island Creek that he bought from his brother James and on which said brother "now lives." Joseph further refers to the land as the former residence of Samuel Henderson, who was possibly a relative of James' mother, Ursula.[20]

At some point after November 1773, James and Mary moved permanently to the Little River area of Ninety Six District between the Broad and Saluda Rivers, South Carolina. The land Williams acquired there and on which he established his plantation was located in what are today Laurens and Newberry Counties. It is likely that Williams and his brother John moved to this part of South Carolina at approximately the same time, since both served in the First Provincial (South Carolina) Congress in 1775 as representatives of the district between the Broad and Saluda Rivers.[21] Once settled in South Carolina, Williams established himself as a farmer, miller, and merchant.[22]

Williams acquired substantial land holdings in Ninety Six District by 1775. In a mortgage dated January 13 and 14, 1775, Williams, describing himself as a merchant and resident of Little River, St. Mark's Parish, mortgaged more than 1,450 acres of land to Rowland Rugeley, merchant, of

[20] Zae Hargett Gwynn, comp., *Estate Abstracts of the Wills and Records of Granville County, NC 1746-1808* (Rocky Mount, NC: Joseph W. Watson, 1973), 38-39. Joseph Williams' will, dated November 3, 1773, was probated May Court 1774. Joseph names his wife, Sarah, and daughter, Mary Williams. He states that if his wife is with child, then that child is to get certain land. Joseph refers to land he bought from his brothers, John and James Williams. The land he bought from brother James Williams was formerly the dwelling place of Samuel Henderson and is located on Great Island Creek. Joseph also describes the land as being where his brother James "now lives."

[21] N. Louise Bailey and Elizabeth Ivey Cooper, eds., *Biographical Directory of the South Carolina House of Representatives, Volume III*: 1775-1790, (Columbia: University of South Carolina Press, 1974-1992), 3: 766-769.

[22] James Williams to Daniel Williams, 12 June 1779, R. W. Gibbes, ed., *Documentary History of the American Revolution: Consisting of Letters and Papers Relating to the Contest for Liberty, Chiefly in South Carolina, From Originals in the Possession of the Editor, and Other Sources,* (New York: D. Appleton & Co., 1857; reprint, Spartanburg, SC: The Reprint Company, 1972), 2: 115. Appendix 3.

Charlestown[23] *(sic)* to secure payment of a debt of £4,700 (South Carolina money) owed to Rugeley. Williams lists the land in three tracts: the first consisting of 1,250 acres[24] on which he now lives located "on both sides of Little River of Saludy" (*sic*, Saluda), the second being 200 acres lately purchased from Peter Strozer, and the third tract containing unspecified acreage recently acquired from Peter Krozert.[25]

In his last will and testament dated June 12, 1780, Williams left substantial tracts of land to his wife and children. The acreage of the tracts specifically listed by their sizes totals 3,550 acres. Williams left several other tracts without stating their acreages. In addition, Williams made specific bequests of his mill and mercantile businesses as well as his 33 slaves. From this information, it is clear that Williams was a substantial landowner in the area in which he lived.[26]

Williams called his plantation "Mount Pleasant." In picking the site for his plantation, Williams chose not only a

[23] Charleston, South Carolina, was referred to in contemporary eighteenth century writings as "Charlestown" or "Charles Town." Its name was not officially changed to Charleston until after the Revolutionary War.

[24] The exact location of Williams' 1,250-acre plantation is shown on the map found in Jesse Hogan Motes III and Margaret Peckham Motes, *Laurens and Newberry Counties South Carolina: Saluda and Little River Settlements 1749-1775: Neighborhood Maps, and Abstracts of Colonial Surveys and Memorials of Land Titles Including a Case Study Jonathan Mote 1727-1763 Migration to Little River*, (Greenville, SC: Southern Historical Press, 1994), 124.

[25] Brent H. Holcomb, abstractor, *South Carolina Deed Abstracts 1773-1778* (Columbia, SC: SCMAR, 1993), 178. Williams also notes that the 1,250-acre tract was "lately purchased" from John Caldwell, another prominent Patriot militia leader in the South Carolina backcountry. It seems likely that the references to "Peter Strozer" and "Peter Krozert" are to the same man.

[26] Will Book A, page 113, Clerk of Courts Office, Caswell County, North Carolina. The few records that survive regarding the administration of his estate in South Carolina provide additional evidence that Williams' holdings there were sizeable. In the Laurens County Estate Book A-I, page 6, there is an appraisal of his estate including 33 Negroes. This appraisal was not filed until July 17, 1788, indicating, perhaps, the disarray of normal affairs in the South Carolina backcountry following the end of British occupation of Charleston in 1782. (Another explanation for the delay in probating his estate in South Carolina, however, may have been the claims the State of North Carolina made on the estate. For a discussion of these claims, *See* footnotes 147-149 and accompanying text.) Mary Williams Griffin, widow of Col. Williams, and her new husband, Joseph Griffin, filed the appraisal. Likewise, there is record on page 20 of that same estate book of an appraisal of 300 acres of land owned by Williams and valued at £100.

location suitable for his mill on the Little River (a tributary of the Saluda River), but also a site with artesian wells from which an abundant flow of water supplied the needs of Williams, his family, his slaves, and livestock. The presence of this source of clean, healthy water was to prove an attraction to Patriots and Loyalists alike during the Revolution as Mount Pleasant was occupied on at least four different occasions, three times by the Loyalists and lastly by Nathanael Greene in the summer of 1781 following his unsuccessful siege of the British outpost at Ninety Six.[27]

Several sources describe Williams as being a devout Presbyterian.[28] The Little River Presbyterian Church founded in 1761 claims Williams as one of its founding members.[29] If this is so, it would be evidence that Williams began his acquisition of land in the area between the Broad and Saluda Rivers long before he moved his family down from North Carolina in late 1773. There are several enticingly interesting grants of land in this area to one or more individuals named James Williams dating from as early as 1756.[30] Efforts to conclusively prove that the grantees are the James Williams who is the subject of this book, however, have not been successful. The grants are too limited in their

---

[27] Greene sent several letters from his camp at Williams Fort on June 20 and 21, 1781, during his withdrawal from the siege of Ninety Six. Dennis M. Conrad, ed., *The Papers of General Nathanael Greene, Volume VIII 30 March-10 July 1781,* (Chapel Hill: The University of North Carolina Press, 1995), 8: 419-432.

[28] *See,* e.g., William Henry Foote, *Sketches of North Carolina: Historical and Biographical, Illustrative of the Principles of a Portion of Her Early Settlers* (New York: Robert Carter, 1846), 270.

[29] The Little River Presbyterian Church (now the Little River Dominick Presbyterian Church) was founded by the Rev. Jesse Creswell in 1761. George Howe, *History of the Presbyterian Church in South Carolina,* (Columbia, SC: Duffie & Chapman, 1870), 1: p 520.

[30] There are a number of grants to a James Williams in the South Carolina Archives which pre-date Williams' taking up permanent residence in South Carolina in late 1773. The grants which are most likely to relate to Williams are as follows [the references given are to the document's location in the Archives' records]: (1) Series Number S213019; Vol. 0007; Page, 00170; Item: 00. November 22, 1756, William Henry Lyttleton, Capt. General, Governor and Commander in Chief of the Province of South Carolina grants, on behalf of King George the Second, 300 acres of land on the "North East side of Saludy on a Creek called Raburns Creek

description of the land, and the records of later conveyances are too meager to definitively tie these grants to Williams. That Williams may have been making forays into the area well before he permanently moved his family into that wilderness seems very plausible, and would provide an explanation for why he would have participated in the formation of a church long before making that move. Also, his early presence in the community would help explain why he was elected to represent the area so soon after he moved there in late 1773. If Williams were in the area early enough to have participated in the founding of the Little River Presbyterian Church in

butting and bounding by Vacant Land on every side" to James Williams. There is no recitation of consideration paid or services rendered; (2) Series Number S213184; Vol. 0008; Page, 00573; Item: 03. Plat dated December 12, 1759, of 100-acre tract belonging to James Williams in Berkeley County and "situate, lying and being in the fork between broad and Saludy rivers and is bounded on a branch of said Saludy river, Called and known by the name of Bush creek and is buting and bounding all round on all sides on vacant Land." The plat was drawn by , D. S.; (3) Series Number S111001; Vol. 0010; Page, 00283; Item, 01. The memorial recites:

> A Memorial exhibited by James Williams, to be registered in the Auditor's office, agreeable to Order of Council, and to a condition of the Grant hereafter mentioned of a plantation or tract of land containing four hundred acres, situate in Berkley County; Bounded on all sides by vacant lands; Survey certified the 3rd of July 1770 and granted the 12th day of Oct. 1771 to the Memorialist, two years from the date. In witness whereof he hath hereunto set his hands the 17th day of Oct. 1770. s/ Jno. Dooly, D. S. s/ Wm. Anderson In the margin of this entry the following appears: "James Williams 400 Acres 20RT: 3/ sterling or 4/ Proc. Money."; (4) Series Number S213184; Vol. 0021; Page. 00478; Item, 02. Plat dated August 25, 1770, of 150-acre tract belonging to James Williams and "situate and being in Craven County, on Reyburn's Creek Butting and bounding N. on land ? to Saml. Millhouse, all other sides bounds on vacant land." The plat was drawn by Jno. Caldwell; (5)Series Number S213184;Vol. 0021; Page, 00477; Item, 01. Plat dated October 15, 1770, of 200-acre tract belonging to James Williams and "situate, lying and being near the head of Beaver Creek in Craven County; Bounding N. W. on James Miller's land, N. on James Douglass' land, and all other sides on vacant land ." The plat was drawn by Wm Glascock, D. S.; (6) Series Number S213184; Vol. 0021; Page, 00469; Item, 02. Plat dated April 15, 1771, of 300-acre tract belonging to Daniel Williams and being "in Barkley (sic) County, in the fork between Broad River and

1761 and to be aggressively amassing land holdings there, he would have been known to most of his new neighbors well before taking up permanent residence there.

Williams' letters to his family written while away with his militia unit clearly depict a man of deep faith. In a letter dated June 12, 1779, Williams tells his eldest son, Daniel, that he is "...by the care of Providence, in the field in defence *(sic)* of my country." Williams urges his son to "... take these hints. In the first place, consider that the eye of God is on you, and to secure His blessing is the only way to make yourself, and those that are concerned with you, happy; for to fear God

Saludy, on the Drafts of a small branch of Bush River called Williams' Beaverdam Branch and bounded Wwardly by land held by John Williams and part vacant, and Ewardly part by land held by Major John Caldwell, and part by Clement Davis, and Swardly by land part laid out to Wm Biggs and part to James Williams, and N. ly by vacant land." The plat was drawn by Enoch Pearson, D. S.; (7) Series Number S213184; Vol. 21; Page, 00476; Item, 01. Plat dated April 22, 1771, of 300-acre tract belonging to James Williams and "situate and being on the Beaver dam, a branch waters of Saludy, in Craven County, Bounded N. on land laid out to George Goggins and on lands of James Williams, laid out do or on S. W. on lands laid out to William Belton, S. E. on land said to be the property of one Winchester, to the E. on land laid out to Elijah Teague, and on land laid out on The Bounty, all other sides bounds on vacant lands." The plat was drawn by Jno. Caldwell, D. S.; (8) Series Number S213184; Vol. 0021; Page, 00475; Item, 02. Plat dated April 4, 1772, of 100-acre tract belonging to James Williams and "situate lying and being on a branch of Beaver Creek, on the N. E. side of Wateree River, in Craven County: Bounded on the E. by Wm Russell's and Drury Arinton's, on the N. W. by vacant and Alexr. Tomb's land, on the S. W. by Thos. Gouger's land, and on the S. by Lewis Clark's land.

Plat was drawn by Jas. Bredin, D. S.; (9) Series Number S213019; Vol. 0021; Page, 000214; Item, 00. Grant dated 12th October 1770, signed by William Bull, granting 400 acres to James Williams, said land being situate in Berkley County, Bounded on all Sides by Vacant Land; and (10) Series Number S372001; Vol. 04VO; Page, 00132; Item: 01. James Williams (but no wife mentioned) deeds to Thomas Creighton for £230, one hundred acres land in the Parish of St. Mark's, Craven County bounded in part by Beaver Dam Creek adjoining lands of James Miller and James Douglass, being part of a 200-acre tract granted to said James Williams. This appears to relate to the land referred to in paragraph 5 above.

is the first and great command."[31] On September 30, 1779, Williams wrote asking his wife to join with him in reliance "... on Him that is able to protect and defend us, in all danger, and through every difficulty; but, my dear, let us, with one heart, call on God for his mercies, and that his goodness may be continued to us, that we, under his blessing, may have the happiness of enjoying each other's society once more."[32] In July of 1780, Williams tries to bolster his family's resolve in the face of the resurgence of Tory militia activity in the backcountry following the fall of Charleston to the British. He makes exaggerated claims as to the forces being marshaled to confront the British and Tories, no doubt in the hope of encouraging her and giving some comfort to her anxiety over his absence from home when Tory units were occupying his plantation and plundering the surrounding area. Williams tells his wife: "The uncertainty of your situation is my great mortification; but let our joint prayers meet in Heaven for each other and our bleeding country."[33]

[31] Appendix 3.
[32] Appendix 4.
[33] Appendix 8.

Chapter Three
Involvement in South Carolina Politics

Williams' public service in South Carolina began with his election to the First Provincial Congress (convened January 11, 1775) for the "District in the Forks Between the Broad and Saludy *(sic)* Rivers." He and his brother John were two of ten representatives from that district. As a member of that Congress, Williams was one of the signers of the "Association" adopted June 3, 1775, when word of the outbreak of fighting in Massachusetts reached Charleston. That Association proclaimed:

> The actual commencement of hostilities against this continent by the British troops, in the bloody scene on the 19th of April last near Boston—the increase of arbitrary impositions from a wicked and despotic ministry—and the dread of insurrections in the colonies are causes sufficient to drive oppressed people to the use of arms. We, therefore, the subscribers, inhabitants of South Carolina, holding ourselves bound by that most sacred of all obligations— the duty of good citizens toward an injured country, and thoroughly convinced that, under our present distressed circumstances, we shall be justified before God and man, in resisting force by force...do unite ourselves under every tie of religion and honor, and associate as a band in her defence against every foe...hereby solemnly engaging that whenever our continental or provincial councils shall decree it necessary, we will go forth and be ready to sacrifice our lives and fortunes to secure her freedom and safety. This obligation to continue in full force until a reconciliation shall take place between Great Britain and America, upon constitutional principles—an event which we most ardently desire. And we will hold those persons inimical to the liberty of the colonies who shall refuse to subscribe this association.[34]

[34] The original of the Association is in the manuscripts collection at the South Carolina Department of Archives and History, Columbia, South Carolina in Series S 131 008. For an excellent article on the Association in South Carolina, See Christopher Gould, *"The South Carolina and Continental Associations: Prelude to Revolution,"* South Carolina Historical Magazine, 87 (1986), 30-48.

The members of the First Provincial Congress appointed Williams and his brother John to "the committee ... for effectually carrying into execution the continental *(sic)* Association."[35]

The Williams brothers actively discharged their duties on this committee. In a letter dated July 24, 1775, Thomas Fletchall (1725-1789), himself a member of the First Provincial Congress but also a prominent South Carolina Tory and militia unit commander who resided in the Fairforest area near Williams' plantation, wrote to Henry Laurens as President of the Council of Safety complaining about the Williams brothers.[36] Fletchall states that he received a letter dated July 4, 1775, from Messrs. John Caldwell, John and James Williams in their capacity as "Committee men" requesting Fletchall to call his militia regiment together in order for his men to sign the "association paper." Fletchall reports that he complied with that request on July 13, but that no member of his regiment would sign the Association, preferring instead, with the men of the regiments commanded by Col. Robert Stark and Col. John Savage,[37] to draft their own resolutions. Fletchall did not include a copy of these separate resolutions in his letter.[38] The content of those resolutions, however, is made clear by Fletchall in the closing of his letter where he states: "I am Resolved and do utterly Refuse to Take up arms against my King untill *(sic)* I find it my duty to do Otherwise and am fully Convinced Thereoff *(sic)*." Fletchall asserts "Some of Our Highland Gentlemen are very aspirering *(sic)* & fond of Commission, Thinking to gitt *(sic)* in favour

[35] William E. Hemphill, ed., *The State Records of South Carolina: Extracts from the Journals of the Provincial Congresses of South Carolina, 1775-1776* (Columbia: South Carolina Archives Department, 1960), 6.

[36] David R. Chesnutt, et al., eds., *The Papers of Henry Laurens*, 15 vols. (Columbia: University of South Carolina Press, 1968-1999), 10: 244-6.

[37] Stark and Savage would later become Whigs and hold commissions in the South Carolina Whig militia. Bobby Gilmer Moss, *Roster of South Carolina Patriots in the American Revolution* (Baltimore: Genealogical Publishing Co., Inc., 1983), 891 and 846 respectively.

[38] *See* Chesnutt, *Laurens Papers*, 10:255-6 for a copy of the "Loyalist Association."

with Gentlemen in Town." Since Caldwell and the Williams brothers are the only people named in the letter as being supporters of the Association, it seems fair to assume that they are the "Highland Gentlemen" of whom Fletchall is complaining and against whom Fletchall is clearly leveling the charge that they over-zealously pursued their duties as committee men in order to curry favor with the political powers in Charleston.

Additional evidence of Williams' early commitment to the Patriot cause arises in the journal kept by Rev. William Tennent. In early August 1775, Tennent, along with William Henry Drayton and others,[39] was sent by the Council of Safety to the upper part of South Carolina to induce the Tories there to sign the Association and to agree to bear arms in the cause of Liberty. In his journal, Tennent chronicles the very modest success their efforts achieved. In an entry dated August 24, 1775, Tennent notes that he lodged at "Mr. James Williams's, one of the committee, an honest and liberal man, who lives in the midst of Cunningham's Company" [Robert Cunningham being one of the most ardent Tories in the upper part of South Carolina].[40] After spending several days in the backcountry "haranguing" the Tories with speeches lasting up to two and a half hours, Tennent returned to Williams' home on August 29. Tennent spent that evening with Williams, and the next day Williams loaned Tennent his saddle horse so that Tennent's horses could recover from their protracted journey through the backcountry. Williams kept Tennent's horses and chaise until September 7, 1775, when Tennent dispatched a man to Williams, returning

---

[39] The other members of the Drayton commission were Oliver Hart, a Baptist minister, Joseph Kershaw, a prominent backcountry merchant, planter, legislator and militia colonel and Richard Richardson. Like Tennent, Reverend Hart kept a diary. *See* William T. Graves, *"Reverend Oliver Hart's Diary of a Journey to the Backcountry,"* Transcribed and Annotated, *Southern Campaigns of the American Revolution,* Vol. 2, No. 4, (April 2005) http://www.southerncampaign.org/mag.php (viewed 9/9/12).

[40] Gibbes, *Documentary History,* 1: 230.

Williams' horse and regaining his horses and chaise, now recovered and restored to good condition.[41]

Williams' connection to the Drayton/Tennent backcountry mission, however, was not limited to hosting Rev. Tennent. Drayton and Tennent's efforts in the backcountry failed to persuade many Tories to sign the Association. In fact, they seemed to have polarized the factions to the point of precipitating imminent civil war between the Whigs and Tories in the South Carolina backcountry. By September 1775, the threat of war induced Thomas Fletchall, the aging Tory, to negotiate a peace with Drayton. Fletchall, on behalf of himself and his followers and in an effort to avoid bloodshed amongst neighbors, promised never to "aid, assist or join" the British troops sent to the colony. Drayton soon learned, however, that Robert Cunningham did not consider himself or his followers bound by Fletchall's agreement. Drayton wrote to Cunningham urging the Tory to reconsider his rejection of the agreement and instructing Cunningham, if he chose to respond, to send his response by Williams.[42] Cunningham's refusal to agree to the same promises made by Fletchall resulted in Cunningham's emergence as the leader of the Loyalists in the South Carolina backcountry who were willing to take up arms in support of their king. Their resolve led to the firing of shots in what became the first Battle of Ninety Six.[43]

Williams and his brother John were again elected as representatives, along with the resolute Loyalists, Col. Thomas Fletchall, Robert Cunningham and thirteen others, of the "Upper District Between Broad and Saluda Rivers (Spartan)" in the Second Provincial Congress (convened November 1, 1775).[44] The election of this diverse group of men with polar opposite views of their political allegiances underscores that, at least at the onset of the Revolution, the

---

[41] *Ibid.*, 1: 232-235.

[42] *Ibid.*, 1: 191-192.

[43] Marvin L. Cann, *"Prelude to War: The First Battle of Ninety Six: November 19-21, 1775,"* *South Carolina Historical Magazine* 76 (1975), 197-214.

[44] Hemphill, *SC Papers*, 24.

political processes in the backcountry accommodated both views. The Williams brothers also served as representatives in the First General Assembly (1776) and Second General Assembly (1776-1778) from that same district.[45]

The session records for the various state legislative assemblies between 1775 and 1780 contain several references to Williams. On March 22, 1776, Captain James Williams was appointed, along with Major Andrew Williamson, Col. John Lewis Gervais, and Captain John Winn, to a committee charged "... to consider, among other things, a proper division of the militia, and how the same may be rendered most serviceable to the public."[46] On March 23, 1776, the Congress ordered £4,000 (South Carolina money) to be paid "... into the hands of Col. John Thomas, Capt. James Williams and Mr. John Prince ... to be expended and laid out, as Commissioners, for erecting and completing ..." the construction of an ironworks on the property of William Wofford, Esq.[47] On April 2, 1776, Williams was granted a leave of absence from the General Assembly for unstated reasons. On April 11, 1776, he was appointed by the General Assembly along with his brother John as one of five commissioners to supervise elections for the "middle or Little District" of Ninety Six.[48]

These early sessions of the nascent state legislature brought Williams into contact with most of the men who were to be the leaders of the South Carolina Whig government and armed forces. His fellow legislative members included Henry Laurens, William Moultrie, Richard Richardson, William Henry Drayton, Christopher Gadsden, John Rutledge, Edward Rutledge, Andrew Williamson, Charles Pinckney, Charles Cotesworth Pinckney, Andrew Pickens, Thomas Sumter, Joseph Kershaw, John Lewis Gervais, John Winn, and Thomas Neel.

---

[45] *Ibid.*, 306, 314.
[46] *Ibid.*, 246.
[47] *Ibid.*, 249.
[48] *Ibid.*, 19, 51.

In 1778, Williams ran unsuccessfully as a candidate for the single seat available in the state Senate representing the Little River District.[49] In the first senatorial election held in South Carolina, Robert Cunningham, the prominent backcountry Tory, soundly defeated him. In his book about the American Revolution, General Joseph Johnson tells the following story about the contest between Williams and Cunningham:

> In the course of this election…when the people were called together, Williams was about addressing the people; before he began, he noticed that Robert Cunningham was standing at his elbow. He said to him, "you stand too close to me." Cunningham coolly replied, without changing his position, "I stand very well where I am." A blow from Williams followed the reply: a fight ensued in which Mrs. Williams, with a true woman's devotedness, took part with her husband by seizing Cunningham by *his cue.*[50] She was gently disengaged by a gentleman present, and the rencontre *(sic)* terminated in Cunningham's favor.[51] (Emphasis in original)

It is easy to imagine the anxiety that Cunningham's election (not to mention his success in the fist fight) caused Williams. For Tory sympathies to be strong enough in his home district to elect the man who had commanded the Tory militia in the first Battle of Ninety Six would have given Williams and the other Whigs in the district ample reason to fear for the safety of their families and property in the midst of such diehard Tory sympathizers.

The last reference to Williams in the contemporary legislative record is an entry for Tuesday, February 8, 1780, for the Second General Assembly. There, notice is taken of Col. Williams' having received £1,000 (South Carolina money) on August 16, 1779, for "provisions for his regiment."[52]

---

[49] Bailey/Cooper, *Biographical Dictionary,* 767.

[50] A braid of hair worn hanging down behind the head usually associated with sailors.

[51] Joseph Johnson, *Traditions and Reminiscences Chiefly of the American Revolution in the South: Including Biographical Sketches, Incidents and Anecdotes,* (Charleston, South Carolina: Walker & James, 1851), 484.

[52] Hemphill, *SC Papers,* 285.

It is interesting to note that Thomas Sumter, like Williams, served as a member of the First and Second Provincial Congresses as well as the First and Second General Assemblies. Sumter represented the District Eastward of the Wateree River. He also served on the committee to execute the Association in Camden District, a responsibility that Williams discharged in his home district.[53] The opportunity for the two men to get to know each another and to serve together in the legislature has a direct bearing on the accusations that Sumter's subordinate, William Hill, later leveled against Williams. It is also interesting to highlight, as previously noted, that it was Williams, not Sumter, who was chosen by his fellow members of the Provincial Congress to serve on the committee to organize the militia and to determine how best to employ it in the service of the newly-formed state.[54] Might Sumter have taken offense at his omission from what surely was viewed as one of the more important committee assignments in the fledgling legislature? Perhaps this early acquaintance gave rise to the rivalry between the two men. At a minimum, it is difficult to believe that Sumter and Williams did not become reasonably well acquainted while serving together in these legislative bodies.

[53] N. Louise Bailey, Mary L. Morgan, Carolyn R. Taylor, eds., *Biographical Directory of the South Carolina Senate* 1776-1985 (Columbia: University of South Carolina Press, 1986), 3: 1567-70. In addition, Sumter served as an elected representative in both the State legislative bodies and the United States House of Representatives and Senate until December 1810, when he retired from public life.

[54] On February 18, 1776, the initial membership of that committee consisted of: "Col. [George Gabriel] Powell, Col. [Charles C.] Pinckney, Col. [Richard] Richardson, Col. [Stephen] Bull, Col. [William] Thomas, Col. [William] Wofford, Col. [Thomas] Neel, Col. [Daniel] Horry, Maj. [James] Mason, Maj. [Joseph] Kershaw, Capt. [LeRoy] Hammond, Capt. [William Henry] Harrington, Capt. [Hezekiah] Maham, Capt. [Arnoldus] Vanderhorst and Capt. Wm Skirving." By resolution passed March 22, 1776, the committee was enlarged to include: "Major [Andrew] Williamson, Col. [John Lewis] Gervais, Capt. [James] Williams and Capt. [John] Winn." Hemphill, *SC Papers*, 246.

Chapter Four
Backcountry Merchant, Miller & Planter

Merchant

Williams refers to himself as a merchant in a number of publicly filed documents. Unfortunately, it appears he left no records or inventories of the goods he sold. Indeed, inventories for backcountry merchants of this era are few and offer little insight into how these merchants conducted their business; how they obtained merchandise; or what precise merchandise they offered to their customers. Intuitively, since most of those backcountry customers were self-sufficient yeoman farmers who had little or no hard currency or specie with which to purchase ready-made goods or luxury items, it seems likely that the merchandise offered was limited to the items that they could not produce for themselves but which, if not absolute necessities, were required to make their lives more bearable. Such items would have included salt, refined sugar, coffee, tea, spices, windowpanes, lead, gun powder, gun flints, gun locks, knives, axes, hoes, plows, hatchets, ceramic ware, saltpeter (which, in its mineral state, was used as a meat preservative and, in its organic state, as an ingredient in gun powder), nails, fish hooks, straight razors, cooking pots and pans, dishes, pewter tableware, glassware and jars, canning lids, paraffin wax, bolts of cloth, sewing needles, thread, buttons, ribbon, quills, ink, writing paper, tobacco pipes, spectacles, and seed grains. That these items were offered by backcountry merchants is confirmed by the few estate inventories of merchants as are available.[55]

By virtue of the letters he wrote his son and wife instructing them on the conduct of his mercantile business while he was away on militia duty, it is known that Williams in fact sold salt

---

[55] *See* Rachel N. Klein, *Unification of a Slave State: The Rise of the Planter Class in the South Carolina Backcountry, 1760-1808* (Chapel Hill: The University of North Carolina Press, 1990); and George Lloyd Johnson, Jr., *The Frontier in the Colonial South: South Carolina Backcountry, 1736-1800* (Westport, CN: Greenwood Press, 1997).

and whiskey.[56] From his letter dated September 30, 1779, to his wife, Williams discloses that he purchased at least some of the salt he sold in blocks that he then ground in his gristmill and sold by the bushel. The presence of 100 gallons of brandy and 69 gun locks in the inventory of his estate indicates that Williams might well have held these items in his stock of merchandise. It is equally possible, however, that these items were held in his capacity as the commander of a backcountry regiment of militia for whom brandy and gun locks would have been essential items for the conduct of war.

With the exception of the brandy and gun locks, the inventories and appraisals of Williams' personal property after his death do not include the large quantities of mercantile items expected in a merchant's estate. The most likely explanation for the lack of merchandise is that the fall of Charleston in May 1780, and the subsequent occupation of the backcountry by the British, cut Williams off from Camden and Charleston, his sources of resupply. What goods he may have had on hand at that time would have been depleted fairly readily by either the purchase of the remaining stock by his neighbors or its loss as plunder to his Tory neighbors emboldened by the British successes. Since neither Williams nor his heirs were hesitant to claim reimbursement from the State for losses suffered during the war, loss of stock due to plunder seems unlikely because no such claims exist. More likely, Williams' neighbors stocked up on whatever goods he had left when the British invasion of the backcountry became inevitable after the fall of Charleston. The likelihood of this latter explanation is enhanced by the presence in Williams' estate of miscellaneous sizable bonds and notes, some or all of which may well have been given in exchange for merchandise purchased on credit. Indeed, Williams stipulated in his will written June 12, 1780, exactly one month after the fall of Charleston, that the "store book & the bonds & Notes & other accounts" were to be collected by his executors and the proceeds used to pay off his debts.[57]

[56] Appendices 2 and 4.
[57] Appendix 7.

Unfortunately, the "store book" is not known to still exist and the inventories of his estate only list the bonds and notes in the aggregate.

Williams borrowed heavily to finance the acquisition of inventory for his business. In January 1775, describing himself as a merchant living on the Little River in the Parish of St. Marks, Williams borrowed £4,700 pounds sterling from Rowland Rugeley, one of Charleston's leading merchants and a fellow member of the first South Carolina Provincial Congress.[58] To secure this debt, Williams pledged a substantial portion of his land holdings including the 1,200 acres he had recently acquired from John Caldwell. On February 13, 1777, Williams borrowed £1,580 (South Carolina currency) from Leroy Hammond, another backcountry merchant and fellow Whig militia officer as well as a member of the South Carolina Provincial Congress.[59] Part of this debt may have been to secure the purchase from Hammond of a 150-acre tract on which an "old store" was located. Whether this is the site at which Williams actually conducted his mercantile business is not known. Also, it is not known whether this "old store" was the site of the skirmish which began at Hammond's Old Store on December 30, 1780, and ended that same day at the fort that Williams had constructed on Mudlick Creek on his Mount Pleasant plantation. Since this debt to Hammond was not secured by land, however, it seems more likely that the debt was incurred to buy merchandise than to buy land. The prevailing practice at the time was to take back mortgages to secure land purchases. On December 3, 1779, Williams borrowed £30,875 (South Carolina currency) from Richard and Wade Hampton, fellow backcountry merchants and Whig militia officers.[60] Again, it is reasonable to think that this debt was incurred to purchase merchandise from the Hamptons since no security was given for the repayment of the debt.

[58] Motes, *Maps and Abstracts*, 125.

[59] *See* records in the South Carolina Department of Archives and History, Columbia, SC: Series: S136002; Box – 146A; Item - 0375A Date: 1789.

[60] *Ibid*, Series: L10018; Year - 1794; Item - 0367A Date: 1794/02/26.

Williams' estate defaulted on the repayment of the debts to both the Hammond and the Hampton brothers. These creditors successfully obtained confessions of judgments from Williams' widow, Mary, and her second husband, Joseph Griffin, in their respective capacities as executrix and executor of Williams' estate, following the restoration of South Carolina's state government after the end of the war. There is no evidence on the public record of what repayment, if any, Williams or his estate made to Rugeley. Rugeley died in Charleston in 1776. Since Rugeley was a Loyalist and his heirs presumably shared his political allegiance, this debt may well have never been repaid. Although the Treaty of Paris of 1783, by which hostilities between Great Britain and the United States were brought to an end, prohibited either side from barring enforcement of debts owed to citizens of opposition, there is no record of any attempt to enforce repayment of that debt either by the heirs of Rugeley or anyone who may have purchased this debt from them.

Miller

Williams also owned at least one mill. In his will, he stipulates that his mill is to be kept by his executors for the use and benefit of his widow during her widowhood or until his youngest son, Washington, comes of age. Williams further stipulated that upon his wife's remarriage or son Washington reaching his majority, the mill was to be sold to the highest bidder among his sons then alive.[61] Williams' widow, Mary, remarried sometime between January 26, 1787, when she conveyed slaves to her son John as "Mary Williams" and April 1, 1788, when she and her new husband, Joseph Griffin, conveyed slaves to her daughter Sarah Griffin.[62] The public record does not disclose when or if Williams' wishes regarding the sale of his mill to one of his sons was ever discharged.

[61] Appendix 7.
[62] Larry Vehorn, compiler, *Laurens County South Carolina Deed Abstracts: Books A-D: 1785-1793 (1769-1793)* (Greenville, SC: Southern Historical Press, Inc., 2004), 57.

The mill is described by Williams in his will as being situated on a 100-acre tract on the north side of the Little River. To date, the only evidence of a mill located on the north bank of the Little River near land known to have been owned by Williams is the ruins of a mill near the crossroads community of Milton in Laurens County, South Carolina. This mill site was improved and used by John Black in the late 18th century as the site for his under-shot mill as well as the location of his retail mercantile business.[63] Black's mill is shown on Robert Mills' 1825 map of Laurens County as being on the north side of the Little River.[64] The ruins of this mill as well a millrace are located just north of the bridge over the Little River on present day Jefferson Davis Road (State Road S-30-38). In the absence of evidence of a mill further down the Little River nearer the old Ninety Six Road as shown on the Mills maps of Laurens and Newberry Counties, it would seem that the site of Black's mill is the most likely candidate for the site of Williams' mill.

What Williams milled is not disclosed in any public records. That he milled salt purchased in blocks is known from his correspondence with his family. That he also milled corn into meal and wheat into flour also is very probable. The indents[65] filed on Williams' behalf by his widow following the war disclose that he provided substantial quantities of both corn meal and flour for the militia.[66] Those indents also disclose another use Williams made of his mill. He provided 150 gallons of whiskey for the militia in October 1779.[67] Since corn mash is an essential ingredient of whiskey, and

---

[63] The South Caroliniana Library, University of South Carolina, Columbia, SC houses a substantial collection of the accounts, records and family papers of John Black.

[64] Robert Mills, *Mills Atlas: Atlas of the State of South Carolina: 1825* (reprint, Greenville, SC: Southern Historical Press, Inc., 1980), Laurens District Map.

[65] When used in this context, an indent was a claim made against the State for goods and services rendered during the war.

[66] Indents from the files at the SC Archives, Columbia, SC: Series Number S108092; Reel 0158; Frame: 00389 (File No. 8554). These records show deliveries by Williams of 1,556 lbs. of flour on April 18, 1779; 800 lbs. of flour and 1,000 lbs. of corn meal in October 1779; and 160 lbs. of corn meal on June 2, 1779.

[67] *Ibid.*

since Williams' estate inventory discloses that he owned a 45-gallon still, there can be no doubt that Williams used corn ground at his mill to provide the mash needed to distill hard liquor at his still. So, to the list of his vocations can be added distiller.

If records of backcountry merchants are rare, records for backcountry millers are even rarer. There is one record, however, that provides interesting insight into the operations of contemporary backcountry millers. George Platt, a Loyalist planter and backcountry miller whose land was located on the Wateree River, filed a claim following the war stating that on his 300-acre plantation, he owned a gristmill "which had constant work in grinding corn." A friend of Platt's filed an affidavit in support of Platt's claim indicating that Platt's gristmill was a very valuable asset as Platt received a "10th bushel for grinding" his neighbors' corn. Platt also hauled his neighbors' corn meal and flour to market using wagons and horse teams he kept for that purpose.[68]

It is very likely that Williams provided these same services and exacted similar fees for his services to his neighbors and customers. His milling and hauling services also would have provided Williams with the opportunity of sending wagons loaded with corn meal, flour, and other farm produce to the market towns of Camden, Augusta, Ninety Six, and Charleston while returning with the merchandise needed to stock his retail establishment. That Williams would have hauled items to and from the backcountry by wagon rather than by barge seems very likely because the Little River led ultimately into the Santee River which did not provide direct access to Camden, Georgetown, or Charleston, the dominant commercial centers of that time.[69]

---

[68] Claim of George Platt, in Great Britain, Audit Office, Transcripts of the Manuscript Books and Papers of the Commission of Enquiry into the Losses and Services of the American Loyalists Held under the Acts of Parliament of 23, 25, 26, 28 and 29 of George III, Preserved amongst the Audit Office Records in the Public Record Office of England, 1783-1790, LII, 156-164, New York Public Library microfilm, cited in Klein, *Unification*, 29 (fn 32).

[69] The Little River of the Saluda flows into the Saluda River which joins with the Broad River to form the Congaree River. The Congaree in turn joins with

There can also be little doubt that Williams used his mill to dress timber. Since he owned at least 3,600 acres of land, most of which probably was virgin timberland when he first occupied it, he would have employed a substantial number of his 33 slaves to clear the land for crops. The resulting timber provided abundant raw material for a sawmill. The lumber it produced provided the enterprising Williams with the opportunity to supplement his income, not to mention supplying his personal need for lumber to construct his home, the slaves' quarters, and the barns and other outbuildings required for the successful operation of a plantation the size of Williams' Mount Pleasant estate.

Planter

Williams' ownership of at least 3,600 acres of land and 33 slaves at the time of his death indicates that he anticipated earning the bulk of his income from farming or ranching or some combination of those activities. With the exception of the corn and wheat he milled at his gristmill, there is little evidence of what other crops, if any, he grew on his plantation. The inventories of his estate list only two cows and calves, no hogs, 14 horses, 16 sheep and 16 geese. The presence of such a small amount of livestock makes it unlikely that Williams was a substantial rancher or that he had intentions of raising significant herds of these animals. These numbers do not even appear to be adequate to provide the meat and dairy products necessary to sustain Williams, his wife, eight children and 33 slaves. It is possible that the small number of such animals listed in the inventories of his estate can be attributed to his having provided supplies to the militia or to loss by plunder to his Tory neighbors. Again, however, the absence of indents or claims against the state for reimbursement of such contributions or losses makes it unlikely that he either provided the meat to the militia or had it stolen by his neighbors.

the Wateree River to form the Santee River. The Santee empties into the Atlantic Ocean between Georgetown in the north and Charleston in the south. There was no port at the point where the Santee flows into the Atlantic.

The answer to how Williams intended to use such a large plantation perhaps lies in Granville County, North Carolina. When Williams' father, Daniel Williams, died there in 1759, he left his heirs tracts of land totaling 2,550 acres, most of which was located in Granville County. An 800-acre tract in Halifax County, Virginia, however, was left by Daniel to be equally divided between his sons, James and Joseph. Son James also was left an additional 400-acre tract in Granville County. Daniel made substantial bequeaths of other personal property to his wife and his seven children. He then directed that all of his debts be paid from the proceeds of the sale of his current crop of tobacco, and that substantial purchases of additional personal property be made from such proceeds to equalize the distribution of his personal property among his seven children. Although the record does not disclose how much money resulted from the sale of his current year's tobacco crop, that crop must have been sizable for Daniel to be so confident that the proceeds from its sale would discharge his debts with enough excess to equalize the distributions of personal property among his children. This indicates that Daniel was a substantial tobacco planter. There can be little doubt that James was reared on a tobacco plantation and grew up knowing how to grow this crop that played such a major role in supporting the planter classes of Virginia and North Carolina.

There is clear evidence that tobacco was being grown in commercially marketable quantities in the South Carolina backcountry by immigrants from North Carolina and Virginia by the 1760s. "Several large quantities of excellent tobacco, made in the back settlements, have been brought to this market," observed a Charlestonian in 1768.[70] By 1769, planters in the backcountry petitioned the General Assembly to establish inland inspection sites to regulate

[70]   *Boston Chronicle,* November 14, 1768, quoted in H. Roy Merrens, ed., *The Colonial South Carolina Scene: Contemporary Views, 1697-1770* (Columbia: University of South Carolina Press, 1977).

tobacco trade.[71] In 1770, Lt. Governor William Bull wrote to Lord Hillsborough stating that "...tobacco, tho' a bulkey commodity, is planted from one hundred and fifty to two hundred miles from Charles Town, where the Emigrants from Virginia find the weed meliorate as they come south; and they cultivate it now with great advantage notwithstanding the distance of carriage to market."[72]

The intention to clear land and ultimately to cultivate tobacco would explain why Williams needed so much acreage and so many slaves. Williams' early involvement in the war and his death only seven years after moving his family to South Carolina perhaps explain why there is little evidence of Williams' having actually grown tobacco at Mount Pleasant. Clearing of land to raise the crops of corn and wheat required to feed his family, slaves, and livestock; the construction and operation of his mill; and the operation of his mercantile and distilling enterprises would have limited the time Williams had to implement any planned tobacco operations. Williams' regular trips to Camden and Charleston with corn and wheat would have given him ample opportunity to transport any tobacco crop he did grow to the markets in those trading centers.

There is one very tantalizing clue that Williams did indeed grow some tobacco at Mount Pleasant. In an indent in his own handwriting filed in April 1779, he lists "1 Tobacker hoxed of flower 1200 net." [Translation: "1 tobacco hogshead of flour weighing 1,200 lbs net"]. A hogshead

---

[71] South Carolina Commons House of Assembly Journal, July 5, 1769.

[72] William Bull to Lord Hillsborough, November 30, 1770, Records in the British Public Record Office Relating to South Carolina, Transcripts, XXXII, 393-396, 402-403. Rachel N. Klein, "Ordering the Backcountry: The South Carolina Regulation," *The William and Mary Quarterly*, 3rd Ser., Vol. 38, No. 4 (October 1981), 663-664. William Bull to Lord Hillsborough, November 30, 1770, Records in the British Public Record Office Relating to South Carolina, Transcripts, XXXII, 393-396, 402-403. Klein, *Unification*, 16, 19, 29, 31-32. Interestingly, the estate records for Benjamin Tutt, a fellow Revolutionary War militia officer, filed in Edgefield County, South Carolina, disclose that Tutt grew a significant amount of tobacco on his plantation in 1790, the year in which he died. The estate records include a return from the sale of Tutt's tobacco crop which was sold at Campobello on April 25, 1791.

was a barrel used to ship tobacco, usually to England. In Virginia, statutes required that the hogshead be 48 inches tall and 30 inches across at either end. It was designed to carry tobacco weighing between 1,000 to 1,500 pounds. That Williams had a spare hogshead to use to ship flour to the militia is a clear indication that, at least before the war cut him off from exporting his crop to England, he intended to grow marketable quantities of tobacco requiring him to make or otherwise acquire hogsheads.[73] If Williams indeed planned to grow tobacco for export, English tariffs and trade restrictions (American colonial exports were required by law to be shipped only to English ports) would have presented a strong incentive for Williams to want to throw off the yolk of English rule. The collapse of even that restricted export market occasioned by the outbreak of war could have fed Williams' ardor for independence from Great Britain's rule.

Williams' possession of a 45-gallon still also makes it highly probable that some of his arable land was planted in the corn needed to produce the mash for distilling into whiskey, not to mention land for growing oats, wheat, barley and hops from which to brew other spirits to appeal to his Scots-Irish neighbors. The production of these crops in quantities sufficient for making spirits would have affected the perfect melding of Williams' mercantile, milling and farming enterprises. Ever the enterprising businessman, Williams would not have missed this opportunity to better his fortunes while providing a service to his fellow backcountry men.

---

[73]   Colonial Williamsburg Teacher Institute, http://www.history.org/history/teaching/tradsamp.cfm (viewed 9/9/12).

Chapter Five
A Backcountry Whig's Library

According to a study by Professor Walter Edgar, private libraries were a rarity in colonial South Carolina.[74] That James Williams possessed a fairly extensive library in backcountry South Carolina in the late 18th Century makes his collection almost unique. An examination of Williams' holdings reveals not only his personal ambitions for his own and his family's education, but also the influences that no doubt shaped this die-hard revolutionary's ideas and ideals for which he sacrificed his life and exposed his family to deprivations and hardships.

The contents of Williams' library are known because Williams took it, along with most of his other valuable movable property, including most if not all of his slaves, to his brother's home in Caswell County, North Carolina. There, on June 12, 1780, he signed his Last Will and Testament describing himself as a "refugee" from Ninety Six, South Carolina. He, like some other South Carolina revolutionaries who suffered the consequences of British occupation of their state following the fall of Charleston on May 12, 1780, tried to remove his property from harm's way as best he could. The plantation of his older brother, Henry Williams, located in Caswell County immediately south of the Virginia border, provided what Williams' hoped would be a place of safekeeping.[75] When Williams died, his brother took an inventory of his estate in North Carolina including

---

[74] Walter Bellingrath Edgar, *The Libraries of Colonial South Carolina*, PhD dissertation, 1969, University of South Carolina.

[75] As it turns out, Williams' choice of Caswell County was not as safe as he hoped. Although none of his property appears to have been compromised, in February 1781, foraging parties from Cornwallis' force raided the storehouse of Williams' uncle, John Williams, in Caswell and made off with an unspecified amount of grain belonging to the public for which the elder Williams was called upon to account. Maybelle Delamar, *Legislative Papers Relating to Revolutionary Service* [Legislative Papers – pp. 80-83 and 206], North Carolina Archives, Raleigh, North Carolina.

his library.[76] It is that inventory that provides the source of our knowledge of the contents of Williams' library. That inventory is set out in annotated form in Appendix 11.

Before trying to draw conclusions from the titles included in Williams' library, however, the question should be asked if these books were Williams' personal library or, since he was a backcountry merchant, were they inventory for his mercantile business. Since Williams made a number of visits to Charleston in his capacity as a representative to the First and Second Provincial Congresses in 1775 and 1776, his repeated presence in the city on official business gave him ample opportunity to frequent the shops of that city's several established booksellers.[77] In addition, it is highly probable that he made other trips to Charleston to obtain goods to sell to his neighbors. He may have seen that having volumes for sale in his business might appeal to some of his backcountry customers who did not have the same opportunity to visit the city to make their own purchases.

Although possible, it seems unlikely that the books were part of Williams' mercantile inventory. Low literacy rates in the days before public education and before education of women was generally practiced would have meant that the customer base for books, especially in the sparsely populated Carolina backcountry, was extremely small. Add to that the expense of books to a population strapped for specie, and it would appear that bookselling would not be the type of enterprise Williams would find attractive. Further, there is no duplication of titles as one would expect in a merchant's inventory. Even in colonial times, commercial success in selling books would have required Williams to anticipate the needs and desires of his customers and to stock multiple copies of the volumes he thought would be popular. With the

<hr/>

[76] The inventory of Williams' estate can be found in the North Carolina Archives under Caswell County Estates, NC, CR.020.508.102.

[77] *See* Edgar, *SC Libraries*, pp. 49-94, regarding booksellers in Charleston during the colonial era. *See also* Hennig Cohen, *The South Carolina Gazette: 1732-1775*, (Columbia: University of South Carolina Press, 1953), 121-156. Cohen listed the titles of many books offered for sale by various Charleston booksellers from their advertisements in the *Gazette*.

exception of the two different editions of Terence's *Comedies*, no two texts are the same. Absence of duplicates strongly suggests careful selection of the texts based on personal criteria, not commercial considerations. Also, the relative scarcity of books on the practical skills that most frontier residents needed such as agricultural practices, bookkeeping, surveying, and mathematics indicates a personal rather than a commercial use for the collection. Books were very expensive luxury items unlikely to appeal to many of Williams' backcountry customers to whom, based on what little can be gleaned from his family correspondence about business matters, Williams sold such items as salt, staple goods and spirits.[78] To the extent that Williams' customers might have included some of the wealthy backcountry planters such as Andrew Williamson, John Lewis Gervais or Andrew Pickens, those men, as members of the General Assembly, would have had their own opportunity to purchase books directly from Charleston booksellers. For a businessman like Williams to tie up substantial capital in speculating on the success of book selling among the largely illiterate population of the backcountry seems improbable.[79]

Assuming the collection to be Williams' personal library, an observation that readily occurs is the heavy emphasis on Greek and Latin texts. This reflects the then prevailing view that a classical education required at least some proficiency in both of these languages. Indeed, the criteria for admission to the few American colleges and universities that existed in the mid to late 18th Century required command of Latin and sufficient proficiency in Greek to be able to interpret

[78] *See* Chapter 4 above.

[79] It is interesting to speculate about Williams possibly having the books as part of a lending library. Professor Edgar cites instances of individuals trying such efforts, largely without success, in Charleston. Apparently, the patrons of such private libraries were notorious for not returning books resulting in checkout deposits sometimes equaling one or two times the cost of the volume borrowed. Edgar, *SC Libraries*, pp. 70-94. *See also* Cohen, *Gazette*, p. 130 for an advertisement dated December 15, 1737, taken out by James Bulloch asking for the return to him of some 14 or 15 titles "...borrowed...and never returned...most of which Books have been out for several Years." It seems very unlikely Williams would have been willing to loan his valuable books to his customers.

the Gospels.[80] The presence of so many such texts and dictionaries in Williams' library indicates that he probably harbored the hope that one or more of his sons might one day attend an institution of higher learning. At the very minimum, he equipped his family with the tools necessary to provide the fundamentals of a classical education by the standards of that era.

Williams' library contained a few books conveying practical knowledge and skills. Texts such as *The Mariners New Calendar, Bookkeeping Methodiz'd* and *The Young Man's Companion* offered instruction in the more practical skills of mathematics, letter writing, surveying, and bookkeeping. All of these skills would have been highly valued by Williams as a merchant, miller, landowner, and father of five young sons.[81] He would have been anxious that his sons learn at least these rudimentary skills to equip themselves for the roles he saw them playing as successors to his farming, milling, and mercantile businesses. In addition, the more practical skills, such as command of mathematics, were becoming important in the curricula of some of America's colleges, influenced by the trend in Scottish universities to emphasize mathematics and the sciences in addition to the classical languages. Again, Williams was equipping himself and his family with the tools necessary for at least a basic education.

---

[80] *See*, for example, Ron Chernow, *Alexander Hamilton*, (New York: The Penguin Press, 2004), 42-43 where the following appears regarding entrance qualifications for aspiring collegians in the 1770s:

> Princeton applicants had to know Virgil, Cicero's orations, and Latin grammar and also had to be 'so well acquainted with the Greek as to render any part of the four Evangelists in that language into Latin or English.'

[81] The Williams family also included three young daughters, but the library contained none of the few books then available that offered instruction on domestic skills such as Eliza Smith's *The Compleat Housewife: or, accomplish'd gentlewoman's companion: being a collection of upwards of five hundred of the most approved receipts in cookery, pastry, confectionary, preserving, pickles, cakes, creams, jellies, made wines, cordials also bills of fare for every month To which is added, a collection of above two hundred receipts of medicines; viz. drinks, syrups, salves, ointments The sixth edition, with very large additions; near fifty receipts being communicated just before the author's death.* This book was frequently reprinted after first appearing in 1727. Edgar found copies of this book in six of the estate inventories he reviewed. Edgar, *SC Libraries*, pp. 235.

Given Williams' strong religious beliefs, the library predictably includes a large number of religious treatises, some written by dissenters from the established Church of England. Three of the works – Henry's *Commentaries*, Boston's *Fourfold State* and Erskine's *Sermons* – appear on the list of 20 recommended works expounded by the great 18th Century evangelist, George Whitefield.[82] As a devout Presbyterian, all of the religious titles in Williams' library would have been essential tools for maintaining the spiritual wellbeing of himself and his family. It is interesting to note that several of the books included daily guides for Bible study and devotionals. Indeed, Burkitt's *Expository Notes* is still available in print and on CD, and touted as instructive in the spiritual life of today's Christians even though Burkitt died in 1703.[83]

One very intriguing omission from Williams' library is Thomas Paine's *Common Sense*, the single most widely distributed political tract in the American provinces. Published early in 1776, Paine's book sold more than 120,000 copies making it, on a *per capita* basis, the bestselling book in American history excluding the Bible.[84] Yet the inventory of Williams' books does not include this pivotal political treatise which has been credited with laying the foundation for the 'self-evident truths' to which Thomas Jefferson subsequently gave such eloquent expression in the Declaration of Independence. The explanation for its absence from the inventory of Williams' library may be simple. As a mere

---

[82] *South Carolina Gazette*, 30 August 1740, abstracted in Cohen, *Gazette*, p. 131 and listed by Edgar, *SC Libraries*, p. 26, n.10. George Whitefield (1714-1770), an English Methodist minister, traveled throughout the American colonies preaching to standing room only crowds everywhere he went and influencing some of the most politically powerful men of the day. It is reasonable to say of him that he was his era's Billy Graham. Arnold A. Dallimore, *George Whitefield: The Life and Times of the Great Evangelist of the 18th Century Revival*, (Edinburgh: The Banner of Truth Trust, 1970, 2 vols.)

[83] *See*, for example, http://www.schooloftomorrow.com/curriculum/computer/curri_comp_bible.asp (viewed 9/9/12) at which Burkitt's text is described as giving "...practical observations on the text, explains the sense of the Scripture and recommends instructive example."

[84] Scott Liell, *46 Pages: Thomas Paine, Common Sense, and the Turning Point to Independence*, (Philadelphia: Running Press, 2003).

pamphlet, his executor may have deemed it too physically unimpressive to warrant inclusion in the inventory. Or, perhaps, its widespread availability rendered it unworthy of inclusion in the inventory. Maybe its message was so powerful an influence on Williams and his family that Williams left his copy of it with his family in South Carolina so that they could draw inspiration from it to continue what Williams recognized would be the protracted struggle for independence resulting from the British taking of Charleston and investment in the Carolina backcountry. Since it is known that several of the Charleston booksellers were Tories, it is possible that Paine's book was not generally available in Charleston, and, therefore, Williams did not own a copy of it.

The total absence from the library of what would have been the "popular literature" of the day such as the works of Henry Fielding, Jonathan Swift, Samuel Richardson, and others is informative. Although as Professor Edgar noted in his dissertation many residents of Charleston and environs had copies of such works in their libraries, backcountry residents would have had little time for reading purely for entertainment.[85] Also missing from Williams' library was most of the classic literature of the age, such as works by Shakespeare, Milton, and Chaucer. These works were available and offered for sale by the Charleston booksellers.[86]

It is interesting that 17 titles of the 30 identifiable books listed in Williams' library are not among the titles listed in Professor Edgar's dissertation as being in at least five of the privately held libraries in South Carolina in the period prior to 1776. Surprisingly, those 17 titles include Samuel Johnson's famous *Dictionary*.[87] It is more surprising that Johnson's

---

[85] Edgar, *SC Libraries*, Appendix II, pp. 227-235, contains a detailed listing of the books held in 5 or more colonial-era South Carolina libraries.

[86] *See*, e.g., Cohen, *Gazette*, Chapter XI.

[87] Johnson's *Dictionary* was held in the Charleston Library Society. Charlestown Library Society, *A Catalogue of Books, Belonging to the Incorporated Charlestown Library Society, with the Dates of the Editions*, (Charleston, SC: Printed for the Society by Robert Wells, 1770). Also, Robert Wells, the Charleston bookseller and printer, offered Dr. Johnson's *Dictionary* for sale as early as June 1755, just months after its publication in April 1755 in England. Cohen, *Gazette*, p. 140.

work is missing from the other South Carolina libraries than that it was included in Williams' library. Although the first collected edition of the dictionary was not published until 1755, it was immediately recognized as a work of genius and almost universally acclaimed as the benchmark against which all other dictionaries of the English language would be judged. Ten of these 17 "unique" titles are religious works; five fall into the category Edgar labels as "practical" works (*i.e.*, dictionaries and practical skills works); and two (Muir's translation of Sallust and Melmoth's translation of Cicero's letters) fall under Professor Edgar's "classical" label.

Possession of these volumes does not mean that Williams or anyone else in his family read them or, having read them, assimilated much of their content. Given that Williams valued the books enough, however, to include them with his other valuable movable personal property taken to his brother's home in North Carolina for safekeeping after the fall of Charleston in May 1780 and the occupation immediately thereafter of his home in the Carolina backcountry, it is highly probable that he and his family did read them. At least as to the numerous volumes of religious instruction, it is safe to assume that the life of the Williams family was informed and guided by the percepts set forth in them.

Certainly, as a merchant and miller, the volumes that included instruction in such skills as bookkeeping, surveying, mathematics, and handwriting would have been essential not only for Williams' children but also for Williams himself. His possession of this library helps to flesh out and give fuller appreciation for the life of wealthy, privileged Carolina backcountry residents in the period just prior to the Revolution. The deaths of Williams and his two eldest sons in the Revolution doubtless meant that whatever hopes and dreams Williams harbored for his sons' higher education were dashed by the practical realities of his surviving sons having to assume the responsibilities of running Williams' plantation, mill, store and distillery at a very early age. It is unlikely that they would have had much opportunity in the hardscrabble Carolina backcountry to read for pleasure's sake.

Chapter Six
Backcountry Militia

The backcountry Whig militia of South Carolina played a substantial role in winning the American Revolutionary War. Without its contributions to victories at the first Battle of Ninety Six in late 1775, King's Mountain in October 1780, Cowpens in January 1781, and numerous other engagements, the conclusion of the war almost certainly would have been delayed and the outcome may have been different. Many people, however, fundamentally misunderstand the nature and function of this militia. They ascribe to it a cohesiveness, discipline, and organization that simply did not exist; at least not during the periods in which the militia enjoyed its greatest successes. Backcountry Whig militia units comprised citizen soldiers who, with few exceptions, were civilians first and soldiers second. The priority of domestic duties and responsibilities undermined the military efficacy of the militia except in times when self-preservation and self-interest dictated devotion to the cause. During times of necessity, however, these units performed well.[88]

In order to place Williams' militia services in their proper context, it is essential to have some rudimentary understanding of some of the major factors that came to bear on the militia as the war progressed. Those factors forced the militia to evolve and adapt as the war took its various twists and turns.

---

[88] For those seeking more detailed examinations of the South Carolina militia, suggested reading includes: Lawrence E. Babits, *A Devil of a Whipping: The Battle of Cowpens* (Chapel Hill: The University of North Carolina Press, 1998); Michael E. Stauffer, *South Carolina's Antebellum Militia*, (Columbia: South Carolina Department of Archives & History, 1991); Jean Martin Flynn, *The Militia in Antebellum South Carolina Society*, (Spartanburg, SC: The Reprint Company, 1991); Ronald Hoffman, Thad W. Tate and Peter J. Albert, eds., *An Uncivil War: The Southern Backcountry During the American Revolution*, (Charlottesville: United States Capitol Historical Society by The University Press of Virginia, 1985); Michael C. Scoggins, *The Day it Rained Militia: Huck's Defeat and the Revolution in the South Carolina Backcountry: May-July 1780* (Charleston, SC: History Press, 2005).

The backcountry Whig militia passed through three distinct stages during the war. The initial stage was one of uncertainty as the Whigs fashioned a new government and tested that government's ability to create and control the military force needed to support its claim to govern. Since there were no land-based British troops in South Carolina at the outset of the war, the most threatening challenges to the Whigs were the presence of significant militia units organized under the old colonial-era laws in areas populated largely by Loyalists, and the presence of a large Indian population on the western frontier. The Whigs effectively met the threat posed by the Tories with the help of the backcountry militia of their own. Ironically, at least in the early stages of the war, the Indian threat was met by militia units which the pension records show to have been manned by both Whigs and Tories, as to a large extent, the Indians posed a substantial threat to all white settlements, Whig and Tory alike.

The second stage occurred during the relative stability that prevailed after the Whigs defeated the backcountry Tory militia in late 1775 and continued until the siege of Charleston in early 1780. It was during this time that the militia enjoyed its highest degree of organization but arguably its lowest degree of military efficacy.

The final stage was one of total instability caused by the British occupation of the entire state following Charleston's fall on May 12, 1780, the collapse of the Whig government, and the outbreak of full-scale civil war between backcountry Tory and Whig sympathizers. It was during this period that the Whig militia had its lowest degree of organizational cohesiveness but it highest degree of efficacy. It was also during this period that Williams made his most enduring contributions to the independence of his country from Great Britain.

Stage One: A Period of Uncertainty, The Whigs Take Power

In early 1775 the colony of South Carolina's nascent,

self-appointed and extra-legal Whig government was faced with many challenges. Not the least of these was establishing its right to organize and control the military force required by every government to support the legitimacy of its claim to govern. The First and Second Provincial Congresses and the Councils of Safety they appointed to exercise legislative and executive powers between sessions of the Congresses grappled with their authority to call out the militia, the only military force then existing in the colony.[89] The records of the proceedings of those Congresses and Councils reveal there was no agreement among the conservatives and radicals as to their goal. Were they establishing a caretaker government that would temporarily exercise power until reconciliation with Great Britain could be achieved? Or were they creating the governmental framework of an independent country?

The militia itself reflected the ambiguity felt by the Congresses and Councils. There were units, especially in the predominantly Tory areas of the backcountry between the Broad and Saluda Rivers, in which the militia was squarely under the control of men such as Thomas Fletchall,[90] Moses

---

[89] The records of the First and Second Provincial Congresses and the Councils of Safety that served under their authority are dispersed in a number of sources. To review all of those records, *See* Hemphill, *SC Papers; Collections of the South Carolina Historical Society*, (Charleston, SC: South Carolina Historical Society, 1858), II: 22-74; *Collections of the South Carolina Historical Society*, (Charleston, SC: South Carolina Historical Society, 1859) III: 35-271; The South Carolina Historical and Genealogical Magazine, Vol. I (1900), pp. 41-135, pp. 183-205, pp. 279-310; Vol. II (1901), pp. 3-26, pp. 97-102, pp. 167-173, pp. 259-267, (Charleston, SC: South Carolina Historical Society, 1900, 1901); John Drayton, *Memoirs of the American Revolution, from Its Commencement to the Year 1776, Inclusive; as Relating to The State of South Carolina: and Occasionally Refering to the States of North-Carolina and Georgia*, Vol. I and II, (Charleston, SC: A. E. Miller, 1821; reprint New York: Arno Press, Inc., 1969); Moultrie, *Memoir;* and A. S. Salley, Jr., *The History of Orangeburg County South Carolina From Its Settlement to the Close of the Revolutionary War*, (Orangeburg, SC: R. Lewis Berry, 1898; Greenville, SC: reprint Southern Historical Press, Inc., 2001).

[90] Col. Thomas Fletchall (1725-1789) was a prominent Tory and militia commander who lived in the Fairforest Creek area of what is now Union County, South Carolina. *See* Phil Norfleet's biographical sketch of Fletchall at http://sc_tories.tripod.com/thomas_fletchall.htm (viewed 9/9/12).

Kirkland,[91] Robert Cunningham[92] and his brother Patrick[93] who refused to subscribe to the Whig Association. These men were adamantly opposed to what they saw as the usurpation of governmental powers from the only legitimate seats of government, the royal governor, his council, and the General Assembly elected under the royal charter.

Perhaps grasping the likelihood of eventual independence from England, the more radical members of the Council such as William Henry Drayton[94] recognized immediately the importance of controlling the military. They knew that without such control the governmental structures established by them would soon collapse. They aggressively set about remedying this deficiency. They authorized the formation of three regiments of provincial troops, two of foot and one of rangers, and appointed as commanders officers who were at least sympathetic to, if not strong proponents of, the views of the radicals.[95] In addition, the Councils actively encouraged the formation of "volunteer companies" of militia. Interestingly, the Whigs did not initially assert the right to call out and regulate the existing militia units under the Militia Act. By calling for the formation of these "volunteer companies," the Whigs were not relying on the mandatory provisions of the

[91] Moses Kirkland (1730-1787) was initially a Whig but quickly changed sides and became an ardent Tory. *See* Phil Norfleet's biographical sketch of Kirkland at http://sc_tories.tripod.com/moses_kirkland.htm (viewed 9/9/12).

[92] Robert Cunningham (1739-1813) an early Tory militia leader who, following the fall of Charleston, won promotion to the rank of brigadier general in the Tory militia, and took part in a number of backcountry engagements including the battles of Hammond's Old Store and Williams Fort. *See* Phil Norfleet's biographical sketch of Robert Cunningham at http://sc_tories.tripod.com/robert_cunningham1.htm (viewed 9/9/12).

[93] Patrick Cunningham was Robert Cunningham's brother and the commander of the Little River Regiment of Tory militia.

[94] William Henry Drayton (1742-1779) was one of the most avid radicals advocating for independence of South Carolina from Great Britain. He was a wealthy lowcountry planter, a gifted polemicist, jurist and member of the Continental Congress from South Carolina. Keith Krawczynski, *William Henry Drayton: South Carolina Revolutionary Patriot,* (Baton Rouge: Louisiana State University Press, 2001).

[95] Command of one regiment of foot soldiers was given to William Moultrie; Christopher Gadsden commanded the other regiment of foot; and William Thomson was given command of the regiment of rangers.

existing militia law passed by the General Assembly elected under the royal charter.[96] After all, this law compelled almost universal participation by free, white males between the ages of 16 and 60.[97] That would include men such as Fletchall,

[96] The last Militia Act passed prior to the Revolution was enacted on June 13, 1747. According to its terms, the Act was to remain in effect for five years. In 1753 the Act was extended for two years and then revived and continued for five years by Act of 1759. Ostensibly, the Act lapsed as of 1764 and there is no record of its having been later revived or extended, but such must have been the case because there were militia units in the field at the start of the Revolution. David J. McCord, Editor, *The Statutes at Large of South Carolina*, Volume the Ninth, (Columbia: State of South Carolina, 1841), 645-663. Furthermore, the resolutions of the First Provincial Congress make it clear that those resolutions were building on an existing set of rules and regulations governing the militia.

[97] In addition to requiring almost universal service by white males between the ages of 16 and 60 (with exemptions from service for certain key functionaries such as members of the Council, the General Assembly, justices, attorneys, clergy, justices of the peace and, interestingly, one white man to attend every ferry in the colony), other significant provisions of the Act specified:

(1) the method for commissioning officers (only the Governor, Lieutenant Governor or President of the Council were empowered to grant commissions);

(2) the limit on the number (6) of musters a captain could call in any year except in time of "insurrection, rebellion or invasion;"

(3) a list of arms each militia man was required to have at his home and to bring with him at each muster ("one gun or musket, fit for service, a cover for his lock, one cartridge box with at least 12 cartridges, filled with good gun powder and ball, a horn or flask, filled with at least a quarter of a pound of gun powder, and shot punch, with bullets proportionable to the gun powder, one girdle or belt, one ball of wax sticking to the end of his cartridge box, to defend his arms in rain, one worm and picker, four spare flints, a bayonet, sword or hatchet...");

(4) that white servants were to be supplied with the required arms by their masters;

(5) restrictions on requiring units to service outside their county, parish or division except in time of emergency and then only three quarters of the company could be called for such outside service;

(6) the powers of officers to impress "any provisions, horses, boats, canoes, pettiaugers and vessels" in any time of emergency;

(7) that the Governor, Lieutenant Governor or President of the Council would have the authority in time of emergency to order the enlistment in the militia of black slaves (to be provisioned by their masters) provided that blacks could not compose more than one third of any militia unit embodied outside of St. Philip Parish, Charleston; or more than one half of any militia unit embodied inside said parish;

(8) the fines, penalties and procedures required to enforce the provisions of the statute.
McCord, *Statutes*, pp. 645-663.

Kirkland and Cunningham, and the companies of Tory sympathizers commanded by them.

The Provincial Congress took a first, cautious step toward asserting its authority to regulate the militia in January 1775. It passed resolutions under which it "*recommended … to all inhabitants of this colony, that they be diligently attentive in learning the use of arms; and that their officers be requested to train and exercise them at least once a month.*"(emphasis added)[98] In June 1775, Congress took a much bolder stance. It enacted a resolution delegating to the Council of Safety the "full power and authority to carry the acts of Assembly for regulating the Militia of this Colony, in all respects, into execution, as in time of alarm." Knowing that men such as Fletchall and Cunningham continued in command of their militia units, however, Congress anticipated that drastic measures might have to be used to deal with them. The Provincial Congress therefore gave the Council of Safety the following authority:

> That if *any just complaint shall be made against any officer in the Militia,* or that there are any vacancies in any of the regiments or companies of Militia in this colony, and that commissions cannot be procured in the usual channel, *the Council of Safety may remove such officer, and forthwith appoint another in his stead, and also appoint officers for filling up such vacancies,* as the case may respectively require.[99] (emphasis added)

This authority vested in the Council the seemingly unfettered power to determine if a complaint was "just." Having made such a determination against any allegedly offending officer, the Council had the power to remove and replace such officer. One can almost see the names "Fletchall," "Kirkland," and "Cunningham" being set forth in the resolution as examples of officers against whom a just complaint might be readily lodged.

[98] Hemphill, *SC Papers,* p. 29.
[99] *Ibid.* p. 54.

Interestingly, when the first Constitution of South Carolina was adopted in March 1776, no express provision authorizing the establishment of a militia was included. Doubtless the Whigs' position was that the inclusion of Article XXIX ratifying "all laws now of force here" had the effect of extending the last Militia Act enacted in 1747, even though that act was passed by an Assembly sanctioned by the Crown. The only nuance would be that the new provincial officers would exercise the powers vested by that act in the royal governor.

Even the second Constitution of South Carolina, adopted on March 19, 1778, failed to expressly empower the General Assembly to establish and regulate the militia. Nonetheless, such powers clearly were claimed by the General Assembly, since on March 28, 1778, it enacted a very detailed new Militia Act.[100] By 1778, the General Assembly would have been totally secure in its authority to regulate a militia. By then the Whigs had unchallenged control of the legislature and executive offices of the State. Although Tory sympathizers still dominated pockets of the backcountry,[101] during the period from late 1775 until the British invasion of South Carolina in early 1780, they could not embody themselves as official militia units. Paradoxically, since the Whigs held unchallenged political power during that period, many Tories served in the militia units as ersatz Whigs in campaigns that no doubt many found distasteful. Self-preservation while living among their Whig neighbors demanded that the Tories make practical compromises in their political principles.

---

[100] McCord, *Statutes*, pp. 666-682. It is interesting to note that this new act expressly forbid the formation of any new volunteer companies and provided for the absorption into the militia of all existing volunteer companies. Volunteer companies having served their purpose early in the life of the new state, by 1778 it was recognized that it was desirable to subject all of the state's citizen-soldiers to the new Militia Act.

[101] A striking example of the continued presence of strong Tory sympathies in the area between the Broad and Saluda Rivers is the election of Robert Cunningham to the state Senate in 1778, even though he was opposed by Williams.

The function of the militia during this period of uncertainty varied substantially from its function in later periods of the Revolution. At the start of the Revolution, with two governments simultaneously claiming the right to govern the Province, neither claimant effectively controlled the militia because, as already noted, many of its units were composed of both Whig and Tory sympathizers. The Whigs immediately recognized this weakness in their claim to govern, and quickly and adroitly moved to put into place an effective military force that they controlled. As almost their first act of government, the Whigs established three regiments of state troops and called for the formation of volunteer militia units. The Council of Safety's control over commissioning of the officers assured that only units commanded by approved officers would be recognized. Numerous such Whig-dominated militia units were formed. Those volunteer units would be governed by the terms of the Militia Act once recognized as legitimate by the Council's commissioning of their officers.

The Tories on the other hand were quickly deprived of their claim to govern. The last royal governor's abandonment of the colony for the safety of a British man-of-war stationed off Charleston and the Whigs' exercise of their controlling votes in the royal legislature to adjourn that body and to reconvene as the First Provincial Congress simultaneously stripped the Tories of both their executive and legislative support. Tory militia commanders such as Fletchall, Kirkland, and the Cunninghams were cut off from any meaningful contact with or support from the Crown.

Deprived of both executive and legislative support, the decision by the backcountry Tory militia to take to the field in support of the Royal governor was doomed to failure. The eventual defeat of the Tory-controlled militia units was inevitable and it occurred in late 1775 at the first Battle of Ninety Six.[102] Following this defeat, the backcountry

---

[102] For an excellent short history of the first Battle of Ninety Six, *See* Lewis Pinckney Jones, *The South Carolina Civil War of 1775*, (Lexington, SC: The Sandlapper Store, Inc., 1975).

Tory militia commanders including Fletchall and Patrick Cunningham were arrested and sent to Charleston.[103] After the successful defense of Charleston in the summer of 1776, the Whig government felt sufficiently safe in its control of the populace to release Fletchall, the Cunningham brothers, and other Tories from imprisonment upon their giving their promise not to take up arms against the Whig government.

The backcountry Whig militia played a determinative role in the first Battle of Ninety Six. Approximately 3,000 backcountry Whig militiamen joined the units commanded by Maj. Andrew Williamson[104] and Col. Richard Richardson.[105] Among their number was a 25-man company raised and commanded by 34-year old Captain James Williams. The sheer numbers of the Whig militia overwhelmed the Tories led by Patrick Cunningham. These Whig militiamen lived in the areas in which the Tory militia was strongest. Their lives and the well-being of their family members depended on the successful suppression of the Tories before full-scale civil war could break out among neighbors over which course South Carolina would follow in the brewing storm. Conditions

[103] Robert Cunningham had been arrested and sent to Charleston under orders issued by William Henry Drayton prior to the Battle of Ninety Six. The grounds for the arrest of Cunningham were provided by his disavowal of the peace treaty which Drayton previously negotiated with Fletchall. Under this treaty, Fletchall agreed on behalf of himself and, ostensibly, on behalf of the men under his command including the Cunningham brothers, not to take up arms in active opposition to the Whigs. The first Battle of Ninety Six was ignited when Patrick Cunningham and his followers intercepted a shipment of arms sent by the Whigs to the Cherokees in an attempt to buy the Indians' neutrality, if not their support, in the brewing conflict between Loyalist and Whig forces. The Whigs maintained that the arms and ammunition were merely part of the ongoing trade with the Indians. Patrick Cunningham, in an attempt to rally his men to rescue his brother from imprisonment, told his men that the arms were being shipped by the Whigs to the Cherokees, not as part of ongoing trade, but to arm the Indians so they could attack the Tories. In truth, the arms were being sent by the Whigs to the Cherokees in an effort at least to negate their overt commitment to the British and hopefully to secure their allegiance to the Whigs.

[104] Andrew Williamson (ca. 1730-1786) was the commanding officer of the South Carolina backcountry militia from the commencement of the war until he took parole from the British in June 1780 following the fall of Charleston.

[105] Richard Richardson (1704-1780) was a backcountry militia leader through much of the war. He was a mediating force in the backcountry against persecution of the Tories.

in late 1775 were perfect for the Whig militia to realize its maximum efficacy by embodying for a short duration in their own neighborhood to protect their own lives and property. These were the conditions under which the backcountry militia best functioned.[106]

Stage Two: A Period of Relative Stability, But Little Success

The defeat of the Tory-controlled militia and the successful defense of Charleston from the British attack in the early summer of 1776 set the stage for the second phase in the evolution of the militia. During the period of relative stability between the early summer of 1776 and the British invasion of South Carolina in the late winter of 1780, the militia units appear to have functioned substantially in accordance with the provisions of the Militia Act. Men were formed into companies, regiments, and brigades commanded by officers either elected by them or, in the case of field grade officers, appointed by the Governor as provided in the Act. Men reported to musters for training and served in the campaigns and battles that occurred during this period, including the largely ineffective campaign against the Cherokees in the late summer and early fall of 1776, the ill-fated Florida campaigns in May-June 1778, the Augusta campaign in December 1778-January 1779, the Battle of Brier Creek in March 1779, the Battle of Stono (June 1779) and the unsuccessful siege of Savannah in September and October of 1779. When tested by the British invasion and capture of Savannah and Augusta in late 1778 and 1779, the South Carolina militia responded well to defend Charleston from Prevost's attempt to take that city in 1779 and to push the British back to the Savannah River, the boundary line

[106] While it is true that Col. William Thomson and his regiment of Rangers participated in the first Battle of Ninety Six, it was the presence of the approximately 3,000 backcountry militia who rallied under Col. Richard Richardson and Major Andrew Williamson that assured the almost bloodless surrender by the far outnumbered members of Patrick Cunningham's Tory command. Jones, *Civil War*, pp. 72-83.

between Georgia and South Carolina. Indeed, a number of backcountry militia units responded to the call to rally to the defense of Charleston when the British landed an overwhelmingly large army under General Henry Clinton and again laid siege to that city in early 1780. Even the units that did not come to the defense of Charleston continued to discharge, at least in part, their duties in the backcountry until after Charleston fell to the British on May 12. Up until that date, they manned the forts and outposts protecting the frontier, and effectively suppressed the backcountry Tories from embodying to support the British forces at Charleston.[107]

Even during this period of relative stability, however, the modern reader must put aside all preconceived notions of traditional military units and the discipline associated with them. These units bore no resemblance to today's National Guard with its thorough military training and government-issued, state-of-the-art weaponry. The Militia Act of 1747 and its replacement in 1778 placed on each man the responsibility of providing his own weapons and ammunition. In that day of hardscrabble yeoman farms, the "citizen soldiers" who made up the ranks of the militia were clearly citizens first and soldiers only as and when emergencies dictated that they assemble for the preservation of themselves and their families. Although some of the wealthier backcountry planters owned slaves upon whom they could rely to do the work required to raise crops and perform the multitude of tasks necessary to sustain life in the backcountry, the vast majority of the rank-and-file members of the militia units were small farmers whose families' continued existence was

---

[107] *See* Letter dated January 28, 1783, from Andrew Williamson to Nathanael Greene with attachment dated April 25, 1780, being a General Report by Captain Benj. Tutt to Williamson regarding the deployment of militia units under Williamson's command in and around Augusta, Georgia. The letter is in the Rare Book, Manuscript, and Special Collections Library, Duke University, Durham, North Carolina. An annotated transcription of it appears at Southern Campaign of the American Revolution, Vol. 2, No. 5 (May 2005), 12 at http://www. southerncampaign.org. (viewed 9/9/12).

totally dependent upon the fruits of their own labor.[108] Such men could not afford to be away from their farms for long periods of time, engaging in what many of them probably deemed meaningless military training. Likewise, they were not well suited to participation in long campaigns far from their homes. The evidence is overwhelming that the most effective use of the militia was made in limited engagements close to the homes of the men doing the fighting against an enemy that posed an immediate threat to the families of those men.[109]

The disastrous campaigns mounted against Florida and Savannah during this period of relative stability amply illustrate the ineffectiveness of using militia far from home on missions of extended duration. On each of these campaigns, men abandoned their units in such numbers as to condemn the campaigns to failure. Their priorities were to provide for and protect their families, not to engage in remote conflicts to achieve what many doubtless viewed as goals and objectives of no immediate personal importance.

It would be a mistake to assume that these traits were unique to the South Carolina backcountry militia. An examination of the militia's actions at the Battle of Camden in August 1780 and again at the Battle of Guilford Courthouse in March 1781 demonstrates that self-preservation and self-interest were paramount concerns to yeoman militiamen. Although fought during a time frame outside this period

---

[108] For an excellent examination of the evolution of agriculture and slavery in the South Carolina backcountry, *See* Klein, *Unification.*

[109] Even during this period of relative stability, the typical militiaman showed up for service bearing his own musket or rifle and riding his own horse. Although the State may have had some sporadic success in obtaining lead, gunpowder, medicines and vittles to at least partially supply the needs of the militia from time to time, most often the men were limited to only the ammunition they brought with them and the food they could forage from the farms unfortunate enough to be in the immediate vicinity of wherever the militia gathered. After the fall of Charleston in May 1780 and the outbreak of civil war between Whig and Tory militia units roaming the backcountry, such foraging usually took the form of each side plundering the farms and plantations of their opponents. If forage was taken from sympathizers, vouchers might be issued allowing the injured party a claim for reimbursement from the government with actual payment on such vouchers being dependent on which of the two governments was left standing at the end of the war.

of relative stability, the actions of the militia units at those engagements fully support the notion that militia were ill-suited to engaging in combat far from home requiring extended absence from their farms and families. Even though the militia units from North Carolina and Virginia should have been (and no doubt were at least partially) motivated at the Battle of Camden by the desire to check Cornwallis' progress in South Carolina before the British could invade their states, they were not on their native soil. There were no South Carolina Whig militia units at Camden. Arguably, had there been South Carolina Patriot militia present, the rout of Gates' army may not have occurred, since the South Carolinians would have had a more vested and immediate interest in the defense of their homes and families. At the Battle of Camden, the militia from North Carolina and Virginia had no such self-interest. When faced with a bayonet attack by the British regular army, they bolted and ran: the ultimate concession to self-preservation and self-interest. Indeed, at the Battle of Guilford Courthouse, the actions of the North Carolina militia, fighting as they were on their home turf, underscore that the instinct for self-preservation trumped whatever vested self-interest they might have felt in defending that specific turf.[110]

Stage Three: A Period of Instability, But More Success

The fall of Charleston, the surrender of the entire southern department of the Continental Army, the capture of a large part of the state's coastal as well as some backcountry militia units, and the resulting collapse of the Whig government in May 1780 mark the beginning of the third period of evolution of the South Carolina militia. Whatever formal structure the backcountry Whig militia may have had before the fall of Charleston, there was none thereafter. There was

---

[110] *See* Lawrence E. Babits and Joshua B. Howard, *Long, Obstinate, and Bloody: The Battle of Guilford Courthouse*, (Chapel Hill: The University of North Carolina Press, 2009).

no Whig government in South Carolina. The state's capitol had fallen, the members of the General Assembly either had been captured and imprisoned or had fled to safety outside the state. Even the governor had been forced to flee the state. Although the General Assembly had endowed Governor John Rutledge[111] with virtual dictatorial powers just before the fall of Charleston, Rutledge had no ability to govern a state in which he could not even reside and from which neither he nor any officers who served under him might reasonably expect any monetary or logistical support. In a very real sense, beginning with the fall of Charleston and thereafter, it was the lot of the men who remained committed to the Whig cause to improvise for themselves the rules that would govern any military units they might choose to establish.

One pervasive element of the units pulled together by the Whigs following the fall of Charleston is that they were composed of men who were refugees. With the rapid establishment by the British of military enclaves throughout the backcountry at Camden, Ninety Six, Rocky Mount, Hanging Rock, Granby, and Augusta, and the rallying to the British by the long-suppressed backcountry Tories, Whigs were forced to make a decision. Either they had to take parole from the British or they had to abandon their farms and plantations to gather in safer environs where they could form units to oppose the British and Tories. Many Whigs such as Andrew Williamson, LeRoy Hammond,[112] Andrew

---

[111] John Rutledge (1739-1800) was the governor of the state of South Carolina at the time Charleston fell to the British on May 12, 1780. Rutledge had fled the city shortly before its surrender to the British. He went initially to Philadelphia to lobby Congress for aid and then returned to Hillsborough, North Carolina where he established an office in exile. Richard Barry, *Mr. Rutledge of South Carolina*, (New York: Duell, Sloan and Pearce, 1942); James Haw, *John & Edward Rutledge of South Carolina*, (Athens, GA: The University of Georgia Press, 1997).

[112] Col. LeRoy Hammond (1729-1790) was the commanding officer of a backcountry militia regiment under the command of Andrew Williamson. Like Williamson, Hammond took parole from the British following the fall of Charleston, but he later reentered the war as a Patriot commander under General Andrew Pickens. LeRoy Hammond was Samuel Hammond's uncle and the brother-in-law of Andrew Williamson.

Pickens[113] and others chose to take parole because they viewed the war as being essentially won by the British, at least in South Carolina and Georgia. Others, however, made what must have been the gut-wrenching decision to abandon their families and homes to gather with like-minded Whigs around Thomas Sumter [114] and James Williams in the Charlotte and Waxhaws areas of northern South Carolina and southern North Carolina or around Francis Marion[115] in the swamps of eastern South Carolina.

The units formed by these men were among the most democratic institutions ever formed in North America. Not only were the officers who commanded these units elected by the men who served under them, but also virtually no action was taken by any of these units without all of the officers having first met in a council of war to reach consensus as to whether or not to engage the enemy. Having decided to engage, the strategy to be used in such engagement then became a matter on which the council members had to reach consensus. The records make it abundantly clear that no action was taken without first having reached such consensus.

There is also clear evidence that dissenters from a particular action were likely to simply abandon the unit without fear of any meaningful consequences. These units were fluid in their composition as men came and went according to their own self-interests, unencumbered by the rigors of traditional military discipline or by the fines and penalties provided in the Militia Act. After all, there was no Whig government to even impose, much less enforce, any such

---

[113] Col. Andrew Pickens (1739-1817) took parole in June 1780 but re-entered the war in late 1780 after the British or Tories burned his plantation. As a man of the utmost honor, he had resisted repeated Whigs' urgings to resume his role as a Whig commander until he felt honorably discharged from the terms of his parole by the burning of his plantation by the British. After the Battle of Cowpens, Governor Rutledge promoted Pickens to the rank of brigadier general.

[114] *See* Anne King Gregorie, *Thomas Sumter*, (Columbia, SC: Press of The R. L. Bryan Company, 1931, reprinted Sumter, SC: Gamecock City Printing, Inc., 2000); Robert D. Bass, *Gamecock: The Life and Campaigns of General Thomas Sumter*, (New York: Holt, Rinehart and Winston, 1961).

[115] *See* Robert D. Bass, *Swamp Fox: The Life and Campaigns of General Francis Marion*, (Orangeburg, SC: Sandlapper Publishing Co., Inc., 1959).

penalties. In a very real sense, men "voted" with their feet (or, most aptly, with their horses' hooves), staying with or leaving units according to their own perceptions of the desirability of any proposed action. Men volunteered their services under different commanders at different times according to whichever commander was engaged in an action to which the men under him subscribed. Even a cursory reading of the pension applications filed by militia veterans discloses that, during this time period after the fall of Charleston, men served with one commander at one engagement and with a different commander at some subsequent engagement. From these records, the strong impression emerges that loyalties to units and commanders were considerably less important to the individual militiaman during this period than commitments to specific military objectives and locales.

Another common element of these units was that they existed by living off the land. Since there was no government from which to obtain pay or supplies except for the very unpredictable supplies that might be provided from time to time by the Continental Army or the state governments of North Carolina or Virginia, the men sustained themselves by plundering the farms and plantations of supposed Tories or by issuing vouchers for claims against a then non-existent government. "Sumter's Wages," or payment by sharing the spoils taken from Tories, became the accepted method of maintaining militia units in the field.

Perhaps no clearer or more succinct statement as to the composition and motivation of the Whig militia following the fall of Charleston can be found than that attributed to Samuel Hammond.[116] In detailing Sumter's action at Blackstock's Plantation in late November 1780, Hammond stated:

---

[116] Samuel Hammond (1757-1842) was a Virginia native who volunteered initially in that province as an infantryman in the battle against the Royalist Governor, Lord Dunmore. From December 1775 to December 1778, he served as a captain in the Virginia militia. He then moved to the portion of the Ninety Six District of South Carolina that later became Edgefield County and was commissioned a captain in the State troops under the command of Col. LeRoy Hammond, his uncle. He fought in many skirmishes and battles including the engagements at: Spirit Creek, Stono Ferry, the siege of Savannah, Hanging Rock, Musgrove Mill, King's Mountain,

To have a clear understanding of this transaction, and of its influence on the success of our revolution, we must recollect that there were three distinct commands of the militia, in the northern portion of South Carolina. The lower under Colonel Marion, the middle under Colonel Sumter, and the upper or western, commanded, sometimes by Colonel James Williams, and, after his death, by Pickens, sometimes by Colonel [Elijah] Clarke and Colonel [John] Twiggs, of Georgia. *This division of our forces, being all militia, was caused by the local residences, families and attachment of the citizens to their own interests.*[117] (emphasis added)

After the fall of Charleston, the backcountry Whig militia units of the Revolutionary War should not be looked at as traditional military units. They were not such units. Rather, they were democratic associations of free-roaming refugees motivated largely by self-preservation and the desire to protect their own families and property. These men came together to fight under such commanders as were in the field at any particular time in pursuit of objectives which each individual man determined for himself were in his best interests. If the objectives were too vague or too far removed from the interests of the individual militiaman, he had a choice to make. He could find a commander pursuing objectives of interest to him. Alternatively, if he resided in a neighborhood somehow not threatened by the presence of Tories, he could retire from combat to work on his farm and support his family until the emergence of some new threat motivated his re-entry into such militia unit as was addressing that threat. Not surprisingly, it was during this period of extreme instability when the need for self-preservation and protection of family and property were highest that the militia enjoyed its greatest successes at places like Williamson's Plantation, Hanging Rock, Musgrove Mill, King's Mountain, Blackstock's Plantation, Cowpens, and Eutaw Springs.

Blackstock's Plantation, Cowpens, Guilford Court House, Augusta, Eutaw Springs and Dorchester. Moss, *SC Patriots*, 408.

[117] Johnson, *Traditions*, 522-523.

Chapter Seven
Williams' Militia Service

Williams was an active participant in the Patriot militia from the start of the war. In November 1775, he raised a company of men from the Little River area of the Ninety Six District who supported the Revolution and served as its captain. This company was a part of the regiment commanded by Major Andrew Williamson.[118] As the backcountry militia expanded, Williams was promoted to lieutenant colonel in 1776 and to colonel in 1779 or 1780 and thereafter served as the regional Patriot militia commander for the regiment in the northeastern part of the Ninety Six Judicial District. From contemporary records and the pension applications of men who served under him, it is known that Williams participated in the first Battle of Ninety Six (November 19-21, 1775),[119] the "Snow Campaign" (December 1775),[120] the Cherokee expedition (July-October 1776),[121] the Patriots' ill-fated third Florida campaign (May-June 1778),[122] the Savannah-Augusta

---

[118] Gibbes, *Documentary History*, 1: 221. Williams is listed in the muster taken November 19, 1775, as being one of 25 captains of militia companies under the command of Williamson. Williams' company is listed in the muster as having 2 officers, 2 sergeants, and 24 privates. The entire regiment commanded by Williamson is listed as consisting of 523 men, including 55 officers, 36 sergeants and 432 privates.

[119] Sarah Downs, Pension Application, 10 December 1838, W21000, National Archives, Washington, DC. This fight was part of the war between the Whigs and Tories to decide political control of the western backcountry of South Carolina.

[120] *Ibid.* The so-called "Snow Campaign" also was a part of the war between the Whigs and Tories to gain political control of the South Carolina backcountry.

[121] James Cunningham, Pension Application, 17 October 1832, S8273, National Archives, Washington, DC.

[122] *The South Carolina Magazine of Ancestral Research*, Vol. XI, No.4, (Fall 1983), 183-4, contains an order dated August 4, 1779, signed by Williams certifying medicines supplied by Dr. George Ross " . . . to the Men, who went out in the Expedition to Florida under the command of Colonel Williamson, By Order of Colonel James Williams." Martha Condray Searcy, *The Georgia-Florida Contest in the American Revolution, 1776-1778*, (Tuscaloosa: University of Alabama Press, 1985).

campaign (December 1778-January 1779),[123] the Battle of Brier Creek (March 1779),[124] the Battle of Stono Ferry (June 20, 1779)[125] and the unsuccessful siege of Savannah (September-October 1779).[126] All of these engagements were conducted while Andrew Williamson was the senior commanding officer of the militia unit in which Williams and the men under his command served. Like Williams, Thomas Sumter also served as one of Williamson's subordinates, at least during the Cherokee expedition in the late summer of 1776.[127]

The fall and winter of 1775 left unfinished business, Whig vs. Tory, to decide who would control the western South Carolina backcountry. Sides were taken, oaths of allegiance given, and the "Snow Campaign" ended in a military defeat of the Tories at the Great Cane Brake in December and the new Whig government in control. It is not known if Williams was personally present at the Great Cane Brake, but testimony from his soldiers clearly indicates he was active in this campaign.[128]

Williamson's command, however, was not without challenge. Although he was in command of the militia in western South Carolina from the inception of the war in

[123]   Cunningham, Pension Application, footnote 121. *See also* James Cannon, Pension Application, 14 May 1833, S32166, National Archives, Washington, DC.

[124]   John Martin, Pension Application, 21 October 1833, S16459, National Archives, Washington, DC.

[125]   James Tinsley, Pension Application, 25 September 1832, S31426, National Archives, Washington, DC.

[126]   *Ibid.*

[127]   E. Alfred Jones, ed., "The Journal of Alexander Chesney, a South Carolina Loyalist in the Revolution and After," *The Ohio State University Bulletin*, Vol. XXVI, No.4, (October 30, 1921). Although Chesney ended his service in the Tory military, like many other backcountry residents, he served in the Patriot militia early in the war for fear of reprisal against himself and his family, including, in Chesney's case, reprisals against his father who also resided in Ninety Six District during the Revolutionary War. *See also* Bobby Gilmer Moss, *Journal of Capt. Alexander Chesney: Adjutant to Maj. Patrick Ferguson*, (Blacksburg, SC: Scotia-Hibernia Press, 2002).

[128]   Patrick O'Kelley, *Nothing but Blood and Slaughter: The Revolutionary War in the Carolinas, Volume One: 1771-1779*, (Lillington, NC: Blue House Tavern Press, Booklocker.com, Inc., 2004), 71-72; Robert D. Bass, *Ninety Six: The Struggle for the South Carolina Backcountry* (Lexington, SC: The Sandlapper Store, Inc., 1978) 121.

late 1775, Williamson only held the rank of major as of mid-1776. Since several of his subordinates (including Williams) had obtained the rank of lieutenant colonel by mid-1776, Williamson's lack of superior rank understandably led to jealousies regarding his command. Francis Salvador[129], a Whig plantation owner residing in Ninety Six District, wrote on July 18, 1776 to then Chief Justice William Henry Drayton of the Council of Safety reporting on Williamson's campaign against the Cherokee Indians. Salvador noted that Williams and others grumbled at being commanded by a major while they held the rank of colonel. Salvador suggested that if Williamson is fit to command the campaign, he deserves "... a much higher rank than any of these classes [meaning Williams and others], who don't object to his person, but his rank."[130] Salvador further

---

[129] Francis Salvador, a Sephardic Jew, was killed by the Cherokee at Esseneca (modern Clemson, SC), on August 1, 1776. Another interesting account of the skirmish at Lindley's Fort appears in a letter dated July 27, 1776, from Rev. James Creswell to Justice Drayton. In this letter, Creswell states:

> The savages have spread great desolation all along the frontiers, and killed a great number. On the 14th (*sic,* 15th) they attacked a part of Colonel Williams' regiment at Lindlay's *(sic)* Fort, but were repulsed, by the loss of one lover of his country, who unfortunately suffered a cruel death by them. This attack was made by about ninety Indians, and 120 white men. Ten of the white Indians were made prisoners, nine of which were painted. They are now safe at Ninety Six, where they will remain, unless released by their brethren.

Gibbes, *Documentary History,* 2: 31; O'Kelley, *Slaughter,* 1: 149-151.

[130] Gibbes, *Documentary History,* 2: 24-27. In his reply dated July 24, 1776, Justice Drayton stated:

> As for my friend, Major Williamson, I long to see him Colonel of the regiment now under his orders. In the station of Major, he does infinitely more honor to it than any Colonel it ever had; of this rank we must say something hereafter. At present the title of Commander-in-Chief of the expedition against the Cherokees, with which he is vested, will give him command of any colonel in his army. According to the military rule, any colonel in his army, though with part, or even the whole of their regiment, are to be considered as volunteers, and they cannot have any authority in the camp or army but what is derived from the Major. However, as in all probability the Major may authorize them to command their several detachments under him, I think they may expect to receive their usual pay while in actual service. But this may be depended upon, that any conduct that shall clash with Major Williamson's orders will be carefully examined into.

Gibbes, *Documentary History,* 2: 29-30.

suggested that the Council of Safety give Williams and the other colonels written orders to put themselves and their men under the command of Williamson.[131] Salvador's suggestions highlight the rivalries that arose at an early stage of the war regarding command of the militia. Those jealousies over the right to command and priority of rank were sounded early and were to prove to be pervasive themes throughout the entire war.

Salvador's letter is also interesting because it gives some details of an attack on Monday, July 15, 1776, on Patriot militia units commanded by Colonels Williams and Liles[132] at Lindley's Fort on Rabun Creek in South Carolina.[133] According to Salvador, 88 Indians and 102 "Scopholites"[134] attacked Williams and Liles, but were repelled. Salvador reports that two of the "... Cherokees' head warriors were killed" and 13 white prisoners were taken in the skirmish and sent by Liles to jail at Ninety Six. Salvador, however, states that:

> ... our men [meaning Williamson and his officers]... are displeased at the people over the river [to wit: Williams

[131] Williamson himself took notice of the lack of cooperation he received from Williams. In a letter dated July 22, 1776, written from his camp at Barker's Creek, Williamson states that he anticipates Col. Williams will join him the following day with 200 men, noting with some peevishness that Williams "...has been at least fourteen days contriving a mode to cross Saluda River." Gibbes, *Documentary History*, 2: 26-27.

[132] This reference could be to either John Lisle (Lyles, Liles) or James Liles, both of whom appear to have been in the South Carolina backcountry as Whig militia officers during this time period.

[133] The term 'fort' was often used in the 1770s to describe fortifications constructed at the plantation of some local resident willing to offer shelter to his neighbors. Upon threat of attack by Indians or opposing militia units, local residents would retreat into the fort for mutual protection. In this case, 'Lindley's Fort' described the plantation formerly occupied by a Tory named James Lindley, who served as an officer in the militia unit commanded by Fletchall. See "James Lindley, Tory" http://mearsm2.tripod.com/Lindley.html (viewed 9/9/12).

[134] A name given to white Tories who dressed up like Indians when attacking Patriot fortifications in the hope of deflecting their neighbors' animosity away from themselves and onto the Cherokees who constituted a constant threat to the frontier settlers prior to and throughout the period of the Revolutionary War. The name derived from Joseph Scoffel, a Tory, who was active in the Loyalist cause from an early period of the war. For an excellent discussion of the "Scoffol Lights", *See* Rachel N. Klein, "Frontier Planters and the American Revolution: The South Carolina Backcountry, 1775¬1782," in Hoffman, *Uncivil War.* 37-69.

and Liles] for granting quarter to their prisoners, and declare they will grant none either to Indians or white men who join them.

The summer military campaign of 1776 addressed the Ninety Six District's immediate security concern: the Cherokees who allied with the British and initiated some attacks on the frontier at the same time as the June 1776 attack by the Royal Navy on Charleston. Once the British threat to Charleston was defeated, the new Rebel government turned its attention to suppressing the Cherokees, something almost all backcountry settlers could agree upon. Coordinated attacks by Virginia, North Carolina, and South Carolina were planned to annihilate the constant threat of a two-front war. Williams' militia was activated under Williamson to attack the lower Cherokee towns. The summer and fall of 1776, from July through October, found the Ninety Six District militia trekking through the North Carolina mountains, burning villages and crops, and attacking all Indians with whom they came into contact. This campaign cowed the Cherokee and pushed them deep into the Smoky Mountains. It is not known if Williams was personally commanding his regiment, but testimony from his soldiers suggests he was active against the Cherokee in this campaign.[135]

Other than references to Williams in the pension applications of men claiming service under him in the skirmishes and battles referred to above, little is known about the details of Williams' personal actions between the battle at Lindley's Fort in July 1776 and January 1779. It was not uncommon for several militia companies of men or parts of several companies to be detached for duties where the whole regiment was not present; in fact, the principal mission of militia was home defense, and in the Ninety Six military district there were constant threats from Tories, Indians, runaway slaves, and bandits. Additionally, law usually limited the time for militia service and the men were needed to run the farms, especially during planting and harvest seasons,

[135] O'Kelley, *Slaughter*, 1: 157-162; 165-169; Bass, *Ninety Six*, 136-143.

and most militia regiments divided service to allow the local subsistence economy to continue to run. Whether Williams was in the field commanding his regiment on any certain day will probably never be known, but Williams was responsible to meet these local threats, respond to the regional and state military command, and balance the family and economic needs of his men. From the written support of loyalty his troops left in the state's records[136] it can be said with certainty that he was successful in this mission

The Americans immediately refocused on the next threat, the British in East Florida, one of the British colonies that chose not to join the Revolution. Gen. Robert Howe's Southern Department Continentals, reinforced by South Carolina and Georgia militia, organized three campaigns to neutralize the East Florida threats and to try to keep control of Georgia's coastal area. East Florida's governor, Patrick Tonyn, had a major problem. With the defeats of the Loyalists in North Carolina, South Carolina, and Georgia, thousands of loyal subjects fled to Crown protection in East Florida, and to St. Augustine, its seat of government. Some of the men were soon organized into Loyalist battalions of militia or provincial troops, but these refugees had roughly doubled the population of the area with no additional sources of food and other supplies. Raiding cattle and rice from the rich Georgia coastal islands was about the only way to feed these refugees, and many of those refugees possessed the skills necessity demanded. Williamson's militia was directed to reinforce the Americans on the third attempt to invade East Florida to stop the raids and ease the threat to Georgia. Williams' regiment made up part of this force.

Gen. Howe gathered his Continental army at Fort Howe on the Altamaha River in May 1778. He waited on Georgia Governor John Houstoun to bring up the Georgia militia from Burke County and for Gen. Andrew Williamson to join him with his Ninety Six District militia. From Gen. William Moultrie's letters, we know that Williamson's militia did not

[136] Appendix 4.

join Gen. Howe's Army until mid-July. Disputes of command had risen amongst the Rebels, which were also complicated by hot weather, sickness, and the lack of reliable supplies. After crossing the St. Mary's River, these troops occupied the ruins of British Fort Tonyn, recently abandoned by the East Florida Rangers. A Council of War of the Continental field-grade officers convened and agreed upon the withdrawal of this Continental force from the St. Mary's River without crossing into Florida; interestingly, neither Gen. Williamson nor Col. Williams was present at this meeting. It appears that Gov. Houstoun and Gen. Williamson determined to march 40 miles further to the St. John's River, but withdrew and started back north. The offensive fizzled with minor skirmishing, and the Georgia coast temporarily returned to the control of the Americans.[137]

Lord George Germain, Secretary of State for the American Colonies and the royal official charged with the suppression of the rebellion in North America, turned his attention southwards and changed strategies of the now-widening world war. Hoping to attract large numbers of loyal citizens to fill new provincial regiments and militia units recruited in the Southern Colonies, the British sent an expedition by sea to Savannah from New York, which quickly fell after a disastrous fight in December 1778. Reinforced by land troops from East Florida, General Augustine Prévost set his eyes on capturing Augusta. This caused a general mobilization of the South Carolina militia to reinforce the Southern Continental army, now under the command of General Benjamin Lincoln who had been appointed by the Continental Congress to replace the inept Gen. Howe as commander in chief of that department of the army.[138]

In a letter dated January 19, 1779, General Williamson writes to Gen. Lincoln that he has ordered Williams and other militia colonels to march detachments from their regiments

---

[137] Searcy, *Georgia-Florida*; Moultrie, *Memoirs*, 206-240; Gordon Burns Smith, *Morningstars of Liberty: The Revolutionary War in Georgia 1775-1783* (Milledgeville, GA: Boyd Publishing, 2006), 104-107.

[138] Wilson, *Strategy*, 69.

to rendezvous with Col. Leroy Hammond in Burke County, Georgia in "... order to check McGirt." Williamson indicates that he intends to join the men himself in crossing over the Savannah River into Georgia, or positioning his troops to be of most advantageous service either helping to protect the Georgia frontiers or confronting the Indians, whom he fears may be induced to attack the frontiers. He notes that the regiments stationed in Ninety Six District "... have done much duty, being obliged to keep a certain number from each regiment constantly on that duty [checking the Indians] as also detachments from each, by rotation to assist in securing the frontiers of the State of Georgia...".[139] If not in the field himself with the detachments from his regiment, Williams would have been responsible for organizing and assigning the men employed in these efforts. These orders from Charleston mobilized Williams' regiment, which took the field in January moving towards Augusta. At the same time, Loyalist Col. James Boyd was detached to the western South Carolina backcountry to recruit loyal subjects and move towards Augusta to meet British Lt. Col. Archibald Campbell. His recruiting efforts were successful. He raised approximately 800 men and started through Williams' territory headed for Augusta. Because of the strong Whig presence forming on the South Carolina side of the Savannah River, Boyd's recruits moved due west, north of Augusta, hoping to circle around the patriot troop positions and come into Augusta from the northwest. Col. Andrew Pickens' militia regiment soon went in pursuit, and Boyd's crossing of the Savannah was delayed at Cherokee Ford and attacked just across the river in Georgia at Vann's Creek. While Williams' militia was helping Gen. Williamson hold the Savannah River at Augusta, Pickens' men crossed the Savannah, joined with

---

[139] Andrew Williamson to Benjamin Lincoln, 19 January 1779, Manuscript Department, The South Caroliniana Library, University of South Carolina, Columbia, South Carolina. The "McGirt" to whom Williamson refers is no doubt Daniel McGirt. *See* footnote 145. The Whigs and Tories fought at Burke Jail on January 26, 1779; however, it is not thought Williams' militia arrived in time to participate in this fight.

Georgians under Cols. Elijah Clarke and John Dooly, and caught up with Boyd at Kettle Creek. After a sharp battle on February 14, 1779, Boyd was killed and many of the Tories were scattered, defected or were captured, although a few hundred eventually made their way to join the British army. This campaign occurred while much of Williams' militia was away and split the loyalties in Williams' home area, already politically divided, and set the stage for the bloody civil war that would last for the next two years.[140]

The British soon withdrew from Augusta, but retained a strong presence in fortified outposts along the lower Savannah River, threatening South Carolina at a dozen ferries. The South Carolina militia maintained a series of camps from Augusta downstream to counter this threat. Williamson detached an army which slowly followed Campbell's withdrawal down the Savannah towards the Georgia coast. Near the mouth of Brier Creek, the Americans, commanded by Continental Gen. John Ashe, camped on the north side of Brier Creek believing that the British were at their posts further downstream at Ebenezer. A portion of Williams' militia regiment camped with this army. On March 3, 1779, the British, marching in a circuitous route, came in behind the American camp, surprising and defeating Gen. Ashe's army. It is not known if Williams was personally present at this defeat, but his troops were there and it is certain that he suffered for the heavy casualties inflicted on his men with the cry of "no quarter" and "remember poor Macalister" offered in retribution of a British soldier killed in Augusta. After the defeat, the American troops that escaped by swimming the cold Savannah or hiding in the swamps gathered on the South Carolina side reeling from their second major defeat since the British invaded Georgia.[141]

Despite the devastating defeat at Brier Creek, the Americans' efforts in Georgia yielded some success. The British evacuated Augusta and their Carolina reinforcements were dispersed.

[140] Smith, *Morningstars,* 141-144; O'Kelley, *Slaughter,* 1: 244-251.
[141] Wilson, *Strategy,* 81-99; Smith, *Morningstars,* 144-147; O'Kelley, *Slaughter,* 1: 253-262.

The efforts of his regiment in Georgia must have yielded some success. In a letter dated March 12, 1779, Col. Andrew Pickens ordered Captain John Irvine to immediately march, with 25 men, to Ninety Six to join Williams in guarding the prisoners held there. Pickens instructs Irvine to receive orders from Williams upon his arrival in Ninety Six.[142] Two days later, however, Pickens again wrote Irvine countermanding his earlier order. Pickens tells Irvine that General [Andrew] Williamson has ordered Pickens to march a "… strong party of my regiment to Cowan's Ferry, on Savannah River …". Pickens instructs Irvine to march two parts of his company to Cowan's Ferry by Wednesday, March 17, "… armed and accoutred *(sic)*, with good horses." Pickens indicates that he has written to Williams to tell him of the changes in Irvine's orders, but that Irvine himself should speak with Williams to explain the change.[143]

On June 3, 1779, Williams wrote to his wife noting that he was in camp and expected to lie there for several days. The lull in action gave Williams time to think of domestic matters. He writes with instructions for his oldest son, Daniel, to put the mill in order in anticipation of the harvest, to plant corn in the "field over the road," and to go to Ninety Six to retrieve a wagon Williams had left there. Williams also desires his wife to send him "… about half-a-pound of cloves and cinnamon by Major Gillam" (the man by whom Williams sent this letter). Williams notes that he has used his supply of these items and finds them a great help to him since "the water is so bad that I make as little use of it as possible." Williams also requests his wife to send him an "...under jacket, for the two that I brought with me are breaking before."[144]

Action must have remained slow at least through June 12, 1779. On that date, Williams wrote a long letter to his eldest son, Daniel. In this letter, Williams gives his son detailed instructions about looking after his mother and

---

[142] Gibbes, *Documentary History*, 2: 109

[143] *Ibid.*, 113. Cowan's Ferry over the Savannah River should not be confused with Cowan's Ford over the Catawba River in North Carolina.

[144] *Ibid.*, 114.

siblings in Williams' absence from home "in defence *(sic)* of my country." Williams instructs his son regarding the care of his plantation, Mount Pleasant, obtaining horses to be sent down to Williams, sending Williams his favorite riding horse by the name of Nancy, putting the saw mill and flour mill in good order, and selling whiskey which Daniel "must raise the price of ... in order to have things as much on average as possible." Williams suggests: "I think you ought to sell it [the whiskey] at two dollars a quart; if by retail, one dollar a half pint. Secure all you can at £35 per 110 gallons."

Williams tells his son that he is sorry to have to report the "melancholy death of Anthony Griffin." On June 11, 1779, Griffin, while out with a scouting party, accidentally shot himself through the head while leaning on his gun. Griffin never regained consciousness. Williams admonishes his son: "This is a fatal consequence of handling guns without proper care; they ought to be used with the greatest caution. The uncertainty of life ought to induce every man to prepare for death."

This letter also offers instructive insight into the practices of militia units functioning in the South Carolina backcountry. Williams tells his son that he has obtained a "fine English mare" that Williams has left with William Adair on Fishing Creek. Williams asks his son to send a man to go for her, or, better, to go for her himself since she is a valuable animal. Williams says that the horse was:

> ... taken from McGirth *(sic)*[145] by Captain Moore,[146] and I bought his right to her; she is a young, full-blooded

[145] This reference is probably to the notorious Tory, Daniel McGirt (McGrith, McGritt), who was born in the area that later became Kershaw County, South Carolina. Like many backcountry Tories, McGirt moved to Florida where he participated in raids into Georgia, and, in the later stages of the war, into South Carolina. There is evidence that McGirt was with Col. Thomas Brown when he invaded the South Carolina backcountry in 1779. Thomas J Kirkland and Robert M. Kennedy, *Historic Camden* (Columbia, SC: The State Co., 1905), 1: 297-305.

[146] This reference is probably to John Moore, a resident of the portion of South Carolina that later became Union County. Moore was active in the Patriot militia under Williamson and others as early as the Snow Campaign. He served as a brigade major under Williams at the Battle of King's Mountain. Bobby Gilmer Moss, *The Patriots at King's Mountain*, (Blacksburg, SC: Scotia-Hibernia Press, 1990), 188.

mare, and has no brand on her unless Adair has branded her since she has been at his house. He [Adair] took her up in favor of Capt. Moore, and since she was carried from camp I traded for her. I want her got home with as little stir as possible, and branded on both cushions with my branding iron; and let it be said that I bought her off a man on Fishing Creek, and paid $1,000. My reason for begging you to go for her is, that it may not be known she is a plunder mare; and when we have the pleasure of meeting, I will put you in possession of all the particulars regarding her. I shall be glad if you put her to the horse as soon as you get her.[147]

Clearly, Williams was concerned that the way he acquired this horse not be a matter of public knowledge. No doubt the rules of ownership by plunder were somewhat imprecise.

The British Gen. Prévost, emboldened by the two easy victories and the threat to Augusta, embarked on a cross-country invasion of South Carolina that would end literally at the gates to Charleston. Gen. Lincoln recalled his army to the relief of Charleston and Prévost withdrew, this time deciding to island hop down the South Carolina coast towards Savannah. To facilitate crossing of the Stono River, the British fortified the approaches to the ferry's crossing and this is where the American commanders decided to attack. Williams' regiment was again engaged on June 20, 1779, in this bloody fight with the rear-guard of Prévost's retreating army. By this time Williams' militia has been in the field over six months, the spring planting season has passed and the Southern Department Continentals have been pushed almost to their destruction.[148]

As previously noted, Williams stood for election to the South Carolina Senate in 1778 only to be thrashed, both politically and physically, by the Tory, Robert Cunningham. This political loss was a harbinger of further difficulties Williams would face. On Friday, September 3, 1779, there is noted in the Journal of the South Carolina House the following:

---

[147] Appendix 3.
[148] Wilson, *Strategy*, 100-131; O'Kelley, *Slaughter*, 1: 291-299.

Dr. Leach presented to the House the Representation, Remonstrance and humble Petition of James Williams, Colonel, and the rest of the field officers, Captains and subalterns of the regiment of Militia commonly called the Little River Regiment in Ninety Six District, also of divers of the privates living within the boundaries of the regimental district whose names are thereunto subscribed, setting forth, as in the said Representation &c.

Ordered, That the Petition and the papers accompanying the same be referred to a Committee. And it is referred to Colonel Hammond, Mr. Patrick Calhoun, Doctor Leach, Major Wise, Mr. Howe, Captain Jones and Mr. John Ewing Colhoun.[149]

Although the exact nature of the petition is not stated in the official legislative records, the text of the petition has been preserved, and it discloses that Williams faced political heat from his Tory rivals even in trying to maintain his role as commander of his militia unit. The text of the petition (uncorrected in spelling and punctuation) reads as follows:

To his Excellency John Rutledge, Esqr., Governor & Commander in chief in & over the State of So. Carolina; the Honourable the Senate & House of Representatives in General Assembly.

Whereas we (the zealous Friends to our Country, & to all who love & distinguish themselves in her Cause) do understand & are exceeding sorry to hear, that there are false & evilly designing Accusations either lying or about to be shortly laid against James Williams, present Colonel in & over Little River Regiment, of which we are a Part; representing him as distressing & very injurious to the Regiment, & designed (as we believe) by the private Enimies of our Country, to deprive us of so worthy a Friend to his Country in general, & good Officer to us in particular; & thereby do a very singular Piece of Service to the common Enimies of America: We do briefly & anxiously remonstrate thus; that we do experimentally know Colo. James Williams to have been a zealous Patriot

---

[149] Hemphill, ed., *SC Papers*, 191-2.

72

from the Commencement of the american Contest with Britain; & to have always stood foremost in every Occasion when called upon to the Defence of his Country. We do further declare, that we have never known said Colo. Jas. Williams to distress any Individual in the Regiment, who voluntarily & judiciously, when legally called upon & commanded to the Field, have turned out in the Defence of their native Rights & Priviledges together with that of their Country; & we do avow it from our Knowledge, that whensoever Colo. Jas. Williams either directly or indirectly, executed any distressing Things, it was upon the stubborn & refractory, whose Practises & Obstinacy declare them inimical to their Country; & that this he did, as being the last promising Effort to reduce them to the dutiful Obedience of loyal & fellow Citizens. Without delaying you; We your humble Petitioners do earnestly beg, that you will hear this our faithful Remonstrance, & proceed with our respected Colo. Jas. Williams, & all such unjust & disaffected Clamours as may come before you against him, as your superior Judgements may direct; only beging leave to conclude with this one Remark, that doubtless you know, that such Clamours are frequently the necessary Effect of Disaffection to the Country.[150]

For reasons not disclosed in the public records, Williams tried to withdraw the petition on September 10, 1779. After debate on Williams' request, it was denied and the petition was ordered to committee with instructions to report thereon at the next sitting of the House.[151] There is no further reference to the petition or any committee action thereon. Since the invasion of the South by the British occurred shortly thereafter, it is reasonable to speculate that more pressing matters occupied the legislature's attention in the interim between September 1779 and the spring of 1780 when Charleston fell to the British, thus bringing the Whig controlled legislature to an abrupt close.

---

[150] Petition, Manuscript Department, The South Caroliniana Library, University of South Carolina, Columbia, SC.

[151] Hemphill, *SC Papers*, 220.

General Lincoln needed a bold offensive to dislodge the British from their deep-water port and principal city of Georgia. The Americans, both Continental and militia, along with the French Fleet, French and allied army, surrounded Savannah and laid siege to the well-fortified city. The siege proceeded normally, with the Americans preparing trenches approaching the British earthworks and heavy cannon bombarding the town. However, disease and fear of the fall hurricane season caused the French Admiral to issue a time ultimatum to storm the British works and end the siege so he could withdraw his exposed fleet to safe anchorage in the Caribbean. The major assault was planned and executed on October 9, 1779. With diversionary attacks around the city, the main American attack proceeded on the western corner of Savannah's defenses at Redoubt #12 and the French at the adjoining Spring Hill Redoubt. Again Williams' regiment was at the siege and participated in the diversionary attacks; the allies' attack faltered after taking heavy casualties making this day one of the bloodiest in the Revolution. The French and Americans withdrew over the next few days leaving the British in firm control of Georgia.[152]

A letter Williams wrote his wife on September 30, 1779, evidences that he had more pressing military concerns as well. Williams wrote this letter from "Camp, 40 miles from Savannah" while engaged with his unit in the siege of Savannah trying unsuccessfully to dislodge the British from that important port. In this letter, however, Williams was more interested in instructing his wife as to matters relating to his plantation and mercantile interests. As a merchant, Williams was anxious about the drying, milling, and sale of salt. He wanted to make sure that the salt was well dried and sold for one hundred dollars per bushel. As to the plantation, Williams "begs" his wife to take a little time to see about the plantation and to make "Samuel" do what is best to be

---

[152] O'Kelley, *Slaughter* 1: 312-353; Alexander A. Lawrence, *Storm Over Savannah* (Savannah: Tara Press, 1979); H. Ronald Freeman, *Savannah Under Siege* (Savannah: Freeport Publishing, 2002); Wilson, *Strategy*, 133-192; Smith, *Morningstars*, 165-177.

done.[153] The Samuel referred to in the letter is not identified by Williams, but it is known that Williams did not have a son by that name. Since Williams gave these instructions to his wife, and not, as he had done previously, to his son Daniel, it is probable that the then 17-year-old Daniel had joined his father in the field by this date.

Williams tells of the continued tribulations of a backcountry militia officer in a letter dated January 4, 1780, to General Andrew Williamson. In this letter, Williams notes that he has assigned a captain, a sergeant, and eight privates in the upper part of his regiment to prevent plundering of the good people by "those fellows" (not identified by Williams). Williams also notes that he is about to "... try to embody a part of the regiment to send to town." Williams' letter was perhaps in response to a call by Williamson and other South Carolina army and militia officers to muster as many men as possible to come to the defense of Charleston. Sir Henry Clinton, the Commander-in-Chief of the British army in America, was soon to invade the South and lay siege to Charleston, which would fall on May 12, 1780. Williams is afraid that the response from his men will not be good. Williams notes:

> I have made it as public in these parts, as possible, about the Governor promising to get salt for the back country; and it has given some satisfaction to the people, but at present it is bad, for many a poor man is obliged to turn out his hogs for the want of salt. To my knowledge some people must suffer greatly. I have sent a pay bill of Capt. J. Gray's[154] with Mr. McNear to get the money, and should take it as a singular favor if it could be got. The Captain deserted his country, and the men will probably lose their money, and I am likely to be a great loser by it

---

[153] Appendix 5.

[154] The "Captain J. Gray" referred to in Williams' letter is probably Jesse Gray, a Tory who rode with SC Loyalist militia Maj. William "Bloody Bill" Cunningham, and who was declared an outlaw in 1785 by Governor Moultrie for "murders, robberies, and other offenses." *See* Robert Stansbury Lambert, *South Carolina Loyalists in the American Revolution*, (Columbia: University of South Carolina Press, 1987), 296.

myself. I have advanced a great part of their wages to them myself. If I could get the money, I am going to that part of the regiment, and will settle with every man myself. If it is possible, I should be glad to get the money, as I am going to that part of the regiment the latter end of this week.[155]

After the fall of Charleston in May 1780, the Patriots' fortune took a very dramatic turn for the worse. Possession of Charleston by British regular army troops emboldened the Tories to action in the backcountry with the full expectation of support from the British. Indeed, General Andrew Williamson, the leader of the Patriot backcountry militia since the inception of hostilities in South Carolina in the fall of 1775, sat inactive with his regiment throughout the siege of Charleston and accepted parole almost immediately after the city's fall to the British.[156] Williamson's acceptance of parole led Clinton, the British Commander-in-Chief in America, to state in his memoir: "Lord Cornwallis ... assured me that the submission of General Williamson at Ninety Six had put an end to all resistance in every district of South Carolina."[157]

Williams also felt the pressure of renewed Tory activity in the backcountry. The Tory journalist David Fanning tells of joining William Cunningham's company of Tories following the fall of Charleston to the British. Fanning says that he and Cunningham decided "... to take Col. Williams of the

---

[155] Appendix 6.

[156] There is some evidence that even though he took up residence in Charleston, Williamson served as a "double agent," passing military information to the Patriots. The intervention of General Nathanael Greene and other prominent Patriots on behalf of Williamson to prevent the confiscation of his property after the conclusion of the war strongly supports the inference that Williamson had served the American cause, even after his defection to the British in 1780. One should not judge Williamson too harshly, as men of the stature of Andrew Pickens, LeRoy Hammond and others who had been active in the Patriot cause were captured and, as part of their parole, agreed not to bear arms again for the Patriots. Thankfully for the Patriot cause, circumstances arose that allowed each of these men to view themselves as released from the limitations of their paroles. Mark M. Boatner, III, *Encyclopedia of the American Revolution* (Mechanicsburg, Pennsylvania: Stackpole Books, 3rd edition, 1944), 866.

[157] Boatner, *Encyclopedia*, 1210.

Rebel militia prisoner … Col. Williams got notice of it and pushed off and though we got Sight of him he escaped us."[158] Although Fanning does not state the date on which this incident occurred, there is evidence that it probably occurred sometime shortly before June 10, 1780. By that date, Tory militia occupied Williams' plantation, Mount Pleasant, and dispatched to Cornwallis the terms of capitulation of the inhabitants of the south side of the Saluda River, including General Andrew Williamson, Col. Andrew Pickens and Col. LeRoy Hammond (but not Williams).[159] Lieutenant Colonel Thomas Brown of the King's Rangers commanded this unit, which included Cunningham as one of its company captains.[160]

If Cornwallis thought that the surrender by Williamson, Pickens, and Hammond would bring an end to conflict in the backcountry of South Carolina, he misunderstood the commitment of Williams and other backcountry Patriot commanders. Although Loyalists in the backcountry became much more active as a result of the surrender of Charleston to the British, the Patriots remained active as well. Most sought refuge in North Carolina, intending to seize every opportunity to harass the Tories. The region descended into all-out civil war with Loyalist and Patriot militia units frequently engaging each other in skirmishes, confiscating each other's crops and livestock, burning each other's homes, and often hanging as traitors those who were unlucky enough to fall into their opponents' hands.[161]

Shortly before the seizure of his plantation in early June 1780, Williams traveled to Caswell County, North Carolina

---

[158] Lindley S. Butler, ed., *The Narrative of Col. David Fanning* (Davidson, NC: Briarpatch Press, 1981), 31.

[159] George H. Reese, compiler, *The Cornwallis Papers: Abstracts of Americana* (Charlottesville: The University Press of Virginia for the Virginia Independence Bicentennial Commission, 1970), 11.

[160] Bobby Gilmer Moss, *Roster of the Loyalists in the Battle of Kings Mountain* (Blacksburg, SC: Scotia-Hibernia Press, 1998), xii.

[161] There are a number of excellent books and articles that document the fearsomeness of the war as fought among the backcountry residents. *See, e.g.,* Hoffman, *Uncivil War.*

where his brother Henry lived with his family.[162]   It appears that Williams, anticipating the invasion of the South Carolina backcountry by the British and the rise of the Tory militia there, removed most of his slaves and personal property from Mount Pleasant and delivered them for safekeeping into the hands of his brother Henry. Williams was in Caswell County from at least June 12 until June 29. While there, Williams prepared his last will and testament dated June 12, 1780. In it, Williams describes himself as a resident of Ninety Six District, but "… now a refugee in North Carolina." Williams names his wife Mary, and children, Daniel, Joseph, John, James, Washington, Elizabeth and Mary, as his beneficiaries. He names his wife; son, Daniel; brother, Henry Williams; and friend, Joseph Hayes, as his executors.[163]

The evidence supporting Williams' removal of slaves and personal property to Caswell County is strong. After Williams' death following the battle at King's Mountain, Henry prepared an inventory of Williams' assets located in Caswell County. An undated estate inventory signed by Henry as executor of his brother's estate indicates that James' estate included 26 slaves (each named in the inventory), 15 horses (each listed by name and description), a large number of books,[164] 2 feather beds, 4 quilts, 40 pounds of feathers, one old silver watch, 1 silver spoon, 14 pewter spoons, 7 pewter plates, 17 earthen plates, 69 gun locks, 2 wagons, 1 man's saddle, 100 gallons of brandy, 1 45-gallon still, 1 Pole axe and 1 dutch Plow, $1,700 of North Carolina currency, $636 of Continental currency, 16 sheep, 16 geese, 2 cows and calves and miscellaneous other personal property.[165] Available estate records do not disclose whether these slaves and items of personal property were physically located in Caswell County or in South Carolina.

---

[162] In a letter dated July 4, 1780, to his wife, Williams states, "… I was at my brother's and settled my family on as good terms as possible, and left him well with his family;" Appendix 8.

[163] Will Book A, p. 113, Clerk of Courts Office, Caswell County, North Carolina. Joseph Hayes, one of the co-executors named by Williams, was Williams' second-in-command of the Little River Regiment. He would assume command of that unit upon Williams' death and serve with distinction at the Battle of Cowpens.

[164] *See* Chapter 5 for a discussion of the holdings in Williams' library.

[165] Caswell County Estates, N.C., CR.020.508.102, James Williams 1780, North Carolina State Archives, Raleigh, NC.

The estate records, however, do contain a separate and different inventory of "part of the estate of James Williams" signed by his wife in her capacity as co-executrix of her husband's estate. The items listed in the inventory taken by Mary differ from the items listed in the inventory taken by Henry. This difference makes it reasonable to assume that Williams removed to Caswell County the items listed in the inventory taken by Henry while leaving the items listed in his wife's inventory in South Carolina for her use in operating the family's plantation, mills, and mercantile businesses as best she could in the face of mounting Tory boldness.[166]

Additional evidence that Williams removed his slaves and personal property to his brother's home in Caswell County, North Carolina arises from an accounting that Henry filed in connection with his administration of his brother's estate. This accounting contains entries beginning as early as November 14, 1780 and runs through May 11, 1782. There are entries for substantial sums expended by Henry to procure, among other things, pork (£628.80 of North Carolina specie spent on January 7,1781), corn (£1,963 of North Carolina specie spent on February 8, 1781), and pork (£636 of North Carolina specie for 318 pounds of pork purchased from William Rice at £200/hundred spent on May 9, 1781).[167] Although these provisions may have been procured by Henry to benefit the widow and her children in South Carolina, a more plausible explanation is that these provisions were obtained to feed the slaves then living on Henry's farm in Caswell County.

---

[166] If Williams did remove part of his property to North Carolina for safekeeping, he would have been following the example of other property owners who found themselves in the path of the British and Tory military units plundering South Carolina. Even Governor John Rutledge urged Col. Daniel Morgan to send troops to Rutledge's plantation in Ninety Six to recover the slaves there and have them brought to North Carolina. Rutledge told Morgan he wanted to have the slaves "...some place where I may, perhaps, make a little by them" until Patriot control of the South Carolina backcountry was reestablished. Haw, *Rutledge*, 145-6.

[167] Caswell County Estates, N. C., CR.020.508.102, James Williams 1780, North Carolina State Archives, Raleigh, North Carolina.

Chapter Eight
Confrontation with Hill

News of the flight from South Carolina of Governor John Rutledge followed quickly by news of the fall of Charleston on May 12, 1780, spread rapidly through the Carolina backcountry. That news, coupled with Britain's existing control of Savannah and East Florida and the immediate establishment in the backcountry of British or Tory controlled enclaves at Georgetown, Camden, Rocky Mount, Granby, Ninety Six, Orangeburg, and other areas of the state, forced the backcountry Whigs to quickly decide whether or not to continue to pursue independence from Britain. Among those forced to decide his future course of action was Brigadier General Andrew Williamson, the commander of the South Carolina backcountry militia. In early June 1780, Williamson called his men together at his home (known as White Hall) on Hard Labor Creek in Ninety Six District to inform them of his decision to lay down his arms and take parole from the British.[168] He saw continued resistance to the British as futile.

The capitulation of General Andrew Williamson to the British resulted in a leadership vacuum among the remaining Patriots who were unwilling to lay down their arms and abandon the quest for independence for their state. One of the likely successors to Williamson's command was Colonel Andrew Pickens, but, at the urging of Williamson, he surrendered his 300-man command at the fort at Ninety Six and accepted parole from the British.[169] Likewise,

[168] *See*, e.g., Samuel Hammond Pension Application, October 31 and November 1, 1832, S21807, National Archives, Washington, DC.

[169] Pickens returned to take a very active role in the Patriot cause following the plundering of his plantation in December of 1780 by Loyalist forces under the command of Major James Dunlop. Pickens, ever a man of the utmost honor and integrity, viewed Dunlop's actions as a violation by the British of the terms of his parole, thus freeing him from the oath of loyalty he was required to take when paroled in June 1780. William Johnson, *The Life and Correspondence of Nathanael Greene (1822)*, 2 Vols. (Charleston, SC: A. E. Miller, 1822, reprinted New York: De Capo Press 1973). Alice Waring, *The Fighting Elder: Andrew Pickens, 1739-1817*, (Columbia, SC: University of South Carolina Press, 1962). Pickens was to play

Williamson's brother-in-law, Colonel LeRoy Hammond, accepted parole from the British shortly after the fall of Charleston.[170] With the state capital captured, the members of the legislature imprisoned or on the run, the governor a refugee in North Carolina, and most of the experienced militia officers under parole, there was no official mechanism by which Williamson's successor as commander of the backcountry militia could be appointed. The void was there to be filled by any man self-assured enough to assert his will to lead and in whom enough men had confidence to follow.

Into this void stepped two Carolina backcountry men, Thomas Sumter and James Williams. That Sumter was the first to assert his claim is indisputable. Sumter, a former Continental Line officer who resigned his commission in September 1778 when the war appeared to be largely over in the South, was rousted out of his lethargy by the burning of his plantation by British troops dispatched by Banastre Tarleton while in pursuit of Colonel Abraham Buford's Virginia Continental Line retreating from Leneud's Ferry near Charleston in May 1780.[171] Sumter fled his plantation shortly before the British arrived. He set up camp within the friendly confines of the Whigs' old and trusted allies, the Catawba Indian Nation, in the "New Acquisition," the area just south of Charlotte, North Carolina.[172] The area Patriot militia leaders and their men gathered at Sumter's camp on Clem's Branch of the Big Sugar Creek in what is today Lancaster County, South Carolina on the line with North Carolina. There a council of war was held by the Whig militia leaders sometime in June.[173] Sumter was elected by those leaders as their 'general'.

---

a major role in the Patriot victory at Cowpens in January of 1781 and in various significant battles and campaigns thereafter.

[170] Like Pickens, Hammond also later broke parole based on Loyalists having violated his property.

[171] Gregorie, *Sumter*, 74.

[172] The "New Acquisition" land was unilaterally ceded by the last of North Carolina's Royal governors to South Carolina shortly before the outbreak of the war.

[173] In his memoir, Richard Winn states that the council at which Sumter was elected as the commander of the backcountry Whig militia occurred a day or two before the Battle of Ramsour's Mill. Since that battle occurred on June 20, 1780, that dates Sumter's election as having occurred on June 18 or 19.

Immediately following the fall of Charleston, Williams, who had been in the field almost continuously from the inception of the war, was in North Carolina delivering his movable property to the safekeeping of his brother. His business in Caswell County completed, Williams returned to the fray. We do not know exactly when Williams returned to South Carolina, but it seems unlikely that he was a participant in the council of war at which Sumter was elected to lead the South Carolina backcountry Whig militia. None of the accounts of that council of war indicate that Williams was present. We do know, however, that Williams had joined the Whigs gathered at Sumter's camp by July 3 when he wrote a letter to his wife from Sumter's camp. We also know that the refugee Whigs who joined Sumter at his camp were men from different areas of the Carolina backcountry, some like Williams, Thomas Brandon, Samuel Hammond, Joseph Hayes, Joseph McJunkin, Benjamin Roebuck, were from the lower, more western region around Ninety Six. Others, like Sumter, the Winn brothers, William Bratton, Edward Lacey, William Hill, were from the more central and upper part of the South Carolina backcountry. As has been noted, when it came to engaging militia in combat, their loyalties most often lay in pursuing objectives that served their self-interest. Therein lay the seeds for the ultimate split between those men loyal to Williams and those loyal to Sumter.

There is no evidence of any rift between Sumter and Williams until after the Battle of Hanging Rock on August 6, 1780. It appears that Williams and those loyal to him were content to remain with Sumter to engage the British and Tories at Rocky Mount and Hanging Rock. After Hanging Rock, however, something occurred that placed a great strain on the cohesiveness of the Whig forces under Sumter. That something was the pending arrival of the forces of the Southern Department of the Continental Army under the command of General Horatio Gates, who was marching his Army to confront Cornwallis. That confrontation would occur on August 15 and 16, 1780, near Camden.

In anticipation of his arrival in South Carolina, Gates contacted Sumter in an attempt to get Sumter to coordinate his movements with Gates' strategy for engaging Cornwallis. Having no formal authority over Sumter, Gates could not order Sumter to join him, and Sumter seemed disinclined to do so. Perhaps sensing that Sumter would not join his force, Gates dispatched some North Carolina and Maryland troops to reinforce Sumter's militia with instructions for Sumter to move down from the Waxhaws to cut off Cornwallis' supply lines and routes of retreat. Sumter moved down to Rocky Mount (which he found abandoned by the British) and the Catawba River to cut off British reinforcements and supplies to Cornwallis at Camden. Sumter's efforts were rewarded with the capture of a number of British troops and supply wagons on the march to join Cornwallis. Interestingly, Sumter's actions placed him and his men in closer proximity to their homes.

Drawing upon their own experiences in joining forces with Continental troops in such unsuccessful undertakings as the Florida expeditions, the first siege of Savannah, the Battle of Brier Creek, and the Battle of Stono, Williams and his followers decided their interests lay elsewhere than engaging Cornwallis at Camden with Gates, or in continuing with Sumter in his foray into the area of his personal interest to harass Cornwallis' supply lines. Their interests lay in facing the British and Tory forces in more limited militia actions in the area of Ninety Six, the deeper backcountry nearer their homes and families who were now exposed to harsh conditions imposed by British occupation and the reinvigorated backcountry Loyalist militia. Sometime after the Battle of Hanging Rock and before the Battle of Camden, Williams and those refugees in Sumter's camp who were allied with him, left Sumter intent on bringing the war to the British and Tories in the area of their personal interest— the area around Ninety Six. Taking their leave of Sumter, Williams and his men went to the camp of Colonel Charles McDowell in search of other Whig forces intent on harassing the British. In McDowell's camp, they found those forces in

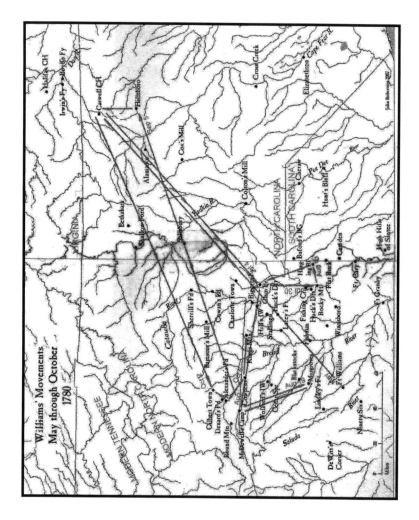

This map depicts Williams' movements following the fall of Charleston on May 12, 1780 and his death near King's Mountain on October 8, 1780.

the persons of Elijah Clarke of Georgia and Isaac Shelby of the far western region of the North Carolina mountains, and the men under their command.

The split of Williams and his followers from Sumter's command gave rise to the savage attack on Williams' character and motives leveled by Colonel William Hill, an officer in the militia commanded by Sumter. In essence, those accusations are that:

1. Williams, having a small number of followers willing to fight under his command, accepted the role as Sumter's commissary only to desert his post and abuse his position of trust by embezzling supplies and ammunition rightfully belonging to Sumter and his command.

2. Having been privately confronted by Col. Edward Lacey regarding the supplies stolen from Sumter's camp, Williams gave his word to return the supplies only to renege once he was free from Lacey's control.

3. Williams took undeserved credit for the Patriot victory at Musgrove Mill and used his participation in that victory to gain promotion to Brigadier General of the South Carolina militia from Governor John Rutledge, South Carolina's Whig governor in exile in Hillsborough, North Carolina, under false pretenses.

4. Asserting his right to command based on his ill-gotten promotion, Williams repeatedly attempted to divert to his home district of Ninety Six the Patriot forces gathering to fight Major Patrick Ferguson's Loyalist troops.

5. Having been unsuccessful in his effort to divert the Patriot troops to Ninety Six, Williams and his small band of followers played an unwelcome and minor role in the Battle of King's Mountain, tagging along behind Sumter's men on the march to King's Mountain even in the face of being pelted by rocks thrown by Sumter's followers in an

active attempt to discourage their participation in the march.

6. Williams was shot shortly after the end of the Battle of King's Mountain by some unnamed Whig because of the distaste for his actions prior to the battle.

There is overwhelming evidence, however, that Hill's accusations against Williams are baseless. That evidence begins with the fact that there is not one example of contemporary support for Hill's accusations against Williams. One fundamental technique for testing the validity of any statement is the presence of independent attestation or corroboration of that statement and, in the case of Hill's accusations, there is no such independent, contemporary attestation. The only negative statements about Williams are made by later generations of historians and writers who have repeated Hill's accusations without having questioned the validity of any of Hill's accusations. Such contemporaneous accounts as do exist are either overtly contradictory to Hill's accusations or silent as to any negative feelings against Williams.

Hill expressly tried to solicit independent support of his view of Williams. On April 23, 1814, Hill wrote to then Governor Isaac Shelby of Kentucky asking him "… please to give me further information respecting Col. Williams being with you previous to the Battle of Kings mountain, and giving you such information as he knew to be false."[174] Shelby's reply does not supply the requested support for Hill's accusations.[175] Indeed, Shelby states that Williams' participation at King's Mountain was a 'welcomed' addition to the Whig forces there. In the official report of the battle submitted shortly after the battle and signed by Shelby as well as William Campbell and Benjamin Cleveland, Williams is credited with having told the gathered Whig forces where to find Ferguson's army.[176] That statement, made within days

---

[174] Lyman C. Draper Manuscript Collection, State Historical Society of Wisconsin, Microfilm, 1VV110.

[175] Appendix 14.

[176] Appendix 12.

of the battle, clearly contradicts Hill's assertion that Williams intentionally misled the Whigs by trying to divert them to Ninety Six, Williams' home territory.

But there exists even stronger evidence that Williams was intent on confronting Ferguson, not in diverting the gathering Whig forces for an attack on Ninety Six. Surprisingly, that evidence comes from the British. In a letter dated October 1, 1780 sent by Cornwallis from his headquarters in Charlotte to Ferguson, Cornwallis says:

> I am informed that Colonel Williams with part of Sumpter's corps marched yesterday from Kerrel's Ford [Sherrill's Ford], giving out that they were going against you. My informant saw only 150, but the enemy told him they had 400 more—that is not good authority. Sumpter has had a quarrel with Williams about command and is gone to Hillsborough to refer it to Gates.[177]

Cornwallis indicated in another letter to Nisbet Balfour that same day that his intelligence of Williams' intention was gathered by a flag of truce he sent Williams at Sherrill's Ford,[178] probably from a drunk officer in Williams' corps.[179]

In his memoirs, Richard Winn, one of Sumter's leading subordinates and one of the men who accompanied Sumter on the trip to Hillsborough that resulted in Sumter's absence from the Battle of King's Mountain, gives his account of the reasons for Sumter's trip. Relating events occurring at a war council shortly before the Battle of King's Mountain, Winn states:

> ... it was unanimously decided that Colonels Winn, Thomas & Capt. Henry Hampton should without delay proceed on to Hillsbough *(sic)* and to use their best Means with the Board of war, Governor John Rutledge & Genl. Gates in procuring Arms Ammunition Camp Utensils & Clothing &c in Order to enable us More fully to prosecute the War in South Carolina. Notwithstanding the necessity

[177] Saberton, *Cornwallis Papers*, Vol. 2, 158
[178] *Ibid.*, 106.
[179] *Ibid.*, 107

and Urgency of the Demand not a Single Article Could be Obtained. Genl. Sumter being present Governor Rutledge Confirmed the Genl. in his Command and so we immediately returned to So. Carolina in the mean time left Colo Lacey in Command, Lacey being inf[orme]d that Majr. Ferguson with a large party of Men was on their March for Charlotte to Join L. Cornwallis was determined to give him battle tho not having more than 300 Men but on approaching the Enemy to his great Joy he found (See Gordon's or Ramsay's history) *in this Action I am well informed no Men in the World could behave more brave that the So. Carolin[ian]s* which was the Case with the Officers & Men for Other Quarters. (emphasis added)[180]

Note that Winn makes no mention of Williams in describing the reasons for going to Hillsboro. In addition, Williams, as a South Carolinian, clearly would have been among the men singled out by Winn for praise as to their actions at King's Mountain. Here again is a direct refutation of Hill's attack on Williams.

Perhaps most convincing of all arguments against Hill's accusations, however, is the complete lack of any corroboration of them in any of the few first-hand accounts left by men who served under Sumter during this period or in any of the pension applications filed by veterans of the Revolution. Richard Winn, Thomas Young, Joseph McJunkin, and Samuel Hammond all left first-hand, eyewitness accounts of their services under Sumter. None say anything derogatory of Williams.

Four hundred and seventeen veterans of the Battle of King's Mountain and/or the engagement at Musgrove Mill lived long enough to file applications for a pension from the federal government for their services in the Revolution.[181]

[180] Winn's memoirs are posted on the Internet at the University of Georgia's website at http://neptune3.galib.uga.edu/ssp/cgi-bin/tei-natamer-idx.pl?sessionid=7f000001&type=doc&tei2id=KRC119 (viewed 9/9/12). A transcription of the memoirs by this writer is posted at http://jrshelby.com/sc-links/winnrichard.pdf (viewed 9/9/12).

[181] Moss, *Patriots of Kings Mountain*. Transcriptions of all of these pension applications can be found posted on the Internet at http://revwarapps.org (viewed 9/11/12).

Not one of these veterans makes a derogatory statement about Williams. Not one of these veterans states that Williams deserted his post or embezzled supplies from Sumter's camp. Not one of these men states that Williams broke his word to Lacey and refused to return supplies to Sumter. Not one of these men states that Williams played anything less than a significant role in the battle at Musgrove Mill or that Williams aggrandized his role in that engagement to gain promotion from Governor Rutledge under false pretenses. Not one of these men states that Williams came into Sumter's camp after the Battle of Musgrove Mill and tried to usurp command from Sumter.[182] Not one of these men states that Williams tried to mislead the Whigs and direct them towards Williams' home near Ninety Six. Not one of these men mention any inexplicable absence of Williams and his men from the forces gathered to face Ferguson. Not one of these veterans states, as Hill asserts, that rocks were thrown at Williams and his followers on the march to King's Mountain for any reason, much less in an attempt to discourage their participation in the forthcoming battle. And not one of these men hints that there was the slightest suspicion that Williams had been murdered by the Whigs after the firing at King's Mountain had ceased.[183] If there were any validity to Hill's

---

[182] That Williams and Sumter disagreed over issues of command, however, cannot be doubted. Even the British were aware that Williams and Sumter had disagreed as evidenced by correspondence from Lord Cornwallis from his headquarters at Charlottetown [Charlotte] , NC on October 1, 1780 when he wrote both Patrick Ferguson and Nisbet Balfour telling them that his intelligence was that Sumter and Williams had a dispute as to command and that Sumter had gone to Hillsborough to consult with Horatio Gates. See, Ian Saberton, Arranger and Editor, *The Cornwallis Papers: the Campaigns of 1780 and 1781 in the Southern Theater of the American Revolutionary War*, 6 vols. (Uckfield, East Sussex, England: The Naval & Military Press Ltd. 2010) 2, 106-7, 158.

[183] The transcriptions of the pension application of veterans of the Battle of King's Mountain as well as pension applications files by many other participants in the Southern Campaigns of the American Revolution can be found at http://www.revwarapps.org (viewed 9/12/12). That veterans were not bashful about accusing their superiors of dishonorable conduct is well illustrated by the accusations of cowardice made against Hill himself in the pension application of Samuel Walker [FPA S3448] not to mention the numerous derogatory

accusations against Williams, it seems incredible that none of these veterans alludes to or even hints at some fact in support of those accusations. No such allusions or hints exist.

The history of the writing of Hill's memoirs also sheds light on the creditability that should be given to them. Correspondence from two of Hill's grandsons, William Randolph Hill and his brother, the noted Confederate General Daniel Harvey Hill, indicates that Hill initially began dictating his memoirs in his old age to William Randolph Hill. W. R. Hill stated in a letter to Lyman Draper dated June 1859, that: "This manuscript was written at intervals by the dictation of my grandfather, Col. (W) Hill of SC in his old age & indeed dotage partly by me when a lad of about 14 years of age and chiefly by a man in the neighborhood employed as an amanuensis."[184] D. H. Hill relates that his father, Solomon Hill, Col. Hill's youngest son, "...tried to prevent him [Col. William Hill] from writing it [the memoirs]. He was in his dotage at the time & my father thought that the egotism of the book was enormous."[185] Further, D. H. Hill wrote to Draper that "The MSS was written by my oldest brother when a boy, the late Col. Wm. R. Hill. He was ashamed even as a boy of its egotism—that accounts for the little interest we have felt for it."[186] An even more scathing assessment of the memoirs was given to Draper by Judge John M. Ross, Hill's grandson-in-law, who said "in the latter part of his life when his body was worn down by disease and his mind very much impaired, he did write a history of Genl. Sumter's campaigns, which was never published, his family knowing that nothing he then wrote was suitable to meet the public notice."[187]

That William Randolph Hill ascribed little credibility to his grandfather's memoirs is amply demonstrated by subsequent events. In 1829, Williams' son and namesake,

---

statements made against General John Ashe for his handling of the forces at Brier Creek or General Horatio Gates for his conduct of the Battle of Camden.

[184] Draper MSS, Sumter Papers, 1VV182. "Amanuensis," in this instance, refers to a person employed to write what another dictates.

[185] Draper MSS, Sumter Papers, 11VV230-235.

[186] Draper MSS, Sumter Papers, 11VV236-239.

[187] Draper MSS, Sumter Papers, 11VV244-245.

James Williams, filed a petition with the South Carolina legislature seeking compensation on behalf of the heirs of Col. Williams for his services during the Revolution.[188] The petition was originally introduced in the House and, after being referred to committees for study, worked its way slowly through the legislative process. In 1833, a joint committee of the House and Senate was appointed to review the petition. On May 29, 1833, the State of South Carolina awarded Williams' heirs the sum of $4,000 for the services of their father during the Revolution. William Randolph Hill was a member of the South Carolina House in 1829 and a State Senator in 1833. It is difficult to believe that he would have allowed this petition to result in favorable action by the legislature if he thought his grandfather's allegations against Williams were merited. Also, Thomas Sumter was alive during most of the time the petition was before the Assembly and, although he was no longer active in politics at this late period of his life, it is equally difficult to believe that he would not have voiced strong opposition to the granting of the petition if he ascribed validity to Hill's allegations.[189]

Although it is impossible to know with any degree of certainty, it is interesting to speculate on Sumter's motives for keeping Hill's memoirs in his possession, unpublished and unexposed to public view, from the time he received them from Hill in 1815 until they were uncovered by Thomas

---

[188] Appendix 18.

[189] The original (and as far as is known, the only) version of Hill's memoirs was sent by Hill to Thomas Sumter. Sumter kept the memoirs in his possession until his death in 1832. After Sumter's death, his grandson-in-law, J.W. Brownfield copied the original, and it is this copy which Sumter's son, Thomas, Jr., certified as being a true copy of the original before its return to William Randolph Hill. What became of the original is not clear. The copy in the Draper MSS appears to be the copy made by Brownfield and it is this copy that was loaned to Draper by the Susan Brownfield, Sumter's great granddaughter. The correspondence between Draper and the Sumter/Brownfield family regarding his obtaining the copy of the memoirs is itself interesting and sheds much light on Draper's prejudices and bias in favor of giving the memoirs unquestioning, full credibility since he promised Susan Brownfield if she would let him copy the memoirs, he would do 'a just yet kind vindication of the truth and justice of history.' The correspondence between Draper and the Sumter/Brownfield family is found in Draper MSS, 18VV beginning at 13 and running throughout the volume.

Sumter, Jr., subsequent to his father's death in 1832. Was Sumter embarrassed by the accusations made by Hill? Did Sumter intend to exercise a form of "pocket veto" by keeping the memoirs in his possession? Was Sumter aware that airing the memoirs during the lifetimes of the men who fought under Williams would expose the memoirs to attack by the only people with firsthand knowledge of the events Hill describes?

The vindication of Williams from Hill's accusations, however, does not hinge on these general observations and surmises. A close examination of each of the charges leveled by Hill disproves their validity.

Hill states that Williams and a "few of his friends or neighbors" came into Sumter's camp shortly after Sumter returned to his camp at Clem's Creek after going to the site of the Battle of Ramsour's Mill on June 20, 1780. Hill states that Williams and his friends came from the north "... securing [plundering] some of the most valuable property." Hill asserts that, since Williams was unacquainted with Sumter or any of his officers other than Hill, Williams sought Hill's help in obtaining some position for him in Sumter's camp. Williams is said to have informed Hill that he [Williams] had no men he could expect to command, but that he wished to be of service to his country. Hill says that he secured an appointment for Williams as commissary for Sumter's troops with responsibility "... to supply the army with provisions." As commissary, Williams had "... under his command ... a Major Miles with 25 men & Horses together with 4 wagons & teams." Hill says that Williams continued in this position until after the Battle of Hanging Rock (which occurred on August 6, 1780). Hill then states that Williams, along with Col. Thomas Brandon (whom Hill identifies incorrectly throughout his *Memoirs* as "Col. Brannon"), "... eloped & had taken a great number of the public horses[,] a considerable quantity of provisions with the camp equipage & a number of men."

According to Hill, Sumter sent Col. Edward Lacey after Williams and Brandon with orders to recover the horses, equipment and other provisions taken by them. Hill reports that Lacey:

... overtook them encamped on the west side of the
Cattawba *(sic)* River & finding their number too great for
him [Lacey] to do any thing by coercive measures he then
got the said Williams to walk with him out of his camp, he
[Lacey] then presented a pistol to his [Williams'] breast
& informed him that if he made any noise to call for assistance he was then a dead man, & after expostulating with
him on the baseness of his conduct he then said Williams
gave his word of honor that he would take back all the public property & as many of the men as he could persuade to
go back. Upon this Col. Lacy *(sic)* not confiding in his word
exacted an oath to the same purpose But so it was that
neither the one or the other had the desired effect, as he
[Williams] took the public property & the men to a place
called the Cherokee ford where there were a number of
North Carolinians encamped with Maj. McDowel *(sic).*

Hill's account, however, only presents one side of the
story. Williams and his followers undoubtedly took with
them some of the supplies from Sumter's camp when they
departed.[190] McJunkin, Brandon, and others of the men
who followed Williams out of Sumter's camp would clearly
have viewed that they had a better claim than Sumter and
his men to the materiel they took. They would have been
justified in that view. According to McJunkin, most of the
ammunition used by Sumter in the summer of 1780 came
from the supplies McJunkin and others under the command
of Thomas Brandon hid when they heard of the fall of
Charleston. McJunkin states:

Before Brandon's defeat,[191] when we heard of the fall
of Charleston, a number of us collected to save a parcel
of powder which had been brought down from Col.

[190] By August 6, Sumter, however, was well supplied not only with the
ammunition supplied by Brandon and his Spartan District militia, but also from the
supplies captured at Ramsour's Mill and Hanging Rock.
[191] This is a reference to the skirmish on June 8, 1780, between Whig
militia forces under the command of Thomas Brandon and Tory forces commanded
by William Cunningham. Patrick O'Kelley, *Nothing but Blood and Slaughter: The
Revolutionary War in the Carolinas, Volume Two: 1780.* (Lillington, NC: Blue House
Tavern Press, Booklocker.com, Inc., 2004), 163-165.

Thomas', & deposited under the care of Col. Brandon. We held a consultation what should be done with it, and we determined to hide it, which was done with some difficulty in hollow logs. Some of this powder was afterwards used in the Battle of Hanging Rock. Some of those Engaged in this business were Col. Brandon, Captn. Samuel Otterson, Lieut. Benjn. Jolly, Joseph Hughes, Wm. Sharp and myself.[192]

Among the six men named by McJunkin as having been involved in hiding the ammunition subsequently used by Sumter, Brandon, Hughes and McJunkin are known to have been with Williams at Musgrove Mill; Otterson was severely wounded at Hanging Rock and was out of action at the time of the battle at Musgrove Mill. Jolly and Sharp probably were with Williams. It is difficult to believe that the men who had provided the supplies would not have felt entitled to take some, if not all, of those supplies with them when they decided to part company with Sumter and follow Williams.

Bear in mind that once Charleston fell in May, there was no civil government in South Carolina, only martial law as imposed by the occupying British military—a government none of the Whigs who refused the protection of the British were going to honor. Consequently, the Whig forces that remained in the field were composed of men who viewed themselves as free to follow whichever leader they thought was most likely to serve their best interests. That a number of the men who initially rallied around Sumter (a resident of the mid-state region of South Carolina, a non-participant in the war for the two years prior to Charleston's fall, and the holder of no officially granted militia rank) chose to follow Williams (a resident of the frontier region of the state around Ninety Six, an unrelenting participant in the Whig militia since the inception of the war, the man with official duties and responsibilities for the defense of the Ninety Six area and probably the highest ranking militia officer who was still in the field in the backcountry) is not surprising. That those men who followed Williams felt entitled to

---

[192] McJunkin, Narrative, Appendix 17.

some portion of the available materiel is even less surprising and, viewed fairly, not in the slightest reprehensible.

Given what is known about Williams' personality and character, Hill's portrayal of him as a sniveling subordinate groveling for some position in Sumter's camp is very difficult to accept. As a man who had been in the field from the beginning of the war with ever-increasing command responsibilities that resulted in his being in command of his own regiment, Williams seems a poor candidate to have lost his self-confidence to the degree described by Hill. More likely, Williams came into Sumter's camp in the same mind-set that appears to have been pervasive in the militia throughout the war. He came as the ranking militia officer in that region of the state and as a participant in perhaps the most democratic institution of its time – the militia. The men in that militia were free to follow whichever leader they found most in tune with their goals and objectives. Most of the time, those goals and objectives were driven largely by self-interest; by a desire to protect one's own family, property, and community.

Another contemporary participant offers a very different view of Williams than that offered by Hill. Joseph McJunkin, then a captain in the Patriot militia unit commanded by Lt. Col. James Steen under Sumter, states that Williams did not join Sumter until after the Battle of Hanging Rock concluded on August 6, 1780.[193] McJunkin says Williams joined Sumter at the same time that Sumter received orders from General Gates on August 14th to cooperate with him in his planned attack on the British at Camden. Williams preferred to march west of the Wateree to Ninety Six District where he lived and had many friends being tormented by the Tories emboldened by the fall of Charleston and by the presence of British troops in the various enclaves established by Cornwallis in the backcountry. McJunkin states that

---

[193] The accuracy of McJunkin's statement as to the date on which Williams joined Sumter, however, is called into question by a letter dated July 4, 1780, from Williams to his wife written from "Camp Catawba, Old Nation." Appendix 8. This was the location of Sumter's camp, which, according to Hill, was located on the Catawba River at Clem's Creek (in what is now Lancaster County, South Carolina) on the boundary line between North and South Carolina.

"the troops joined with Sumter or Williams just as their own inclinations led them." Also joining the unit under Williams was Col. Thomas Brandon, another Patriot who had served under Andrew Williamson in the South Carolina backcountry, Joseph Hayes, Williams' second in command of the Little River Regiment, Lt. Col. James Steen, Benjamin Jolly, Samuel Otterson, Joseph Hughes, Joseph McJunkin, and Capt. Samuel Hammond and others.[194]

Williams' strong desire to raise troops to attack the Tories in Ninety Six District is evident in his letter dated July 4, 1780, addressed to his wife. In this letter, Williams tells his wife: "… I pray God that I may have the happiness of seeing you my love at Mount Pleasant in the course of this month, with a force sufficient to repel all the Tories in the upper part of South Carolina." Williams states his awareness "… that many false stories are in circulation in our country to the disheartening of our friends in that quarter [Ninety Six] of the State." Williams then proceeds to paint a very optimistic picture of the strength of the American military forces on their way to relieve the inhabitants of South Carolina. He gives specific (and very inflated) numbers for the troops under the command of, or being raised by, DeKalb, Wayne, Smallwood, Caswell, Rutherford, and Sumter, and states that there is a very large French fleet on the South Carolina coast. This confident assessment of the forces being marshaled to confront Cornwallis was intended to bolster the resolve of those Patriots oppressed by the Tories and British troops in the backcountry. Williams assured his wife that "… under the blessing of God … we will soon relieve our distressed family and friends; so bear up with fortitude till that happy day comes."[195]

---

[194] The composition of Williams' troop is borne out by numerous pension applications of veterans who claimed service under the above named officers. *See also* Bailey, *Commanders*, 262. The author has compiled a table in which he attempts to assign the various men thought to have been at the Battle of King's Mountain. That table appears as Appendix 13. That table demonstrates that there were a substantial number of men from both South and North Carolina serving under Williams at that battle.

[195] Appendix 8.

Williams had good reason to be very concerned about his wife and family. On July 10, 1780, Williams' plantation, Mount Pleasant, was occupied by the British and Tories for a second time. Ferguson and his Tory troops seized the property and dispossessed Mrs. Williams and her family. In diaries kept while serving under Ferguson on his expedition to pacify the South Carolina backcountry and gain recruits for the Tory militia, both Lt. Anthony Allaire and Dr. Uzal Johnson note that Ferguson spent the evening of July 10 at Col. Williams' plantation. Each state that Mrs. Williams and the children were at home, but were "treated with the utmost civility." Neither journalist states that Williams' plantation was plundered by Ferguson or his troops, but, based on diary entries regarding Ferguson's occupation of other Whig properties, it is reasonable to assume that Ferguson and his men helped themselves to whatever provisions and horses the plantation had to offer. That those offerings may have been negligible and not worth mentioning would lend further support to the speculation that Williams already had removed most of his personal property and slaves to the safety of North Carolina, well in advance of Ferguson's arrival. Both Allaire and Johnson described Col. Williams as being a "Rebel," Dr. Johnson noting that Williams commands a "Battalion of Rebels and is a very violent, persecuting man."[196] Lt. Allaire observed that Col. Williams was away "with the Rebels, and is a very violent, persecuting scoundrel."[197] Words of high praise indeed when spoken by the enemy.

Williams wrote his letter dated July 4, 1780, from Sumter's camp on the Catawba River. He states that he is in Sumter's camp and that Sumter's force numbers about 500 South Carolinians, with the expectation that Sumter will cross the river that day to join an additional 500 militiamen from Mecklenburg County, North Carolina. The fact that Williams was in Sumter's camp as early as July 4 clearly favors Hill's

[196] Bobby Gilmer Moss, ed., *Uzal Johnson, Loyalist Surgeon: A Revolutionary War Diary* (Blacksburg, SC: Scotia Hibernia Press, 2000), 43.
[197] Allaire's Diary is set forth in an appendix to Draper, *King's Mountain*, 500.

statement over McJunkin's as to the date Williams came into Sumter's camp. Williams' letter, however, does not refer to any commission he obtained to serve as Sumter's commissary or in any other office. Whether or not Williams left Sumter's camp sometime after July 4 and returned at some later time more consistent with McJunkin's statement will probably never be known.

The participation of Patriots of the stature of Thomas Brandon, Joseph Hayes, James Steen, Joseph McJunkin, Samuel Hammond, and the men serving under them with Williams in the march to Ninety Six District casts substantial doubt on Hill's characterization of Williams' actions. Further doubt arises from the fact that none of these men abandoned Williams after the confrontation that Hill alleges occurred between Williams and Lacey. Another explanation might be that Sumter and Williams, both of whom had served as colonels in command of their own militia regiments, and both of whom were ambitious to succeed General Andrew Williamson as the general officer in command of the militia in that part of the state, simply disagreed as to what step to take next in support of the Patriot cause. In keeping with the democratic manner in which militia units operated at this time, it is logical to believe that the men encamped with Sumter on Clem's Creek simply chose which leader they wished to follow. That Williams and those choosing to go with him fell victim to Hill's ire is not surprising. Bearing in mind that militia units were loosely organized groups of men whose primary connection was common interests in protecting their families and property, it seems likely that Williams, Brandon, Hayes, Roebuck, Steen, McJunkin, Hammond, and their men were more interested in returning to their home areas to confront the Tory militia units operating there than in remaining with Sumter in the New Acquisition.[198]

[198]   At least one historian gives some credence to this view. In her biography of Sumter, Dr. Gregorie characterizes the decision to split their forces as being mutually agreed upon by Sumter and Williams. She states:

On the march to the Waxhaws, Sumter was joined by his commissary, Colonel James Williams. While encamped at Cane Creek, it was agreed that Williams should take such of the troops as would accompany him and march through the region now comprised in the counties of York, Spartanburg, and Laurens. At the same time Sumter should descend the Wateree and co-operate with Gates, who was advancing through the pine barrens toward Camden. Gregorie, *Sumter*, 97.

Dr. Gregorie states that the basis for the dispute between Williams and Sumter was that Williams "made off" with camp horses, provisions, and camp equipment. Gregorie, *Sumter*, 97. How Williams and the men who elected to go with him were to conduct a campaign without horses, provisions or camp equipment, however, is an issue that neither Dr. Gregorie nor Hill, chose to address.

Chapter Nine
Musgrove Mill

In the predawn hours of Saturday, August 19, 1780, a band of 200 mounted Patriot militiamen from the Carolinas and Georgia completed an overnight 40-mile trek from their camp at Smith's Ford on the Broad River to within several miles of Edward Musgrove's mill on the Enoree River.[199] Their objective was to attack what they thought was a similarly-sized force of South Carolina Tory militia camped at Musgrove Mill. When they arrived, they learned from a local sympathizer that the Tories had been reinforced during the night by 300 British Provincials. Finding themselves outnumbered by more than 2 to 1 and unable to affect a retreat on their exhausted horses, the Whigs quickly formulated a plan to take up a defensive position hoping to avoid detection by the British long enough to recuperate sufficiently to retreat or, if unsuccessful in avoiding detection by the enemy, to engage them as best they could. Contact was made and the ensuing rout of the Provincial and Tory forces[200] at Musgrove

---

[199] Musgrove Mill State Historic Site is located on south side of the Enoree River in Laurens County, South Carolina, off of SC Highway 56. The site is just across from the point of conjuncture of the Spartanburg, Union and Laurens county lines. The exterior of the visitors' center for the Site is an interpretation of Edward Musgrove's colonial-era home and is located adjacent to the home's original location. The mill site is located below the visitors' center on the south bank of the Enoree River. Only parts of the foundation and the dam structures remain. The Historic Site now incorporates land on which interpretative demonstrations are held on the north side of the river across from the visitors' center. The actual site of the battle, however, is yet to be proven. It is known that most of the battle took place on the north side of the Enoree in what is today Spartanburg County, with perhaps a portion of the battleground lying in Union County. The conclusion of the battle took place on the south side of the Enoree in Laurens County. Present day Highway 56 is believed to lie very close to where the colonial-era road lay at the time of the battle.

[200] Because of the awkwardness of referring to the Provincial and Tories forces jointly, the term "Loyalist" will be used occasionally when referring to these forces collectively. A distinction, however, must be drawn between the Provincials and the Tories. The terms "Provincial" or "Provincials" are used to refer to forces made up of Americans who formally enlisted in the British army and who served in units composed entirely (or almost so) of their fellow American Loyalists. Provincial

Mill provided a desperately needed boost in morale to the Whigs who were in danger of being completely overrun in South Carolina. Coming just three days after the crushing defeat of the Continental Army's Southern Department under General Horatio Gates[201] at Camden[202] and one day after the thrashing of Patriot forces under Colonel Thomas Sumter[203] at Fishing Creek,[204] the victory at Musgrove Mill demonstrated to the much maligned Whig partisans that they were capable of successfully confronting the better trained and equipped British and Loyalist forces that controlled most of South Carolina and all of Georgia and were preparing to invade North Carolina. Although the Patriots' hasty retreat from Musgrove Mill resulted in no gain of territory, the

units were trained, clothed, equipped and disciplined in the same manner as regular British army units. Often, Provincial forces were commanded by British regular army officers. The terms "Tory" or "Tories" are used to refer to militia or partisan forces consisting of Americans who remained loyal to the King and Great Britain. The militia or partisans were citizen soldiers who came together when called to serve under officers who were men of prominence in their local communities but who were not professional soldiers. The term "British" is used in reference to the professional British regular army.

[201] Horatio Gates (1728/9-1806) was born in England and served as an officer in the British Army. He was with Braddock at his defeat in the French and Indian War. He became a friend of George Washington and settled in Virginia. Upon the outbreak of the Revolution, he was commissioned as a brigadier general in the Continental Line. He was credited with the defeat of Burgoyne at the Battle of Saratoga while commanding the Northern Department of the Continental Army. He was sent to command the Southern Department in the summer of 1780 and suffered a humiliating defeat at the Battle of Camden in August of that year. On December 2, 1780, in Charlotte, he was replaced by Nathanael Greene as commander of the Southern Department. Golway, *Greene*, 238.

[202] The Battle of Camden is summarized in O'Kelley, *Slaughter* 2: 256-277. A more detailed description of the battle is offered in Kirkland/Kennedy, *Camden*.

[203] Thomas Sumter (1734-1832) was a lieutenant colonel in the 2nd (later, 6th) Rifle Regiment of South Carolina State Troops in the spring and summer of 1776. He and his regiment were later transferred to the Continental Line. He resigned his commission as a Continental officer on September 19, 1778, and remained inactive until after the fall of Charleston in May 1780. The South Carolina backcountry Whig partisans rallied around Sumter once he retook the field after the British burned one of his plantations. He was promoted by Governor John Rutledge to the rank of Brigadier General in October 1780 and thereafter was the ranking officer of the South Carolina militia until the end of the war. Bass, *Gamecock*; Gregorie, *Sumter*.

[204] The Battle of Fishing Creek is summarized in O'Kelley, *Slaughter* 2: 277-286.

psychological importance of Whig partisans' standing up to and defeating the Loyalist forces steeled the nerve of the Patriots throughout the southern backcountry. That resolve would be needed for their decisively important involvement in the battles at King's Mountain and Cowpens—two battles that were pivotal in America's struggle for independence from Great Britain.

Reconstructing the details of the Battle of Musgrove Mill presents some challenges. There are only four first-hand accounts of it from the Whigs' perspective. The descriptions given by those four participants vary significantly. Only the short report given by James Williams, one of the commanders of the Patriot militia, was written contemporaneously.[205] The only other militia commander present at the battle who is known to have given his account of it is Col. Isaac Shelby.[206] He wrote his account in 1814, thirty-four years after the events he describes. At that time, Shelby was 64 years old and serving the second of his two non-consecutive 4-year terms as governor of Kentucky.[207] The most detailed account of the four was given by Samuel Hammond, one of Williams' subordinates.[208] Unfortunately, Hammond's account bears no date and the original appears to have been lost. The sole known source of his account is its purported transcription given by Johnson

[205] Appendix 10.

[206] Isaac Shelby (1750-1826) was a Patriot militia officer. He was the first Governor of the State of Kentucky, being elected in 1792. Boatner, *Encyclopedia*, 1001. S. Roger Keller, *Isaac Shelby: A Driving Force in America's Struggle for Independence* (Shippensburg, PA: Burd Street Press, 2000).

[207] Shelby's account, annotated by the author, is set forth in full in Appendix 15. Shelby & Hart Collection #659z in the General and Literary Manuscripts, Manuscripts Department, Wilson Library, The University of North Carolina at Chapel Hill.

[208] Hammond's account reads as follows:

Before this affair a few days, Colonels Williams and Bratton, of South-Carolina, Colonel Clarke, of Georgia, Colonel Isaac Shelby, of the Virginia or Holston settlement, McCall, Hammond and Liddle of the Ninety Six brigade, formed a junction in the State of North-Carolina, near General McDowal's rendezvous, _____ county. General McDowal was consulted on the propriety of making an excursion into South-Carolina, to look at the enemy, and to commence operations against their out-posts, if they should be found assailable with our force. The general countenanced the proposal, and stated that he would co-operate with us, if he saw any opportunity for doing good by the joint force. Two active and enterprising men were sent in, to look at and obtain intelligence as to the position of the outposts of the enemy nearest to us. Having received information from those men that there was a party at Musgrove Mill, on Enoree river, that was altogether tories, and not over two hundred in number, it was determined to march with all possible dispatch to attack them. Information was given to General McDowal, and our little band was put in motion. We marched twenty or twenty-five miles, on the 16th; halted and fed and refreshed for an hour, and after dark set out upon our march again. In the course of the night, Colonel Bratton turned off the line of march, intending to pass through his own neighborhood, and to fall in with us again before day. This was injudicious in every point of view, for it afforded more than a double chance to the enemy of gaining intelligence of our approach, and a probability of our not falling in with them, or of their aiding us in the affair; and this proved to be the case, for they did not rejoin us until the affair was over. General McDowal advanced a few miles, but declined joining in the enterprise. Our march was silently and skillfully conducted, and we arrived near the post about daylight. It was agreed by Colonels Williams, Shelby and Clarke, that the command should be conjoint; the plan of operations was agreed upon; and, as the precise situation of the enemy's camp had not been clearly discovered, it was determined to halt half a mile from the place, and send in two men to be relied upon, to reconnoiter the post and obtain the information wanted. They performed the duty-saw the situation of the enemy-found them on the opposite side of the river from our position, and, unfortunately, on their return, fell in with and were fired upon by a patrol of the enemy. Thus disappointed in the hope of surprising them, it was resolved to send in sixteen well mounted, expert riflemen, to fire at the enemy, and draw them on to attack us upon the hill. This was done; our horses were picketed three hundred yards in the rear beyond the hill, and we were formed a little upon the descent, towards the enemy, Each colonel took his station to command his own men. The sixteen sent out, were, in retreating, to fall on the left flank of the enemy, and from their horses keep up a fire upon them. As they advanced, this command was united to Captain Shadrick Inman, of Georgia—a like number placed on the right flank, with the same orders. There were sixteen men left, also, as a main guard, on our horses; this reduced our whole effective force, including officers, to about __ men. These were placed in one line, in scattered or open order, and were ordered not to fire until the enemy were within fifty yards, and also to be governed by a single shot from Colonel Shelby; to be steady and take good aim. Being thus prepared, the enemy were drawn out. They came, flushed with the hope of an easy victory, in full trot. Reinforcement had joined them the day before, of which we had no information; Colonel Innis and Major Fraser, with one hundred and fifty regulars—York volunteers—had joined the tories.

They advanced in three columns—the regulars, commanded by Major Fraser, in the centre—the militia on the right and left. Advancing, at the distance of one hundred and fifty yards, they displayed and gave us a fire, which was not returned but from our flanking parties. They then

in his *Traditions and Reminiscences* published in 1851.[209] The inability to completely authenticate Hammond's account has caused some historians to disregard it. Hammond also made a very brief mention of the battle in his pension application

advanced with trailed arms; their columns displayed, and were allowed to come within forty yards, when the signal was given, and their ranks thinned. They fell back, and before a second fire they formed and again advanced. On the second fire, they fell back in confusion. The fire then became brisk, and was kept up on our side. The tories saw the regulars fall back in disorder, and they also gave ground in confusion, and in fact without any thing like pressure on our part.

Our troops, encouraged by this disorder, rushed on with more boldness than prudence. The mounted riflemen on both flanks charged into the ranks of the retreating foe, and they fled and re-crossed the river in great disorder. On our part, we were so scattered and out of order, that it was determined to halt, form, and send for our horses to cross the river. This caused a necessary pause, during which we received information, by express, that General Gates had been defeated and his army dispersed; that Colonel Sumter, after much success, had been overtaken by the enemy, and also defeated and his army dispersed; and to crown all, that Colonel Ferguson was advancing towards us, and within a few miles, with a considerable force. Thus circumstanced, we were compelled to give over further pursuit, and seek our own safety by a hasty retreat.

The result of this little affair was a clear speck in the horizon, which would have been otherwise very much overcast. We had one captain—S. Inman—a brave man and good officer, with four men killed and eleven men wounded. The British lost Major Fraser, and eighty-five men killed; Captain Innis and several other officers wounded, the number not known. One captain of regulars, two captains of tories, and seventy-three privates–mostly York volunteers–were taken prisoners. Our retreat was hasty, and continued, without halting, day or night, to feed or rest, for two days and nights. We entered North-Carolina, and passed down towards Charlotte with our prisoners. Colonel Shelby left us near Greenville, and we encamped near Charlotte, with a few continental troops who had escaped from Gates' defeat. We made a stand here, to collect more men from the defeat, and form for a further expedition. Here the prisoners were committed to Major S. Hammond, while Colonels Williams and Clarke returned to the western frontier of South-Carolina. The prisoners were conducted to Hillsborough' and delivered up there. This little affair, trifling as it may seem, did much good in the general depression of that period. Our numbers continued to increase from that time, and all seemed to have more confidence in themselves.

[209] Johnson, *Traditions,* 519-522.

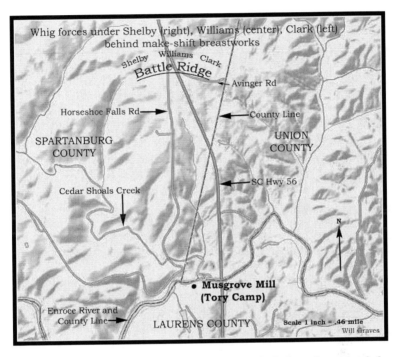

Archeology performed in 2012 has established that the site of the initial engagement at the Battle of Musgrove Mill (August 19, 1780) took place on a hill approximately 1.45 miles from Edward Musgrove's mill on the Enoree River. Artifacts of that engagement have been found concentrated in portions of the area labeled Battle Ridge.

filed in November 1832.[210] The final Patriot account was given by Joseph McJunkin, another subordinate of Williams'. McJunkin makes only passing reference to his involvement at Musgrove Mill in his pension application dated December 25, 1833.[211] At age 82, he gave a somewhat more detailed description in the narrative he dictated in 1837 to his grandson-in-law, the Reverend James Hodge Saye.[212]

[210] The relevant part of Hammond's pension application reads as follows: In August 18 or 19 was with Col. Williams of Carolina, Clark of Georgia & Col. Shelby from over the mountains in the Battle of Musgrove Mill on Enoree River Ninety Six District. The Enemy were defeated, Col. Innis commanding officer of British wounded, Major Fraser 2nd in command killed, a number of prisoners taken who were committed to Applicant's Care & Safety. Conveyed to Hillsborough N. Carolina. While at that place received the appointment of Major with a Brevet commission as such from Gov. Rutledge with orders to command the militia from Col. L. Roy Hammond's Regiment of Ninety Six. Had conference with Board of War & obtained from Mr. Pen an order on the commissaries & Quartermasters for the So. Western frontiers of North Carolina, for Rations of provisions & forage, for the S. Carolina & Georgia militia, who might assemble for active service. *See* footnote 168.

[211] The relevant part of McJunkin's pension application reads as follows: I then fell under the Command of Col. Williams & hearing at Smith's ford that the British & Tories were encamped at Musgrove Mill on Enoree River marched 40 miles that night & attacked the Tories as day broke and defeated them on 20th August 1780, and at the Close of this action we received Word that both Sumpter & Gates were defeated, which Caused us to abandon the Idea of Crossing the River to attack the British; having passed Ferguson's on our right we retreated towards the mountains. *See* Appendix 17, 271.

[212] The relevant part of McJunkin's 1837 narrative reads as follows: Col. Williams, Col. Steen and myself one of his captains, with those who had a disposition to annoy the British and Tories at Ninety Six, by various marches went up to Smith's Ford on Broad river, & lay one day & on the evening of the 18th of August, took up our line of march for Musgrove Mill. On our march we were overtaken by Francis Jones, who informed us of the defeat of Gen. Gates & Sumter's defeat. Continuing our march, & leaving Col. Ferguson a little to our right, reaching the Tory camp, 300 strong, forty miles from Smith's Ford, at the dawn of day, & commenced the fight; killed a great many, took many prisoners, & marched forty miles to North Tiger. The reason of our rapid march to North Tiger was this: The Tory prisoners told us, that there 400 British soldiers under the command of Col. Innis, encamped just over the river; and Knowing that Col. Ferguson whom we had just passed a little on our right, must also have heard our firing, & not knowing but that they would break in upon us (who were only about 150 strong), & serve us worse than we did the Tories. We got our water as we passed the brooks, & hunger was so great that we pulled green corn and ate it as we marched. Draper MSS, Sumter Papers, 22VV153-203, *also* Appendix 17, 284.

From the opposite perspective, the infamous Tory David Fanning gave the only account known to have been made by any of the participants defeated by the Whigs at the Battle of Musgrove Mill.[213] In addition to Fanning's brief acknowledgment of the battle in his memoirs, there are several references to it in diaries or correspondence from British or Tory sources that help establish the date of the engagement and the identities of the Provincial and Tory forces that participated in it.

Drawing from these various accounts, sometime after the Battle of Hanging Rock on August 6, 1780, Williams, Colonel Thomas Brandon,[214] Lieutenant Colonel James Steen,[215] Captain Samuel Hammond, Captain Joseph McJunkin, and their followers decided to leave Sumter's camp near Fishing Creek. There is no record of the exact number of men who accompanied Williams when he left Sumter's camp. Prior to their departure, Sumter received communications from Gates urging Sumter to join forces with him in his planned

---

[213] Fanning's account reads as follows:
... after the British american Troops had taken possession of ninety six I continued scouting on the Indian lines untill Colonel Innis forwarded his march up to Musgroves Mill on the Innoree River. I then Joined them with a party of 14 men the morning following the picketts were attacked by a party of Rebels. Col. Innis ordered us to advance and Support them which we did, and followed them untill we arrived where the main body lay in ambush under the command of Colonel Williams. Col. Innis was unfortunately wounded with Several other officers. We engaged them for Some time and then Retreated about a mile and a quarter where we encamped and in the night marched off towards ninety Six under the command of Captain Depister, and the next morning I and my Small party Returned back to the Indian lines. Butler, *Fanning*, 32.

[214] Thomas Brandon (1741-1802) was a South Carolina Patriot militia officer who served under James Williams at Musgrove Mill and King's Mountain and under Thomas Sumter at Blackstock's and later engagements. Phil Norfleet has a biographical note covering Brandon posted at http://sc_tories.tripod.com/thomas_brandon.htm (viewed 9/9/12). *See also* Moss, *SC Patriots*, 95.

[215] James Steen (1734-c.1781) was a successful planter who, at the time of the Revolution, resided in the Thicketty Creek area of what was once the northern part of Union County (formed in 1785) and is now part of Cherokee County (formed 1897), SC. He is believed to have been stabbed to death in Rowan County, NC, while trying to arrest a Tory. Moss, *SC Patriots*, 894.

invasion of South Carolina aimed at Camden. In keeping with
the independent mindedness of the Carolina backcountry
militiamen,[216] Williams and his followers evidently determined
that they would be better employed harassing the British
positions in the more western portions of the State where
they, their families, and friends resided.[217] They withdrew to
the camp of Colonel Charles McDowell[218] at Smith's Ford on
the Broad River where they found Colonel Isaac Shelby from
the Watauga region of western North Carolina and Colonel
Elijah Clarke[219] from Georgia with their men. Shelby and
Clarke shared Williams' interest in harassing the British and
Loyalists in the deep backcountry of South Carolina: Shelby
because his western North Carolina home was threatened
by Major Patrick Ferguson's aggressive recruitment of Tory
militia, and Clarke because of his consuming interest in
liberating Augusta from British control. While at McDowell's
camp, Williams, Shelby and Clarke learned of the Tories
gathering at Musgrove Mill. Recognizing their opportunity
to strike a blow against His Majesty's forces, they determined
to attack the Tories.

The exact nature of the Tory encampment at Musgrove
Mill is not known. It does not appear to have been a fortified
position permanently garrisoned by either Tory or Whig
forces. Although the road and ford just east of the mill would
have been a strategically important point of access into and

[216] Chapter 6 above.

[217] Sumter also argued to Horatio Gates that his forces were better
used in stopping reinforcements and supplies from coming in from Ninety Six,
controlling the British at the Wateree-Catawba River and controlling the British
and Loyalists in the backcountry than in joining Gates' force near Camden. Sumter
convinced Gates of the wisdom of his strategy, and Gates reinforced Sumter's forces
by assigning to him 100 Maryland Continentals, 300 North Carolina militiamen and
artillery. Johnson, *Traditions*, 296; Kirkland/Kennedy, *Camden*, 1: 152.

[218] Colonel (later General) Charles McDowell, 1743-1815, was a
commander of North Carolina Whig militia after the fall of Charleston in 1780.
William S. Powell, ed., *Dictionary of North Carolina Biography*, 6 vols. (Chapel Hill, NC:
The University of North Carolina Press, 1979-1996), 4: 142.

[219] Elijah Clarke (1733-1799) was the North Carolina born commander
of Whig militia forces from the backcountry portions of Georgia. He participated in
the engagements at Kettle Creek, the first Cedar Spring, Musgrove Mill, Blackstock's
Plantation and the several sieges of Augusta. Boatner, *Encyclopedia*, 233-234.

out of this part of the backcountry, there is no record of Musgrove Mill being occupied on a continuous basis by either party. The mill's position near the road and ford makes it logical to assume that British, Loyalist, and Whig forces used the mill from time to time to grind corn into meal and wheat into flour, the basic staples of a backcountry militiaman's and soldier's diet.

On the occasion of the battle, Musgrove Mill probably was serving as a gathering area for local Tory militia commanded by Colonel Daniel Clary.[220] In early August, Clary had been ordered by Col. John Harris Cruger,[221] commander of the British regulars at Ninety Six, to muster his Dutch Fork Militia Regiment in support of Ferguson's force.[222] The exact strength of Clary's command is not known, but estimates are that he had at least 100 men with him at Musgrove Mill on August 18.

In his account, Shelby tells of a Captain William Hawsey, "an officer of considerable distinction among the Tories," being wounded at the height of the battle. Since Hawsey is not known to have been a member of Clary's regiment,

[220] Daniel Clary was a prominent backcountry militia officer residing in the area of Ninety Six District that later became Newberry County. His property was confiscated at the end of the war but he successfully petitioned the State Legislature to be allowed to remain in South Carolina where he regained prominence after the war. Bobby Gilmer Moss, *The Loyalists in the Siege of Fort Ninety Six* (Blacksburg, SC: Scotia-Hibernia Press, 1999), 23-24.

[221] John Harris Cruger (1738-1807) was a provincial officer from New York who accompanied Lt. Col. Archibald Campbell in his successful expedition against Georgia in late 1778 and early 1779. He participated in the defense of Savannah in October 1779. He succeeded Nisbet Balfour as commander of the British and Loyalist forces at Ninety Six. He successfully defended that location against the siege mounted by Nathanael Greene in the late spring of 1781. He was at the Battle of Eutaw Springs on September 8, 1781. He participated in the defense of Charleston for the remainder of the war. At the conclusion of peace, his New York properties having been confiscated, he removed to London where he lived out his life. Boatner, *Encyclopedia*, 310-311.

[222] Cruger to Cornwallis, 4 August 1780, Cornwallis Papers, P.R.O. 30/11/63: 13-14. In referring to the Dutch Fork militia, Cruger is making reference to the Loyalist militia serving in the area between the Saluda and Broad Rivers in what was called the Saxe-Gotha area of South Carolina. This area was originally settled primarily by German Lutherans and the term "Dutch Fork" is thought to be a corruption of "Deutsch Fork."

Hawsey's presence strongly suggests that other Tory units were gathering at the mill. The best estimate is that all together there were about 200 Tories at the mill as the sun rose on August 19, 1780.

Sometime during the late evening of the 18th or early morning hours of the 19th, the Tories were joined by about 300 Provincials under the command of Colonel Alexander Innes.[223] Like the Tories under Clary, Innes' force was under orders from John Harris Cruger to reinforce Ferguson.[224] Innes' force included about 100 men of his South Carolina Royalist mounted regiment, a light infantry company of the New Jersey Volunteers, and a detachment from the 1st Battalion of Delancy's New York Brigade, part of John Harris Cruger's own regiment.[225] There is also evidence that the

---

[223] Alexander Innes was an officer and official of the British provincial forces in North America. Given the rank of Lt. Col., he commanded the South Carolina Royalists when that unit was formed in February 1779. *See* Moss, *Chesney*, 109-110.

[224] Cruger to Cornwallis, n.d. [17 August 1780], Cornwallis Papers, P. R. O. 30/11/63: 93.

[225] The composition of Innes' command is taken from the account given by Roderick Mackenzie, a British officer who in 1787 published a short book entitled *Strictures on Lt. Col. Banastre Tarleton's History*. In his book, Mackenzie takes Tarleton to task for failing to even mention the battle fought at Musgrove Mill. Though Tarleton was not involved in the battle, Mackenzie's view was that a proper history of the Southern Campaign by a "correct historian" would necessarily have to include an account of the battle at Musgrove Mill. Roderick Mackenzie, *Strictures on Lt. Col. Banastre Tarleton's History*, (London: R. Faulder, 1787). Mackenzie's account of the battle reads as follows:

An action which a detachment from the garrison of Ninety Six had with an American corps, upon the 19th of August, 1780, would certainly have excited the attention of a correct historian.

Lieutenant Colonel Tarleton's forte as an author, seems to be compilation; he might therefore have given the American account of this affair, either from Ramsay, or from the Scots Magazine of December, 1780; but as it has entirely escaped his attention, you may depend upon the following statement, as it comes from unquestionable authority.

The Americans, under Colonels Williams, Shelby, and Clarke, were strongly posted on the Western banks of the Enoree; their numbers have not been precisely ascertained, probably five hundred. The detachment of British troops, commanded by Lieutenant Colonel Innes, consisted of a light infantry company of the New-Jersey volunteers, a captain's command of Delancy's, and about one hundred men of the South Carolina regiment mounted. The troops passed the river, the infantry drove the

Loyalists may have been using Musgrove's house or the area around his home as a field hospital caring for men wounded in the skirmishes between the Whigs and Loyalists at Cedar Spring,[226] Wofford's Iron Works[227] and probably Hanging Rock[228] as well as other recent backcountry engagements. Doctor George Ross is known to have been at Musgrove Mill treating the injured and wounded Loyalists at the time of the Battle of Musgrove Mill.[229]

When the Whigs under Williams, Shelby, and Clarke departed McDowell's camp on August 18, their intelligence was that Ferguson and his force of Tory militia numbering more than 1,000 men were encamped somewhere between McDowell's camp at Smith's Ford and Musgrove Mill.[230] To avoid encountering this much-larger force, the Whigs traveled in the woods until complete darkness and then took to the road to cover ground more quickly. Arriving about one and a half miles from the ford of the Enoree River near Musgrove Mill just prior to first light on the morning of the 19th, the Whigs received word from a local sympathizer that the Tories had been reinforced during the night by Innes and his troops.

enemy at the point of the bayonet, and the horse, though but lately raised, and indifferently disciplined, behaved with great gallantry; but in the moment of victory, the commandant, Major Fraser, Captain Campbell, Lieutenants Chew and Camp, five out of the seven officers present, were wounded by a volley from the Americans. The British troops, consequently unable to avail themselves of the advantages which now offered, were conducted by Captain Kerr to the Eastern side of the river, where they remained till reinforced by Lieutenant Colonel Cruger.

The text of Mackenzie's book is posted at
http://home.golden.net/~marg/bansite/src/strictures1.html (viewed 9/9/12).

[226] O'Kelley, *Slaughter* 2: 197-199.

[227] *Ibid*, 233-236.

[228] *Ibid*, 221-233.

[229] In his diary, Dr. Uzal Johnson, a Loyalist surgeon under Ferguson's command, has an entry dated August 10, 1780, in which he reports that the wounded from the engagement at Cedar Spring were sent to Musgrove Mill on the Enoree River to be attended by Dr. Ross. Moss, *Uzal Johnson*, 53-54.

[230] This intelligence was wrong. On the night of the 18th-19th of August, 1780, Ferguson and his men were camped at Colonel Richard Winn's plantation near Winnsboro, SC, some 55 miles due east of Musgrove Mill. Moss, *Uzal Johnson*, 57-58. Consequently, Ferguson was too far away from the Whig's path of march to be an immediate threat to them.

The Provincial forces under Innes' command were not Tory militia. They were well-trained and equipped Provincials schooled in the discipline and tactics of the regular British army and dressed in the uniforms of the regular army. Their presence presented the Whigs with a significantly different challenge than the Whigs had anticipated when they began their trek the evening before.

To further complicate matters, a scouting party sent out by the Whigs encountered a Loyalist scouting party. Shots were exchanged between the two parties. The advantage of surprise that the Whigs had hoped to have over their enemy was lost.

Finding themselves outnumbered and deprived of the benefit of surprise, Shelby, Williams, and Clarke hurriedly held a council to decide how to proceed. Because they had traveled all night at a breakneck pace, their men and horses were exhausted. Retreat was not an option. The commanders decided to take up a defensive position at the top of the wooded hill that rose up from the river on its north slope.[231] They deployed their men behind trees in a 300-yard-long line that straddled the road leading to the ford of the Enoree. Each of the colonels commanded his own men with Shelby's men being posted on the American right flank, Williams'

---

[231] Charles Baxley noticed that the 1786 map of Spartan District (the "Benson Admeasurment Map"), owned by the Spartanburg County Historical Association, depicts the site of the battle as being about 2.7 miles north of the ford of the Enoree River. Baxley made the estimate by applying the map's scale to the distance between the ford and the symbol used by the cartographer to mark the spot of the battle. Baxley notes that the fact that the cartographer placed the battle this far from the ford should be given credence because the cartographer would have visited the area within six years of the battle and probably based his placement of the symbol on statements from area residents who had been on the battlefield immediately after the battle. Baxley indicates that such placement of the battle would have it occurring at the very top of a long rise up from the ford rather than at the top of an intermediate hill currently interpreted as the site of the Whig's defensive position. Although not quite so far removed from the ford as the 1786 map places it, very recent archeology indeed indicates that the battle was fought further from the ford on the Enoree River than has been previously thought. See the map on page 105.

men in the center and Clarke's men on the left flank.[232] It is likely that some of the men cut bushes and limbs to form a makeshift breastwork on the crest of the hill filling in the gaps between the trees and providing a modicum of cover to those militiamen unfortunate enough to find themselves treeless.[233]

Having lost the element of surprise and being deprived of the option of immediate retreat, the colonels devised a strategy that would take maximum advantage of their position.[234] Captain Shadrach Inman of Clarke's command along with about 15 of his men was sent forward under instructions to proceed to the river and fire upon the enemy. If the enemy chose to return fire and engage Inman's troops, he was to feign retreat and lead the Loyalists into the heart of their compatriots' defensive line on the timbered ridge. Inman and his men were to file off to their right (*i.e.*, the left flank of the American line) as they retreated up the hill toward where their compatriots waited to ambush the advancing enemy. Inman's small force was matched by a like number of mounted riflemen posted on the Patriots' right flank under the command of Captain Josiah Culbertson.[235] The mounted riflemen on each flank were to bring cross fire to bear on the enemy as they advanced up the hill.

Taking the bait dangled by Inman and his men, the Loyalists crossed the river and deployed in ranks within 150 to 200 yards of the Americans. They commenced firing while advancing in formation in their usual disciplined fashion. Firing uphill, they apparently overshot the Whigs and consequently inflicted few casualties on them.[236] The fact that they commenced firing far in advance of the 100-yard effective range of their Brown Bess muskets indicates that

---

[232] James Hodge Saye, *Memoirs of Major Joseph McJunkin: Revolutionary Patriot* (Richmond, VA: Watchman and Observer, 1847; Spartanburg, SC: reprint A Press, Inc., 1977), 15.

[233] In his account, Shelby mentions that the men throw up a breastwork. Shelby's account, however, is the only one that mentions a breastwork.

[234] Exactly who came up with the strategy is not known.

[235] Saye, *McJunkin Memoir*, 16.

[236] *Ibid*, 16.

perhaps Inman and his men stayed exposed to fire from the Loyalists in a position well in front of the Whig line and that perhaps the Loyalists were unaware of the presence of the larger Whig force at the time they opened fire on Inman and his men. Another possibility is that the Loyalists deployed and opened fire early in an attempt to intimidate the Whigs by displaying their numbers and flashing the much-feared bayonets with which they no doubt intended to charge the Americans at some point during the engagement. Whatever the reason for it, this premature fire filled the battleground with smoke, obscuring the Loyalists' view of the defensive position of the Whigs. The Whigs, on the other hand, were instructed to hold their fire until the Loyalists got within a range of 50 to 60 yards. They stayed protected behind their trees and makeshift breastwork: they had no intention of deploying in formal battle lines and exposing themselves openly to their enemy's fire or bayonet charge.

When the Whigs opened fire, they exacted a gruesome toll on the Loyalist officers and men. The first volley from the Americans rocked the Loyalists causing a momentary retreat. The Loyalists quickly regrouped only to take a second volley that caused them to break in disorderly retreat to the opposite side of the river. The disorganized retreat probably resulted from so many of the officers being seriously wounded and removed from the battlefield. Among the seriously wounded were Innes, Major Thomas Fraser, Captain Peter Campbell, Captain William Hawsey, Lieutenant William Chew, and Ensign John Camp. Command of the retreating Loyalist forces devolved to Captain George Kerr of Delancy's New York Brigade. Kerr was one of only two Loyalist officers not wounded in the fight.[237] Once he had his troops back on the south side of the Enoree, Kerr was able to establish a rear

---

[237] The other Loyalist officer who evidently emerged from the battle unwounded was Colonel Daniel Clary, the Tory militia commander who was gathering his Dutch Fork Militia Regiment at Musgrove Mill. Clary, who continued to reside in the Carolina backcountry after the war, related his experience at Musgrove Mill to his neighbors. As he later told the story, at some point during the battle two Whig militiamen grabbed his horse's bridle intent on taking him prisoner. Without hesitation, he had the presence of mind to say to his would-be captors in a stern

guard to cover a more organized retreat of his force from their original encampment at Edward Musgrove's house and mill.

David Fanning says the Loyalists retreated about a mile and a quarter before they encamped.[238] This statement varies somewhat from Williams' statement that the Whigs chased the British and Tories about two miles. The two statements, however, may not be as inconsistent as they seem if Fanning measured the retreat from the site of the Tories' original camp while Williams measured the Whigs' chase from the spot where the Americans sprung their ambush.

Williams reported that during the 15 minutes the battle lasted the Loyalists suffered 60 killed on the battlefield, the greatest part he identified as being "British." Since there were no regular British troops at the battle, he was doubtless referring to the red-coated Provincial forces under the command of Innes. Williams' estimate of 60 killed on the field is known to be overstated because, in his official report, he states that Innes and Fraser were among those killed. Both of these men survived their wounds and later returned to active duty. In addition to those killed, 70 prisoners were taken by the Americans. No estimate of the wounded was given by Williams or in the Loyalist reports, but it is reasonable to assume that a substantial portion of the troops were wounded during the battle.[239] Williams listed the American losses as three killed on the field and eight wounded, one of whom was thought to be mortally wounded.[240] From the other accounts, Captain Shadrach Inman, who led his mounted troops into the fray and was shot down while pursuing the

---

and commanding voice: "Damn you, don't you know your own officers?" When the intimidated Whigs released the bridle, he made good his escape. John Belton O'Neall, *The Annuals of Newberry, Historical, Biographical and Anecdotal* (Charleston, SC: S.G. Courtenay & Co., 1859) 71, 313.

[238] Butler, *Fanning*, 32.

[239] The staff of the Musgrove Mill State Historic Site estimates the British and Tory casualties as being 63 killed, 90 wounded and 76 taken prisoner. *See* SCAR, Vol. 1, No. 1, September 2004, 14 posted at www.southerncampaign.org/newsletter/v1n1.pdf (viewed 1/30/10).

[240] The Historic Site staff estimates the Whig casualties at four killed and eight or nine wounded. *Ibid.*

retreating enemy, is known to have died from his wounds.

The reason the casualties suffered in the engagement were so disparate was that the Americans, with the exception of Inman and his troops, never exposed themselves to open fire until they emerged from their cover to chase the retreating enemy from the field. The Whigs stayed behind cover firing their rifles and muskets with deadly accuracy at close, effective range. The Loyalists, on the other hand, armed only with notoriously inaccurate muskets, fired prematurely and from exposed ranks. Their red-coated ranks presented an easy target for the concealed Whig marksmen. Marching up the slope to the Whigs' position at the top of the hill, the Loyalists never were able to deploy the bayonet charge so feared by the backwoodsmen.

Musgrove Mill is one of the few recorded uses by the backcountry Whigs of ambush tactics, perhaps learned from encounters with their Cherokee and Creek adversaries in the earlier Indian campaigns. While the engagements at Ramsour's Mill,[241] Williamson's Plantation,[242] Rocky Mount,[243] Hanging Rock,[244] and even Fishing Creek[245] were clearly not traditional affairs with formal lines of opposing forces drawn up in face-to-face combat as would be mandated under traditional 18th century rules of war, neither were any of them engagements in which one force exposed itself by deploying in ranks in accordance with the rules while the other force remained concealed and protected behind defensive positions. One very valuable lesson that the backcountry soldiers clearly learned at Musgrove Mill was that there was great advantage to defending a position affording cover when facing an attacking force deployed in ranks. This is a lesson that was applied to full advantage on numerous occasions by

---

[241] O'Kelley, *Slaughter* 2: 180-187.

[242] *Ibid.* 190-197. The Battle of Brattonsville is also known as Huck's Defeat and the Battle of Williamson's Plantation. Scoggins, *Huck's Defeat.*

[243] *Ibid.* 211-216.

[244] *Ibid.* 221-233.

[245] *Ibid.* 277-284.

the backcountry militia. Even at King's Mountain[246] where the Whigs were the attackers, however, they were able to adaptively apply the lessons learned at Musgrove Mill by taking full advantage of the protection offered by the trees on the slopes of King's Mountain rather than trying to advance up the mountain in formation. They knew full well that doing so would have had disastrous consequences.

After the battle, the Whigs initially intended to press ahead to attack the British and Loyalist forces occupying the star fort at Ninety Six. At some point, however, either immediately before the commencement of the fight or immediately after the Loyalists had been chased from the field, the Whigs learned of the defeats of Gates at Camden and Sumter at Fishing Creek. This disturbing news, coupled with their genuine but misplaced apprehension that Ferguson with his troop of 1,000 Tories was in the immediate vicinity, convinced the Whigs that their best option was to retreat as quickly as possible. Shelby indicates that he retreated into the North Carolina mountains, leaving the prisoners taken at Musgrove Mill in the custody of Clarke. Clarke, too, decided to effect his retreat leaving the prisoners in the custody of Williams to deliver them. Sometime prior to September 5, 1780, Williams delivered the prisoners to the remnants of Gates' Continentals assembled at Hillsborough, North Carolina, thereby bringing the Battle of Musgrove Mill to a most advantageous conclusion for the victorious Whigs.

On September 8, 1780, North Carolina Governor Abner Nash issued an order permitting Col. Williams to recruit up to 100 horsemen to "act against the enemy." Had Williams been promoted to general as of September 8, Governor Nash's order would have been issued to him with that rank. The order reads as follows:

Hillsborough, September 8, 1780
Nash to Col. James Williams

[246] Lyman C. Draper, *King's Mountain and its Heroes: History of the Battle of King's Mountain October 7th, 1780, and the Events Which Led to It* (Cincinnati: Peter G. Thompson, 1881; reprint, Johnson City, TN: The Overmountain Press, 1996).

Sir:

You are desired to go to Caswell County, and to such other counties as you think proper, and use your best endeavors to collect any number of volunteer horsemen, not exceeding one hundred, and proceed with them into such parts as you judge proper, to act against the enemy, and in this you are to use your own discretion. You may assure the men who turn out with you that they shall be entitled to all the advantages and privileges of militia in actual service, and that it shall be considered as a tour of duty under the militia law, they serving the time prescribed by law for other militia men. All Commissaries, and other staff-officers, are required to grant you such supplies as may be necessary.

In getting your men, you are to make no distinction between men already drafted and others; and, in case of need, you are to impress horses for expresses, and other cases of absolute necessity.

S/ A. Nash.[247]

To aid him in recruiting and paying these horsemen, the North Carolina legislature granted Williams $25,000 for which his estate was later required to account.[248]

In a letter dated September 20, 1780, Governor Rutledge reports the discouraging state of military affairs to South Carolina's congressional delegation in Philadelphia. He notes that except for a force of about 200 under Sumter at Salisbury, the "little Party under Marion & a few at Cross Creek,[249] under Col. Harrington," there are no South Carolina Patriots in the field. He tells the delegates, however, he has:

... seen Col. James Williams whose affair with Innis (not killed, as you have heard, but recovering of his wound) was truly brilliant—He is gone on with a Determination to distinguish himself as a Partisan, & I believe he will—I have put both him & Sumter (*each of whom may be of service but*

---

[247] Gibbes, *Documentary History*, 2: 138.

[248] Walter Clark, ed., *The State Records of North Carolina*, Vol. XXI¬ 1788-'90 (Goldsboro, NC: Nash Brothers Book and Job Printers, 1903), 74-5.

[249] Cross Creek is the name used for what is now Fayetteville, NC.

they will never agree) under Genl. Smallwood's Command.[250]
(Emphasis added)

Rutledge's observation that Sumter and Williams "will never agree" is a clear indication that the rivalry, if not outright animosity, between the two men was well known to, and understood by, Rutledge. Indeed, Rutledge's statement hints at his intent to use the rivalry between the two to animate the South Carolina backcountry militia's resistance. It also is interesting to note that as late as September 20, Rutledge was still referring to Williams as "Colonel." Clearly, if Rutledge did promote Williams to brigadier general, that promotion occurred some time after September 20.[251]

Williams in fact recruited in Caswell County and other North Carolina counties. At least six men filing pension applications assert that they were from Caswell County, North Carolina, and served under Williams at the Battle of King's Mountain.[252] One

---

[250] John Rutledge to Delegates, Hillsborough, 20 September 1780, South Carolina Historical and Genealogical Magazine, Vol. XVII, No.4, October 1916, 136-139. This is a reference to William Smallwood (1732-1792), the Continental Army general appointed by Washington to succeed DeKalb, who died from wounds suffered in the Battle of Camden. According to an earlier portion of Rutledge's letter, North Carolina gave Smallwood command of its militia. This command was in addition to his duties as a general in the Continental Army. When Nathanael Greene assumed command of the Continental Army in the South, he appointed Frederich von Steuben as his second-in-command. Smallwood objected to serving as a subordinate under von Steuben, so Greene reassigned Smallwood to Smallwood's home state of Maryland. Boatner, *Encyclopedia*, 1013.

[251] Exactly when (and if) Governor Rutledge commissioned Williams a brigadier general is not known. The author has not found a copy of a commission granting Williams such rank. Except for Hill's assertions as to Williams' promotion and references to him as "General Williams" appearing in Allaire's diary and several pension applications filed by militia veterans under the 1832 federal pension act, there is no contemporary support for his holding such rank. Unfortunately, Rutledge's correspondence has not been collected and a definitive answer to whether or not he promoted Williams may lie in as yet undiscovered correspondence.

[252] Moss identifies John Douglas, Elisha Evans, David Mitchell, Jacob Neely, Benjamin Newton and Matthew Pryor, Sr. as being from Caswell County, North Carolina. Several of these men also state in their applications for pensions that they had served under Captain John Graves of Caswell County at the Battle of Camden and were on their way home from that battle when Col. Williams recruited them to join his force. Joseph Neeley identifies himself as being a resident of Person County, North Carolina at the time he fought at King's Mountain, and Richard and

applicant from Person County, North Carolina (which adjoins Caswell), and two from Stokes County, North Carolina (which is separated from Caswell only by Rockingham County), also claimed to have served under Williams at King's Mountain. In addition, it is likely that Williams sent newly brevetted Major Samuel Hammond to recruit in other North Carolina counties closer to the border with South Carolina. Hammond says in his pension application that he accompanied Williams in delivering the prisoners taken at Musgrove Mill to Hillsborough. While in Hillsborough, Hammond received an "… appointment of Major with a Brevet commission as such from Gov. Rutledge." Hammond states that he went to Rowan County, North Carolina; established a camp there; and issued a call to the "…Carolina & Georgia Refugees" to assemble there. Hammond says that the number of men who responded to that call "…by the last week in September was considerable & made the largest proportion of Col. Williams' command in the Battle of King's Mountain."[253]

Williams left North Carolina intent on confronting the forces led by Patrick Ferguson. Ferguson, the British officer

Thomas Shipp identify themselves as residents of Stokes County, North Carolina at that time. Moss, *Patriots at King's Mountain.*

[253] Samuel Hammond Pension Application, *see* footnote 168. Hammond attached a copy of the flyer he used to issue the appeal for recruits. The flyer is captioned "A Call to Arms: Beef, Bread & Potatoes, Higgins' Plantation, 2nd Sept. 1780" and reads in part as follows:

The undersigned [Hammond] has just returned from Hillsborough to this neighborhood. While there he obtained an order on the Companies and Quartermasters upon this frontier for supplies of provisions and forage for such of the patriotic Citizens of South Carolina & Georgia as might be embodied for actual services and being informed that there is a number of you, resting with patriotic friends in the Two adjoining Counties no doubt anxiously looking for an opportunity to embody for the performance of duty, but without the power or means of supporting yourselves or your horses from your own resources I have thought your wishes would be forwarded by Establishing of a Camp at a rallying rendezvous at a convenient place for your assemblage, and to be ready when occasion might offer to give our aid for the recovery of Our County.

I have with this view formed a Camp at Higgins' Plantation a few miles from Capt. Brannon's Tavern, near the road leading westwardly to Torrence's Crossroads, where we will be supplied with the needful…. I Have some other good news. Come and hear it.

in command of a force largely comprising Provincials and Tories, had occupied Williams' plantation in June, displacing Williams' wife and children from their home. Williams clearly had a score to settle with Ferguson. In late August and early September, Ferguson had been dispatched by Lord Cornwallis to the western regions of North and South Carolina to recruit Loyalists to join Cornwallis' army and to suppress continued Whig resistance in those areas. Having subjugated South Carolina and inflicted a resounding defeat on the Southern Department of the Continental Army at Camden, Cornwallis now turned his attention to adding North Carolina to the list of southern colonies restored to British rule.

As the first step in implementing his plan, in late September of 1780, Cornwallis invaded Charlotte, North Carolina, with the main body of his army. That move met with heavy resistance as the Whigs were unwilling to allow the British to occupy Charlotte without causing Cornwallis considerable harassment. Ferguson, whose forces comprised the left wing of Cornwallis' army, was not with Cornwallis in Charlotte but was still in the west discharging his duties recruiting additions to his force and suppressing the Whigs in that area. Ferguson's isolation from the protection of Cornwallis provided just the right opportunity for the convergence of forces allied against him. Not only were Williams and the South and North Carolinians under his command out looking to track down Ferguson, but the forces under four other men were looking as well. They included: Isaac Shelby and John Sevier from the western portions of North Carolina that had been threatened by Ferguson; the forces from western Virginia under William Campbell which had been alerted to the threat the British posed to that State; and the forces of Georgia refugees led by Col. Elijah Clarke who had fled to the relative safety of North Carolina after an unsuccessful attempt to retake Augusta. All these converged to constitute a force of militia intent upon taking on Ferguson before he could rejoin Cornwallis in Charlotte. That reunion was destined never to occur. A different fate awaited Ferguson and his men on the top of King's Mountain.

Chapter Ten
On to King's Mountain

The convergence of the Whig militia forces allied in their determination to prevent Ferguson and his Army from rejoining Cornwallis in Charlotte occurred at the Cowpens in South Carolina on October 6, 1780. There an estimated 1,500 Whig militiamen assembled with Colonels Williams, William Campbell, Isaac Shelby, John Sevier, Joseph McDowell, and Benjamin Cleveland, and Majors William Chronicle and Joseph Winston. Although the eyewitness accounts vary as to the precise details, these men met in a council of war sometime in the late afternoon or early evening of Friday, October 6 to designate a leader to take the overall command of the pending attack on Ferguson and to agree upon a strategy for engaging him. They knew that Ferguson was encamped on the top of King's Mountain intent on rejoining Cornwallis at Charlotte.

The council designated William Campbell of Virginia as an overall commander, primarily because he had the largest group of men at the Cowpens and had come the furthest to join the fray. The decision was made that since Ferguson was on his way to Charlotte, time was of the essence in bringing on the confrontation. The strategy agreed upon involved the designation of a force of approximately 900 of the best mounted and armed men to make a forced march to engage Ferguson the next day before he could leave his encampment. The balance of the troops gathered at the Cowpens was to follow the horsemen on foot and join them as soon as possible. This force of approximately 900 men rode all night and most of the next day and engaged Ferguson at approximately three o'clock in the afternoon of Saturday, October 7, 1780, in a fierce battle in which Ferguson was killed and his entire force either killed, wounded, or taken prisoner by the Whigs.

In this battle, Williams would suffer the wounds from which he died the next day. It seems particularly ironic given the extreme sacrifice that Williams made at King's Mountain, that his participation in that battle should have given rise to the harshest of Colonel William Hill's attacks on him.

According to Hill, Williams came into Sumter's camp on Indian Land on the east side of the Catawba River immediately following his promotion to brigadier general, had his commission read to the assembled officers and men, and attempted to assert his right to command Sumter's unit. Hill relates:

> ...[M]uch to his well deserved mortification they [Sumter's men] all to a man knowing his recent conduct in deserting his post & embezzeling *(sic)* the public property as before mentioned refused to have any thing to do with him or his commission & if he had not immediately left the camp he would have been stoned out of it—he then went up to the settlement in North Carolina on the Yadkin River where he engaged about 70 men—such as did not choose to do duty under their own officers by promising them that if they would go with him to South Carolina they could get as many Negroes & horses as they chose to take from the Tories.[254]

No clearer illustration of the distinction between militia and regular army can be offered than as described by Hill in this passage. To ascribe to a militia unit anything like the organization, structure, or discipline of a regular army unit is to totally misunderstand the militia. Taking at face value Hill's description of the reception Williams received, the refusal of Sumter and his men to acknowledge the right of Williams to command would be unimaginable in a regular army unit. According to Hill, Williams had obtained promotion to brigadier general from Governor Rutledge. If true, this made Williams clearly the highest-ranking officer in Sumter's camp. Yet Sumter, Winn, Hampton, Thomas,

---

[254] Hill, *Memoirs of the Revolution*, (Columbia: The Historical Commission of South Carolina, 1921, 2nd printing, 1958), ed. A.S. Salley, Jr., 17. Hill's memoir is set forth in its entirety in Appendix 15.

Middleton, Hill, Lacey, and others not identified by Hill are alleged to have refused to serve under Williams. Such insurrection in the regular army would have been an offense subject to the severest punishment. Yet Sumter and his men had no reason to fear such punishment because militia units were not subject to the same disciplinary rules as would have been applicable in the Continental Army.

Hill and the other officers under Sumter then called a meeting "... in order to deliberate on some plan respecting General Sumter's commission as it was protested by Williams." The meeting, which Hill refers to as a "Convention," designated five officers to go to Governor Rutledge in Hillsborough to plead Sumter's position. Sumter was to go with them but was "... not to make his appearance until the business was decided."[255]

Hill's observation is interesting because, throughout his narrative, Hill treats Sumter as if he were not a participant in any dealings with Williams. As noted previously, Hill alleges that when Williams first came into Sumter's camp in July, Hill interceded for Williams because Hill knew Williams better than anyone else in camp. This assertion plants doubt as to Hill's version of events, if for no other reason than that Williams and Sumter served together as representatives from the backcountry in the only four South Carolina legislative bodies assembled in the period from 1775 to 1778. Further, both had been extremely active field-grade militia officers from the start of the war. It is difficult to accept that two such active politicians and high-ranking militia officers would not be well acquainted. Yet Hill does not relate a single direct interaction between Williams and Sumter. Hill would have his reader believe that Sumter and Williams were strangers to one another, and that Sumter somehow maintained the detached aloofness of someone unsullied by even the need to acknowledge Williams' existence, much less have any direct contact with him.

[255] *Ibid.*, 18. Hill names those selected as Gen. Richard Winn, Col. Henry Hampton, Col. Thomas [probably Col. John Thomas, Jr.] and Col. Middleton [probably, Col. Charles Middleton]. Hill states he could not recall the name of the fifth officer designated to accompany Sumter to Hillsborough.

Among the documents relating to this time period is a letter dated October 2, 1780, from Williams to General Horatio Gates, who continued to command the Continental Army in North and South Carolina until December 1780 when he was replaced by General Nathanael Greene. Williams wrote this letter from Burke County, North Carolina. In it, Williams states that he is about 70 miles from Salisbury, North Carolina, on the Catawba River with about 450 men in pursuit of Colonel Ferguson. Williams states that he has dispatched men to different quarters to gather intelligence. From those efforts, he reports that Col. Clarke from Georgia has taken Augusta with 800 men, but finding it impossible to hold Augusta, has retreated with all his men to Ninety Six. Further, Williams reports that he has learned of the arrival at Burke Court House of Colonels McDowell and Shelby with 1,500 men and Col. Cleveland with 800 men. Williams states that he hopes to join these groups on October 3 to take up the pursuit of Ferguson.[256]

This letter from Williams either has been ignored by historians or treated as further evidence of the validity of Hill's charges that Williams was a self-aggrandizing opportunist. Indeed, adding all the troops listed by Williams would mean that the Patriots would soon have a force of 3,550 men to confront Ferguson. That no such number of men was involved in the preparations to engage Ferguson is not disputed. It is important to note, however, that the only number Williams states as being of his own personal knowledge is the approximately 450 men with him. The number of troops under the command of the other colonels is based on intelligence gathered by men serving under Williams. Although Williams asserts in his letter that Gates may depend upon the intelligence he has gathered, it seems unduly harsh to ascribe to Williams any malicious motive in passing this information on to Gates. The essence of Williams' report to Gates is correct in that Clarke, Shelby,

---

[256] Banastre Tarleton, *A History of the Campaigns of 1780-1781 in the Southern America*, (Dublin: Colles, Exshaw, *et al*, 1787; reprint, North Stratford, NH: Ayer Company Publishers, 1999), 194.

McDowell and Cleveland were all converging with their men, albeit with far fewer men than asserted by Williams. The slow and unreliable methods of communication coupled with the understandable anxiety accompanying the anticipated confrontation with Ferguson's forces provide a more likely explanation for Williams' misinformation than any overt intent to mislead Gates or to aggrandize Williams' role in the coming engagement with Ferguson.

In the absence of Sumter and the other senior officers who accompanied him on his trip to lobby Gov. Rutledge for promotion, command of Sumter's regiment fell to Hill and Lacey. Shortly after assuming command, Hill and Lacey learned that a large number of men from the west were marching with the intent of meeting Ferguson and his Tory militia. Hill states that Williams and Brandon again came into their camp and tried to assert his right to command the force. Hill says that he informed Williams "... that there was not an officer or man in the whole army that would submit to his command as his recent conduct was such that no officer or sett *(sic)* of men would submit to such an officer." Concerned that they would soon have to engage Ferguson's superior force, however, Hill decided he "... would endeavour *(sic)* to bring them [Williams and his men] in to an action as it was probable by this measure that some of them would meet a fate they so well merited." Hill notes that Lacey approved this plan but only if some way could be devised that would engage Williams and his men "... without paying respect to Williams' commission." Hill's account continues as follows:

> I then proposed as Cols Grimes & Hamright *[sic]* had that day joined us with a small party of North Carolinians, we would suppose the army to be three divisions, the North Carolinians one, Williams' & Brannon's [*sic*, Brandon's] men one, & the South Carolinians the third & that we would choose a Major General over the whole & that all orders should be assigned by all the Officers[.] [T]he following morning those propositions were offered to Williams but he spurned them & intimated that by virtue of his commission he would command the whole—upon this

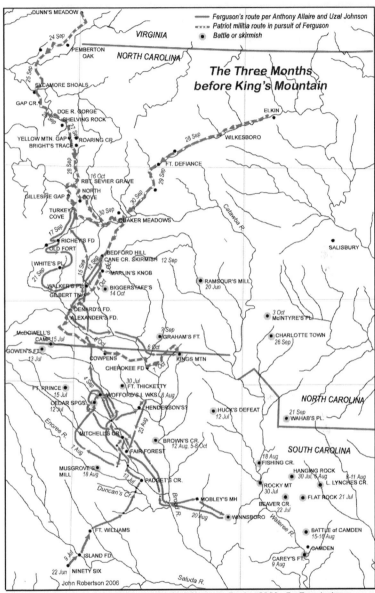

From Christine Swager, *The Valiant Died*, Heritage Books, 2006. By Permission.

he was told to absent himself & not attempt to march with us or the North Carolinians, as the consequences would be serious, he then agreed to the proposition, accordingly we elected the officer that was to act as before mentioned, that day our spies came in & informed us that the mountain men were marching in a valley between a large & small Mountain.... But strange to relate, that the very same day on the morning of which we had this information [to wit: the information regarding Ferguson's whereabouts] your author missed Williams & Brannon [*sic*, Brandon] out of the line of march & being informed that they had taken a pathway that led to the mountain. Nothing more was heard of them until evening after sunset—your Author being on the water we then discovered them coming to the camp— he then enquired of them which way they had been as they had not been with the army the greater part of the day. They appeared unwilling to give the Information I desired however upon insisting further Williams replied that they had been with the mountain men & that they were a set of fine men & well armed, upon being questioned where we were to form a junction with them, the answer was at Lawsons fork on the old Iron works, I then remarked that would be marching directly from Ferguson & that undoubtedly the design of these men was to fight Ferguson, that he [Ferguson] had sent to Cornwallis at Charlotte for Tarleton [Major Banastre Tarleton] with his horse and infantry and that this reinforcement might be expected in a day or two which would enable him to form a junction with the grand Army and that if this battle was not fought before the reinforcement came the certain probability was that it never would be fought... and that he was now in So Ca. & had been a bitter & cruel enemy, that it appeared as if Heaven had sent those men from the mountains to punish so great & cruel Enemy; & he the said Williams, appeared by these remarks to be for some moments embarrassed, but when he came to his speech, he acknowledged, that He had made use of deception to get them [the overmountain men] to go to Ninety Six ... I inquired of him if they had any cannon with them ... his answer was in the negative, & added that such men with their Rifles would soon reduce that Post [the Tory-controlled fort at Ninety Six].... I then used the freedom

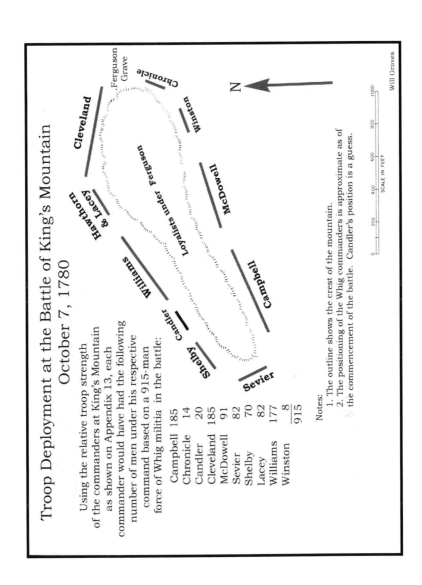

Troop Deployment at the Battle of King's Mountain
October 7, 1780

Using the relative troop strength
of the commanders at King's Mountain
as shown on Appendix 13, each
commander would have had the following
number of men under his respective
command based on a 915-man
force of Whig militia in the battle:

Campbell 185
Chronicle 14
Candler 20
Cleveland 185
McDowell 91
Sevier 82
Shelby 70
Lacey 82
Williams 177
Winston 8
915

Notes:
1. The outline shows the crest of the mountain.
2. The positioning of the Whig commanders is approximate as of
the commencement of the battle. Candler's position is a guess.

SCALE IN FEET

Will Graves

to tell him that I plainly saw his design was to get the Army in his own settlement as well as to get some of his property (and plunder the Tories) from thence. In the course of the conversation he [Williams] said with a considerable degree of warmth, that the No. Ca. might fight Ferguson or let it alone, & that our business was to fight for our own country—I then informed him that notwithstanding he had used such unwarrantable means to avoid an action that I hope under Providence that I would prevent his design.[257]

Lacey rode to meet the overmountain troops, allegedly to redirect their march. Hill accuses Williams of going among the officers and men trying to persuade them to join him in his planned march to confront the Tories at Ninety Six. Hill states that he went behind Williams urging the men to stick with the plan of joining up with the overmountain units to fight Ferguson before Cornwallis and Tarleton from Charlotte could reinforce him. Hill ascribes to Williams the design of seeking to motivate the men to plunder the Tories in Ninety Six rather than fight for their country. Hill says he addressed the army, telling those who wished to fight for their country with him to parade to the right and those who wished not to fight but to gain plunder, to parade to the left. Hill relates that, to his "... great surprise the greatest part of the army paraded to the right ...."[258]

The militia under Hill and Lacey marched to Cowpens to meet with the overmountain men. Hill says Williams and the few men who stayed with him, seeing that their safety lay with the larger group, joined the march toward Cowpens. Hill asserts Williams and his men had to hang back because Hill's rear guard held them in such unfavorable light as to throw stones at them in an attempt to run them off.

Hill relates that the meeting in Cowpens between Colonels Campbell, Cleveland, Shelby, Lacey, Hambright, and Hawthorne resulted in Col. Campbell assuming

---

[257] Hill, *Memoirs*, 19-20.
[258] *Ibid.*, 22.

"… nominal command over the whole [.] [T]his was done in courtesy as he & his men had come the greatest distance & from over the mountain." Nine hundred thirty-three of the best-mounted men were selected from the available troops to ride ahead of the main Army to engage Ferguson at King's Mountain before he could be reinforced. Interestingly, Hill was not among the 933 men so selected. Williams and his men were selected. Hill attributes his omission to his not being fully recovered from wounds he suffered at Hanging Rock.[259] Hill does not disclose who made the selection of the men chosen to participate. The fact that Williams and his men were selected, however, casts some doubt on Hill's assertion that Williams was universally distrusted not only by the officers and men of Sumter's unit, but also by the colonels commanding the other units that participated in the battle.

Hill reserved one final insult to Williams' reputation. Even though he was not present at the battle,[260] Hill purports to have insight into Williams' demise. Hill summarizes the end of the battle and Williams' death as follows:

> By this time (toward the end of the battle), the Americans were within shot of the whole of their (the Tory's) camp chiefly under cover of rocks & trees. Col. Ferguson being killed the second in command sued for peace. About this time Col. Williams with his small party came up the side of the mountain, at which time a number of white handkerchiefs were seen holding up in the camp & yet a number of men not knowing the intention of this signal continued their fire & it was some time before the officers could get them to cease firing. At this moment this Col. Williams was killed. It is generally supposed & believed that it was done by some of the Americans, as many of them had been heard to promise on oath that they would do it

---

[259] *Ibid.*, 22.

[260] *Ibid.*, 22. Hill states he was "…with the rear guard" as he was still recovering from his wounds sustained at Hanging Rock. Hill entrusted command of his unit to his subordinate, Lt. Col. James Hawthorne. By rear guard, it is reasonable to assume Hill is referring to the men congregated at Cowpens but not one of the approximately 933 well armed and mounted men chosen to advance rapidly from Cowpens to King's Mountain to engage Ferguson.

when they had an opportunity which promises were made at the time the dispute took place before mentioned, so that the Historians that have hitherto written of these transactions must have had very incorrect information—as it is a fact that after the attempt to deceive Col. Campbell & other Officers he dare not appear before them neither at the council of Officers at the Cowpens nor at the other near the mountain.[261]

Except for the statements of Hill as confirmed by Sumter's later review and passive acquiescence of them, no other contemporary accounts even note the existence of any grounds to impugn Williams' actions or motives. For example, in their official report filed shortly after the battle, Colonels Campbell, Shelby, and Cleveland directly contradict several of Hill's charges against Williams. In their report, the surviving commanders note that they marched to the Cowpens "... on the Broad river, in South Carolina, where we were joined by Col. James Williams, with four hundred men, on the evening of the 6th of October, *who informed us, that the enemy lay encamped somewhere near the Cherokee Ford,*[262] *of Broad river, about thirty miles distant from US.*"[263] (Emphasis added)

This statement contains no hint of any attempt by Williams to misdirect the units that converged at Cowpens to plan the attack on Ferguson. On the contrary, the other commanders credited Williams with having informed them exactly where Ferguson's camp was located. Further, they also credited Williams with bringing 400 men, not the small number of miscreants that Hill alleges followed Williams.[264]

---

[261] *Ibid.*, 23-24.

[262] This ford was in the direct path of the route leading from Cowpens to King's Mountain.

[263] The full text of the official report appears in Appendix 12 and as an appendix to Draper, *King's Mountain*, 522-24.

[264] Tarleton, *Campaigns*, 194. It is very likely that the men credited to Williams included Lacey, Hawthorne and other of Sumter's followers, but their inclusion does not negate the fact that they were there and that Williams was the highest-ranking officer in their group. As such, Williams was entitled to "command" of the group, even if the personal loyalties of some inclined them to strongly prefer Sumter to Williams.

Indeed, none of the veterans of the Battle of King's Mountain who lived long enough to file applications for pensions cast any aspersions on Williams' conduct before, during or after the battle. Far more of such veterans proudly claimed service under Williams and his lieutenants at the battle than claimed service under Lacey, Hawthorne, or Hill.

Joseph Kerr, a civilian spy working for Williams, provides persuasive evidence for Williams' having been the source of the information of Ferguson's whereabouts. In his pension application, Kerr gives an amazingly detailed statement as to what Williams and the other colonels knew about the location of Ferguson's camp. Kerr states:

> The Declarant [Kerr] ... joined Col. Williams as a spy.... By this time [late September or early October, 1780] ... Col. Steen, who commanded the South Carolina "Refugee," had joined Col. Williams, from there they marched near to the Cowpens in order to join what were called the "Overmountain troops" under the command of Cols. Sevier, Cleveland and Shelby. Col. Steen informed the other Officers that this Declarant was known to him as a faithful and efficient spy, as a true friend to his Country, and one in whom the utmost confidence could safely be reposed. Cols. Sevier, Cleveland, Shelby and Steen then held a council in the presence of this Declarant. They knew that Ferguson with his British and tories was then stationed about twenty miles from them, at Peter Quin's old place about six or seven miles from King's mountain and between said mountain and where our troops then were. The result of the council held by the officers was that this Declarant should go and reconnoiter Ferguson's position, which he did. He found the British and tories encamped about one hundred yards apart and their arms stacked up, and no centinels [*sic*, sentinels]. This Declarant gained easy access to them by passing himself off for a tory, as tories were then numerous in that part of the Country. He believes, but in this he may be mistaken, that Ferguson's strength including british and tories was not exceeding fifteen hundred. He ascertained from the tories that they intended, on the evening of that day to go from Quin's old place to the top of King's mountain in order

to remain there a few days in order to give protection to all the 'rebels' who would join Ferguson's standard. After obtaining this information and making these discoveries, this Declarant returned next day to Cols. Sevier, Shelby, Cleaveland and Steen having stayed all night at the house of a Tory who lived about ten miles from Quin's old field. He reached our encampment about Sunset. The officers immediately collected round this Declarant in order to ascertain what his discoveries had been. He gave a brief, but circumstantial, account of them to the said Sevier, Shelby, Cleaveland, Steen and *Williams, whose name has been unintentionally omitted, in his last references to the officers. Williams was present at each council that was held.* The conclusion was that they would march that very night in the direction of King's Mountain a distance, he believes, of about twenty seven miles; perhaps twenty six miles. Sevier, Cleaveland, Shelby, Steen & Williams with their troops, reached King's mountain the next day (having marched all night) about 10 O'clock and completely surprised Ferguson and his troops by surrounding them, Sevier occupying one position, Cleaveland another, Williams another, Shelby another and Steen another. The engagement he thinks lasted about one hour, he may be mistaken. The defeat of Ferguson was complete. About two hundred and fifty were killed on the ground; about seven hundred and fifty taken prisoner, the balance Escaped. They were principally Tories. We lost about twenty five men killed on the ground—many wounded—of which number was Col. Williams who was wounded in several places. A mortal wound in the groin, as this Declarant believes, terminated his life on the next day after the battle before 12 O'clock. This Declarant well remembers conversing with him after the battle. He knew he must die, and did so, cheerfully resigned to his fate.[265] (Emphasis added)

Some have discredited Kerr's statements because he clearly confuses the sequence of battles in which he claims to have played a role. He places the Battle of Blackstock's Plantation (that occurred on November 20, 1780) before the Battle of King's Mountain and the Battle of Williamson's Plantation (also

---

[265] Joseph Kerr, Pension Application, 4 September 1832, S4469, National Archives, Washington, DC.

called the Battle of Brattonsville or Huck's Defeat that occurred on July 12, 1780) after the Battle of King's Mountain. He also refers to Captain Huck as "Hook" and states that he was under a "Capt. Barnett" in his discussion of the Battle of Williamson's Plantation. He states that Capt. Barnett was in command of a few South Carolina Patriot "refugees" then in Mecklenburg County, North Carolina. No commander by that name is known to have participated in that engagement. It is possible that the "Capt. Barnett" to whom Kerr refers is Col. William Bratton (1742-1815), one of the militia commanders known to have participated in the Battle of Williamson's Plantation. Kerr made his declaration when he was 72 years old. That he, like many other elderly men making claims for benefits under the various pension acts, may have been of failing memory would not be surprising. His detailed recollection of the events occurring at the time of the Battle of King's Mountain, however, should not be given significantly less weight because he mistakenly reversed the order of two other, less significant engagements. Certainly, Kerr's recollections are entitled to the same credence as those of Hill, written sometime between 1810 and 1814 when Hill was 69 to 73 years of age.[266]

Throughout his narrative, Hill repeatedly refers to Williams and the "few men" who chose to follow him. The evidence, however, is otherwise. Of the various participants listed by Dr. Moss in his *The Patriots at Kings Mountain*, approximately 131 fought under Williams or officers under his command including Brandon, Roebuck, Hammond, Thompson, Steen, and Anderson. Approximately 62 men served under Sumter's subordinates, Lacey, Hill (who was

---

[266] According to the inscription on his tombstone, Hill was born in 1741 and died December 1, 1816. He is buried in the Bethel Presbyterian Church yard near Clover, York County, South Carolina. Hill's introduction to his *Memoirs* is dated February 1815. In that introduction, Hill states that he has been waiting "near 30 years" for some "fitly qualified" person to write a history to rectify the mistakes which prior historians have made concerning the Battle of King's Mountain. Because no one else has corrected the record, Hill states that he has undertaken to "rectify the mistakes that have unhappily been made." Hill, Memoirs, 4-5. Since October 7, 1810 marked the 30th anniversary of the Battle of King's Mountain and 1813 marked the 30th anniversary of the Treaty of Paris, Hill probably wrote his Memoirs sometime between 1810 and 1814.

not present at the battle, having turned his command over to his lieutenant, James Hawthorne, because Hill was still recovering from wounds sustained at Hanging Rock), Bratton, or Liles. The participants listed as having fought under other commanders present at King's Mountain break down as follows: William Campbell (139), Joseph McDowell (68), Sevier (62), Cleveland (138), Shelby [including Winston's command] (58), Chronicle (11) with approximately 190 participants not attributed to any particular commander.[267]

A contemporary account also indirectly supports the view that Sumter's men did not universally hold Williams in contempt. In reporting the defeat of Ferguson at King's Mountain, General William Lee Davidson (1746-1781), a brigadier general of the North Carolina militia, wrote on October 10, 1780 to his superior, General Jethro Sumner, that he had learned of the Patriot's victory at King's Mountain from "Mr. Tatum (*sic*, Tate),[268] who was major in General Sumter's late command." Tate's account included Williams among those colonels[269] who participated in the battle and acknowledged that Williams was mortally wounded.[270] Tate in no way disparages Williams' role in the battle. Although too much weight should not be attached to Tate's failing to disparage Williams, it is difficult to believe that Tate, being one of Sumter's field officers whom Hill says universally despised Williams, would include Williams among those who participated in the battle without at least some qualification of the credit due him. It would have been more in keeping

---

[267] Moss, *Patriots at Kings Mountain.* The number of participants serving under particular officers was compiled by the author and not by Dr. Moss. Any errors in attribution are solely those of the author.

[268] The officer referred to is Maj. Samuel Tate, not "Tatum" as given in the transcription of Davidson's letter. Davidson notes in his letter that the man erroneously identified as Tatum was a "... brigade major...in the action." Samuel Tate was a brigade major with Lacey and Hawthorne's men at King's Mountain and is the only person who matches Davidson's description. Moss, *SC Patriots*, 244.

[269] The list of commanders given by Tate to Davidson was, as listed in Davidson's letter, "Colonels Campbell, Cleveland, Shelby, Sevier, Williams, Brandon, Lacey, &c."

[270] William Davidson to Jethro Sumner, 10 October 1780, Tarleton, *Campaign*, 196.

with Hill's view of Williams for Tate simply to ignore Williams' role and to omit him from those participating in the battle.

Persuasive evidence that Hill's accusations against Williams were at best overstated and at worst untrue, arises from Sumter's own actions after the Battle of King's Mountain. Immediately following that battle, Sumter took back into his command Col. Thomas Brandon, the very man Hill names in his memoir as aiding Williams in the alleged embezzlement of the provisions and horses from Sumter's camp.[271] Brandon's return was so lacking in acrimony that Brandon was the officer upon whose advice Sumter relied when selecting William Blackstock's plantation as the site to confront Tarleton in late November 1780.[272] Sumter also accepted the return of Joseph McJunkin and Samuel Hammond,[273] both of whom, though not named by Hill in his memoir, clearly were with Sumter and left with Williams and Brandon when they departed Sumter's camp shortly before the battle at Musgrove Mill. Not only did Sumter allow these men (and the units they commanded) back under his command, but also, in the case of McJunkin, Sumter promoted him to the rank of major sometime after the Battle of King's Mountain and prior to the Battle at Blackstock's.[274] For Sumter to so readily accept back into his command men who only two months before had participated in the embezzlement of camp provisions and horses stretches credulity. For Sumter to promote one of those participants to field officer rank is a clear acknowledgment that Sumter ascribed no such culpability to the actions of Williams and his followers.

[271] Hill, *Memoir*, 16. This contains the accusation of Brandon's duplicity with Williams. Bass, *Gamecock*, 103. Bass describes Brandon's role in the Battle at Blackstock's Plantation on November 20, 1780.

[272] Bass, *Gamecock*, 103.

[273] Hammond, Pension Application, *see* footnote 168.

[274] Saye, *McJunkin Memoir*, 28.

Chapter Eleven
Williams' Death

Contemporary accounts of Williams' death are given in the memoirs and pension applications of those who claimed either to have served under him at the Battle of King's Mountain or to have opposed him there. Thomas Young gave the most vivid and, perhaps, accurate description of Williams' demise. He wrote:

> On the top of the mountain, in the thickest of the fight, I saw Col. Williams fall, and a braver or a better man never died upon the field of battle. I had seen him once before that day; it was in the beginning of the action, as he charged by me full speed around the mountain; toward the summit a ball struck his horse under the jaw when he commenced stamping as if he were in a nest of yellow jackets. Col. W. threw the reins over the animal's neck-sprang to the ground, and dashed onward. The moment I heard the cry that Col. Williams was shot, I ran to his assistance, for I loved him as a father, he had ever been so kind to me and his little son, Joseph. They carried him into a tent, and sprinkled some water in his face. He revived, and his first words were, "For God's sake boys, don't give up the hill!" I remember it as well as if it had occurred yesterday. I left him in the arms of his son, Daniel, and returned to the field to avenge his fall. Col. Williams died next day, and was buried not far from the field of his glory.[275]

Pensioners Joseph Hughes and John Whelchel both state that Williams was not wounded until very shortly after the Tories had surrendered. Hughes says that he was "… at King's Mountain, where General Williams was mortally wounded after the British had raised their flag to surrender,

---

[275] Thomas Young's memoir was first published in *Orion Magazine*, October and November 1843, and was transcribed and published on the Internet by Phil Norfleet, http://sc_tories.tripod.com/thomas_young.htm (viewed 9/9/12). Thomas Young was born in 1764 and died 1848. He is buried in the Old Union Church Cemetery, Union County, South Carolina.

by a fire from some tories."[276] Whelchel states, "Colonel
Williams received his fatal shot immediately after the enemy
had hoisted a flag to surrender."[277] Ensign Robert Campbell
claims in his pension application that "Colonel Williams was
shot through the body, near the close of the action, in making
an attempt to charge on Ferguson; he lived long enough to
hear of the surrender of the British army, when he said: 'I die
contented, since we have gained the victory.'"[278]

Williams' opponents, however, also took note of his death.
The backcountry Tory journalist Alexander Chesney claims
in his diary that he fought at King's Mountain. He claims
to have seen Ferguson himself kill Williams immediately
before Ferguson was recognized and pierced with seven balls.
Contrary to several of the Patriot accounts, Chesney states
that Ferguson mortally wounded Williams *before* the Tories
surrendered. Chesney notes that the surrender by the Tories
did not occur until Ferguson's second in command, Capt.
Arent Schuyler DePeyster, assumed command.[279] Allaire noted
Williams' death at King's Mountain, but he does not purport
to know the circumstances of his demise. Allaire, however,
refers to Williams as "Brigadier-General Williams" which
indicates that the British were aware of Williams' promotion
to that rank and attached some significance to it.[280] Perhaps,
however, that significance arises only out of the natural desire
any vanquished army would have to at least have inflicted a
mortal wound on the highest ranking officer of the opposition.

The battle began about 3 P.M. and was concluded about
4 P.M. on Saturday, October 7, 1780. During that time,
it is estimated that of the approximately 1,100 Whigs who
participated in the battle, 25 to 30 died and 60 were wounded.
Of the approximately 1,100 Tories, an estimated 150 were killed,

---

[276] Joseph Hughes, Pension Application, 20 September 1832, FPA S31764,
National Archives, Washington, DC.

[277] John Whelchel, Pension Application, 3 September 1832, FPA W6498,
National Archives, Washington, DC.

[278] Robert Campbell, Narrative recorded in Vol. 15, Pages 100-104 of the
Colonial and State Records of North Carolina. Posted on the Internet at http://
docsouth.unc.edu/csr/index.html/document/csr15-0068 (viewed 9/14/12)

[279] Moss, *Chesney*, 136.

[280] Allaire, *Diary*, 510.

an equal number wounded and 600 to 700 taken prisoner. Along with the other wounded fighters, Williams spent that evening and night on the top of the mountain. There was little to eat and, except for the camp equipment captured from Ferguson's corps, there were no tents, equipment, or other materials to accommodate the needs of the healthy survivors, much less the needs of the wounded. Having marched from Cowpens throughout the night of the 6th and morning of the 7th in order to catch Ferguson at King's Mountain, the Patriots were understandably exhausted with little energy to care for the wounded or bury the dead. Thomas Young stated, "Awful indeed was the scene of the wounded, the dying, and the dead on the field, after the carnage of that dreadful day."[281] Another Patriot soldier, John Spelts, described the scene as follows: "The groans of the wounded and dying on the mountain were truly affecting, begging piteously for a little water; but in the hurry, confusion and exhaustion of the Whigs, these cries, when emanating from the Tories, were little heeded."[282]

Receiving news shortly after the battle that Tarleton was on his way to King's Mountain with his corps, the Patriot commanders employed the same tactic they had used many times before following engagements with the enemy: they marched their troops toward the relative safety of the western part of North Carolina. This retreat involved retracing part of the march they had made the day before the battle, traveling on the road leading from King's Mountain to Cowpens. According to Bailey, those caring for Col. Williams reached a farm owned by Jacob Randall near Deer's Ferry on the Broad River by late afternoon. There, Bailey says, Williams died on Sunday, October 8, 1780. His body was buried sometime later that day when the group stopped for the evening to rest and to eat the sweet potatoes they dug up at the abandoned plantation of a Tory named Matthew Fondren.[283]

---

[281] Young, *Memoir.*

[282] Drayer, *Kings Mountain*, 308

[283] J. D. Bailey, *Some Heroes of the American Revolution*, (Spartanburg, SC: Band & White, 1924), 107-111. Bailey states that Fondren's plantation was located near the eastern bank of the Broad River and a little north of Buffalo Creek.

Chapter Twelve
Williams Family Tribulations Continue

The tribulations of the Williams family did not end with Williams' death. In late October 1780, Lieutenant Colonel Moses Kirkland, an ardent backcountry Tory militia leader from the earliest days of the Revolution, occupied Williams' plantation yet again and dispossessed Williams' widow and six small children.[284] On November 22, 1780, Robert Cunningham, Williams' old political adversary in the race for the State Senate in 1778 (and winner of the fist fight that allegedly occurred between them), was appointed by Lord Cornwallis as a brigadier general and given command of the Ninety Six District loyal militia. Shortly after participating in the victorious engagement against the Whigs at Long Canes on December 12, 1780, Cunningham joined Kirkland at Mount Pleasant.[285] Kirkland and Cunningham either fortified the plantation or occupied fortifications Williams himself constructed prior to his death. The Tories prepared to hold the plantation against Patriot attempts to retake it. Mary Williams and the six children[286] still living with her sought shelter in outbuildings located on other tracts owned by Williams.[287] When the Whigs defeated Cunningham

---

[284] Kirkland sent dispatches from Williams' plantation to Cornwallis beginning as early as October 31, 1780 and continuing until the Patriots retook the plantation at the end of December 1780. Reese, *Cornwallis Papers*, 35, 39, 41, 51, 53

[285] Bailey/Morgan, *Biographical Directory* 1: 353-355. *See also* O'Kelley, Slaughter 2: 381-383, for discussion of the engagement at Long Cane.

[286] Williams' two oldest sons, Daniel and Joseph, were with him at King's Mountain. Daniel served as a captain in the militia. Young, *Memoir*.

[287] In a poignant (albeit not necessarily factually correct) tribute to their grandmother, Mary Wallace Williams Griffin's grandsons erected a tombstone to mark her grave that reads as follows:

Mrs. Mary (Wallace) Williams, widow of the hero of King's Mountain, Revolutionary War, Col. James Williams. Mrs. Williams was left with 8 small children. The Tories took possession of her house and most of her property after the death of Col. Williams and drove her out with her little children, forcing them to abandon their home and all their comforts. She had to take shelter in an outhouse a few miles off. When the Tories were forced to leave, they burned down her mill, houses, and many other

at Williams Fort on December 31, 1780, Cunningham allegedly burned to the ground the home and mills located there. There is also a strong possibility that the victorious Patriots commanded by Col. William Washington burned the fortifications on Williams' plantation to prevent their subsequent occupation again by the Tories as the opposing militia groups' fortunes waxed and waned in the Carolina backcountry.[288]

Even though only 18 or 19 years old, Williams' oldest son Daniel continued to serve as a captain in the Little River Regiment of Whig militia. Joseph Hayes, Williams' friend, co-executor and second-in-command, assumed command of the regiment. This regiment played an important part in the Battle of Cowpens fought in January 1781.[289]

On November 19, 1781, Hayes and about 35 of the men in the regiment were at a blockhouse or 'fort' on or near Hayes' Edgehill Plantation when Captain William Cunningham and his Loyalist militia attacked it. Captain Daniel Williams and his younger brother Joseph were with Hayes. Caught by surprise, Hayes and his men retreated into the blockhouse and returned fire. In the skirmish that followed, at least one

---

valuables. On Oct. 1781 at Hays (sic, Hayes) Station, her two oldest sons, Daniel and Joseph, were murdered in cold blood by the Tories, just twelve months after the death of her husband, and some years after that her oldest son John was supposed to be poisoned while on a visit to Virginia, and although she encountered many troubles, hardships, and losses, through the assistance of a Kind Providence and great energy she succeeded in raising the balance of her children well and seeing them respectably married and settled near her.

    James Leland Bolt and Margaret Eltinge Bolt, *Family Cemeteries Laurens County, S.C.,* (Greenville, SC: A Press, 1983), 2: 94-95.

    [288] If Mount Pleasant was destroyed, the strong probability exists such destruction was the work of the Patriots. Alexander Chesney, the Tory, notes in his journal that, after he escaped from the Patriots following the Battle of King's Mountain, he raised a company of men and marched them to Col. Williams' house on the Little River to join up with SC Loyalist militia General Robert Cunningham. Chesney says that when his company drew near to Williams' house, they found that Cunningham had already abandoned it and SC Patriot militia Major Benjamin Roebuck, had taken possession of it. Roebuck took Chesney and his company prisoner, paroled them to Ninety Six District where they were exchanged. It seems likely that if Cunningham had destroyed the improvements at Mount Pleasant, Chesney would not have been lulled into approaching so closely as to allow Roebuck to take him prisoner. Moss, *Chesney.*

    [289] Babits, *Devil of a Whipping,* 73-77.

Loyalist and one Patriot were killed. When Cunningham set the blockhouse on fire, Hayes surrendered with the agreement that he and his men would be treated as prisoners of war. Cunningham, however, did not honor the terms of surrender. He immediately hanged Hayes, Daniel, and several others. Joseph Williams (then only 14 or 15 years old), who knew Cunningham, is said to have run to him asking: "Capt. Cunningham, how shall I go home and tell my mother that you have hanged brother Daniel?" Cunningham is alleged to have answered that Joseph would not have that melancholy duty. He hanged Joseph along with Hayes, Daniel and the others.[290]

One final tribulation remained for the Williams family. In administering the estate of his deceased brother, Henry

---

[290] Differing versions of this story are told in numerous accounts of the backcountry horrors occurring during the Revolutionary War. *See*, e.g., J. B. O'Neall, "Random Recollections of Revolutionary Characters and Incidents;" *Southern Journal and Magazine of Arts*, Vol. 4, No.1, (July 1838), 40-45; Draper, *King's Mountain*, 468; David Ramsay, *History of the Revolution of South Carolina from a British Province to an Independent State*, 2 vols. (Trenton, NJ: 1785) 2: 40-47. A contemporary account of the Battle of Hayes Station is set forth in a letter dated December 2, 1781, from LeRoy Hammond to Nathanael Greene, (Nathanael Greene Papers, Manuscripts Department, Perkins Library, Duke University, Durham, NC). Another interesting reasonably contemporary account of this engagement is contained in a letter dated December 14, 1784, from Aedanus Burke, a judge, to Governor Benjamin Guerard. Burke informs Guerard of the lynching of Matthew Love, a Tory alleged to have been with Cunningham at Hayes Station. Burke relates Cunningham's expedition in the South Carolina backcountry in the winter of 1781 had resulted in the murder of a number (said to be 50) of the "friends of the Country" and the burning of many Patriots' farms and plantations. Judge Burke states:

... Cunningham...came at length to a House in which were an American party of 35 men commanded by Colo. Hayes. These refusing to surrender at discretion an attack commenced & a hot fire kept up, with some Loss on both Sides, for about three hours; the British party possessed themselves of the out buildings, & at last set fire to the house in which Colo. Hayes was posted. In this distressful Situation they refused to surrender at discretion; reasonable terms were offered; that they should march out, lay down their arms & be treated as prisoners of war until exchanged; & a Capitulation was formally signed & interchanged. The Americans had no sooner marched out & laid down their Arms, but the British seized Colo. Hayes, & with the Capitulation in his hand, pleading the terms of it & begging for Mercy, they hanged him to the limb of a tree & then fired a Bullet thro' him. Captn. Williams the second in Command, was treated in the same manner. After which Cunningham, with his Own hands slew some of the prisoners & desired his men to follow his example. A most cruel slaughter of the prisoners ensued; nineteen of them were butchered & the rest escaped their fate by means too tedious now to mention.

A man by the name of Love, who had dwelt in the district before & since the war & had married there, was one of Cunningham's party, & a principal actor in this tragical business. Love traversed over the ground where lay the dead & the dying, his former neighbours & old Acquaintances, & as he saw Signs of Life in any of them, he ran his sword thro' & dispatched him. Those already dead he stabbed again: & when others seemingly without Life, pierced by the point of his Sword were involuntarily convulsed with the pain, to these he gave new wounds; lest any in so dreadful a Calamity might sham death to avoid it. Many other Circumstances of barbarous insult to the dead bodies of Colo. Hayes, Captn. Williams & others are related by Major Downs, Major Mulwee, Captn. Saxon & sundry other gentlemen of great worth & honor, who were witnesses of this Massacre, but fortunately escaped it; some thro' the good will of a Neighbour, & others by the intercession of their own slaves.

Love was thenceforth held in universal execration, yet he some time ago ventured to return into the vicinity of Ninety Six. He was taken up, & a Justice of the peace committed him to Goal, thinking that such barbarity did not come under the treaty of peace, so as to shelter him from prosecution. The State's Attorney laid the Affair before the Court of Sessions, who over ruled the prosecution; I being of opinion That under the Treaty, his Conscience & his feelings alone stood responsible for what was alleged; & on motion of his Council he was discharged. I then observed that there was no appearance, no look of disapprobation directed against a man so generally detested: all seemed to be reconciled. The determination on Love's Affair closed the business of the Sessions, & the Court immediately adjourned to the 26th of April next.

A party of men as respectable for Services & good Character as any in the district, composed of the fathers, Sons, & brothers and friends of the slain prisoners, had attended Court, & waited until the Judge had left the Court House, & arrived at his Lodgings. And then without tumult or noise made Love a prisoner & put him on horseback: they proceeded on, & tho' the house where they supposed the Judge had entered, led directly to the place where they intended to convey him, yet they took a Circuit another way to the skirts of a wood, where they arrived under the limb of a tree, to which they tyed one end of a rope, with the other round his neck, & bid him prepare to die; he urging in vain the injustice of killing a man without tryal, & they reminding him, that he should have thought of that, when he was slaughtering their kinsmen. The Horse drawn from under him left him suspended til he expired.

Thus I have related this unhappy Affair as I have heard it, & I can assure your Excelly., that whatever appearance this transaction may have to the contrary, the people of Ninety Six wish ardently to forget the injuries of the War, provided those do not return among them, that have committed wanton acts of barbarity. Many plunderers and other mischievous people now set down among them without molestation; nor can I learn that there exists resentment against any man who acted like a Soldier & fought them in fair open action. But it is to be lamented that such men as Love is described to have been, will be so infatuated as to return among the Citizens, & thus prevent the restoration of the publick tranquility.

Williams of Caswell County, North Carolina, submitted an accounting to the State of North Carolina for the $25,000 that it had given to Williams to raise militia in Caswell and surrounding counties of North Carolina. The accounting was submitted to and reviewed by a committee of the North Carolina legislature with the following report:

> Mr. John Macon from the Committee … to whom was referred the accounts of Col. James Williams, Deceased, Reports as follows: That it appears to your Committee that the said Williams had received Twenty-Five Thousand Dollars out of the Treasury to enable him to carry on an expedition against the Common Enemy and that upon examining the aforesaid account we find a balance due the State of Four Thousand, Three Hundred & Twenty nine and a half Dollars, all which your Committee humbly submit.
> S/ J. Macon, Chr.
> The House taking the said Report into Consideration Concurred therewith, Whereupon, Resolved that Mr. Henry Williams, Executor of the said James Williams, Deceased, pay into the hands of Robert Lanier, Esquire, Treasurer of the District of Salisbury such balance.[291]

Henry Williams died before he could resolve the matter. Williams' son John, however, continued to pursue it. On November 7, 1788, John Williams filed the following petition with the North Carolina General Assembly:

> To the Honorable, the General Assembly of the State of North Carolina:
> The Memorial and Petition of John Williams, eldest surviving son of James Williams, late of South Carolina, Deceased, Humbly Sheweth that the Father of your Memorialist took an early and active part in the late contest for American liberty, that in or about the month

---

This letter is in Records of the General Assembly, Governor's Messages, No., 313, South Carolina Archives, Columbia, SC and was reproduced in the South Carolina Historical Magazine, Vol. 88, No.1, (January 1987).

[291] Walter Clark, ed., *The State Records of North Carolina* Vol. XVI: 1782 1783 (New York: AMS Press, 1968-1972), 85-86.

of September in the Year 1780, he was supplied by your State with a sum of Money for the purpose of raising and marching Men to oppose the Enemy, who were then in force and moving toward Virginia, for which sum he was to be accountable. That he did raise in the County of Caswell and elsewhere (as Your Memorialist has been informed) a considerable Number of Men, and March'd them to King's Mountain, where he was instrumental in defeating the British troops & torys, commanded by that brave, and active officer, Ferguson, on the 7th day of October of the same Year, but he lived not to enjoy the fruits of the Victory, for about the close of the Action he fell and died. That he left a Widow and Eight Children, in their infancy, that his eldest two sons were afterwards Murdered by a party of Tories, that no part of the Money furnished as aforesaid ever came to the hands of his family but was fully applied as Your Memorialist verily believes in raising and Marching the men as aforesaid, that during part of the War, the Enemy kept a Garrison at his House, that they took and destroyed the Whole of his live Stock and Household furniture and five Valuable Slaves, which were never afterwards recovered, that the remains of the Estate is scarcely sufficient to payoff the Just claims against it, and that it would be particularly distressing to the Family now to be called on to account for that sum as they are not possessed of the vouchers which the deceased probably might have had at the time of his death.

In tender consideration whereof your Memorialist humbly prays that your Honors will be graciously pleased to take the Subject matter under consideration and grant unto the Family of the said James Williams deceased, such relief as to your Honors may seem Just, and your Memorialist will pray so.

S/ John Williams[292]

On November 20, 1788, the Committee to which this petition was submitted issued its report stating:

[292] The original of this petition is located in the North Carolina General Assembly Sessions Records, Nov-Dec. 1788, Box 3, House Joint Resolutions 3 Nov.-6 Dec. 20 Nov. 1788, in the North Carolina Archives, Raleigh, NC. This petition is entirely in the handwriting of John Williams with few strikethroughs or misspelled words, indicating that Col. Williams and his wife probably used his library (*see* Appendix 11) to educate their children.

Williams' memorial, erected by the Daughters of the American Revolution, at the Cherokee County Administration Building, Gaffney, South Carolina. The inscription reads: "Col. James Williams/ Hero of the Battle of King's Mountain/ 1780/ Erected by/ Daniel Morgan Chapter/ DAR/ 1917."

That by a Resolution of the General Assembly passed at Hillsborough [in] 1780, the said Petitioner's father, James Williams, was authorized to draw the Sum of twenty-five thousand Dollars from the Treasury of this State, conditioned that the money would be applied in raising Troops for the defence of this State then invaded by the British Army.

That your Committee are inclined to believe the money was applied to that particular Purpose as he was Soon after the reception of thereof seen in action at the Battle of King's Mountain at the head of three or four hundred Men, where he gloriously fell.

Your Committee therefore begs leave to recommend that a Resolution be passed, releasing & acquitting the said James Williams, his Heirs, Executors or administrators from the aforesaid draft.[293]

The committee's recommendation was accepted, and the North Carolina legislature forgave the unaccounted for balance of the $25,000 it had advanced Williams for the raising of troops in North Carolina.

---

[293] *Ibid.* The report bears notations that it was read and concurred in by both the House and Senate and is signed by the respective clerks of those bodies, all on November 20, 1788.

Chapter Thirteen
Williams Acclaimed

On October 27, 1780, General George Washington issued a general order from his headquarters at Totowa as follows:

> The General has the pleasure to congratulate the army on an important advantage lately obtained in North Carolina[294] (*sic*, South Carolina) over a corps of 1400 men, British troops and new Levies, commanded by Col. Ferguson. The militia of the neighbouring country under Colonels Williams, Shelby and others having assembled to the amount of 3000 men detached 1600 of their number on horseback to fall in with Ferguson's party on its march to Charlotte; they came up with them at a place called King's mountain, advantageously posted, and gave them a total defeat, in which Colonel Ferguson with 150 of his men were killed—800 made prisoners, and 1500 stand of arms taken. On our part the loss was inconsiderable. We have only to regret that the brave Col. Williams was mortally wounded.
>
> These advantages will in all probability have a very happy influence upon the Successive operations in that quarter. It is a proof of the Spirit and resources of the country.[295]

History does not disclose why Washington chose to single out Williams and Shelby for recognition. Given how poorly the war was proceeding in the South following the fall of Charleston and Gates' defeat at Camden, it is probable that Washington sensed an opportunity to boost the morale of the citizenry, army, and militia in the South. He saw the victory at King's Mountain (and Williams' death in it) as raw morale-building material too precious to pass up. Washington's words

---

[294] At this time, both North and South Carolina claimed that the battleground at King's Mountain was located within its borders. King's Mountain sits on the border between the two states, but the actual battleground is located in South Carolina.

[295] *See* fn 3 supra.

of recognition and praise for Williams, however, would have been particularly troubling to Sumter and his supporters, especially as time passed and the importance of the battle at King's Mountain became clearer. Sumter's absence from the single most important militia engagement to occur in the southern backcountry must have been the source of bitter disappointment to a man as strong-willed, egocentric, and independent as Sumter.

Williams' participation in, and death at, the Battle of King's Mountain became the stuff of legends. Poems and songs were written to commemorate the tale. General Joseph Johnson preserved one of the old songs called the "Battle of King's Mountain" as follows:

Old Williams from Hillsborough came,
To him the South-Carolinians flocked again.
We marched to the King's Mount, Campbell was there,
Shelby, Cleveland and Colonel Sevier
Men of renown, sir, like lions so bold,
Like lions undaunted, ne'er to be controlled.
We set out on our march that very same night;
Sometimes we were wrong, sometimes we were right;
Our hearts being run in true liberty's mould,
We valued not hunger, wet, weary nor cold.
On top of King's Mountain, the old rogue we found,
And like brave heroes, his camp did surround;
Like lightning the flashes, like thunder the noise,
Our rifles struck the poor Tories with sudden surprise.
Old Williams, and twenty-five more,
When the battle was o'er, lay rolled in their gore;
With sorrow their bodies we interred in clay,
Hoping, to heaven, their souls took their way.
This being ended, we shouted amain,
Our voice was heard seven miles on the plain;
Liberty shall stand—the Tories shall fall,
Here is an end to my song, so God Bless you all! [296]

---

[296] Johnson, *Traditions*, 491.

Chapter Fourteen
Why a Whig?

Why was Williams such a die hard, uncompromising Whig from the outset of the War? Having made that choice in the early days of the Revolution when he may well have been caught up in the often irrational euphoria and optimism that accompanies the early stage of most wars, why did he remain a Whig after the fall of Charleston? That sobering event caused many Whigs, some of whom—such as Andrew Williamson, Andrew Pickens and LeRoy Hammond—had played prominent roles in the armed rebellion, to lay down their arms and take protection from the British.

Williams presents a particularly intriguing challenge in positing answers to these questions. He and his family lived in the only area of the province in which the Loyalists had such a strong presence that they felt emboldened to actually take up arms in support of the royal government in 1775. That area's Tory militia, led by Col. Thomas Fletchall, Robert Cunningham and others, presented a significant threat to the Whigs until Fletchall and Cunningham were arrested and the Tory militia scattered by Whigs during the Snow Campaign in late December 1775. Even after that defeat of the Tories, the region between the Saluda and Broad Rivers where Williams lived remained a hotbed of Tory sentiment. Robert Cunningham's defeat of Williams in the 1778 State Senate election in the area and the rapid raising of Tory militia units there after the fall of Charleston provide abundant evidence of continued Tory dominance in that region.

As a merchant and miller intent on earning at least a portion of his income selling goods and services to his neighbors, and as a substantial planter with a home, family, slaves, crops and other valuables all vulnerable to plunder by his Tory neighbors, why did self-interest not dictate to Williams that, at a minimum, he remain neutral until after the authority of the Whig government was established in late 1775? Likewise, why did self-interest not dictate that he at least consider taking parole after the fall of Charleston in May 1780? He did neither. Instead, Williams threw aside what arguably might have been in the best personal interest of himself and his family and openly cast his lot with the Whigs. Why? Some clues to the answers lie in the inferences that can be drawn from his actions and the multitude of social and political countercurrents that influenced him as a backcountry planter/merchant/miller. Other clues can be gleaned from what sparse written record he left.

British Military Ineffectiveness — Lack of Military Presence

One factor that may well have influenced Williams and other Whigs was the lack of any regular military presence of the British in the backcountry. Although there is yet no definitive evidence that Williams served in the Cherokee campaigns of 1759-1761, he nevertheless would have been fully aware of the failure of Governor William Henry Lyttelton's 1759 campaign, Colonel Archibald Montgomery's 1760 campaign, and Colonel James Grant's 1761 campaign to deal effectively with the threat of Indian uprisings in the Carolina backcountry. Although the British declared each of these campaigns a "success" in quelling the Indian threat, none resulted in any meaningful diminution in the ability of either the Cherokees or the Creeks to wage war. No decisive engagements occurred in these campaigns. These two tribes continued to present the most immediate threat to backcountry security in the early 1770s. The inability of the British military to provide significant protection to the backcountry settlers from the Indian threat would have led many of those settlers, already prone to being self-reliant, to place little or no value on the prospect of future British assistance. The backcountry settlers knew that dealing with the almost daily threat posed by Indian uprisings would be their collective responsibility.

This feeling of the futility of relying on the British to defend them must have been strongly reinforced by the total withdrawal of all British regular forces from the Carolina backcountry following the end of the French and Indian War in 1763. The closest British garrison of any size was stationed in St. Augustine in East Florida in the territory ceded to England by the Spanish as part of the settlement of that war. The absence of any meaningful presence of British troops in the backcountry also would have removed any restraining influence such a presence might have had on the settlers. Just as there was no British army to deal with the threat of Indian uprisings, there was no army to quell the settlers' enthusiasm for taking up arms in the coming drive to separate the colonies from Great Britain.

Lack of Desire for British Military Presence in the Backcountry

It is highly likely that Williams and the majority of his backcountry neighbors would not have welcomed the intervention of the British army in dealing with the Indian threat. The frontier settlers would have been justifiably concerned that any troops the British sent into the backcountry would have to be housed and fed at their expense. While the quartering of troops in the coastal cities and towns of North America may well have been an immediate cause for concern among the residents living in those areas, at least those residents' proximity to alternative sources of food and housing would not have presented a threat to their ability to survive. In the backcountry, where many small farmers barely grew enough to sustain themselves and their families, the burden of having to provide food and shelter for a large army moving through their region would have deprived them of such sparse provisions as they may have been fortunate enough to lay aside for their own sustenance. That such fears were justified was amply proved when the British invaded the backcountry after the fall of Charleston and resorted to appropriating the food stores and housing of the frontier residents to sustain the army. Such script or IOUs as may have been issued in compensation for those appropriations

Memorial at Hayes Station where two of James Williams' sons, along with the other Whigs listed on the memorial, were killed by South Carolina Loyalist militia Major William ("Bloody Bill") Cunningham.

would have been of little value to these frontiersmen when faced with the immediate need to replenish their precious food stuffs and provide shelter for their families.

British Attempts to Limit White Settlers' Encroachment on Indian Lands

Another British action that put backcountry settlers such as Williams at substantial odds with the mother country was King George III's proclamation of October 7, 1763. Following its successful termination of the French and Indian War, Great Britain wanted to appease the North American Indians, a large proportion of whom had fought on the side of the French. King George and his ministers realized that one reason the Indians sided with the French was that the French were traders who, unlike the English colonists, did not send waves of settlers to encroach on the Indians' land. In an attempt to mollify that concern, the king proclaimed that henceforth the Indians were not to be molested or disturbed in their possession of such lands as had not been heretofore ceded to or purchased by Britain. All other Indian lands were to be "reserved to them, as their Hunting Grounds."[297] The proclamation further placed a ban on all settlements beyond the headwaters of any of the rivers that fall into the Atlantic Ocean. This band was to remain in effect "until our [the King's] further Pleasure be known." Specific grants made by treaty with, or purchase from, the Indians would be required to obtain access to the vast regions beyond the crest of the eastern mountains. Such unilateral assertion by the King of the right to limit expansion of the frontier was a substantial, tangible limitation of the heretofore unrestrained "right" that frontiersmen, such as many of Williams' neighbors and customers, claimed for themselves and their children. There is no evidence that Williams himself ever claimed squatters' rights to any land, but such was a common practice among the specie-starved pioneers who settled the Carolina backcountry. As a businessman intent on growing

[297] Appendix 1.

his mercantile and milling business, anything that slowed the settlement of the backcountry and the continued expansion of the boundaries of the frontier would have been adverse to the personal interests of Williams. Furthermore, by the 1770s there was a well-established tradition throughout the American colonies of farmer families meeting their ever-expanding need for new land to accommodate the requirements of future generations by expanding southward and westward into Indian territories. Williams harbored these same expectations for his children's future prospects.

Reaction to British Attempts to Ally Themselves with the Cherokee

The attempts by John Stuart, the royal agent to the Cherokee Indians, and other royalists to gain the Cherokee's allegiance to the Crown in the very early stages of the conflict with the colonists would also have been a matter of grave concern to Williams. Fear that the British might arm the Indians in an attempt to force the colonists to fight a two-front war posed a real threat to the security of the interior parts of the State.

Influence of the North and South Carolina Regulator Movements

Williams came from a part of North Carolina that was heavily involved in that colony's Regulator movement. Orange County North Carolina was the center of that province's Regulator movement. Granville County where Williams lived from the time his parents moved there when he was very young until, at age 33, he moved to South Carolina, adjoined Orange County. Williams would have been well aware of the Regulators' grievances against the colonial government's exaction of high taxes payable in scarce specie; remote courts; corrupt sheriffs and other public officials; high lawyers' fees for effecting land transfers and other routine business transactions; nonexistent representation of the yeoman farmer class in the colony's legislative body; and

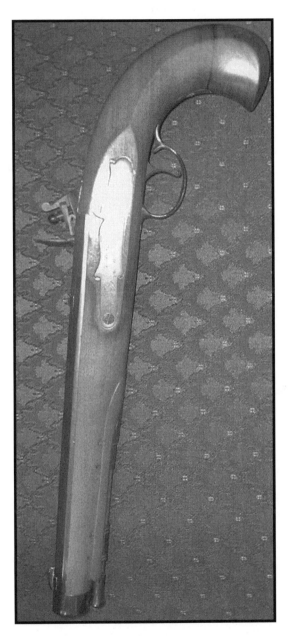

Reproduction of one of two pistols presented to Williams' family by the North Carolina General Assembly in appreciation for his services in the Revolutionary War. The original pistols given to the Williams family after the Battle of King's Mountain are said to have been used by Capt. Daniel Williams at Hayes Station. Rather than suffer those pistols to fall into the hands of Maj. William Cunningham, the commander of the Tory forces, Daniel is said to have thrown them into the burning remains of the Station before his surrender to Cunningham. The pistol is on loan for public display at the Musgrove Mill State Historic Site in Laurens County, SC.

other complaints that culminated in the Battle of Alamance on May 16, 1771. At that battle the state militia, under the command of the royal governor, ruthlessly put down the Regulator rebellion and hanged seven of their leaders. As the nephew of both Judge Richard Henderson and lawyer John Williams (two of the victims of the Regulators' protest actions), if Williams played any role in the Battle of Alamance, he would have done so as a member of the governor's militia rather than as a Regulator. However, he would have been well aware of the Regulators' complaints and the legitimacy of those complaints against a government that drew its authority from the Crown of England.[298]

Similarly, the Regulation as fought in South Carolina influenced Williams. Unlike North Carolina's Regulation that centered on grievances against the colonial government, South Carolina's Regulation involved the suppression of backcountry lawlessness by frustrated landowners. Prior to the formation of vigilante groups of landowners who dubbed themselves Regulators, gangs of thieves and bandits victimized the backcountry unrestrained by any attempt of the colonial government in Charleston to enforce the laws on the frontier. Like their North Carolina counterparts, the South Carolina Regulators also complained of under-representation in the colonial legislature, remote land registration, and lack of courthouses and jails on the frontier; however, their primary grievance was the indifference of the colonial government to the establishment of any semblance of the rule of law in the backcountry. Having acquired substantial landholdings in that lawless backcountry, Williams likely looked upon the seeming indifference of the colonial government to the plight of the frontiersmen as a genuine threat to his own personal fortune and that of his family.[299]

---

[298] For an excellent discussion of the North Carolina Regulation, *See* Marjoleine Kars, *Breakings Loose Together: The Regulator Rebellion in Pre-Revolutionary North Carolina*, (Chapel Hill: The University of North Carolina Press, 2002).

[299] The South Carolina Regulation is covered in Richard Maxwell Brown, *The South Carolina Regulators* (Cambridge, MA: Harvard University Press, 1963); and Rachel N. Klein, "Ordering the Backcountry: The South Carolina Regulation," *William & Mary Quarterly*, 3rd ser., 38 (1981).

Williams' Early Engagement by the Whigs: Whig Support of Wider Democratization in South Carolina

The emergence of the Whigs as the major political force clearly offered Williams the opportunity to participate in a meaningful way in the new government the Whigs proposed for South Carolina. By designating Williams, his brother John, and many other backcountry men of influence as representatives in the first Provincial Congress that met in Charleston in January 1775, the coastal region power brokers who assembled that Congress secured the loyalty of many of these men. The majority of those power brokers were, or grew to be, Whigs or, at a minimum, Whig sympathizers. Although not all the members of the first Provincial Congress ultimately chose to become Whigs, many did cast their lot with the Whigs because it was the Whigs who proposed a radical departure from the old colonial legislative approach totally controlled by the powers in London supported by a provincial assembly composed almost exclusively of members of the wealthy, privileged upper class of coastal planters, lawyers and merchants. The inclusion of Williams in this first Provincial Congress must have had a profound influence on his loyalty to the Whig cause thereafter. Albeit as only one of many members of the newly formed Whig power base, the intoxicating allure of such inclusion would have been difficult for someone as ambitious as Williams to ignore.

The Charleston Whigs' inclusion of men such as Williams in the first Provincial Congress reflected the Whigs' commitment to restructuring the legislature to allow more representation of backcountry interests and to address some of their complaints, such as the lack of courts, justices of the peace, and sheriffs. These concessions to the backcountry, however, were by no means driven by eleemosynary or self-sacrificing motives. The lessons of both the North and South Carolina Regulations could not have been misunderstood by the men who wished to wield the power in the new political system they saw emerging from the unrest among the colonists. They knew that if they did not address some of the backcountry complaints and share some of their power with the now more populous backcountry regions of the State, they ran the risk of having that power taken from them by force.

More importantly, the coastal power brokers needed the active support of the backcountry region for at least three basic reasons. First, by 1775 the coastal region's population included substantially more enslaved blacks than whites. In the event of a slave uprising, the backcountry militia's participation in its suppression would be essential. Although there were a few substantial slave holders such as Williams in the backcountry, in 1775 the vast majority of the residents of that region were yeomen farmers who owned few, if any, slaves. The backcountry's population was overwhelmingly white and therefore represented a significant manpower pool from which to form militia to come to the aid of the coastal areas in the event of a slave insurrection. Secondly, if satisfactory conciliation with Great Britain could not be effected and war resulted, the Whigs knew that the British were most likely to attack South Carolina by sea. Charleston was one of the most important port cities in North America. It was logical to anticipate (as indeed would prove to be the case) that the British would attack Charleston early in the war in an attempt to cut off the southern colonies from vital supplies. Clearly, backcountry militia support would be needed if there were to be any hope of successfully defending the coastal regions of the colony. Thirdly, the presence of a substantial force of Cherokee and Creek warriors on the frontier presented the potential for having to fight a two-front war in the event armed hostilities broke out with Britain. Again, the lessons of the recently concluded French and Indian War would not have been lost on the coastal elites. In that war, the participation on the side of the French by a substantial majority of the Native American eastern tribes had threatened to tilt the outcome of the war in favor of the French. Since the end of the war, it had been the English who had plied the Indians with trade goods to curry their favor; it had been King George who had issued the 1763 proclamation declaring a line of demarcation in an attempt to protect Indian lands; and it had been the English who had appointed agents to live among the Indians to keep a constant finger on the pulse of Indian concerns. Were the Indians to be aroused to action by the British against the colonists, the backcountry militia would be required to bear the burden of protecting the coastal regions from Indian attack. All of these factors argued strongly for the inclusion of the backcountry population in the political process that would be necessary to defeat the British in the event of war. As the owner of 33 slaves himself and as a resident of an area close enough to the perils presented by the Indians to cause him to construct a fort on his own plantation, Williams had much in common with the interests of the coastal region power brokers.

Lord Dunmore's Freeing of Slaves

As the owner of more than 30 slaves, Williams would have reacted very negatively to John Murray, the 4th Lord Dunmore, the last royal governor of Virginia, encouraging indentured servants and black slaves to abandon their masters and enlist in his army in exchange for their freedom. Since Dunmore's action occurred very early in the conflict between Britain and her colonies, Williams and other slave owners would have had ample reason to fear that their slaves would rise up against them and fight for the Crown. Although similar proposals to free slaves in exchange for their serving in the military would be raised by some Whigs such as Col. John Laurens, Jr., in the latter stages of the war, no such proposals were being entertained by the Whigs at the time Lord Dunmore actually implemented his plan in 1775.[300]

---

[300] *See*, e.g., Boatner, *Encyclopedia*, 775-777, 1148.

Lack of Cosmopolitan Influence on Williams

Unlike many of the coastal upper class who had been educated or traveled in England, Williams had no cosmopolitan experience. There is no evidence that he had ever been beyond the borders of Virginia, North and South Carolina. Consequently, while men like the Rutledge brothers, Henry and John Laurens, William Henry Drayton, and even Thomas Sumter might be expected to have their commitment to the Whig cause tempered by their exposure to and tangible awareness of the sophisticating influences of ties to the motherland, Williams had no such ties. This lack of cosmopolitan influences may well have caused Williams not to fully appreciate, and indeed to be indifferent to, whatever benefits would be lost by severing ties with Great Britain. Likewise, few of the items Williams and his fellow backcountry residents required for daily life came from England. Loss of trade connections with England may have had some minimal impact on Williams' activities as a merchant but it is doubtful that loss of those ties would have had much influence on him.

Scotch-Irish/Presbyterian Influences

Although Williams was of Welsh ancestry, a substantial portion of his neighbors was of Scotch-Irish ancestry. Much has been written about this breed of independent-minded folk predisposed by their long suffering under various administrations to dislike and distrust the English. Much less is made of the abuses of the Welsh by the English, but those abuses were not significantly different from those inflicted on the Scotch-Irish.[301] Both groups suffered repression of their language, religion, and cultural and ethnic heritage. The consequence of this repression was that neither the Scotch-Irish nor the Welsh harbored much affection for the English.

[301] *See*, e.g., A. H. Dodd, *The Character of Early Welsh Emigration to the United States* (Cardiff: University of Wales Press, 1953).

Like his Scotch-Irish neighbors, Williams was a devout Presbyterian adamantly opposed to the Anglican Church and its status as the official state church of Great Britain and its colonies. The hierarchical structure of the Anglican Church with its vicars, bishops, and archbishops all subject to the rule of the Archbishop of Canterbury and ultimately to the Crown as head of the Church was antithetical to the democratic governance of the Presbyterian Church. Furthermore, firebrand Presbyterian preachers like Alexander Craighead of Mecklenburg County in North Carolina relentlessly preached from their pulpits the betrayal suffered by Presbyterians when the English broke the Solemn League and Covenant. To win the support of the Scot Presbyterians for Parliament against Charles I and his Irish Catholic allies in the first English Civil War in 1643, the English Parliamentarians had entered into the Covenant promising the Scots that the Scottish system of church government would be adopted in England. Parliament's failure to honor the Covenant was still a very real issue and grounds for grievance among the Scotch-Irish.[302]

On a less theoretical and theological basis, the vestry acts imposed taxes to support the Anglican Church; taxes which were due and payable by all the Crown's subjects including backcountry residents like James Williams. Williams and his neighbors certainly resented these taxes, even though there is little evidence that any serious effort was made by the Royal government to actually collect such taxes in the more remote regions of its domain. More immediately offensive to the residents of these regions were the marriage acts requiring marriages to be performed by Anglican clergy or government officials appointed by the Royal government in Charleston. Under these laws, the many marriages performed in the

---

[302] *See*, e.g., C. Gregg Singer, *Theological Interpretation of American History* (Philadelphia, PA: The Presbyterian and Reformed Publishing Co., 1981, 1964); Alexander Craighead, *Renewal of the Covenants, National and Solemn League; A Confession of Sins; An Engagement to Duties; and a Testimony; as They Were Carried on at Middle Octorara in Pennsylvania, November 11, 1743, 1748* [a collection of sermons] (Philadelphia: 2nd ed., 1748, 1743: Cerlox Bound Photocopy Series. Edmonton, AB, Canada: Still Waters Revival Books, n.d.).

backcountry by Presbyterian, Baptist, Methodist, Lutheran and other sectarian ministers—without Anglican sanction—were illegal, and the children born to such unions were, at least as far as the law was concerned, illegitimate.

These vestry and marriage laws were particularly irritating to the frontiersmen. Even if the frontiersmen had been inclined to seek Anglican sanction of their marriages, there was no permanent presence of the Anglican Church on the frontier. To make matters worse, the Anglican missionaries, such as the Reverend Charles Woodmason, who made occasional forays into the backcountry were completely ignorant of, and unsympathetic to, the challenges of frontier life and the accommodations the frontiersmen were forced to make to survive there. It is not difficult to understand why the backcountry residents found little sustenance for their spiritual needs from the likes of Reverend Woodmason.[303]

Like many of his fellow backcountry neighbors, Williams was driven to meet his spiritual needs by actively participating in the formation and construction of a church. In Williams' case that church was the Little River Presbyterian Church, formed in 1761.[304] Williams is listed as one of the founding elders of this church even though he did not move his family from North Carolina to his South Carolina plantation until late 1773. His participation in its founding, at a time when he was making the preliminary efforts to establish a residence in the area, shows his commitment to the spiritual well-being of himself and his family. The predominantly Scotch-Irish composition of the congregations of backcountry Presbyterian churches such as the Little River Presbyterian Church would have assured that Williams communed among men and women who held no love for the English.

---

[303] Charles Woodmason, (Richard Hooker, ed.), *The Carolina Backcountry on the Eve of the Revolution: The Journal and Other Writings of Charles Woodmason, Anglican Itinerant*, (Chapel Hill: University of North Carolina Press, 1953).

[304] The Little River Dominick Presbyterian Church still exists today on a site 500 yards north of its original location. The original sanctuary of the church was located near Williams' Mount Pleasant plantation in what is today Newberry County, South Carolina. *See* fn 29, supra. Howe, *Presbyterian Church.*

Countervailing Influences

Not all of the factors bearing on Williams, however, argued for his becoming a Whig from the outset of the war. As already noted, he lived in the middle of Tory territory. His neighbors and potential customers in the area between the Saluda and Broad Rivers were more likely to be Tories than Whigs. Further, his main creditor was a Tory. On January 10, 1775, Williams borrowed the princely sum of £4,700 sterling from Rowland Rugeley, a prominent Charleston merchant and Tory.[305] This loan was secured by a mortgage on substantially all of Williams' real estate including his plantation, Mount Pleasant. Coming as it did just prior to the start of the first session of the first Provincial Congress, this loan at least raises the specter that Rugeley might have been trying to influence Williams toward the Tory position. Whatever Rugeley's motivation, it did not work to sway Williams. By taking up arms for the Whig cause, Williams immediately exposed his entire fortune. Rugeley died in Charleston in 1776. There is no indication, however, that Rugeley's heirs ever attempted to enforce their lien on Williams' estate even though Article 4 of the Treaty of Paris stipulated that "it is agreed that creditors on either side [of the conflict between the United States and Great Britain] shall meet with no lawful impediment to the recovery of the full value in sterling money of all bona fide debts heretofore contracted".

Fall of Charleston

The factors already discussed had some bearing on Williams' decision to become a Whig at the start of the

---

[305] In addition to his role as a merchant in Charleston, Rugeley enjoyed some renown among his contemporaries as an author having published *Miscellaneous Poems and Translations for La Fontaine and Others* (Cambridge, London: Fletcher and Hobson, J. Kearsly, 1763) and *The Story of Aeneas and Dido Burlesqued: From the Fourth Book of the Aeneid of Virgil* (Charleston, SC: Robert Wells, printer, 1774). Little is known of Rugeley's life. He is thought to have been born in 1735 in England and to have emigrated to America in 1766. He died in Charleston in 1776. Robert Bain, Joseph M. Flora, Louis D. Rubin, eds., *Southern Writers: A Biographical Dictionary* (Baton Rouge: Louisiana State University Press, 1979).

war. None of those factors, however, provide a satisfactory answer to why he chose to remain an uncompromising Whig once Charleston fell in May 1780. Prominent backcountry Whigs such as Andrew Williamson, Andrew Pickens, John Winn, LeRoy Hammond, and others saw the British taking of Charleston and the subsequent establishment in the backcountry of British military strongholds at Ninety Six, Camden, Rocky Mount, Granby, and elsewhere as signs that further armed resistance to the British would be futile. Those men who took protection from the British promised that they would no longer fight the British. By giving their parole they avoided being incarcerated as prisoners of war or worse, being tried for treason. Although some of these men would reenter the war as Whigs after real or perceived violations of the terms of the parole by the British, Williams never wavered in his commitment. Why?

After the fall of Charleston, Williams wasted no time removing his personal property from his exposed backcountry plantation in the heart of Tory country to the relative safety of the plantation of his brother, Henry, in Caswell County, North Carolina, just below the Virginia line. By June 12, 1780, Williams had deposited with his brother most of his slaves, livestock, books, and other moveable valuables. Such swift action highlights that Williams harbored little or no doubt that he would continue to fight against the British. It would have taken almost all of the time between the news of Charleston's fall on May 12 until June 12 to organize and effect the removal of this personal property from harm's way.

Fear of Reprisal for Past Transgressions Against his Tory Neighbors

One possible clue to why Williams remained such a die-hard Whig lies in the letter Williams wrote to his son Daniel on June 12, 1779. In that letter, Williams tells his son that he has traded with Captain John Moore for a mare. Moore got the mare by plunder from Daniel McGirt, a notorious backcountry Tory and reputedly an excellent judge of

166

horses. Williams tells his son to go get the horse, bring her back to Mount Pleasant, and brand her on both cushions with Williams' brand. If asked, Daniel was to say that his father acquired the mare by purchase from a man on Fishing Creek, paying $1,000 for her. Williams states: "My reason for begging you to go for her is, that it may not be known she is a plunder mare …". Having benefited, at least indirectly, from the plunder of his Tory neighbor, would Williams have been worried that his surrender to British law would subject him to prosecution, if not persecution, by his Tory neighbors? This seems an unlikely full explanation for Williams' continued attachment to the Whig cause. Why would he feel any more exposed to Tory claims for retribution than Williamson, Pickens, Hammond, Winn, or any of the other former Whigs who took parole from the British following the fall of Charleston? Had Williams engaged in more egregious offenses against his neighbors than other backcountry Whigs? There is no record of any such activities by Williams. However, having been in the field participating in almost every major campaign from the inception of the war, it is very likely that Williams and the men under his command made liberal use of the opportunity to supply their needs from the larders of their Tory neighbors, thereby creating legitimate concern that their activities might come home to roost.

His Rivals Take the Field

Another compelling reason for Williams' determined dedication to the Whigs would have been the re-emergence of his old political nemesis, Robert Cunningham, the Tory who defeated Williams in the 1778 State senatorial race in his home region. Although Cunningham was not allowed to take his seat following his election in 1778, the mere fact that he remained on his plantation in South Carolina and immediately came forward in support of the British following the fall of Charleston would have given Williams good reason to fear for the safety of his family and himself. Cunningham, his brother Patrick, and their cousin William (later to be known as "Bloody Bill" Cunningham) were close neighbors of Williams and were bound to seek outlets for the four years of pent-up frustration they had experienced while the Whigs dominated the State. Robert Cunningham found expression for his frustration by accepting a commission as brigadier general of the backcountry Tory militia. Bloody Bill found expression for his frustration by commanding a group of Tory banditti that terrorized the backcountry even well after Cornwallis' surrender at Yorktown effectively ended Britain's offensive prosecution of the war.

That Williams' fears of reprisals from his Tory neighbors were well-founded was quickly confirmed. The loquacious Tory David Fanning states that the first act he and Bloody Bill Cunningham took following the fall of Charleston was to embody some men to capture Williams. They went immediately to Williams' plantation to take him prisoner, but Williams had been forewarned and made his escape in sight of his pursuers. Fanning, Cunningham, and their men then joined Captain Richard Pearis, who took the fort at Ninety Six and accepted the surrender of General Andrew Williamson, and two companies of Whig militia at Williamson's plantation known as White Hall. Williams' narrow escape, however, left his plantation exposed. It was promptly occupied by Thomas Brown, the Tory commander of a regiment of provincials in the Southern backcountry. Brown held Mount Pleasant until Major Patrick Ferguson and his troop of Tory provincials came there on their way into the backcountry to recruit more Tories to join the King's forces.

Long Established Friendships/ Comradeship with Fellow Militiamen

No small factor bearing on Williams' steadfastness as a Whig would have been his unwillingness to suffer the loss of honor and standing among his comrades in arms that would have resulted from his taking parole from the British. Williams raised a company of men to fight in the first Battle of Ninety Six in the late fall and early winter of 1775, and he had remained in the field continually since that date in command of his Little River Regiment of Whig militia. The men making up that regiment would not only have been Williams' friends and neighbors, but also the men who had answered Williams' repeated calls to duty as he led them into engagements during the 1776 Cherokee Campaign, the Florida Campaign in the late spring of 1778, the Augusta Campaign in the winter of 1778-1779, the Battle of Brier Creek in March 1779, the Battle of Stono in June 1779, the Siege of Savannah in the fall of 1779, and, at the time of the fall of Charleston, the guarding of the approaches to Augusta at the Cupboard Swamp and Spirit Creek bridge. Although other men may well have seen that common sense dictated that they lay down their arms following the fall of Charleston, Williams' aggressive commitment to the cause and his men required him to remain in the field even in the face of seemingly insurmountable odds.

More specifically, Williams' close friendship with Joseph Hayes, his second in command of the Little River Regiment, would have restrained any impulse Williams might have entertained to take protection. The evidence suggests that Hayes had been with Williams since the beginning of the war. Hayes accompanied Williams on his trip from Mount Pleasant to Caswell County, North Carolina, to deliver his personal property into the safekeeping of his brother in late May and early June 1780. There Hayes agreed to serve as Williams' executor. The support of such a good friend would have been a bulwark to any man's will to continue on the path of realizing the common goals they had shared for the five years they had been in the field together. It is easy to imagine these two strong-willed men mutually bolstering each other's resolve.

Commitment to Family

The key to understanding Williams' steadfastness, however, lies not in some cold analysis of what was in his personal best interest but in his relationship with his family and his understanding of his obligations to them. Although Williams left little written record of his political beliefs and inclinations, his letter to his eldest son, Daniel, written June 12, 1779, provides the clearest insight into his motivation. In that letter he states:

> I am, by the care of Providence, in the field in defence of my country. When I reflect on the matter, I feel myself distracted on both hands by this thought, that in my old age I should be obliged to take the field in defence of my rights and liberties, and that of my children. God only knows that it is not of choice, but of necessity, and from the consideration that I had rather suffer anything than lose my birthright, and that of my children. When I come to lay down in the field, stripped of all the pleasure that my family connections afford me at home—surrounded by an affectionate wife and eight dear children, and all the blessings of life—when I reflect on my own distress, I feel for that of my family, on account of my absence from their midst; and especially for the mother, who sits like a dove that has lost its mate, having the weight of the family on her shoulders.

Even though this was written before the fall of Charleston, it is unimaginable that the author of such words would turn his back on the cause for which not only he, but also his family, had sacrificed so much. With a wife who, in addition to holding their family together, had run his plantation, store, and mills during his long absences and with a family of eight young and impressionable children ranging in age from 17 to 1, Williams had to stay the course. To do otherwise would have been a compromise with his principles that, from all the available evidence, was never seriously considered by Williams. In Williams' view, he was a Whig because in opposing the British he was defending the liberty that he held to be the birthright not only of himself but, more importantly, of his children.

Afterword

James Williams was a committed Patriot. He fought steadfastly for the independence of the United States from Great Britain. His commitment to independence endured when the faith of other erstwhile Patriots faltered in the face of the resurgence of Tory activities in the Carolina backcountry following British victories at Charleston, Camden, and Fishing Creek. Men with far greater resources such as Andrew Williamson abandoned what, in the summer and autumn of 1780, must have seemed a lost cause to many Patriots in the Carolina backcountry. Time after time from the start of hostilities in 1775 through October 7, 1780, Williams unhesitatingly responded to the call of duty, leaving his family and property exposed to assault and plunder by his Tory neighbors.

On October 8, 1780, Williams paid the ultimate price for his uncompromising dedication to his country. For that country to consign him to an inaccurate and dismissive reference on the battleground on which he gave his life is disheartening. This is especially true since such consignment is based solely on highly dubious, self-serving accusations belatedly made by a man bitterly disappointed by his absence and that of his mentor from what proved to be one of the pivotal battles of the war.

Perhaps the model set by George Bancroft, considered by many to be the father of American analytical history, will serve future generations of historians. Bancroft probably had full knowledge of Hill's accusations, yet he disregarded them and wrote of Williams:

> Among those who fell [at King's Mountain] was Colonel James Williams of Ninety Six, a man of an exalted character, of a career brief but glorious. An ungenerous enemy revenged themselves for his virtues by nearly extirpating his family; they could not take away his right to be remembered by his country with honor and affection to the latest time.[306]

[306] Bancroft, *History*, 10:339.

What Williams' Tory enemies could not do, Hill did with his accusations. Williams' dogged commitment to the Patriot cause entitles him to a better legacy than that fashioned for him by Hill. While Williams' role as one of nine commanders of the Patriot militia forces at the battle does not entitle him to be known as "the Hero of King's Mountain," he is entitled to be included, without caveat or reservation, among the many heroes who selflessly served his country in its fight for independence. Indeed, his legacy should rate him among the pantheon of South Carolina's Revolutionary era military heroes, men such as Francis Marion, Thomas Sumter, Andrew Pickens, John Laurens, William Henderson and William Moultrie.

Appendices

1. Royal Proclamation of 1763 by George III
2. Letter from Williams to his wife: June 3, 1779
3. Letter from Williams to his son, Daniel Williams: June 12, 1779
4. Petition filed September 10, 1779, by Officers and Men serving under Williams' command in the Little River Regiment of the South Carolina militia
5. Letter from Williams to his wife: September 30, 1779
6. Letter from Williams to Gen. Andrew Williamson: January 4, 1780
7. Last Will and Testament of James Williams: June 12, 1780
8. Letter from Williams to his wife: July 4, 1780
9. Williams' Report on the Battle of Musgrove Mill
10. Letter from Williams to Major General Horatio Gates: October 2, 1780
11. Books in Williams' Library
12. Official Report of the Battle of King's Mountain
13. Table of King's Mountain Whig Militia Listed According to Commanding Officer
14. Account of Property Lost at Hayes Station
15. Isaac Shelby's Account of his Exploits During the Revolutionary War
16. William Hill's *Memoirs*
17. What Did McJunkin Really Saye?
    A. McJunkin's Pension Application
    B. McJunkin's Narrative: Draper MSS, Sumter Papers 23VV153-203
    C. McJunkin's Statement: Draper MSS, Sumter Papers 23VV203-212
18. Petition filed by Williams' heirs for his services during the Revolutionary War and Actions of South Carolina Legislative Committees
19. A Concurrent Resolution passed by the South Carolina Senate and concurred in by the House
20. Account of the re-burial of Col. Williams' body

Appendix 1

Royal Proclamation of 1763 by George III

Whereas We have taken into Our Royal Consideration the extensive and valuable Acquisitions in America, secured to our Crown by the late Definitive Treaty of Peace, concluded at Paris, the 10th Day of February last; and being desirous that all Our loving Subjects, as well of our Kingdom as of our Colonies in America, may avail themselves with all convenient Speed, of the great Benefits and Advantages which must accrue therefrom to their Commerce, Manufactures, and Navigation, We have thought fit, with the Advice of our Privy Council, to issue this our Royal Proclamation, hereby to publish and declare to all our loving Subjects, that we have, with the Advice of our Said Privy Council, granted our Letters Patent, under our Great Seal of Great Britain, to erect, within the Countries and Islands ceded and confirmed to Us by the said Treaty, Four distinct and separate Governments, styled and called by the names of Quebec, East Florida, West Florida and Grenada, and limited and bounded as follows, *viz,*

First—The Government of Quebec bounded on the Labrador Coast by the River St. John, and from thence by a Line drawn from the Head of that River through the Lake St. John, to the South end of the Lake Nipissim; from whence the said Line, crossing the River St. Lawrence, and the Lake Champlain, in 45, Degrees of North Latitude, passes along the High Lands which divide the Rivers that empty themselves into the said River St. Lawrence from those which fall into the Sea; and also along the North Coast of the Baye des Chaleurs, and the Coast of the Gulf of St. Lawrence to Cape Rosieres, and from thence crossing the Mouth of the River St. Lawrence by the West End of the Island of Anticosti, terminates at the aforesaid River of St. John.

Secondly—The Government of East Florida bounded to the Westward by the Gulf of Mexico and the Apalachicola River; to the Northward by a Line drawn from that part of the said River where the Chatahouchee and Flint Rivers meet, to the source of St. Mary's River, and by the course of the said River to the Atlantic Ocean; and to the Eastward and Southward by the Atlantic Ocean and the Gulf of Florida, including all Islands within Six Leagues of the Sea Coast.

Thirdly—The Government of West Florida bounded to the Southward by the Gulf of Mexico including all Islands within Six Leagues of the Coast, from the River Apalachicola to Lake Pontchartrain; to the Westward by the said Lake, the Lake Maurepas, and the River Mississippi; to the Northward by a Line drawn due East from that part of the River Mississippi which lies in 31 Degrees North Latitude to the River Apalachicola or Chatahouchee; and to the Eastward by the said River.

Fourthly—The Government of Grenada, comprehending the Island of that name, together with the Grenadines, and the Islands of Dominico, St. Vincent's and Tobago. And to the end that the open and free Fishery of our Subjects may be extended to and carried on upon the Coast of Labrador, and the adjacent Islands, We have thought fit, with the advice of our said Privy Council to put all that Coast, from the River St. John's to Hudson's Streights, together with the islands of Anticosti and Madelaine, and all other smaller Islands lying upon the said Coast, under the care and Inspection of our Governor of Newfoundland.

We have also, with the advice of our Privy Council thought fit to annex the Islands of St. John's and Cape Breton, or Isle Royale, with the lesser Islands adjacent thereto, to our Government of Nova Scotia.

We have also, with the advice of our Privy Council aforesaid, annexed to our Province of Georgia all the Lands lying between the Rivers Altamaha and St. Mary's.

And whereas it will greatly contribute to the speedy settling of our said new Governments, that our loving Subjects should be informed of our Paternal care, for the security of the Liberties and Properties of those who are and shall become Inhabitants thereof, We have thought fit to publish and declare, by this Our Proclamation, that We have, in the Letters Patent under our Great Seal of Great

Britain, by which the said Governments are constituted, given express Power and Direction to our Governors of our Said Colonies respectively, that so soon as the state and circumstances of the said Colonies will admit thereof, they shall, with the Advice and Consent of the Members of our Council, summon and call General Assemblies within the said Governments respectively, in such Manner and Form as is used and directed in those Colonies and Provinces in America which are under our immediate Government: And We have also given Power to the said Governors, with the consent of our Said Councils, and the Representatives of the People so to be summoned as aforesaid, to make, constitute, and ordain Laws, Statutes, and Ordinances for the Public Peace, Welfare, and good Government of our said Colonies, and of the People and Inhabitants thereof, as near as may be agreeable to the Laws of England, and under such Regulations and Restrictions as are used in other Colonies; and in the mean Time, and until such Assemblies can be called as aforesaid, all Persons Inhabiting in or resorting to our Said Colonies may confide in our Royal Protection for the Enjoyment of the Benefit of the Laws of our Realm of England; for which Purpose We have given Power under our Great Seal to the Governors of our said colonies respectively to erect and constitute, with the Advice of our said Councils respectively, Courts of Judicature and public Justice within our Said Colonies for hearing and determining all Causes, as well Criminal as Civil, according to Law and Equity, and as near as may be agreeable to the Laws of England, with Liberty to all Persons who may think themselves aggrieved by the Sentences of such Courts, in all Civil Crises, to appeal, under the usual Limitations and Restrictions, to Us in our Privy Council.

We have also thought fit, with the advice of our Privy Council as aforesaid, to give unto the Governors and Councils of our said Three new Colonies, upon the Continent full Power and Authority to settle and agree with the Inhabitants of our said new Colonies or with any other Persons who shall resort thereto, for such Lands, Tenements and Hereditaments, as are now or hereafter shall be in our Power to dispose of; and them to grant to any such Person or Persons upon such Terms, and under such moderate Quit-Rents, Services and Acknowledgments, as have been appointed and settled in our other Colonies, and under such other Conditions as shall appear to us to be necessary and expedient for the Advantage of the Grantees, and the Improvement and settlement of our said Colonies.

And Whereas, We are desirous, upon all occasions, to testify our Royal Sense and Approbation of the Conduct and bravery of the Officers and Soldiers of our Armies, and to reward the same, We do hereby command and empower our Governors of our said Three new Colonies, and all other our Governors of our several Provinces on the Continent of North America, to grant without Fee or Reward, to such reduced Officers as have served in North America during the late War, and to such Private Soldiers as have been or shall be disbanded in America, and are actually residing there, and shall personally apply for the same, the following Quantities of Lands, subject, at the Expiration of Ten Years, to the same Quit-Rents as other Lands are subject to in the Province within which they are granted, as also subject to the same Conditions of Cultivation and Improvement; *viz,*

To every Person having the Rank of a Field Officer—5,000 Acres.

To every Captain—3,000 Acres.

To every Subaltern or Staff Officer—2,000 Acres.

To every Non-Commission Officer—200 Acres.

To every Private Man—50 Acres.

We do likewise authorize and require the Governors and Commanders in Chief of all our said Colonies upon the Continent of North America to grant the like Quantities of Land, and upon the same conditions, to such reduced Officers of our Navy of like Rank as served on board our Ships of War in North America at the times of the Reduction of Louisbourg and Quebec in the late War, and who shall personally apply to our respective Governors for such Grants.

And whereas it is just and reasonable, and essential to our Interest, and the Security of our Colonies, that the several Nations or Tribes of Indians with whom We are connected, and who live under our Protection, should not be molested or disturbed in the Possession of such Parts of Our Dominions and Territories as, not having been ceded to or purchased by Us, are reserved to them or any of them, as their Hunting Grounds—We do therefore, with the Advice of our Privy Council, declare it to be our Royal Will and Pleasure, that no Governor or Commander in Chief in any of our Colonies of Quebec, East Florida or West Florida, do presume, upon any Pretence whatever, to grant Warrants of Survey, or pass any Patents for Lands beyond the Bounds of their respective Governments as described in their Commissions: as also that no Governor or Commander in Chief in any of our other Colonies or Plantations in America do presume for the present, and until our further Pleasure be known, to grant Warrants of Survey, or patents.

And We do further declare it to be Our Royal Will and Pleasure, for the present as aforesaid, to reserve under our Sovereignty, Protection, and Dominion, for the use of the said Indians, all the Lands and Territories not included within the Limits of Our said Three new Governments, or within the Limits of the Territory granted to the Hudson's Bay Company, as also all the Lands and Territories lying to the Westward of the Sources of the Rivers which fall into the Sea from the West and North West as aforesaid.

And We do hereby strictly forbid, on Pain of our Displeasure, all our loving Subjects from making any Purchases or Settlements whatever, or taking Possession of any of the Lands above reserved without our especial leave and License for that Purpose first obtained.

And, We do further strictly enjoin and require all Persons whatever who have either willfully or inadvertently seated themselves upon any Lands within the Countries above described, or upon any other Lands which, not having been ceded to or purchased by Us, are still reserved to the said Indians as aforesaid, forthwith to remove themselves from such Settlements.

And whereas great Frauds and Abuses have been committed in purchasing Lands of the Indians, to the great Prejudice of our Interests, and to the great Dissatisfaction of the said Indians: In order, therefore, to prevent such Irregularities for the future, and to the end that the Indians may be convinced of our Justice and determined Resolution to remove all reasonable Cause of Discontent, We do with the Advice of our Privy Council strictly enjoin and require, that no private Person do presume to make any purchase from the said Indians of any Lands reserved to the said Indians, within those parts of our Colonies where, We have thought proper to allow Settlement: but that, if at any Time any of the Said Indians should be inclined to dispose of the said Lands, the same shall be Purchased only for Us, in our Name, at some public Meeting or Assembly of the said Indians, to be held for that Purpose by the Governor or Commander in Chief of our Colony respectively within which they shall lie: and in case they shall lie within the limits of any Proprietary Government, they shall be purchased only for the Use and in the name of such Proprietaries, conformable to such Directions and Instructions as We or they shall think proper to give for that Purpose: And we do, by the Advice of our Privy Council, declare and enjoin, that the Trade with the said Indians shall be free and open to all our Subjects whatever, provided that every Person who may incline to Trade with the said Indians do take out a Licence for carrying on such Trade from the Governor or Commander in Chief of any of our Colonies respectively where such Person shall reside, and also give Security to observe such Regulations as We shall at any Time think fit, by ourselves or by our Commissaries to be appointed for this Purpose, to direct and appoint for the Benefit of the said Trade:

And we do hereby authorize, enjoin, and require the Governors and Commanders in Chief of all our Colonies respectively, as well those under Our immediate Government as those under the Government and Direction of Proprietaries, to grant such Licenses without Fee or Reward, taking especial Care to insert therein a Condition, that such License shall be void, and the Security forfeited in case the Person to whom the same is granted shall refuse or neglect to observe such Regulations as We shall think proper to prescribe as aforesaid.

And we do further expressly conjoin and require all Officers whatever, as well Military as those Employed in the Management and Direction of Indian Affairs, within the Territories reserved as aforesaid for the use of the said Indians, to seize and apprehend all Persons whatever, who standing charged with Treason, Misprisions of Treason, Murders, or other Felonies or Misdemeanors, shall fly from Justice and take Refuge in the said Territory, and to send them under a proper guard to the Colony where the Crime was committed of which they, stand accused, in order to take their Trial for the same.

Given at our Court at St. James's the 7th Day of October 1763, in the Third Year of our Reign.

GOD SAVE THE KING

Appendix 2

Letter from Williams to his wife: June 3, 1779

James Williams to His Wife:

CAMP, HEADQUARTERS, June 3, 1779.
My Dear,
I have nothing more than I have enclosed of the 1st instant.

As to the news, our army is very strong, and in high spirits. There was a probability of an action the other day, and it appeared to be the hearty desire of every man to come to action; but it was not thought expedient by the General,[307] and we returned to camp. We are now laying in camp, where I expect to lay for several days. As to particulars, I refer you to Major Gillam.[308]

I desire that Daniel[309] will use his utmost endeavors to have the mills in the best order against harvest. I was speaking to him in regard to trying to plant that field over the road in corn; but that I submit to him, and he may do as he pleases. I hope that the utmost care will be taken by him to save the crop that is planted. My wagon that I rode in with, is at Ninety Six; send Daniel to bring it home, and have it put under a shed. I purpose to sell it when I return home.

I desire you, my dear, to send me about half-a-pound of cloves and cinnamon by Major Gillam; what I brought I have used, and find it a great help to me. The water is so bad that I make as little use of it as possible. Major Gillam has come to bring a relief for the men that are here. If it is possible, I should be glad that you could send me an under jacket, for the two that I brought with me are breaking before.

---

[307] The "General" referred to is probably General Andrew Williamson under whose command Williams served until Williamson capitulated and accepted parole sometime in June 1780.

[308] Probably a reference to Robert Gillam, Jr. (1760-1813) who served as a sergeant, captain and major in Williams' Little River Regiment. Moss, *SC Patriots*, 358.

[309] This is probably a reference to Williams' eldest son, Daniel.

I am, dear wife, with respect, your ever loving husband till death,

Jas. Williams

(From Gibbes, *Documentary History*, 2: 114)

Appendix 3

Letter from Williams to his son, Daniel Williams: June 12, 1779

James Williams to Mr. Daniel Williams

CAMP, HEADQUARTERS, June 12, 1779.
Dear Son,
This is the first chance I have had to write you.

I am, by the care of Providence, in the field in defence of my country. When I reflect on the matter, I feel myself distracted on both hands by this thought, that in my old age I should be obliged to take the field in defence of my rights and liberties, and that of my children. God only knows that it is not of choice, but of necessity, and from the consideration that I had rather suffer anything than lose my birthright, and that of my children. When I come to lay down in the field, stripped of all the pleasure that my family connections afford me at home—surrounded by an affectionate wife and eight dear children, and all the blessings of life—when I reflect on my own distress, I feel for that of my family, on account of my absence from their midst; and especially for the mother, who sits like a dove that has lost its mate, having the weight of the family on her shoulders.

These thoughts make me afraid that the son we so carefully nursed in our youth may do something that would grieve his mother. Now, my son, if my favor is worth seeking, let me tell you the only step to procure it is the care of your tender mother—to please her is ten times more valuable than any other favor that you could do me in my person. I hope that when you come to reflect on the duty of a son to a tender parent, you will take every step to establish that connection, which will add to my happiness; for it is a pleasure to me to know that I have a son who is able to manage my business and plantation affairs. Make it your study to be obliging to your mother, being careful not to do anything that may grieve her. Take the utmost care of every thing that falls under your care, so that you may receive, on my return, my thanks, and have the blessing of being a faithful and dutiful son to his trust. I would have you consider yourself filling one of the most important posts that could be confided in you; and if you should manage well, it will greatly rebound to your praise. After these serious thoughts, I beg that you will take these hints. In the first place, consider that the eye of God is on you, and to secure His blessing is the only way to make yourself, and those that are concerned with you, happy; for to fear God is the first and great command.

The next command is, to honor thy father and mother. Now, the only way to do this, is not to do anything that will grieve or oppress them. Be kind to your brothers and sisters, and careful to manage the business to the interest of the family. Your care and good conduct in the management of my plantation adds greatly to my happiness; and I can promise you, that you shall feel the good effects of it, for I have the pleasure to hear by your tender mother's letter to me, that you are doing very well, and business goes on well. I am happy to hear it.

I have wrote several times about trying to get a few good horses. I expect by this time you have made the trial; if you have been successful in procuring some, I shall be glad to hear how many, and what sort they are, and I will send some good man to bring them down. If unsuccessful in your effort, no matter. I want Nancy brought to me at that time to ride. Try to have the mares in as good order as possible; be careful that they are all well fed; let them be used as little as possible.

I have traded for a fine English mare, which is on Fishing Creek, at Mr. Wm. Adair's; the order is enclosed for her. I wish you could get a man to go for her, or spare the time to go yourself, as she is a valuable animal. If you go, Mr. Adair will, doubtless, be saying something about her. She was taken from McGirth[310] by Capt. Moore,[311] and I bought his right of her; she is a young, full-blood mare, and has no brand on her unless Adair has branded her since she has been to his house. He took her up in favor of Capt. Moore, and since she was carried from camp I traded for her. I want her got home with as little stir as possible, and branded on both cushions with my branding iron; and let it be said that I bought her of a man on Fishing Creek, and paid $1,000.

My reason for begging you to go for her is, that it may not be known she is a plunder mare; and when we have the pleasure of meeting, I will put you in possession of all the particulars regarding her. I shall be glad if you put her to the horse as soon as you get her. On all necessary occasions get Mr. Griffin to help you about the plantation. Regarding the horses I wrote you about, you may either come or let it alone, just as you please, as I can send for them if you have any agreeable to my direction.

I am sorry to have to inform you of the melancholy death of Anthony Griffin, which took place on the 11th instant, while out with a scouting party. Alighting from his horse, and leaning on his gun, it accidentally went off, shooting him through the head. He never spoke after the accident. This is a fatal consequence of handling guns without proper care; they ought to be used with the greatest caution. The uncertainty of life ought to induce every man to prepare for death.

As for news, I have nothing more to communicate than what I wrote last to your dear mother. I hope every thing will be done to have the mill in as good order as possible, to grind up the wheat; and as soon as you can, supply the saw mill with timber, as I desire to put in operation. In regard to whiskey, I think you must raise the price of it, in order to have things as much on an average as possible. I think you ought to sell it at two dollars a quart; if by retail, one dollar a half pint. Secure all you can at £35 per 110 gallons. I am in hopes

---

[310] Daniel McGirt. *See* footnote 145.
[311] Probably John Moore. *See* footnote 146.

of being at home by the 1st July, to see my family. I shall be glad to hear from you by every opportunity.

Son, I think if you manage matters well, and I am spared, I can put affairs in such a state that, under the blessing of God, we may stand in as good a position as any family in the State. Pray, let no pains be spared to make every edge cut, and have the crops secured in the best manner, as much depend on them.

Now, my son, I must bid you farewell. I commit you to the care of Providence, begging that you will try to obtain that peculiar blessing. May God bless you, my son, and give you grace to conduct yourself, in my absence, as becomes a dutiful son to a tender mother and the family. I am in reasonable good health at present, and the regiment as much so as could be expected. The death of Griffin is much lamented. I hope in God this will find you, my son, and your dear mother and the children, all well. My best compliments to you all, and all enquiring friends.

I am, dear son, with great respect, your affectionate father,

Jas. Williams

(From Gibbes, *Documentary History*, 2: 115)

Appendix 4

Petition filed September 10, 1779, by Officers and Men serving under Williams' command in the Little River Regiment of the South Carolina militia[312]

---

[312] The names of the signatories have been alphabetized for convenience. Spellings of names have been preserved as closely as possible to how they appear on the petitions with "?" indicating that there is uncertainty as to the name of the signatory resulting from difficulty deciphering the handwritten signatures. The document set out above results from the melding of two known versions of the petition, each signed by different members of the Little River Regiment. Because of the missing signatures of a number of other known Whig members of the regiment (including that of Williams' very close friend and second in command of the regiment, Joseph Hayes), there is thought to be at least one additional version signed

To his Excellency John Rutledge, Esqr., Governor & Commander in chief in & over the State of So. Carolina; the Honourable the Senate & House of Representatives in General Assembly.

Whereas we (the zealous Friends to our Country, & to all who love & distinguish themselves in her Cause) do understand & are exceeding sorry to hear, that there are false & evilly designing Accusations either lying or about to be shortly laid against James Williams, present Colonel in & over Little River Regiment, of which we are a Part; representing him as distressing & very injurious to the Regiment, & designed (as we believe) by the private Enimies of our Country, to deprive us of so worthy a Friend to his Country in general, & good Officer to us in particular; & thereby do a very singular Piece of Service to the common Enimies of America: We do briefly & anxiously remonstrate thus; that we do experimentally know Colo. James Williams to have been a zealous Patriot from the Commencement of the american Contest with Britain; & to have always stood foremost in every Occasion when called upon to the Defence of his Country. We do further declare, that we have never known said Colo. Jas. Williams to distress any Individual in the Regiment, who voluntarily & judiciously, when legally called upon & commanded to the Field, have turned out in the Defence of their native Rights & Priviledges together with that of their Country; & we do avow it from our Knowledge, that whensoever Colo. Jas. Williams either directly or indirectly, executed any distressing Things, it was upon the stubborn & refractory, whose Practises & Obstinacy declare them innimical to their Country; & that this he did, as being the last promising Effort to reduce them to the dutiful Obedience of loyal & fellow Citizens. Without delaying you; We your humble Petitioners do earnestly beg, that you will hear this our faithful Remonstrance, & proceed with our respected Colo. Jas. Williams, & all such unjust &

by yet another group of Williams' supporters. The two versions melded above are from different repositories, one in the Manuscripts Collections at the South Caroliniana Library at the University of South Carolina and the other in the collections of Duke University (item #5767, Manuscript Dept., Wm. M. Perkins Library, Durham, NC).

disaffected Clamours as may come before you against him, as your superior Judgements may direct; only beging leave to conclude with this one Remark, that doubtless you know, that such Clamours are frequently the necessary Effect of Disaffection to the Country.

Signed by the following members of the Little River Regiment:

James Absom
Benjamin Adair
Isaac Adair
James Adair
James Adair Jr.
James Adair Sr.
John Adair
John Adair, Sr.
Joseph Adair
Joseph Adair, Jr.
Joseph Adair, Sr.
William Adair
George Akins
John Akins
Jacob Anderson
William Arthur, Capt.
Henry Atwood
Nath Barrett
William Bean
William Blake
John Bourland
Hugh Boyd
William Boyd
Joseph Brown
George Campbell ?
Thomas Campbell
William Campbell
Abner Casey
George Casey
Levi Casey, Lt.
Peter Casey
Samuel Casey
Adam Chambers
James Craig
William Craig
Matthew Cunningham
James Dardenman

George Davis
William Davis
Jeremiah Dial
John Dial
William Dial
Josias Dickson
James Dillard
Jacob Duckett
Joseph Duckett
James Dugan
Robert Dugan, Lt.
Thomas Dugan, Capt.
Samuel Ewing
Thomas Ewing
John Finney
Abolom Filby ?
James Gambel
John Gambel
John Glenn
Benjamin Goodman
John Gray
William Gray
Alexander Greer
Isaac Greer
James Greer
John Greer
John Greer, Jr.
Josiah Greer
John Hewston
James Howerton
John Howerton, Jr.
George Hughes
William Hughes
James Huddleston
William Huddleston
John Johnson
Robert Johnson

James Johnston
Robert Johnston
John Jones
Hugh Killpatrick
James Lindsay
John Lisdin ?
Robert Long
Arthur McCracken
Samuel McCracken
Thomas McCracken
Andrew McCrary
Matthew McCrary, Lt.
John McCrary, Jr.
John McCrary, Sr.
Matthew McCrery
Robert McCrery, Lt. Col.
Thomas McCrery, JP
James McCrecken ?
Hughes Manford
Richard Mark
Robert Miller
James Montgomery
Samuel Murray
William Murray
Benjamin Nabers
Ringal Odell
Andrew Owens
James Owens

John Owens
Arthur Park
James Ralley
John Ramage
Joseph Rammage
Elijah Rhodes
John Robinson
Williams Simmons
Garrard Smith
John Speaks ?
John Stacks
James Stak
Edward Stapleton
William Stark
Ejeniah Verjen (Virgin?)
Joseph Verdiman ?
James Virgin
Benjamin Watson
David Watson
John Watson
Barrack Williams
Daniel Williams
John Williams
Phillip Whitten
William Wilson
Ambros Witten ?
Robert Wilton
George Young

Appendix 5

Letter from Williams to his wife: September 30, 1779

Col. Williams to Mrs. Williams

CAMP 40 MILES FROM SAVANNAH, Sept. 30, 1779.
Dear Wife,

I wrote a letter last night to you, my love, that gave you the best intelligence that I have been able to get. I have every reason to believe that the matter is settled before this; and as you may in confidence depend that whenever I am able to get the truth of matters I will transmit it to you, by express. I beg that you may bear with fortitude my absence; and let us with humble confidence rely on Him that is able to protect and defend us, in all danger, and through every difficulty; but, my dear, let us, with one heart, call on God for his mercies, and that his goodness may be continued to us, that we, under his blessing, may have the happiness of enjoying each other's society once more.

I mentioned in my last letter about the salt. I beg that you may have it well dried and ground in the mill and then you are to sell it for one hundred dollars per bushel. Let Sam have the wheat sown as soon as possible, and I beg that you may take a little time to see about the plantation, and make Samuel do what is best to be done. As to Lea, I hope you will let no one have her without an order from me in writing, and signed by me. My compliments to you, my dear, and my children and friends.

I am, dear wife, with great respect, your ever loving husband, until death,

Jas. Williams

(From Gibbes, *Documentary History*, 2: 122)

Appendix 6

Letter from Williams to Gen. Andrew Williamson: January 4, 1780

To General Williamson

14th Jany. 1780 [this appears on the reverse of the text of the letter]

Mount Pleasant January 4, 1780

Dear Sir

I rec'd your favor by Master Gorge (?, could be "George") & have carefuly (*sic*, carefully) observed the contence (*sic*, contents). I have had a Capt., 1 sargent (*sic*, sergeant) & 8 picked men out in the upper part of My ridgment (*sic*, regiment) for some time, in order to prevent those felers (*sic,* fellows) from plundering the good pepel (*sic,* people) & to have them taken & brout (sic, brought) to Justice. I am a bout (*sic,* about) to try to IMbody (*sic,* embody) a part of the ridgment *(sic)* to send to town.[313] How they will turn out, I can't tell, but I fear but Poorly. I have Made it as publick (*sic,* public) in these parts a bout (*sic,* about) the governor promising to get Salt for the back Cuntery (*sic,* Country) as posbel (*sic,* possible), and it is given some satisfaction to the pepel (*sic,* people), but at the present it is bad for many poor men is oblidge (*sic,* obliged) to turn out his hogs for the Want of Salt. To My knowledge, some pepel *(sic)* Must Suffer greatly. I have sent a pay bill of Capt. Jms. (? could be Isaac or John) Gray's[314] (? could be Graiss or Graift) With Mr. McNear (?) to get the money & should take it as a singlar (*sic,* singular) favor if it could be got. The Capt. Deserted his Cuntery (*sic,* Country) & the Men is Like to have their Money. & I am likly (*sic,* likely) to be a greatly Lueser (*sic,* loser) by it my Self. I have advance (*sic,* advanced) [a] great part of the Wages to them My Self. If I culd (*sic,* could) git (*sic,* get) the Money I am a guine (*sic,* going) to that part of the ridgment *(sic)* & Will my self seter (*sic,* settle) with Every Man my self. It is possible I should be glad to get the Money as I am a guine (*sic,* going) to that part of the ridgment (*sic,* regiment) the Later (sic, latter) End of this Weak (sic, week).

> I am Dear Sir your Most
> Respectfull & Hubel Sert.
> Jas Williams

(Transcribed from the original in the Gibbes Collection folder #153, Box 2, S213089, South Carolina Department of Archives and History, Columbia, SC)

---

[313] The reference is probably to Charles Town (Charleston) since in January 1780, the British had landed south of Charleston to begin their siege of that city.

[314] Someone named "John Gray" signed the Little River Regiment petition dated September 10, 1779. No other name on that list seems to fit, but "John Gray" may or may not be the person referred to by Williams in this letter.

Appendix 7

Last Will and Testament of James Williams dated June 12, 1780

In the Name of god, Amen. I James Williams of the State of So Carolina & of Ninty (*sic,* Ninety) Six District but Now in the State of North Carolina as a refuge [*sic*-refugee] & at [blank space]. I being att (*sic,* at) present in My proper hilth (*sic,* health) & of sound Mommomary (*sic,* memory) but considering that it is apointed (*sic,* appointed) for all Men once to die [?], I Done ordain this to be My Last Will & Testament.

First, In the great sence [*sic,* sense] of humility, [I] give my sole (*sic,* soul) to god that gave it [to] me that first in & through the merits of Christ the Savor of Man quine (*sic,* kind) & then My body to be Decently buried att the Descreson (*sic,* Discretion?) of My Executors here after to be Mentioned.

Item the first: it is My Will & Desire that all My Just debts be pad (*sic,* paid).

Item the Second: I lend to My beloved Wife, Mary Williams, During her Natural Life, a part of the track [*sic,* tract] of Land that I live on [on] Litel (*sic,* Little) river in Ninty (sic, Ninety) Six District bounded as folers (*sic,* follows), that is to say, on the south side of the river beginning on the river below the Mill Where the Line crosses the river & from thence along the Line of the Land bout (*sic,* bought) of John Caldwell to a great branch thence with the branch to the Ninty Six Road from thence along the road to Where it intersex (*sic,* intersects) the fore mentioned Line & so along the Line to mi (*sic,* my) pond att the Land bout of John Caldwell & Land swoft (*sic,* swapped) With Gil Turner, N. Land released of Daniel Simson for the term of the release & I give an (*sic,* and) bequeath to My beloved Wife, Mary Williams, a Child part of My Moveabel (*sic,* moveable) a State (*sic,* estate) to be equally devided (*sic,* divided) by Lot att the Descreson of My Executors and betwixt My beloved Wife and My Children then Living.

Item 3: I give & bequeath to My Son Daniel Williams the following tracks (*sic,* tracts) of Land as follows: The Land bout of William containing 250 Acres [of] Land bout of Robin Jonston Estate 900 acres, Land bout of William Brison 75 acres and all that part of track of Land that was bout of William Johnston below the Milling house that lays on the North side of the Charlestown road thought to be about 80 acres & a Child part of all My Moveabel a state When he arive (*sic,* arrives) to the age of Twenty One years.

Item 4: I give & bequeath to My Son Joseph Williams? [could be a fraction] following tracks of Land, the track of Land I bout of Luke [might be Luther ?] Lenard 250 Acres track bout of Seamore 100 Acres & a ? that part of the Land bout of Caldwell that lays below the still house branch Except 100 Acres that is to be reserved for the Mill that Joins the Mill below the branch & that part of the Land I bout of William Johnston that lays the south side of the Charles town road & a Child part of all My Moveabel a state to be given up to him att his arriving att 21 years of age.

Item 5: I give & bequeath to My Son John Williams all of that track of Land that I bout of Caldwell that lays below the road & the great branch & that bout of Peter Stroshar by Computation 600 Acres & a Child part of My Moveabel a state att his arrival to the age of 21 years.

Item 6: I give & bequath (*sic,* bequeath) to My Daughter Elizabeth Williams that track of Land bout of Capt. Towls Late Hutcherson's & a Child part of all My Moveabel estate to be Delivered to her on her marriage (spelled "marge"), if the Marriage [is] agreable (*sic,* agreeable) to the Desires of the Executors.

Item 7: I give an[d] bequath to My Daughter Mary Williams that track of Land in bush river bout of Col. Hammons with the old store Containing 150 Acres & a Child part of all My Moveabel a state to be Delivered on her Mariage (*sic,* marriage) if agreable to Executors.

Item 8: I give an[d] bequath to my Daughter Sary Williams as Mutch (*sic,* much) Cash out of My a state be for (*sic,* before) the Divison (*sic,* Division) is made as Will purtch (*sic*, purchase) her a track of Land Equal in Value to Either of her Sisters' Land Mentioned above & a Child part of all My Moveabel a state to be Delivered on her Maridg (*sic*, marriage) if agreable to the Executors.

Item 9: I give an[d] bequath to My son James Williams all that part of the Land bout of John Caldwell on the Northern Side of Litel river above the Williams branch by Computation 500 Acres & a Child part of My Moveabel a state to be Delivered on his ariving of age—

Item 9 (*sic*): I give and bequeath to My son Washington Williams all that track of Land Lent to My beloved Wife During her Natural Life & the Land bout of James Cook by Computation 600 Acres & a Child part of all My Moveabel a state to be Delivered att his arival at 21 years of age.

It is My Will an[d] Desire that as sone (*sic*, soon) as conivent (*sic*, convenient) after My Death that all My Lands that is not Willed a Way, that is to say, old James Johnston & the Land I bout of William Johnston on the Bever (*sic*, Beaver) Dam & my Stalons (*sic*, stallions) & Still & Wagon & horses & horses ? Should be sold att publick (*sic*, public) sail (*sic*, sale) & the N? book & the bonds & Notes & other a Counts (*sic*, accounts) collected, the Money arising there from is to Discharge my Debts & the balance to be devied (*sic*, divided) a Mong (*sic*, among) My beloved Wife & My Eight Children or sutch (*sic*, such) of them as is then alive, as to My Wagons, there is one red? Wagon & 8 Work Horses to be reserved for the youes (*sic*, use) of My family & My beloved Wife is to have 2 Carige (*sic*, carriage) horses & the Carige for the youes of the family & Eatch (*sic*, each) of My Children to be furnish[ed] With a good riding horse & a breading (*sic*, breeding) Mare as the Executors May think proper. My Mill & the 100 Acres of Land Joining it on the North side of the river is to be capt (*sic*, kept) for the youes of the family During My beloved Wife['s] WiderWhood (*sic*, widowhood) or till the Washington Williams comes of age & then she is to be Sold att the highest bides a Monge (*sic*, among) My Sons then alive, & it is my Will that If [any] of My Children should Die Without an heir (?) be four (*sic*, before) they arive att 21 years of age that thare (*sic,* their) part of this Shall be Equale (*sic,* equally) Divided a Mong My Children then alive.

It is My Will that My beloved Wife Mary Williams & My Son Daniel Williams, & My Brother Henry Williams & Joseph Hays, be apointed by Me My Executors to carry this my Last Will & Testament in to Execution. Signed With My hand & Sealed With My Seal this 12 Day of June 1780.

S/ Jas Williams

Signed & Sealed in the Present [*sic,* presence] of Witnesses houes (*sic,* whose) Names is Written (?) under a Next: William Rice; James Goodman; James "X" Cook (His Mark)

Caswell Sept. First 1780[315]

The Execution of this Will was proved in open Court upon The oaths of William Rice & James Goodman Two of the Witnesses Thereto & on Motion Ordered to be registered. Test. William Moore, Clerk

(Recorded in Book: A Page 113, Caswell County, North Carolina, Register of Office, Yanceyville, North Carolina)

Appendix 8

Letter from Williams to his wife: July 4, 1780

Mr. Williams to Mrs. Williams
CAMP CATAWBA, OLD NATION, July 4, 1780

Dear Wife,

My anxiety for you and my dear children, far exceeds anything that I am able to express; not knowing your distress but I trust in God that His guardian care has been over you

---

[315] This date makes no sense—Williams was still alive on September 1, 1780. Is it possible that his brother, Henry Williams, received a false report of his death sometime prior to September 1, 1780, and mistakenly filed his will prematurely? Caswell County's court records show that the will was not offered for probate until the December session of the Court of Quarter Sessions and Common Pleas. Perhaps, the date was written in error at some later date.

for your protection; I have earnestly requested the favor of heaven on you. I have had some accounts from you, but they were very imperfect. I pray God that I may have the happiness of seeing you my love at Mount Pleasant in the course of this month, with a force sufficient to repel all the Tories in the upper part of South Carolina.

I have been informed that many false stories are in circulation in our country to the disheartening of our friends in that quarter of the State. I give the true state of things touching our army, and you, my love, and all my friends, may depend on it to be the truth. I was at my brother's and settled my family on as good terms as possible, and left him well with his family.

I left there on the 29th of last month; that day, Major General DeKalb and General Wayne and Smallwood, with the Maryland and Pennsylvania troops to the amount of 3,000, and 2,500 from Virginia, are on the march from Roxbury in order to join Major General Caswell with about 2,000 North Carolina militia, and about 200 regular light horse; on the whole 7,700, that is now in motion, and will be at Camden in the course of six or seven days, which may put a different face on matters. And there are 5,500 Virginia militia marching that will be here shortly, (and 2,000 North Carolina militia, under General Rutherford, that is to march to Ninety Six,) with some South Carolina militia commanded by Col. Sumter, to the amount of 500, now in camp at this place, and are expected to cross the river to-day, with about 500 of the Mecklenburg militia. Over and above all these, there are 4,000 more North Carolina militia to march as soon as harvest is over.

On the whole, I expect we will shortly meet the Tories, when they must give an account of their late conduct. I can assure you, my dear, that there is a large French Fleet and army on our coast. I think, from these circumstances, that our affairs are in a flattering condition at present.

I expect you have heard of Moore's defeat, in the fork of the Catawba by a detached party from General Rutherford, under Capt. Falls, not exceeding 350, that defeated 1300

Tories, and took their baggage, with about 500 horses and saddles and guns, and left 35 on the field dead. Since that General Caswell has defeated the English at the Cheraws, and cut off the 71st Regiment entirely.

I can assure you and my friends that the English have never been able to make a stand in North Carolina yet, and they have slipt their time now, for they are retreating to Charlestown with all rapidity. From this you may see, under the blessing of God that we will soon relieve our distressed family and friends; so bear up with fortitude till that happy day comes.

I hope in God this will find you, my dear wife, and my children all well My compliments to you and my children and friends that inquire about me. Myself and Capt. Hays, Daniel and the boys are all hearty; God be blest for His mercy to us.

The uncertainty of your situation is my great mortification; but let our joint prayers meet in Heaven for each other and our bleeding country. The Rev. Mr. Simson has had his house and every thing he had but the clothing the family had on destroyed, and he is in camp with me and Mr. Croghead, and is part of my family in camp. Mr. Simson, Mr. Croghead, and Capt. Hays, join me in our compliments to you, my love and friends.

I am with great regard your loving husband till death,
Jas. Williams
N. B.—As for family affairs do as you may think best.

(From Gibbes, *Documentary History*, 2: 135)

Appendix 9

Williams' Report on the Battle of Musgrove Mill

Col. Williams, Col. Shelby & Col. Clarke with a party of South Carolinians and Georgians in Number about Two Hundred, March'd from the North Side of Broad River on the 17th August in Order to attack Two Hundred Tories on the Innere (*sic*, Enoree) R[iver] at Musgrove's Mills, but on the Night of the 18th the Tories was were reinforced by Col. Innis with Two Hundred Regular Troops and One Hundred Tories, our party meant to Surprise them, but were discovered[:] this obliged us to send a small party of Horse to reconnoiter them, and if found they were in a disposition to attack us, they were ordered to Skirmish with them and lead them on to our main body.

And being formed across the road, our line Extended at least 300 Yards in length, on a Timbered Ridge, and Twenty Horse was were ordered on each flank, waiting the Enemy's Approach. They Advanced within 200 Yards and formed a line of Battle, and moved on within the distance of 150 Yards, and then began a very heavy fire.

But Col. Williams gave orders that not a man should fire untill (*sic*) the Enemy came within Point blank Shot, and every man take his Tree, and not fire untill (*sic*) Orders were given, and that every Man take his Object sure, and not to fire till the Enemy was within 80 Yards distance. A warm fire began that lasted about 15 Minutes, which when our brave friends to their Distressed Country, Obliged the Enemy to retreat, and we drove them about Two Miles.

We Kil'd dead on the field 60 of the Enemy the greatest part British, and took 70 Prisoners, among the Killed was a Major Frazer of the British, one British Captain and Three Torie (*sic*) Captains, Col. Innis of the British by report mortally Wounded by Two balls one in the neck, the other broake broke his Thigh.

Our loss in this Action was only Three Killed on the field, Eight Wounded, one of which is Mortal

Hillsborough 5th Sept. 1780

Jas. Williams

(The full report was published in the *Pennsylvania Packet*, September 23, 1780, "by Order of Congress," 3)

Appendix 10
Letter from Williams to General Horatio Gates: October 2, 1780

Burk [*sic*] County, 2nd October 1780

Dear Sir

I am at present about 70 Miles from Salisbury, in the Fork of the Catawba, with about 450 horse Men, in pursuit of Col. Ferguson.

On my crossing the Catawba River, I dispatched to different Quarters Expresses for Intelligence, & this Evening I was favoured with this glorious News that you may depend on to be Fact: That Colo. Clark, of the State of Georgia, with 100 Rifle Men, forced his way through So. Carolina to Georgia. On his way there he was joined by 700 Men, & has made his way to the Town of Augusta, and taken it with a large quantity of Goods; but not finding it prudent to continue there, has retreated to the upper parts of S. Carolina, in Ninety Six district, and made a Stand with 800 brave Men.

And this Moment another of my Expresses is arrived from Cols. McDowell and Shelby: They were on their way near Burk (*sic,* Burke) Court House, with 1500 brave Mountain Men, & Col. Cleveland was within 10 miles of them with 800 Men, and was to form a Junction with them this day. I expect to Join them tomorrow, in pursuit of Col. Ferguson, and, under the direction of heaven, I hope to be able to render your honour a good account of him in a few days. I hope that we in a short time shall have the upper parts of So. Carolina & Georgia in Our possession.

I am, Dr. sir,

Your most huml. Servt.

James Williams

To His Excelly. Major-general Gates

(Clark, *State Records*, XC: 94; Tarleton, *Campaigns*, 194)

Appendix 11
Books in Williams' Library[316]

1 Large Bible
*1 **Burkitt's Expository** [Expository notes, with practical observations, on the New Testament of our Lord and Saviour Jesus Christ: wherein the sacred text is at large recited, the sense explained, and the instructive example of the blessed Jesus, and his Holy Apostles, to our imitation recommended: the whole designed to encourage the reading of the Scriptures in private families, and to render the daily perusal of them profitable and delightful.* By William Burkitt (1650-1703), a vicar and lecturer in Dedham, England.]

6 Voliams, Henry's Comment [*Family Bible Containing the Old and New Testaments, and the Apocrypha with Notes Explanatory and Practical Carefully Selected from the Commentary of the Rev. Matthew Henry.* By Matthew Henry (1662-1714) a Nonconformist minister and commentator; born at Broad Oak, Flintshire, Wales; died at Nantwich, Cheshire. His reputation was largely based on this work which was first printed in London in 5 volumes in 1708-1710.]

2 Vol. Ainsworth Dictionary [*Thesaurus Linguae Latinae Compendiarus. Or a Compendius Dictionary of the Latin Tongue. Designed for the use of the British Nation.* By Robert Ainsworth (1660-1743), English schoolmaster and author.]

1 Holyork's do [*A large dictionary in three parts I. The English before the Latin, containing above ten thousand words more than any dictionary yet extant, II. The Latin before the English, with correct and plentiful etymological derivations, philological observations, and phraseological explications, III. The proper names of persons, places and other things necessary to the understanding of historians and poets in the whole comprehending whatsoever is material in any author upon this subject, together with very considerable and ample additions, carried on by a diligent search into and perusal of very*

---

[316] The bold text below indicates the exact wording of the entry made in the inventory of Williams' library as made by his brother and executor, Henry Williams. The bracketed entries are an attempt to identify each book specifically listed in the original inventory of the library.

many authors both ancient and modern, whereby this work is rendered the most complete and useful of any that was ever yet extant in this kind performed by the great pains and many years study of Thomas Holyoke. By Francis Holyoake (1567-1653), rector in Southam (Warwickshire), England. Francis began the Dictionary, but died before its completion. Likewise, Francis' son, Thomas Holyoke (1616-1675), an English clergyman, worked on the Dictionary, but it was Thomas' son, Charles Holyoke (dates unknown) who finally published the first edition of the Dictionary in 1676.]

1 Jacob's do Law [*A New Law-Dictionary: Containing, The Interpretation and Definition of Words and Terms used in the Law; and Also the Whole Law, and the Practice Thereof, Under All the Heads and Titles of the Same. Together With Such Informations Relating Thereto, as Explain the History and Antiquity of the Law, and Our Manners, Customs, and Original Government. Collected and Abstracted From All Dictionaries, Abridgments, Institutes, Reports, Year-Books, Charters, Registers, Chronicles, and Histories, Published to This Time. And Fitted for the Use of Barristers, Students, and Practicioners of the Law, Members of Parliament, and Other Gentlemen, Justices of Peace, Clergymen, &c.* By Giles Jacob (1686-1744) English legal lexicographer.]

2 Vol. Johnson's Dictionary [*A Dictionary of the English Language: In Which The Words are deduced from their Originals, And Illustrated in their Different Significations By Examples from the best Writers. To Which Are Prefixed, A History of the Language, And An English Grammar.* By Samuel Johnson (1709-1784) the premier lexicographer of the English language, poet and critic. This dictionary was not printed in the United States until 1818, so the edition in Williams' library would have been one of the editions known to have been printed either in London or Dublin prior to 1780.]

2 Olde dictionary's English Latin [Since no author or compiler is listed, it is impossible to say definitively which of a number of works these might be, but, based on the seminal work done by Professor Walter Edgar, it appears likely that at least one of these dictionaries was Adam Littleton's *Linguae Latinae Liber dictionarious.* According to Edgar that title appeared in 12 other colonial era libraries of South Carolinians.[317]]

1 Macknight's Harmony [*A Harmony of the Four Gospels in which the natural order of each is preserved with a Paraphrase and Notes.* By James Macknight (1721-1800) Presbyterian minister, moderator of the Kirk of Scotland, author of religious treatises.]

6 Vol. Doddrige's, Paraphrase [*The Family Expositor: Or, a Paraphrase and Version of the New Testament with Critical Notes and Practical Improvement of Each Section.* By Philip Doddridge, D. D. (1702-1751) an English Non-conformist minister and author.]

3 Vol. Burn's Justice [*The Justice of the Peace and Parish Officer.* By Richard Burn (1709-1785) an English legal writer.]

3 Vol. Erskin's Sermons [Either *Sermons Upon The Most Important And Interesting Subjects* by Ebenezer Erskine (1680-1754) or *The Sermons and Other Practical Works by the Late Rev. Ralph Erskine.* By Ralph Erskine (1685-1752). Ebenezer and Ralph were brothers. Ebenezer was a chief founder of, and both were ministers in, the Secession Church (form of dissenters from the Kirk of Scotland) which, long after their deaths, united with other Presbyterian denominations to form the United Presbyterian Church.]

6 Vol. Watson's Horace [*The Odes, Epodes, and Carmen Seculare of Horace, translated into English prose, as near as the two languages will admit. Together with the original Latin from the best editions. Wherein the words of the Latin text are put in their grammatical order ... with notes ... The whole adapted to the capacities of youth at school, as well as of private gentlemen.* By David Watson, M. A. (1710-1756)]

2 Vol. Cooke's Terence [*Terence's Comedys Translated into English, with Critical and explanatory Notes. To which is prefixed a dissertation on the Life and Writings of Terence, containing An Enquiry into the Rise and Progress of dramatic Poetry in Greece and Rome, with Remarks on the comic Measure.* Translated by Thomas Cooke (1703-1756)]

[317] Edgar, *SC Libraries.*

1 Fitz Gerald's Terence

1 Anderson's Remonst [*A Remonstrance against Lord Viscount Bolingbroke's Philosophical Religion, addressed to David Mallet Esq., the publisher.* By the Reverend George Anderson (1676-1756), Minister of the Tron Church, Edinburgh.]

1 Boston's Fourfold State [*Human Nature in Its Fourfold State of Primitive Integrity, Entire Depravity, Begun Recovery and Consummate Happiness or Misery.* By Thomas Boston (1676-1732), a Presbyterian minister much influenced by the Rev. Henry Erskine, the father of Ebenezer and Ralph Erskine.]

1 Vol. Attorney's Pocket Book [probably, *The attorney's compleat pocket-book. Containing above four hundred of such choice and approved precedents, in law, equity, and conveyancing, as an attorney may have occasion for ... By the author of the Attorney's Practice Epitomized.* Author unknown. The British Library has in its catalogue an edition printed in 1764 with the above title.]

3 Vol. Sherlock's Discourse [one or more of the following works of the Rev. William Sherlock, *A Discourse Concerning the Happiness of Good men, And the Punishment of the Wicked In The Next World: A Discourse Concerning the Divine Providence: A Practical Discourse Of Religious Assemblies: A Practical Discourse Concerning a Future Judgment, Under the Following Heads: Via: I. The Proof of Future Judgment. II. Concerning the Time of Judgment. III. Who Shall be Our Judge, IV. The Manner and Circumstances of Christ's Appearance,* By William Sherlock, D. D. (1641-1707), dean of St. Paul's Cathedral, London and author of many religious treatises.

1 Book Sed Vol. Human Understanding [probably either the work by that name written by John Locke (1632-1704) or David Hume (1711-1776); most likely the former since it was a popular title in colonial era libraries. A search of the British Library's catalogue, however, reveals that there were a number of other works available in the 18th Century in which the words "Human Understanding" appear in the title.]

1 Vol. Melmoth's Letters [one of the following: *The Letters of Marcus Tullius Cicero To Several of His Friends with remarks by William Melmoth: or The Letters Of Pliny The Consul: With*

Occasional Remarks. By William Melmouth, Esq: or *The Letters of Sir Thomas Fitzosborne, on several Subjects.* By William Melmoth ('Fitzosborne' was the pseudonym of William Melmoth the Younger (1710-99), English Classical Scholar.]

1 Book Confessions of Faith

Bennet's Oratory, 2 Vols. [*The Christian Oratory: or the Devotion of the Closet in two volumes.* By Benjamin Bennet (1674-1726).]

1 Horn Book

1 a practical, Christian Perfection [*A Practical Treatise upon Christian Perfection.* By William Law (1686-1761), an English, Anglican theologian and author.]

1 Sermon Book

1 Sermon Book, Lectures of Selected Subjects

1 Book Disenting Gentleman's Letters [*A Dissent from the Church of England Fully justified: And Proved the Genuine and Just Consequence of the Allegiance Due to Christ. The dissenting gentleman's answer to the Reverend Mr. White's three letters; in which a separation from the Establishment is fully justified; the charge of schism is refuted and retorted. The dissenting gentleman's second letter to the Reverend Mr. White, in answer to his three letters, in which his various misrepresentation of the Dissenters are corrected. The dissenting gentleman's third and last letter to the Reverend Mr. White. The dissenting gentleman's postscript to his three letters to Mr. White. By The Dissenting Gentleman (Rev. Micaiah Towgood).* Micajah Towgood (1700-1792), a Dissenting minister. (John Wesley wrote of Towgood's book: "I think the most saucy and virulent satire on the Church of England that ever my eyes beheld.")]

1 Book the young man's Companion [Either, *The newest Young man's companion, containing a compendious English grammar, instructions to write variety of hands, with copies both in prose and verse. Letters on compliment, business, and several other occasions. Forms of indenture, wills, testaments, letters of attorney, bills, receipts, releases, acquittances, &c. Arithmetic and book-keeping, in an easier way than any yet published. A compendium of geography, describing all the empires, kingdoms and dominions of the whole world. To which is added a description of the several counties of England and Scotland, their produce, market-towns and* *market-days. The management of horses, being directions to cure and prevent most distempers which are incident to horses. The art of painting in oil.* By Thomas Wise (?), (no information except the name and the description "accountant" could be found for this author in the catalogues of both the British Library and the Library of Congress) or *The instructor; or, Young man's best companion. Containing spelling, reading, writing, and arithmetic, in an easier way than any yet published. Instructions to write variety of hands, with copies. How to write letters on business or friendship; forms of indenture, bonds, bills of sale, receipts, wills, leases, releases, &c. Merchants accounts, and a short and easy method of shop and book-keeping; with a description of the product, counties, and market-towns in England and Wales, and a list of fairs according to the new style. The method of measuring carpenters, joiners, sawyers, bricklayers, plasterers, plumbers, masons, glasiers, and painters work. How to undertake each work, and at what price; the rates of each commodity, and the common wages of journeymen, with the description of Gunter's Line, and Coggeshall's Sliding-rule. The Practical Guager made easy; the art of Dialling, and how to erect and fix dials, with instructions for dying, colouring, and making colours; and some general observations for gardening every month in the year.* By George Fisher (?)[318]]

1 Book Pilgrim's Progress [This is probably John Bunyan's masterpiece by that name of which there were numerous copies offered for sale by the Charleston booksellers in the 18th Century, but it might be *The New Pilgrim's Progress: Or, the Pious Indian Convert, Containing a faithful account of Hattain Gelashmin, ... who was baptis'd into the Christian Faith by the name of George James ... Together with a narrative of his ... travels among the savage Indians for their conversion, etc.* By James Walcot, in which he gave a detailed account of South Carolina in 1740. Walcot was an Oxford graduate who traveled in Jamaica and South Carolina.]

1 Book of Marchant Accompts [Since James Williams was a merchant and miller in the Carolina backcountry, this may

---

[318] See L. C. Karpinski, 'The Elusive George Fisher, "Accomptant" - writer or editor of three popular arithmetics' in Scripta Mathematica (N.Y., 1953) in which Karpinski speculates as to the identity of George Fisher.

be a reference to his own book of accounts. However, given the way in which the word "accounts" is spelled, it seems more likely that the book referred to is *Book-keeping Methodiz'd: Or, A Methodical Treatise Of Merchant-Accompts, According to the Italian Form...To which is added...I. Descriptions and Specimens of the Subsidiary Books...II. Monies and Exchanges...III. Precedents of Merchants Writings...IV. The Commission, Duty, and Power of Factors. V. A short History of Trading Companies...VI. The Produce and Commerce of the Tobacco Colonies. VII. A Dictionary...* By John Mair (1702/3-1769)]

1 do Mair's Sallust [*Sallust C. Crispi Sallustii Bellum Catalinarium et Jugurthinum, ex optima atque accuratissima Gottlieb Cortii editione expressum. Or, Sallust's history of Catiline's conspiracy and the war of the Jugurtha, according to the excellent and accurate edition of Gottlieb Cortius. With an English translation as literal as possible and large explanatory notes. . . By John Mair.* By John Mair (also known as John Major) (1469-1550) Scottish theologian and historian, Professor of Theology at the University of Paris, Principal at the University of Glasgow and later Provost of St. Andrews' University in Scotland. John Knox was one of his students and said of Mair that he was "… held as an oracle on matters of religion."]

1 do a Treatise Concerning the Lord's day [*A Treatise Concerning the Sanctification of the Lord's Day Wherein the Morality of the Sabbath, … is Maintained … Containing Also Many Special Directions and Advices … Proper for Families. by J. W. Minister of the Gospel in Dundee.* By John Willison (1680-1750), minister of the Church of Scotland, Dundee, Scotland. Willison was a staunch defender of the Church of Scotland and preached ardently against the schisms that fragmented the church into Baptists, Methodists, Reformed Presbyterian, etc.]

1 Book Richard Aesop's [No edition with someone named Richard or Richards is listed in either the British Library or the Library of Congress. There is an edition listed in the British Library as having been edited and contributed to by Samuel Richardson, the novelist. That edition is entitled *Æsop's Fables. With instructive morals and reflections [by Samuel Richardson] … And the life of Æsop prefixed, by Mr. Richardson.*]

205

1 do Tatler Sed Vol [Possibly, *The Tatler or Lucubrations of Isaac Bickerstaff, Esq. In 4 Volumes.* By Sir Richard Steele. Joseph Addison, & Jonathan Swift were among the contributors to this periodical. Bound editions of the periodical began to appear in 1711 and some are still in print today. Sir Richard Steele was the publisher of the periodical and he used the pseudonym of Isaac Bickerstaff. Steele revealed his identity in the last issue of the periodical published in 1711. Steele assumed the voice of Isaac Bickerstaff, a fictitious character created by Swift. The noted author, Walter Scott, said of the Tatler that it was "… the first of that long series of periodical works which have enriched our literature with so many effusions of genius, humor, wit, and learning."]

1 Book The Mariners New Calendar [*The Mariner's New Calendar. Containing The Principles of Arithmetick and Practical Geometry; with the Extraction of the Square and Cube Roots: Also Rules for finding the Prime, Epact, Moon's Age, Time of High-Water, with tables for the same. Together With Exact Tables of the Sun's Place, Declination, and Right Ascension: Of the Right Ascension and Declination of the Principal Fixed Stars: Of the Latitude and Longitude of Places; A large Table of Difference of Latitude and Departure, for the exact Working a Traverse. The Description and Use of the Sea-Quadrant, Forestaff and Nocturnal; The Problems of Plain Sailing and Astronomy, wrought by the Logarithms, and by Gunter's Scale; A Rutter for the Coasts of England, Scotland, Iceland, France, &c.: And the Soundings coming into the Channel: With Directions for Sailing into some Principal Harbors. By Nath. Colson, Student in the Mathematicks.* By Nathaniel Colson (fl 1674).]

17 Books, Containing Latton & greak [17 Latin and Greek Books]

Appendix 12

Official Report of the Battle of King's Mountain

Official Report of the Battle of King's Mountain

A Statement of the proceedings of the Western Army, from the 25th of September, 1780, to the reduction of Major Ferguson, and the army under his command.

On receiving intelligence that Major Ferguson had advanced as high up as Gilbert Town, in Rutherford county, and threatened to cross the mountains to the Western waters, Col. William Campbell, with four hundred men from Washington county, of Virginia; Col. Isaac Shelby with two hundred and forty men from Sullivan county, North-Carolina, and Lieutenant-Col. John Sevier, with two hundred and forty men from Washington county, North-Carolina, assembled at Watauga on the 25th of September, where they were joined by Col. Charles McDowell, with one hundred and sixty men from the counties of Burke and Rutherford, who had fled before the enemy to the Western waters.

We began our march on the 26th, and on the 30th, we were joined by Col. Cleveland, on the Catawba River, with three hundred and fifty men from the counties of Wilkes and Surry. No one officer having properly a right to the command-in-chief, on the 1st of October, we despatched an express to Major General Gates, informing him of our situation, and requested him to send a general officer to take command of the whole. In the meantime, Col. Campbell was chosen to act as commandant till such general officer should arrive.

We reached the Cow Pens, on the Broad River, in South Carolina, where we were joined by Col. James Williams, on the evening of the 6th October, who informed us that the enemy lay encamped somewhere near the Cherokee Ford of Broad River, about thirty miles distant form us. By a council of the principal officers, it was then thought advisable to pursue the enemy that night with nine hundred of the best horsemen, and leave the weak horses and footmen to follow as fast as possible. We began our march with nine hundred of the best men about eight o'clock the same evening, marched all night, and came up with the enemy about three o'clock P.M. of the 7th, who lay encamped on the top of King's Mountain, twelve miles north of the Cherokee Ford, in the confidence they could not be forced from so advantageous a post. Previous to the attack, in our march the following disposition was made:

Col. Shelby's regiment formed a column in the centre on the left; Col. Campbell's another on the right; part of Col. Cleveland's regiment, headed by Major Winston and Col. Sevier's, formed a large column on the right wing; the other part of Col. Cleveland's regiment composed the left wing. In this order we advanced, and got within a quarter of a mile of the enemy before we were discovered. Col. Shelby's and Col. Campbell's regiments began the attack, and kept up a fire on the enemy while the right and left wings were advancing forward to surround them. The engagement lasted an hour and five minutes, the greatest part of which time a heavy and incessant fire was kept up on both sides. Our men in some parts where the regulars fought, were obliged to give way a small distance two or three times, but rallied and returned with additional ardour to the attack, and kept up a fire on the enemy while the right and left wings were advancing forward to surround them. The troops upon the right having gained the summit of the eminence, obliged the enemy to retreat along the top of the ridge where Col. Cleveland commanded, and were there stopped by his brave men. A flag was immediately hoisted by Captain Dupoister, the commanding officer, (Major Ferguson having been killed a little before,) for a surrender. Our fire immediately ceased, and the enemy laid down their arms—the greater part of them loaded—and surrendered themselves to us prisoners at discretion. It appears from their own provision returns for that day, found in their camp, that their whole force consisted of eleven hundred and twenty-five men, out of which they sustained the following loss:—Of the regulars, one Major, one captain, two lieutenants and fifteen privates killed, thirty-five privates wounded. Left on the ground, not able to march, two captains, four lieutenants, three ensigns, one surgeon, five sergeants; three corporals, one drummer and fifty-nine privates taken prisoners.

Loss of the tories, two colonels, three captains, and two hundred and one privates killed; one Major and one hundred and twenty-seven privates wounded and left on the ground not able to march; one colonel, twelve captains, eleven lieutenants, two ensigns, one quarter-master, one adjutant, two commissisaries, eighteen sergeants and six hundred privates taken prisoners. Total loss of the enemy, eleven hundred and five men at King's Mountain.

Given under our hands at camp,

WILLIAM CAMPBELL,
ISAAC SHELBY
BENJAMIN CLEVELAND

The loss on our side–

Killed –		Wounded –	
	1 colonel,		1 Major,
	1 Major,		3 captains,
	1 captain,		3 lieutenants,
	2 lieutenants		55 privates
	4 ensigns,		62 total
	19 privates		wounded
	28 total killed		

(First published in the *Virginia Gazette*, Nov. 18th)

Appendix 13

Table of King's Mountain Whig Militia Listed According to Commanding Officer

Footnotes at end of table

	James Williams	William Campbell	William Chronicle	(James McCall) Elijah Clarke[1]	Benjamin Cleveland	Joseph McDowell	John Sevier W6011 (widow)	Isaac Shelby	-? (Hawthorn/ Lacey)	Joseph Winston	Unidentified[3]
1	Joseph Alexander S15355	James Alexander W12190	Robert Barkley W17252	Robert Bean	Travice Alexander	Philip Anthony S6800	Capt. Jesse Beene	Joseph Bealer	Maj. John Adair W2895	William Bailey R372	John Abston R14 [Pittsylvania Co. Va.—WC]
2	Capt. Robert Anderson	Robert Anderson W2579	Andrew Barry (Berry)	John Black R890	David Allen S16601	Alexander Bailey S32101	Capt. Jacob Brown	Andrew Beaty S2989	John C. Adams W8312	Lt. Adam Binkley S1890	John Adams R41 [Louisa Co., Va.—WC]
3	Jacob Barnett (killed)	William Anderson	William Beard S2370	Maj. William Candler	John Amburgay R174	Charles Baker S31536	John Brown (killed)	Jacob Biffel S3003	Hugh Allison R157	William Conner S30955	Alexander Aiken [unk SC—TS/JW]
4	Samuel Blair S3009	William Anderson R206	Jacob Beeler S5277	Capt. Patrick Carr	John Anderson W9329	Joseph Ballew S31541	Joseph Brown S17291	Henry Blevins W1703	Capt. Robert Anderson	William Hooker W10119	Absalom Baker S35184 [unk NC]4
5	John Blassingame S30576	Robert Baker S16628	Samuel Caldwell W528	John Crawford R2470	Lawrence Angel S31519	— Berry (killed)	William Brown S31563	Sgt. William Carr	Matthew Armstrong	Benjamin Jones S7076	Robert Bean [Watauga area of NC (TN)—JS]5
6	John Boyce	Benoni Banning	Enoch Gilmer	Maj. John Cunningham W6752	Elihu Ayers R335	— Berry	James Campbell S30310	John Caswell S3133	William Armstrong		Andrew Bigham S1639 [Mecklenburg Co., NC—under Col. John Hampton at KM]6 unk
7	Richard Brandon W21714	Lt. William Bartlett	William M. Gilmer	Capt. William Hammett R4528	Daniel Bailey R369	Enoch Berry W8128	Jeremiah Campbell S3131	Moses Cavett R1820	Lt. John Bird s1890		John Black R890 [Elbert Co., Ga.—unk]
8	Col. Thomas Brandon	Capt. David Beattie	Robert Henry	Richard Heard W4229	Robert Ballew S10350	William Bradley W8399	William Depriest S8319	John Craig R2426	Joseph Black		James Blair S22125 [Burke Co., NC—JM]
9	William Brandon W71	Ensign John Beattie	Matthew Leeper W26205	Peter Helton R4854	George Barker S37710	Capt. Jonathan Camp	Ebenzer Fain R3421	Alexander Crockett R2496	Laird Burns S3091		Essius Bowman [unk—Capt. Joel Lewis—JM]

	James Williams	William Campbell	William Chronicle	(James McCall) Elijah Clarke[1]	Benjamin Cleveland	Joseph McDowell	John Sevier W6011 (widow)	Isaac Shelby	Thomas Sumter[2] (Hawthorn/Lacey)	Joseph Winston	Unidentified[3]
10	George Brooks S31574	William Beattie	Alexander McLaen S17575	James Lochridge W472	Capt. John Barton R12277	George Cathey S16699	Smith Ferrill S1513	Robert Crockett S30353	Joseph Carroll W9778		John Boyd [Lincoln Co., NC—BC]
11	Capt. Gabriel Brown	Joseph Black	William Rabb	Lt. Col. James McCall	Thomas Becknel S12985	Capt. Mordecai Clarke W25591	John Fields R3529	Nathaniel Davis S30366	John Chittam S10116		Lt. John Boyer S32125 [96 SC—TS/JW]
12	Jacob Brown, Jr. W833	Lt. William Blackburn (killed)		John Patterson S17626	___ Benge (killed)	John Collins, Sr. W6735	Peter Finn S32244	William Delaney	James Clinton S2437		Gerard Brandon [unk, SC—TS/JW]
13	Joseph Brown, Jr. W5744	George Blane R929		Thomas Price W1076	David Benge S38530	Isaac Conner S10465	John Franklin, Jr. R3756	Maj. William Edmondson	James Coiel S31624		Capt. John Brandon [unk, NC]
14	William Caldwell W22727	James Blevens S32121		Peter Strozier R10279	Obahiah M. Benge R743	Adam Crum S8260	Nathan Gann S1820	Capt. James Elliott	John Copland S30966		Josiah Brandon[7] [Tory captured at KM] [Rowan Co., NC—JM]
15	Lt. Joel Callahan	Charles Bowen S16055		Peter Tramel R10674	Thomas Biecknell R12399	Maj. Joseph Dickson	Richard Gentry W8844	Thomas Elliott R3294	George Cunningham W2071		Joseph Brymer W5947 [Abbeville, SC—TS/JW]
16	James Campbell R1644	Reece Bowen (killed)			John Blackwell S2083	Joseph Dobson, Jr. W19187	John Gilleland	John Fagan	Capt. John Cunningham R2425		Andrew Bryson R1389 [Iredell Co., NC—JM]
17	Samuel Carson	Michael Boyers S3022			David Blalock S3011	John Duckworth S6805	William Good W1413	Joshua Hamilton S2608	John Curren		James Busby W2995 [Goochland Co., Va—WC]
18	Ephraim Cassel R1792	John Broddy			Daniel Blevens S31555	John Dysart S3315	Alexander Greer	Francis Haney S32292	James Elliot		Lt. Thomas Caldwell [Washington Co., Va—WC]
19	Coleman Clayton W6692	Thomas Brown W8381			John Boyd R1089	Capt. Alexander Erwin	James Gregory R4292	Robert Hansley S4323	Andrew Floyd S21757		Capt. John Campbell [Washington Co., Va—WC]
20	Samuel Clowney W9391	William Bulen			William Boyd S45878	Capt. Edmund Fear	John Grier S1906	Abrah Horton W7778	William Gaston S32265		Solomon Campbell[8] S39287 [unk, SC?]
21	Josiah Culbertson S16354	Meshack Burchfield S16668			Hawkins Bracket R1121	John Forbis W25591	Elisha Hadden R4412	Hall Hudson R5331	John Gebie		William Campbell [unk—SC]
22	Robert Culbertson S21722	Capt. David Campbell			John Bradley S31575	Abraham Forney W9976	Lt. Samuel Handy S1911	Joseph James (alias, Rogers) S32340	Joseph Gilmore W355		Maj. William Candler [unk, Ga.—JW]

	James Williams	William Campbell	William Chronicle	(James McCall) Elijah Clarke[1]	Benjamin Cleveland	Joseph McDowell	John Sevier W6011 (widow)	Isaac Shelby	Thomas Sumter[2] (Hawthorn/Lacey)	Joseph Winston	Unidentified[3]
23	Capt. Samuel Culbertson	Joseph Campbell, Jr. S2414			Benjamin Brown S16327	James Furgason S1816	Gideon Harrison S2602	John Jones R5719	Ralph Griffin S16389		Lt. Andrew Carothers [unk. NC (now TN)-JS/IS]
24	William Daugherty W3229	Lt. Patrick Campbell			Capt. John Brown	Preston Goforth (killed) [Col. Andrew Hampton]	Esli Hunt S7054	James King S4477	Thomas Hawkins S10796		Thomas Carothers S35809 [unk. --NC]?
25	Henry W. Deshasure S16362	Ensign Robert Campbell			Humphrey Brunfield S8105	Lt. Col. Frederick Hambright R4505[10]	Dempsey Hunter R5399	Thomas Laughlin W9112	Col. James Hawthorn		Capt. Patrick Carr [unk Ga. IS/JW]
26	Capt. James Dillard S6797	Lt. William Crew			William Burch W26976	Capt. John Hardin Hambright W932	John Moses Johnson R5666	John Long	Capt. John Henderson R4869		William Carson S9305 [York Co., SC --TS/JW]
27	John Dollarhide R3001[1]	Capt. Gilbert Christian			John Burns S9118	Capt. John Hardin	Richard Keele S1977	Capt. Samuel Martin S9003	Col. William Hill[2]		Giles Landon Carton R1756
28	Capt. John Douglas	John Clarke R1990			Thomas Cadle R1579	Edward Harris R4683	John Kusick	Lt. George Maxwell	Capt. John Hollis S21827		John Caruthers S32163 [prisoner of the Tories at KM]
29	Felix Earnest W7066	Capt. Andrew Colvill			Ephraim Carter S8152	Capt. John Harvey [Hardy?]	Lt. Isaac Lane R6137	Thomas Maxwell	David Howe S13422		John Clark R1965 [unk Va--WC]
30	Potter Enlow W11912	James Conn S15386			William Carter S9133	Capt. Thomas Hemphill	Michael Mahoney	William McCormack R6648	Berry Jeffers W10145		Ensign William Cocke [Washington Co., Va--WC]
31	Elisha Evans S6830	Ensign James Corry (killed)			Zachariah Carwill S9310	Joseph Henry W10096	John McQueen S30577	Samuel McGaughy W9981	James Johnson W9088		William Coombs W8757 [Wilkes Co., NC--BC]
32	John Fields S8471	Samuel Covey S3190			Isaiah Case S16692	Daniel Horton S1834	Burt Moore W2155	William McKinney S16470	John Kelly R5845		Capt. Thomas Cowan W18922 [Rowan Co., NC--JM]
33	Lt. William Giles	Lt. William Crabtree			William Cavinder W6903	Francis Hughes S075	William Moore S2858	Thomas Morrell S4241	John Kincaid W12029		Joseph Cox S41494 [Sury Co., NC--BC]

	James Williams	William Campbell	William Chronicle	(James McCall) Elijah Clarke[1]	Benjamin Cleveland	Joseph McDowell	John Sevier W6011 (widow)	Isaac Shelby	Thomas Sumter[2] (Hawthorn/ Lacey)	Joseph Winston	Unidentified[3]
34	Samuel Gilkey R4019	James Craig, Jr.			Josiah Chandler W159	George Hughey S21306 [Capt. James Withrow & Col. A. Hampton]	Patrick Murphy	Capt. John Pemberton	John Knight R6026		William Cox [Watauga River, NC (TN)—JS/IS]
35	William Goodlet W8857	John Craig S16740			John Childress S3146 [states that JW in command at KM]	William Jewell S1837	Jacob Norris	John Peters	Capt. Hugh Knox W10180		John Crawford R2470 [unk Ga.]?
36	William Grant W1757	Capt. Robert Craig			Capt. John Cleveland	John Jones W373	James Ownbey W3712	John Ross S31336	Col. Edward Lacey		Colbay Creed S32194 [prisoner of the Tories at KM] [Surry Co., NC]
37	Capt. William Grant	Andrew Creswell S1948			Capt. Robert Cleveland	Joseph Jones S2652	Capt. James Pearce W5529	George Rutledge	Thomas Large R6164		Andrew Cresson W6767 [Surry Co., NC—BC]
38	William Gray R42213	James Crow			Capt. Joseph Cloyd	Capt. George Ledbetter [Col. Hampton]	Abel Pearson S3661	Capt. John Sawyers	William Large R6165		John Crossland S18784 [unk, SC]
39	Charles Hamilton R4512	Joseph Culton S16742			Reuben Coffey S46916	Samuel Lusk W8092	Capt. Thomas Price	Ensign John Sharp	Andrew Lofton		Maj. John Cunningham W6752 [unk SC]
40	Martin Hammond	Edward Darten S30983			James P. Collins R2173	Samuel Mackie W7385	William Price W1072	Evan Shelby, Jr.	Capt. Thomas Lofton S17114		William Davenport R2678 [Surry NC—BC]
41	Maj. Samuel Hammond S21807	Lt. William Davidson			George Cox	Capt. Joseph McDowell	Maj. Charles Robertson	Isaac Shelby, Jr.	Christopher Loving S38153		William Davis W8653 [York, SC]
42	Samuel Hand W10	Ensign Henry Dickenson			John Cox S21124	James McWhirter R6818	Lt. William Robertson S4790	Capt. Moses Shelby	Edward Martin W21746		John Dellinger W19180 [Lincoln NC—JM]
43	Lt. Col. Joseph Hayes	Ensign Nathaniel Dryden (killed)			William Crain S1753	Danza Metcalf W4280	George Russell	James Simms S4840	Andrew McAllister R6602		David Dickey [Col. Wm. Graham] [unk NC—JM]
44	George Hays W7635	Capt. James Dysart			Snead Davis S32205	Warner Metcalf W4281	Abraham Sevier S1589	Zebulon Smith S1876	William McElhaney R6697		John Dickey W3962 [Rowan NC—JM]

	James Williams	William Campbell	William Chronicle	(James McCall) Elijah Clarke[1]	Benjamin Cleveland	Joseph McDowell	John Sevier W6011 (widow)	Isaac Shelby	Thomas Sumter[2] (Hawthorn/ Lacey)	Joseph Winston	Unidentified[3]
45	Robert Henderson S31738	Lt. Andrew Edmondson (killed)			William Davis W8657	Samuel Moore	James Sevier S45889	John Wallace S17178	John McKennon R6751		David Duff [either TS or JW] (killed)
46	Robert Henson R4902	Lt. Robert Edmondson [younger]			William Dudley R3105	William Morrison W1455	Joseph Sevier	Capt. Thomas Wallace W11739	Capt. James Meek		Timothy Duick [unk]
47	John Hicks	Lt. Robert Edmondson (killed) [older]			Edward Dugless S3297	James Murphy R7512	Capt. Robert Sevier	William Walling S1935	John Miller S38950		Capt. Josiah Dunn R3145 [Ga?][US?]
48	Daniel Higdon W25769	Samuel Edmondson			Alexander Dunn R3142	Jesse Nevill S21899	Capt. Valentine Sevier, Jr. W6012	Frederick Shelby Blwt 40920	Capt. John Mills		Jacob Eberhart S31661 [Burke Co., NC—JM]
49	Benjamin Hollingsworth	William Edmondson			Mastin Durham S1197	Walter O'Neill S7281	George Sherrill S3902	Benjamin Webb S3487	Capt. John Moffett		Arthur Erwin [Unk, either NC or SC]
50	Samuel Houston W7810[14]	Capt. William Edmondson (killed)			Thompson Epposon W7115	Thomas Patten S32429	Ute Sherrill R17811	George Webb W6445	Samuel Marrow W21825		James Espey S31668 [Capt. Isaac White] [Tryon Co., NC—JM]
51	Ambrose Hudgens R4321	Robert Elder S12865			John Fox, Sr. R3734	Maj. James Porter [Col. Hampton]	John Michael Saltpeter W3730	Capt. Jonathan Webb	David Morton S21380		Capt. Samuel Espey S6824 [Col. Graham] [Linclon Co., NC—JM]
52	Lt. Joseph Hughes S31764	Andrew Evans S3341			Capt. Jesse Hardin Franklin	William Robertson	William Steele	Moses Webb S35113	Lt. Col. John Nixon		Nathaniel Ewing [Capt. James Hawston (Houston?)] [NC—JM]
53	William Humphreys W4000	Andrew Evans W10019			Peter Fulp W5278	John Simmons R9578	Capt. James Stinson	Alexander Young S35755	Capt. Joseph Palmer		Lt. Alexander Faris S3344 – [York Co., SC—TS/JW]
54	John Ingram R5483	Hugh Ewin			Lt. Martin Gambrill W7504	John Smart [Col. Hampton]	Capt. Christopher Taylor R10420		Robert Patrick W21925		Andrew Ferguson S32243 [unk]
55	John Jefferies, Sr. S18055	Barnabus Fair S12895			David Gentry W7511	Capt. Daniel Smith	Maj. Jonathan Tipton W1098		James Ramsey R8570		Lt. George Finley [Capt. Andrew Lewis][15] [unk Va.—WC]

	James Williams	William Campbell	William Chronicle	(James McCall) Elijah Clarke[1]	Benjamin Cleveland	Joseph McDowell	John Sevier W6011 (widow)	Isaac Shelby	Thomas Sumter[2] (Hawthorn/Lacey)	Joseph Winston	Unidentified[3]
56	Benjamin Jolly	John Findley			Benjamin Glover S16829	George Taylor	John Wallace S32572		William Shaw R9446		John Fisher W25580 [prisoner of Tories at KM]
57	Benjamin Jones R5746 [Col. Anderson]	Frederick Fisher S20364			William Glover W929	James Thompson S32014	Capt. Samuel Ware		Capt. John Steele		John Fitzpatrick W7276 [Surry Co., NC—BC]
58	Capt. John Jones	James Forgason R3664			Lt. Charles Gordon	Samuel Thornton R10571	John Watson S16287		James Stuart W8762		Micajah Frost S31043 [under Capt. Finley] [Washington Co., Va,—WC]
59	James Jordan S32346 [Gen. JW at KM]	James Fugate S15846			Benjamin Guess S32283	Capt. David Vance	Samuel Weaver S3516		Maj. Samuel Tate		Joel Galliher [Washington Co., Va.—WC]
60	Robert Kell S32355	Jonathan Fugate R3625			Capt. Moses Guess S1197	Christopher Waggoner R10995	Capt. Samuel Williams		Robert Walker		James Glenn S21768 [Col. Graham]
61	Lt. Samuel Kelso R5853	George Gamble S10720			William Guest W21239	Henry Wakefield W35	Capt. James Wilson		William Watson		Col. William Graham S8624 [Tryon Co., NC—JM]
62	William Kenedy (Kennedy) S2695	Bellingsby Gibson S1761			John Hammon S9559	William Walker S32573	Robert Young R19322		William White W8995		William Griffis R4323 [96 SC-- TS/JW]
63	William Kennedy, Sr	Samuel Gibson W9450			Joel Hampton R4547	William Watson S7831					John Hall S30451 [Patrick Co., Va—WC]
64	Joseph Kerr S4469	Francis Gilley R035			Andrew Hannah W794	Maj. Joseph White					Col. Andrew Hampton [Rutherford NC]
65	William Love W956	James Gilliland S15852			Paul Henson	John Wilfong S7951					Capt. William Hammett R4528 [Wilkes Co., Ga—JS/IS]
66	Thomas Mann R6876 [Col. Anderson]	Ensign Nathaniel Gist			Capt. Benjamin Herndon	James Williams S31487					Robert Hanna [unk]
67	Joseph Marler R6934 [Col. Robert McCreery][6]	Richard Gist			Maj. Joseph Herndon	Capt. James Withrow S7945 [Col. Andrew Hampton]					Benjamin Hardin, Jr. S32293 [Col. George Davidson][7] [Rutherford Co., NC—JM]
68	Capt. Salathiel Martin W1044	Andrew Goff			George Hillen S7006	Capt. Samuel Wood					Jeremiah Harrold S17467 [Orangeburg, SC --TS/JW]

	James Williams	William Campbell	William Chronicle	(James McCall) Elijah Clarke[1]	Benjamin Cleveland	Joseph McDowell	John Sevier W6011 (widow)	Isaac Shelby	Thomas Sumter[2] (Hawthorn/Lacey)	Joseph Winston	Unidentified[3]
69	Lt. James Martindale R6979[18]	Miles Goforth R4092			George Hodge W4234						Richard Heard W4229 [Wilkes Co., Ga—JS/IS]
70	Samuel Mayes W2140	James Gray S8594			David Hogan R5101						Peter Helton R4854 [Surry Co., NC—BC]
71	Silas McBee S7202	William Green W24319			Thomas Hood S4379						Lt. Thomas Henderson W10102 [York SC‐IS or JW]
72	Capt. Vardry McBee	Philip Greever			John Horton W367						John Henry (killed)[19]
73	David McCance S16464[20]	John Harris W24391			Howell Hunt R5396						Capt. Malcolm Henry S16866 [York Co., SC] [Col. Graham]
74	Capt. John McCool W9546	Israel Hayter			James Isbell W7863						Moses Henry R4382 (mortally wounded)[Col. Graham] [Lincoln Co., NC—JM]
75	Samuel McElhaney W12455[21]	Henry Henigar			Capt. William Jackson						Lt. James Hill W3815 [Col. Graham] [Tryon Co., NC—JM]
76	Stephen McElhenney S21368	Leonard Hice S8713			Alexander Johnson R15508						Thomas Hill W663 [Col. Graham] [Lincoln Co., NC—JM]
77	Daniel McJunkin W9190	George Hise R5044			Lt. Samuel Johnson (Johnston) W5012						Conrad Hise W4453 [Capt. Stevens] [Mecklenburg Co., NC—unk]
78	William McKnight S32407	Ensign James Houston S1914			John Judd						Jacob Hise R5045 [Washington Co., NC—JS/IS]
79	William McMaster R21675	Ensign John Houston			Rowland Judd						George Hofstalar S15176 [Col. Graham] [Rowan Co., NC—JM]
80	William McMenamy S9013	Peter Hughs W7823			Ensign Christopher Kerby S32356						Charles Holland S7027 [Capt. Strain?] [96, SC—JW]

	James Williams	William Campbell	William Chronicle	(James McCall) Elijah Clarke[1]	Benjamin Cleveland	Joseph McDowell	John Sevier W6011 (widow)	Isaac Shelby	Thomas Sumter[2] (Hawthorn/ Lacey)	Joseph Winston	Unidentified[3]
81	Capt. John McMullen W4287 [Caswell NC]	Capt. Thomas Kennedy S31185			Charles Kilgore						John Houser W9650 [Surry Co., NC—BC]
82	Lt. David Mitchell W7460 [Caswell NC]	James Keys S15907			James Lefoy S10971						John Hudgins R7515 [Chatham Co, NC—unk]
83	William Mitchell S4221 [Caswell NC]	George Kincannon			Moses Lawson W5019						William Thrift Hughlett W4996 [Surry Co., NC—BC]
84	Charles Moore W24005	Ensign James Laird			Capt. William Lenoir S7137						Pendleton Isbell [SC unk—TS/JW]
85	Maj. John Moore W9205 [son]	Abner Lee R6257			Lt. James Martin Lewis						Lt. Arthur Johnson W10152 [Capt. Woodson] [Brunswick Co., Va—WC]
86	Maj. John Moore W9206 [widow]	James Logan			Capt. Joel Lewis W780						Capt. James Johnson [Lincoln Co., NC—JM]
87	Joseph Neeley S31879 [Caswell NC]	Charles Love R6466			Maj. Micajah Lewis						John Johnston W7942 [Col. Watson] [York Co., SC—TS/JW]
88	Jacob Neely S7264 [Caswell NC]	Thomas Lovelady W8065			John Livingston R6393						Martin Johnston W436 [Culpepper Co., Va—WC]
89	Benjamin Neighbors S19000	Humberton Lyon			Joseph Logan R6413						Martin Johnston W436 [Culpepper Co., Va. -WC]
90	Benjamin Newton S16493 [Caswell NC]	William Maxwell R7046			William Lowe S13795						Capt. William Johnston [Lincoln NC -JM]
91	Lewis Sanders Nobles R7683	John McClain S31853			Thomas Majors S30564						Freeman Jones W7900 [prisoner of the Tories at KM]
92	Thomas Palmer	Joseph McClaskey W1449			Jacob Martin S7172						Gabriel Jones S36652 [Surry NC—BC]

	James Williams	William Campbell	William Chronicle	(James McCall) Elijah Clarke[1]	Benjamin Cleveland	Joseph McDowell	John Sevier W6011 (widow)	Isaac Shelby	Thomas Sumter[2] (Hawthorn/Lacey)	Joseph Winston	Unidentified[3]
93	Elisha Parker S11354	Capt. John McClure W25692			Obediah Martin R6976						Thomas Jones R5735 [Charlotte Co., Va—WC]
94	William Prewett R8460	John McCroskey S2781			Philip Mason S8994						John Kanselar [Col. Thompson][unk SC]
95	Primes R8486	Lt. Thomas McCulloch			Thomas May R7057						Devault Keller S32358 [Col. Beard] [96SC—TS/JW]
96	Matthew Pryor, Sr. S3747 [Caswell NC]	John McCullock S7204			Rice McDavis R6685						Alexander Kelso W9493 [in NC unit at KM]
97	Capt. John Putnam	William McFerren S2791			Capt. William Meredith						Capt. Robert Kennedy [Washington Co., Va—WC]
98	Samuel Quinton, Sr. S32461	Alexander Meek S7218			James Meritt S21883						David Kerr R5890 [Abbeville SC—TS/JW]
99	James Renick S14262	Lt. Samuel Meek			Martin Mooney S38234						Lt. Andrew Kincannon [Washington NC—JS/IS]
100	Maj. Benjamin Roebuck	William Moore S25312			George Morris R7411						David Kirkwood W29916
101	John Scott S32508	Sgt. Edward Murphey S1569			Capt. Abraham Moss [DeMoss?]						Samuel Lamme R6103 [Cpt. Patrick Buchanan] [Augusta Co., Va—WC]
102	William Sharp	Lt. Lewis Musick			Hanse Nelson W1462						Claiborn Laurence R6196 [Surry NC –BC]
103	Adam Skains S11404	Lt. Samuel Newell R7617			John Norris R7700						James Lindsay [prisoner of Tories at KM]
104	Robert Starke, Jr.	Capt. Joshua Nichols S32414			William Overstreet						William Logan [Col. Graham] [Rutherford Co., NC—JM]
105	Lt. Col. James Steen[2]	Alexander Outlaw			David Owen						David Long W2 [Rowan NC—JM]

	James Williams	William Campbell	William Chronicle	(James McCall) Elijah Clarke[1]	Benjamin Cleveland	Joseph McDowell	John Sevier W6011 (widow)	Isaac Shelby	Thomas Sumter[2] (Hawthorn/Lacey)	Joseph Winston	Unidentified[3]
106	Henry Story S32537	Robert Paris S31287			Edmund Paine S3624						William Maclean, M. D., unk
107	John Story W1507	Ensign Jarres Phillips			Henry Parks S31898						Charles Mattocks [Capt. John Mattocks]
108	John Sutherland S39098[23]	Martin Pruitt, Jr. S32455			John Parmly S30637						Capt. John Mattocks [Lincoln NC—JM] (killed)
109	Lt. Josiah Tanner W9503	William Purselly R8523			James Patterson W10861						Lt. Col. James McCall[24]
110	Burwell Thompson S3801	Abraham Reed S4052			Capt. Joseph Phillips						James McCallon S2779 [York Co., SC—TS/JW]
111	Capt. John Thompson	Ensign John Reid W26946			William Profitt R8499						Abraham McCorkel [SC unk]
112	Stephen Thompson S1595	John Rhea			Joseph Reed W1484						Francis McCorkle [Rowan Co., NC—JM]
113	William Thompson W1001	Amos Richardson			Elisha Reynolds W4060						John McCullough S32404 [Mecklenburg Co., NC—JM]
114	Golden Tinsley S18246	Capt. Bethuel Riggs S17046			William Ridley S41980						John McCutchen [prisoner of the Tories at KM]
115	Abraham Toney R10642	Lt. William Russell			James Roberts W4063						Henry McDaniel R6678 [Bedford Va –WC]
116	William Tramell W6312	John Scott S32509			John Rose W18824						John McFatrick W9556 [Edgefield SC—TS/JW]
117	Jacob Van Hook S9509	Samuel Scott R9307			Thomas Scott W5997						John McGuire R6728 [Spartanburg SC—TS/JW]
118	Benjamin Warford W8977	Benjamin Sharp S17086			Joseph Seamons S3909						Joseph McKenzie [SC unk]
119	George Watkins	John Skeggs			Capt. James Cheppard						Lt. Col. Charles McLean [Tryon Co., NC—JM]

Appendix 13

	James Williams	William Campbell	William Chronicle	(James McCall) Elijah Clarke[1]	Benjamin Cleveland	Joseph McDowell	John Sevier W6011 (widow)	Isaac Shelby	Thomas Sumter[2] (Hawthorn/Lacey)	Joseph Winston	Unidentified[3]
120	Davis Whelchel R11388	Edward Smith W9301			Richard Shipp R9515						Ephraim McLean [Tryon Co., NC—JM]
121	Francis Whelchel, Jr. R11300	Jonas Smith S7565			Thomas Shipp S7487						Redmon McMahan R6785 [Craven Dist. SC—TS/JW]
122	Francis Whelchel, Sr.	James Snodgrass			Edmund Simpson S21974						David Miller [Tryon Co., NC—JM]
123	John Whelchel W6498	William Snodgrass S[no number]			Daniel Siske						Capt. James Miller [Col. Hampton—BC]
124	William Whelchel	James Stagel R10208			John Spelts S14548						Robert Miller W5376 [Chester SC—TS/JW]
125	Gillam Wilbanks	Joseph Starnes W7600			John Stonecypher S16539						John Moore W4035 [York SC—TS/JW]
126	William Wilbanks R11508	Nicholas Starnes W26445			George Thomason S7712						Thomas Moore S1858 [Granville, NC—JW]
127	Capt. Daniel Williams (son of James Williams)	William Sulcer W9687			John Tilley W4832						Peter Morris [Burke Co., NC—JM]
128	Joseph Williams (son of James Williams)	Thomas Toms			Ishmael Titus R10623						John Neill R7578 [Rowan Co., NC—JM]
129	Nathan Williford S32066	James Vance S7782			Lt. Richard Vernon (killed)						William Newton R7636 [Tryon Co., NC—JM]
130	Maj. Thomas Young S10309	Samuel Vance S1882			John Vickers R10938						William Nolen S30623 [Fairfield Dist., SC—TS/JW][25]
131	Capt. William Young W10008	James Weir R11287			Isaac Walker S3446						Benjamin O'Bannon S31886 [Mecklenburg Co., NC—?]
132		Benjamin White			Samuel Wallace R11071						Thomas Oliver [Culpepper Co., Va—WC]

	James Williams	William Campbell	William Chronicle	(James McCall) Elijah Clarke[1]	Benjamin Cleveland	Joseph McDowell	John Sevier W6011 (widow)	Isaac Shelby	Thomas Sumter[2] (Hawthorn/ Lacey)	Joseph Winston	Unidentified[3]
133		Lt. Matthew Willoughby			William Walton, Sr.						George Oxer R7851 [unk Va.,—WC]
134		Ensign William Willoughby			George Wheatley W9886						Arthur Patterson, Jr. [prisoner of Tories at KM]
135		Joseph Wilson			John Wilson W2391						Arthur Patterson, Sr. (reported to have been killed at KM) [prisoner of Tories at KM]
136		Jonathan Wood			Lt. David Witherspoon						John Patterson S17626 [Lincoln Co., NC—JM]
137		William Wossom S18670			John Witherspoon S3610						Thomas Patterson [prisoner of Tories at KM]
138		Ambrose Yancey S46059			Lewis Wolf W4403 [Capt. Joseph Phillips]						William Patterson [prisoner of Tories at KM]
139		Samuel Young S32621									Capt. Robert Patton W4758 [Burke Co., NC—JM]

The following men also cannot be assigned as having served under a particular commander at KM and would appear in the "Unidentified" column if the table were to be extended to include them in tabular form, but to save space and paper, I have elected to simply list them. The addition of these men to the "Unidentified" column brings the total of those men to 189. These men are as follows:

Reuben Pennel W5519 [Col. Armstrong] [Surry Co., NC—BC]; **Maj. Robert Porter** R8352 [Rutherford Co., NC—JM]; **William Porter** [Rutherford C., NC—JM]; **Solomon Prewitt** W1315 [unk Va.,—WC]; **Edward Prichard** W8536 [Wake Co., NC -- ?]; **James Quinton** [unk SC—TS/JW]; **Joseph Ratchford** W3866 [York SC—TS/JW]; **William Rawls** S47905 [unk NC—JM]; **Ezekiel Reynolds** S2013 [Capt. Francis] [Surry Co., NC—BC]; **Reuben Roberts** W1492 [unk—NC] ; **Thomas Robertson** [Rutherford Co., NC—JM]; **Martin Luther Roler** [Shenandoah Va.—WC]; **Benjamin Rowan** [unk SC—TS/JW]; **Adam Runyon** R9082 [Botetourt Va.—WC]; **Philip Sailors** R9143 [Capt. Daniel McKissick] [Lincoln Co., NC—JM]; **Andrew Salisbury** S18195S [Col. Taylor] [Richland SC—TS/JW]; **Thomas Scott** R9313 [Guilford SC—TS/JW]; **Robert Shannon** R9420 [Lincoln NC—JM]; **Adam Sharp** [prisoner of the Tories at KM]; **George Shelton** S4670 [Capt. McElhanney] [Buncombe NC—JS/IS]; **Joseph Sidebottom** W8727 [Hampton Va—WC]; **Maj. Richard Singleton** [Rutherford Co., NC—JM]; **Henry Slappey** W6073 [Col. Wade Hampton] [unk SC—TS/JW]; **Benjamin Smith** S38387 [Chesterfield VA—WC]; **David Smith** W25006 [unk NC]; **John Smith** S4852 [Col. Shepherd] [Surry Co., NC—BC]; **Capt. Minor Smith** [Wilkes or Surry, NC—BC]; **Nathan Smith** R9816 [Frederick Co., Va—WC]; **David Stephenson** R10141 [unk SC]; **Peter Strozier**[26] R10279 [Wilkes Co., Ga—JS/IS or JW]; **Thomas Townsend** S31428 [Capt. Daugherty] [Henry Co., VA—WC]; **Peter Tramel** R10674 [Orange Co., NC—JW]; **Henry Trollinger**[27] W4087 [Orange Co., NC]; **John Tubb** S32560 [Camden Dist., SC—TS/JW]; **William Twitty** [Lincoln Co., NC—JM]; **John Waddle** R10978 [Augusta Co., Va—WC]; **John Wallace** S9517 [Col. Barbour] [Laurens SC—JW]; **John Wallace** W955 [York SC—TS/JW]; **John Wallace** R11064 [unk SC]; **William Walton, Jr.** S17184 [Amherst Co., Va—WC]; **Nathaniel Watson** S3454 [Surry Co., NC—BC]; **Lt. Samuel Watson** [unk SC—JW]; **William Watson** R11207 [unk Va.—WC]; **John Wear** S1781 [unk Va.—WC]; **Capt. John Weir** [Lincoln Co., NC—JM]; **Capt. Isaac White** [Lincoln Co., NC—JM]; **Capt. Joseph White** [Rowan Co., NC—JM]; **Lt. Thomas White** [Lincoln Co., NC –JM]; **Vincent White** R11445 [unk NC]; **Lt. Frederick Williams** R11603 [Guilford Co., NC—JW]

Footnotes

[1] Elijah Clarke was not at King's Mountain but a number of the men who served under him claimed to have been under the command of Joseph McDowell, Isaac Shelby and/or James Williams, all of whom had cooperated with Clarke in prior engagements. Any of Clarke's men who were at King's Mountain are most likely to have been under the

[2] Thomas Sumter was not at King's Mountain. He was in Hillsborough NC meeting with SC Governor John Rutledge. He had turned over command of his men to Col. Edward Lacey and Col. William Hill. Hill, however, was still recovering from wounds and he, in turn, has turned over command of his men to Col. James Hawthorn.

[3] I have noted in brackets the county and/or state from which the veteran is believed to have served; the commander under whom he states he served, if any; and my guess as to which commander at KM the veteran is most likely to have served under. WC=William Campbell; JS=John Sevier; IS=Isaac Shelby; JM=Joseph McDowell; and JW=James Williams.

[4] This man is unlikely to have been at KM. His application has conflicting statements in that he says he was wounded at Gates Defeat and stayed in the hospital some time recovering. The next battle he lists after making this statement is the battle of Cowan's ford. He lists KM among the battles he participated in without giving any specifics or stating under whom he served.

[5] Moss says Bean was under Elijah Clarke at KM but Clarke was not at KM (interestingly, Moss himself does not list Clarke on his roster of KM participants).

[6] This man was probably not at KM. He says he was at KM in the 2nd NC Regt. under Col. John Hampton—no such unit or commander is known to have been at KM.

[7] It is not clear why Moss listed him as a Whig at KM since he states in his PA that he fought at KM as a Loyalist. Prior to and after KM he fought as a Whig.

[8] This applicant claims to have been severely wounded at Camden (4 wounds); could he have recovered in time to have been at KM?

[9] Moss speculates that he was under JW at KM.

[10] The applicant's son applied for the pension in his own right, but there was no provision for pensions benefiting children of veterans.

[11] This man says he served under Cleveland at KM, but he also says he was in Capt. John Douglas' Company at KM and Douglas was one of James Williams' captains.

[12] He is included because he is listed by Bobby Moss, but in his own memoir, Hill says that because he was still recovering from his wounds, he gave command of his men to Hawthorn. Hill says he was with the second group of primarily foot militia that arrived after the battle was over.

[13] This applicant says he was under Campbell and Cleveland, but all the junior officers he names, i.e., Mulwee and Entrekin were under James Williams.

[14] He states that he was under the command of Col. Edward Lacey and Col. Williams at King's Mountain, and that Williams shared command of the troops there.

[15] Moss does not list Capt. Andrew Lewis as having been at KM.

[16] McCreary or McCreery is known to have served under James Williams, but he was not at KM.

[17] Moss does not list Col. George Davidson as a participant at KM.

[18] His application was accepted, but his widow's later pension application was rejected because his was improperly granted because he failed to submit admissible evidence.

[19] Moss, p.118 lists him as killed at KM.

[20] This man says he was under Lacey and Williams at KM.

[21] This man says he was under Lacey at KM but that James Williams had command.

[22] He is listed on the 1909 Monument at KM as being killed in the battle at KM, but that is very probably not correct.

[23] Although this applicant does not state explicit whom he served under at KM, he says he was a resident of Caswell County during the War. My guess is he was one of the recruits James Williams got after Musgrove's Mill. This opinion seems reasonable since McCall served under Elijah Clarke at the siege of Augusta which was not lifted until Sept. 17, 1780, when Clarke, his men and a large number of their relatives and supports retreated from Augusta toward NC seeking refuge.

[24] I do not believe McCall was at KM.

[25] This man seems unlikely to have been at the Battle of KM. He states in his application that he was in a skirmish at the cross roads near King's Mountain.

[26] James Williams purchased part of the plantation he owned in 96 District from someone of this name.

[27] This man is erroneously included in Moss' KM Roster. He says in his application he was at Shallow Ford at the time of the KM battle.

Appendix 14

Account of Property Lost at Hayes Station

Account sworn to May 22, 1783 by John Williams listing property in possession of his two brothers killed at Hayes Station

An Account of Sundry Articles Lost at Col. Hays Station Novr. 18, 1781 the property of Capn. Daniel Williams and Joseph Williams

Two Saddles and bridles 25. 0. 0
1 Rifle gun 40. 0. 0
1 pair of pistols and Holsters 16. 5. 0
3 Blankets 09.15. 0
2 Great Coats 35. 0. 0
1 pair plated spurs 3. 5. 0
2 Hatts 10. 0. 0
1 Coat Jacket and 2 pair Breeches 29. 5. 0
To 214 yds Manchaster Velvet 13. 0. 0
To 2 pair of shoe buckles. 9.15. 0
To 2 pair of ? Buckles 4.17.0
To 3 pistols 12. 2. 6
To 2 pair of Shoes 4.17. 6
To 1 pair Saddle Baggs . . . . <u>6.10. 0</u>
£239.12. 6

To [pair of] stock Buckles. 6.10.0
To 1 large glass. 20.0.0
To 2 Breeches. . . . . <u>6.10.0</u>
33.10. 0
<u>239.12. 6</u>
272.12. 6

Received the 22nd Sept 1785 full satisfaction for this acct
S/ Mary Williams
No. 669   S/ John Williams

[On reverse side of this document is the following]
Ninety Six District
John Williams made Oath before me that the Within Articles Belonged to his two Brothers that was murdered when Col. Hay's Station was taken by Wm Cunningham and his party & that to the best of his knowledge they were all taken by the Enemy & none of them ever After Got.

John Williams
Sworn the 22nd of May 1783
Levi Casey
No. 6 £276.12/6 (*sic*)

(Transcribed from the original by the author. South Carolina Archives, Columbia, SC: Series Number: S108092; Reel: 0158; Frame: 00272)

Appendix 15

Isaac Shelby's Account of his Exploits During the Revolutionary War[319]

[319] Isaac Shelby (1750-1826), a Maryland native, was appointed a colonel of the Patriot militia in Sullivan County, North Carolina in early 1780. (Sullivan, along with five other counties in what was then western North Carolina, was ceded by North Carolina to the federal government in 1788 and subsequently became the state of Tennessee when that state was formed in 1796). Along with John Sevier (1745-1815), Shelby commanded the so-called Overmountain Men in their participation in the various engagements in the western portions of Georgia and the Carolinas during the latter stages of the Revolutionary War. After the war, Shelby held a number of important political offices including serving as the first governor of Kentucky. (Sevier was the first governor of Tennessee.)

In August 1814, while serving as governor of Kentucky, Shelby wrote the following account of his involvement in the Revolutionary War. The account was written in response to a request from Col. William Hill (1741-1816), the founder of Yorkville, South Carolina and a noted Patriot militia officer who served under, and was a particular friend of, General Thomas Sumter. Col. Hill was writing his own history of the Revolution as fought in the Carolina backcountry and he solicited Shelby's input.

The original of this account, along with some of the correspondence between Shelby and Hill, is held in the Shelby & Hart Collection #659z in the General and Literary Manuscripts, Manuscripts Department, Wilson Library, University of North Carolina at Chapel Hill. The following transcription of that document was made from a photocopy of the handwritten original and consequently may contain errors of interpretation. The footnotes were added by me.

Shortly after the fall of Charlestown in May, 1780, the enemy had well over run the States of Georgia & So. Carolina and had advanced to the borders of No. Carolina—General Charles McDowell of the latter State made a requisition of Colonel Isaac Shelby & Col. John Sevier to march a body of men from the Western Waters to aid in repelling the enemy who were in considerable force under Major Ferguson—It was in the month of July of the same year Col. Shelby & Col. Sevier marched with the regiments of Sullivan & Washington Counties[320] and formed a junction¬ with General McDowell, on Broad River with which force he was able to check the advance of the Enemy Commanded by Ferguson, an officer of great experience and enterprise as a partisan who headed a force of British and Tories amounting to upwards of three thousand men.

Very shortly after this acquisition of force, General McDowell detached Col. Shelby & Lieut. Col. Elijah Clarke with six hundred men to attack and carry a British post on Thicketty garrisoned principally by Tories & commanded by Capt. Patrick Moore [321]—The American detachment consisted of six hundred men who appeared before the British garrison & instantly surrounded it on the morning of the 22nd July, 1780,[322] just at day light. Capt. William Cocke,[323] was sent in with a flag by Col Shelby to demand a surrender of the Garrison. Capt. Moore at first refused to surrender, but on being warned by Capt. Cocke of the consequences of the garrison being stormed by the Americans he surrendered although his post was made doubly strong by abbetees (*sic, abattis*) well constructed around it. Our men took one

[320] These counties later comprised part of what became the State of Tennessee.

[321] Moore was a native of Virginia of Irish decent. Settling in South Carolina, he became a Tory officer and died in 1781. Moss, *Chesney*, 140.

[322] Shelby's date for this engagement is incorrect. The attack on the old French and Indian War era Fort Anderson, later called Fort Thicketty near Thicketty Creek in modern day Cherokee County, SC, occurred on July 30, 1780. Col. Charles McDowell, Col. Andrew Hampton, and Major Charles Robertson (Col. John Sevier's second in command), along with Shelby, were the Patriot officers present at this engagement.

[323] William Cocke (1748-1828), one of the officers in Sevier's regiment.

hundred prisoners of the enemy & two hundred stand of arms that were all charged with bullets & buck shot. This surrender was a fortunate event as the place was capable of sustaining an attack from double our force of small arms.

At this time Major Ferguson, with an army of three thousand Tories & British with a small squadron of horse commanded by Major Dunlap,[324] lay encamp[ed] some miles south of Warford's Iron Works[325] in the edge of South Carolina. General McDowell detached Colonel Shelby with Lieut. Col. Clarke &. Col. Joseph McDowell [326] with seven or eight hundred horse men to reconnoiter the Enemy's camp and cut off any at his foraging parties which might fall in their way—Col. Shelby with this light party, hung upon the Enemy's lines for several days—until the morning of the 22nd of July[327] just at day light at the Cedar Springs he fell in with a re¬connoitering party from the enemy's camp of about the strength of his own party and near Warfords Iron Works, Commanded by Major Dunlap—an action severe and bloody ensued for near an hour when, the enemy's main body came up, and the Americans were obliged to give way, with the loss of near twenty men & some valuable officers.

[324] James Dunlop (?-1781), a Tory officer particularly notorious among the North and South Carolina populace as being very brutal. Dunlop led a mounted Loyalist troop who fought at Cedar Spring—Peach Orchard—Wofford's Iron Works and later at Cedar Creek, NC, where he was wounded. He was shot, left for dead and survived to be captured at Beattie's Mill and later murdered. Moss, *Chesney*, 148-150 (Moss refers to him by the name James Dunlap).

[325] Wofford's Iron Works on Lawson's Fork Creek in the Glendale section of Spartanburg County, SC, near where Glendale Road (S-42-30) crosses the creek.

[326] Joseph McDowell (1756-1801), a Patriot militia officer from North Carolina. Although Shelby indicates that Joseph McDowell commanded a unit at this engagement, other records indicate that, in addition to Shelby and Clarke, the only other unit commander present at Cedar Spring was Col. William Graham (1742-1835), a Virginia native who was appointed a colonel of militia from Tryon County, NC.

[327] Again, Shelby has confused the dates of this engagement. This engagement took place on August 8, 1780. It is sometimes referred to as the second Battle of Cedar Spring, Greene's Spring, Wofford's Iron Works, Buffington and/or the Peach Orchard. The site is located in present day Spartanburg County, South Carolina on Lawson's Fork of the Pacolet River.

Colonel Clarke was taken prisoner.[328] It was believed our men killed more than double that number of the Enemy as they brought off upwards of fifty prisoners mostly British regulars with one lieutenant and one ensign—General McDowell lay at that time 25 miles or upwards distant on the north side of Broad River at the Cherokee ford with the main army. The enemy made great efforts to regain the prisoners and continued their pursuit for several miles—often occasioned our party to form and give battle while the prisoners were hurried on ahead, by which means the Americans made good their retreat to Genl. McDowell's headquarters with all the prisoners on one of the warmest days ever felt.

General McDowell continued to maneuver on the north side of Broad River, not being in force to attempt an attack upon Ferguson camp, until the 18th of August[329] at which time he received information that five hundred Tories were encamped at Musgrove Mill on the Bank of the Enoree River.[330] Colonel Shelby & Lieut. Col. Clarke were again selected by General McDowell to head the detachment destined to cut up that party of Tories. McDowell's camp was then at Smith's ford of Broad River forty miles or upwards from the Tories encamped at Musgrove—Major Ferguson lay about half way with all his force and only two or three miles from the route our party had to travel.[331] They commenced

[328] It is doubtful that this statement is true since Col. Clarke was one of the commanders present at the Battle of Musgrove Mill which occurred on August 18, 1780. If true, Clarke effected his escape from captivity in time to be at Musgrove Mill. Some accounts do indicate that Clarke was wounded at Cedar Spring, but, if so, his injuries did not prevent his full participation at Musgrove Mill only 10 days later.

[329] Other accounts place this date in doubt. The correct date for the departure of the Patriots from Smith's Ford is probably August 17, 1780. This is based on the entry in Anthony Allaire's diary stating that an express arrived in Ferguson's camp at Winn's plantation (some 40 miles from Musgrove Mill) at 7 o'clock PM on August 19, 1780, informing Ferguson of the action at Musgrove Mill. Although possible for a rider to have covered the distance between the two locations in the time described, it seems more likely that the express was sent the day following the battle.

[330] The site of Edward Musgrove's mill is now a South Carolina state historic park located off South Carolina Highway 56 in Laurens County.

[331] Ferguson's camp was much further away than the Patriots thought. From Anthony Allaire's diary, it is known that Ferguson was camped at Winn's plantation (near present day Winnsboro, SC) some 40 miles from Musgrove Mill.

their March from Smiths ford at sun about one hour high on the evening of the 18th of August, 1780, with seven hundred picked men well mounted, amongst whom were several of the field officers of McDowell's Army who volunteered their services and they were joined by Col. Jno. Williams[332] and his followers making all together a force of between seven and eight hundred picked men—They traveled through the woods until dark, then took the road, and traveled fast all the night great part of the way in canter, never stopped even to let their horses drink, & arrived within half a mile of the enemy camp just at break of day, where they were met by a strong patrol party of the enemy, coming out to reconnoiter—a sharp fire commenced in which several of the enemy fell & they gave back to their camp; at this juncture a country man who lived in sight came up & informed Colonel Shelby that the enemy had been strongly reinforced the evening before with six hundred regular troops, from Ninety Six, the queens American regiment from New York commanded by Col. Innes—The Americans after a hard travel all night of forty miles or upwards were too much broke down to retreat, they prepared for a battle as fast as possible, by making a breast works[333] of logs and brush which they completed in half an hour, when the Enemy's whole force appeared in full view, their lines lay across the road upwards of half a mile in length, a small party under Capt. Shadrack Inman[334] had been sent on to scrimmage with the Enemy as soon as they crossed the river (for their Camp was on the south side at Musgrove plantation)—Capt. Inman had orders to give way

---

[332] Williams moved to Ninety Six District of South Carolina and took an active role as a Patriot militia in the South Carolina backcountry from the inception of the war until his death on October 8, 1780, from wounds suffered the day before at the Battle of King's Mountain. Throughout this account, Shelby erroneously refers to Williams as "John" instead of James.

[333] No other contemporary account of the battle refers to the Patriots having erected any sort of breastworks. Given the short time the Patriots would have had between the initial contact with the Tories and the firing of the first shots, it seems unlikely that any substantial breastworks could have been constructed. It is more likely that the Patriots took up positions behind trees at the top of the hill above an old Indian field which led up from the mill site.

[334] No information about him has been located.

as the enemy advanced—when they came within 70 yards of our breast works, a heavy & destructive fire commenced upon them. The action was bloody & obstinate for upwards of an hour and a half. The Enemy had gotten within a few yards of our works: at that juncture Colonel Innes who commanded the enemy was badly wounded and carried back, and every other regular officer except one Lieutenant of the British was either killed or wounded when the enemy began to give way, just at that moment also Capt. Hawsey[335] an officer of considerable distinction among the Tories was shot down near our lines while making the greatest efforts to animate his men. The Tories upon the fall of Capt. Hawsey broke in great confusion, the slaughter from thence to the Enoree River about half a mile was very great, dead men lay thick on the ground over which our men pursued the enemy—In this pursuit Capt. Inman was killed while pressing the enemy close in his rear—great merit was due to Capt. Inman for the manner in which he brought on the action—and to which the success of the day was greatly to be attributed. This action was one of the hardest ever fought in the United States with small arms. The smoke was so thick as to hide a man at the distance of twenty yards—Our men took two hundred prisoners during the action, and would have improved the victory to great advantage, their object was to be in Ninety Six[336] that night distant 25 or 30 miles and weak and defenseless. But just after the close of the action an

[335] Shelby's account (which William Hill largely copied verbatim in his *Memoirs*) is the only eyewitness account that mentions this officer. The British and Tory officers known to have been present at the battle were: Lt. Col. Alexander Innes (South Carolina Royalists), Major Thomas Fraser (South Carolina Royalists), Captain Peter Campbell (New Jersey Volunteers), Captain James Kerr (1st Battalion of DeLancey's Brigade of New York Loyalists), Captain Abraham DePeyster (Ferguson's corps), Lt. William Chew (New Jersey Volunteers), Lt. John Camp (New Jersey Volunteers), Colonel Daniel Clary (head of the local Tory militia) and Captain David Fanning (local Tory militia). According to Anthony Allaire, Innes sent an express on August 19, 1780, to Ferguson at Winn's plantation informing Ferguson

[336] There was an earthen star fort at the village of Ninety Six. At the time of the Battle of Musgrove Mill, the fort was garrisoned by the British, but possession of that fort changed hands several times during the course of the war.

express arrived from General McDowell with a letter to him from Governor Caswell informing of the defeat on the 16th of our Grand Army under General Gates near Camden. In this situation to secure a safe retreat was a most difficult task our small party broke down with fatigue two hundred British prisoners[337] in charge, upwards of forty miles advance of General McDowell who retreated immediately and dispersed upon the receipt of the news of Gates's defeat—Ferguson with 3000 men[338] almost directly in their rear. It required all the Vigilance and exertion which human nature was capable of to avoid being cut to pieces by Ferguson's light parties—it was known to Col. Shelby that he had a body of dragoons and mounted men. That would endeavor to intercept him which caused him to bear up towards the mountains. The enemy pursued as was expected fifty or sixty miles until their horses broke down and could follow no further—It is to be remarked that during the advance of upwards of forty miles and the retreat of fifty or sixty, the Americans never stopped to eat, but made use of peaches and green corn for their support. The excessive fatigue to which they were subjected for two nights and two days effectually broke down every officer on our side that their faces & eyes swelled and became bloated in appearance as scarcely to be able to see.

This action happened at the most gloomy period of the revolution just after the defeat and dispersion of the American army, and is not known in the history of the Revolution. After our party had retreated into North Carolina clear of their pursuers, Colonel Shelby crossed the mountains to his own country and left the prisoners taken in the action in the possession of Col. Clarke to carry them on to the North until they could be safely secured; he gave them up shortly after to Colonel John Williams[339] to conduct them to Hillsborough in

---

[337] Shelby's estimate of the number of prisoners taken at Musgrove Mill is too high. The report filed by James Williams contemporaneously with the battle lists 70 prisoners as having been delivered by him to Hillsborough, NC.

[338] Shelby's estimate of the size of Ferguson's Corps is greatly exaggerated. Most sources put Ferguson's Corps at roughly 1,100-1,300 men, at this time.

[339] Sic, the reference should be to Colonel James Williams.

North Carolina, at this period there was not the appearance of a Corps of Americans embodied anywhere to the Southward of Virginia—In this action the Americans loss was small compared with that of the enemy who over shot them as they lay concealed behind their breast works. The loss of Capt. Inman was much regretted, he fell gloriously fighting for his country on the 19th of August, 1780, with many other brave spirits who volunteered their services on that occasion and defeated the enemy far superior in force to their own.

The defeat of General Gates, the surprise and complete dispersion of General Sumpter & the dispersion of Genl. McDowell's Army, no appearance of an American corps existed to the Southward of Virginia, & many of the Whigs from the Carolinas and Georgia with General McDowell at their head retreated to the west side of the Allegany Mountains for refuge from a pursuing foe—It was at this gloomy period of the revolution that Colonel Shelby, Colonel Sevier, Colonel Campbell [340] and General McDowell who had fled to their country began to concert a plan for collecting a force & making a forced march to surprise Major Ferguson with his party who had advanced up to the foot of the Mountains on the East side and threatened to cross over and lay waste the Country on that side for their opposition to his Majesties' arms.

The Americans once more in pursuance of their plan which they had concerted on the Western waters began to collect on Doe River in the edge of the mountains that separates the Eastern from the Western waters about the 24th of September, 1780—at which place Colonel Shelby, Colonel Sevier & Colonel Campbell with their regiments and General McDowell with his followers rendezvoused, but previous to their march from Doe River it was discovered that a certain Crawford[341] and one or two others had deserted to the enemy—They proceeded however on their proposed route to the top of the Yellow Mountain—but here it was

---

[340] William Campbell (1745-1781), Virginia militia officer.

[341] James Crawford, who along with Samuel Chambers, deserted the Patriot forces on or about September 27, 1780. They were members of Sevier's troops. The Patriots feared that these men would betray their intentions to Ferguson.

determined in a council of officers as useless to attempt to surprise Major Ferguson, and they concluded to file off to the left—through mountains almost impassable, get in the enemy's front and act as circumstances might enable them to do—fortunately on the first day they got clear of the mountains on the east side—They fell in with Colonel Cleveland[342] an officer of great zeal in the cause of liberty, with 400 men, who had embodied in the Northern Counties of North Carolina, with a view to join any other American party that might be collected to oppose the advance of the enemy—The next day they fell in with Colonel John Williams[343] and sundry other field officers of distinction from So. Carolina, with their followers who has also advanced with a view to join any Americans collected to oppose the Enemy, having all together about four hundred men—The whole then moved on towards Gilbert Town[344] where it was expected Ferguson's Army lay—It was now discovered that the American Army thus accidentally collected without a head, was a mere confused mass, incapable of performing any great military achievement. The officers Commanding regiments assembled and determined that a Commanding officer was expedient, but the Senior officer[345] of the army was unpopular and as the campaign was a volunteer scheme it was discovered that those who had the right to command would not be chosen—It was determined to send for General Morgan,[346] or General Davidson,[347] to take the command

[342] Benjamin Cleveland (1738-1806), North Carolina militia officer.

[343] Sic, James Williams.

[344] The site of Gilbertown is located approximately three miles north of modern day Rutherfordton, NC and is marked by an historical marker. http://www.ncmarkers.com/Results.aspx?k=Search&ct=btn (viewed 9/9/12).

[345] The officer alluded to is NC Patriot militia General Charles McDowell.

[346] General Daniel Morgan (1736-1802), Continental Line officer from Virginia. Since Morgan was not promoted to the rank of brigadier general until October 30, 1780, Shelby is probably incorrect in his recollection that application was made to Morgan for appointment of a commander for the forces gathered to face Ferguson.

[347] William Lee Davidson (1745-1781), North Carolina Continental Line officer appointed as brigadier general following the capture of General Griffith Rutherford at the Battle of Camden. Davidson was killed on February 1, 1781, opposing Cornwallis' troops at the Battle of Cowan's Ford.

and General Charles McDowell proposed to undertake this mission and actually set out in pursuit of one of those Generals—During their sitting it was proposed that until General Morgan or General Davidson arrived that the officers composing that board should meet once a day & determine upon the movements of the army—this being agreed to, it was also proposed and agreed to that Col. Campbell should be appointed officer of the day to execute the plans adopted by the Commandants of regiments.

These regulations being adopted the army marched into Gilbert Town. Ferguson had left it two or three days. The Americans pursued upon his trail which appeared for some distance as if he intended to take shelter under the walls of Ninety Six—in order to move with greater velocity in their pursuit the American officers spent the whole of Thursday night in selecting their best men, best horses and guns, & by daylight on Friday morning were ready to pursue with nine hundred and ten picked men well armed and mounted on good horses—the residue about seven hundred of weak horses and foot men, were directed to follow as fast as possible—the Americans pursued hard on the Enemy's trail all day on Friday without lighting until they arrived at the Cowpens just at dusk, here they killed some cattle, stayed an hour and roasted some beef then resumed their pursuit. The night was very dark but it was discovered that Ferguson had changed his rout and that instead of Ninety Six, his object appeared to be to set in the rear of Lord Cornwallis, who lay at Charlotte, in North Carolina with the British Grand Army—& that his making this circuit was merely to gain time to collect his Tories who had been suffered to go to their homes before it was known that the Americans had collected to oppose him—At the Cowpens Colonel Williams and his men left the Army & started just after dark to go to attack six hundred Tories said to be collecting at Major Geiles's[348] but a few miles distant from that place. The Colonel was

---

[348] It is not clear to whom this refers. It may be someone named William Giles who, according to Draper in his King's Mountain treatise, was a member of James Williams' command and a resident of Union region of South Carolina.

much importuned to abandon that object but refused in the morning however just at day light on the army arriving at the Cherokee ford of Broad River, Colonel Williams with his men came up in the rear this was a welcome sight as from the sign on the enemy's trail the American army had gained ground greatly upon him and the conflict was growing to a crisis—This was Saturday morning and at sun rise it began to rain hard. The army however continued unremittingly to pursue its main object, traveled hard all day through the rain, until they got within a few miles of the enemy where he lay encamped on Kings Mountain, and where he had only arrived late the evening before—On gaining information of the position of Major Ferguson's Army, the American line of battle was formed as follows—Colonel Campbell's regiment headed by himself formed the center column to the right; Colonel Shelby's regiment commanded by himself formed the center column on the left. The right wing was composed of Colonel Sevier's regiment, Col. McDowell's regiment, Col. Winston's regiment & commanded by Col. Sevier in front. The left wing was composed by Col. Cleveland's regiment, Colonel Williams' regiment, Colonel Lacey's regiment & Colonel Brannum's[349] regiment, & headed in front by Col. Cleveland himself, in this order the American Army advanced in four lines until it arrived in sight of the Enemy's Camp on Kings Mountain at three o'clock in the afternoon of Saturday the 7th day of October, 1780. The two center columns then wheeled to the right and left formed a front, marched up and attacked the enemy, while the right and left wing were marching round. The action then became general and lasted one hour and a half. The Americans had upwards of sixty killed and wounded—and they killed and took of the Enemy eleven hundred and five—three hundred and seventy five of them were left weltering in their Gore upon Kings Mountain among the latter Major Ferguson himself, he fell in the close of the action—about the same time or shortly before Colonel

[349] This is evidently a reference to Col. Thomas Brandon (1741-1802), a member of James Williams' command.

Williams was mortally wounded of which he died.[350]

The American Army from this period was successful to the end of the Revolution. In November of 1781, General Marion[351] received information that 4 or 500 Hessians in Garrison at Colliton Hall near Moncks Corner, were in a state of insurrection; he detached Col. Mayam[352] of the Dragoons, Colonel Shelby and Colonel Sevier, with a party of eight hundred men to attack the post. The party was commanded by Colonel Mayam. They appeared before the British Garrison early on the 26th day of November, 1781. The Hessians had been sent to Charlestown the day before, under an apprehension of their disaffection. But the British in the Garrison amounting to one hundred and fifty surrendered at discretion under the impression that the Americans had Artillery—this post was six or eight miles below the Enemy's Grand Army at Ferguson's Swamp commanded by General Stewart.[353] The Detachment were all mounted and carried the prisoners by turns through the woods on their horses and arrived the night after about one o'clock' at General Marion's headquarters in the Swamp of the Santee River,

---

[350] Williams died on October 8, 1780, and was buried where he died. What were believed to be his remains were dug up in the early part of the 20th Century and reburied in front of the Cherokee County Administration Building in Gaffney, South Carolina. The site is marked by a memorial erected by the Daughters of the American Revolution.

[351] Francis Marion (1732-1795), "The Swamp Fox," a legendary South Carolina militia general officer. *See* fn 115 supra.

[352] Hezekiah Maham (1739-1789), South Carolina militia officer who served under Francis Marion.

[353] Alexander Stewart (1741-1794), British officer who, as a lieutenant colonel, commanded the British forces at the Battle of Eutaw Springs fought on September 8, 1781. Stewart was slightly wounded in the elbow at this engagement. At the time Shelby references, Stewart still held the rank of lieutenant colonel and he was not the commander of the British forces in Charleston. Those forces were commanded by Major General Alexander Leslie. Boatner notes that Leslie's rank at this time was uncertain. Clinton had evidently promoted him to what Boatner refers to as the 'local rank' of lieutenant general since he refers to him by that rank in correspondence as early as September 1781, but Lord Germain refers to him in his correspondence to Clinton as a brigadier general in a letter dated January 1781. Leslie is listed as a regular army major general on the official War-Office publication, *A List of all the Officers of the Army...1780.* Boatner, *Encyclopedia,* 618.

at the distance of near fifty miles from where the British surrendered.[354]

General Stewart sent a strong detachment, to regain the prisoners but could not come up with them.

The Enemy's whole army retreated to Charlestown two days after the reduction of the post at Colliton Hall and never came out again during the Revolution.

Appendix 16
William Hill's Memoir

For near 30 years, I have been waiting with hopes that some person fitly qualified both in abilities and knowledge of facts, would have undertaken to rectify some great mistakes, which have been made by the historians who have wrote on the revolution in So-Ca-. Charity will oblige me to suppose that the misrepresentations that have been made was owing to correct information being wanted, and not by design; but whatever was the cause, the fact is that great misrepresentations have been made and one in particular of the action of Kings Mountain in this State, and as the result of that battle, was one grand link in the great chain of Providence & events that broke the plans of the enemy, to hold the Southern states as British provinces, it ought to be handed down to posterity, and more especially as we are now engaged in war, to support our independence—it

---

[354] No reported battle corresponding to Shelby's description of this engagement has been located. The closest found is the following description given by the National Park Service:

> December 1, 1781: Encounter at Dorchester, South Carolina. After the Battle of Eutaw Springs, Nathanael Greene departed the area. British forces are now commanded by Major John Doyle who takes over from a wounded Alexander Stewart. Greene launches an assault at Dorchester located 15 miles northwest of Charleston and defended by 850 men. The British fail to realize that Greene has only 400 men under his command and hastily retreat to Charleston after destroying what they are unable to carry with them. British forces are so concerned about a Patriot attack upon the city that they take the extraordinary step of arming black slaves.

http://www.nps.gov/revwar/revolution_day_by_day/1781_bottom.html (viewed 9/12/12).

is the design of the author to rectify the mistakes that have unhappily been made: and I do declare to the readers, that it is not from any peculiar motive or design of the author to be known as a historian (as I am conscious I am not qualified for the task)—I can relate facts (which I know of my own certain knowledge) in the naked dress of truth—and it hath so happened that there is not now alive any other person, that can write so fully of so many facts as I can—and as no other has undertaken the task, that hath the same knowledge, I have with reluctance taken it upon myself—In the reading of both military & Civil, or Legislative transactions the designing eye (and more especially these who are yet alive that had any agency in the transactions) will see that there was a Providence that overruled the actions of men, who brought forth means to carry forth the great work—It will be seen that Genl. Sumter who had the merit of first, genl. officer, that made any opposition to the enemy after the fall of Charleston, they having overrun the Country; and all So. Ca. had submitted to their power except the new acquisition, now York district,—that Genl. Sumter was prevented from being with the party at Kings Mountain, and having then the chief command, that he was necessarily absent by reason of the treacherous conduct of an officer, that is the only one of So. Co. that is named by the historians, and at the same time the only officers that was instrumental to bring about that great event, is not mentioned—and altho' it is disagreeable to state facts that may hurt the character of the dead or wound the feelings of the living yet it is the duty of the Historian:—and the duty of the living, if their friends acted improperly, is for them not to follow their example— That the present generation may copy after the laudable example of their forefathers and make use of all the means which God & nature hath given them:—and to hold that independence purchased so dearly by their fathers, and have a proper trust in that Power who governs the affairs of nations, is the Prayer and wish of the author —

(Signed) Wm. Hill

Feby. 1815—

Shortly after the fall of Charleston which happened the 12th- of May 1780 the British had advanced above Camden to the Waxsaw & fixed a post at Rocky Mount, and Granby, on the Congarees, Orangeburg & &ᶜ. At that time all the upper division of the State was commanded by Genl. Pickens as Genl. Williamson that had the chief command previous to that time, turned a traitor to his country. & went to the enemy then in Savannah, & made his peace with them—Previous to the fall of Charleston, at that time there being a considerable quantity of arms & ammunition deposited at a fort in Ninety Six District, the British commander Earl Cornwallis, commissioned a certain Capt. Parris, that commanded about 80 tories, to go ahead of his troops to take the submissions of all the Americans that was disposd. to become British subjects. to this Parriss & his small party of Tories. did Genl. Pickens submit & surrender the beforementioned fort. together with all the military stores. And likewise marched several hundred men with their arms. & surrendered to the said Parriss —— When these events came to be known, to the citizens in the new acquisition, now Yk. Dt. the two Cols. commanding that dist. namely Watson & Bratton, as it was then the custom to have two Cols. to a Regiment, they then appointed a meeting of the Regt. at a place called Bullocks creek meeting house. At this meeting, they did not encourage the men, but much the reverse, by telling them that they had hitherto done their duty. But it appeared to them that any further opposition to the British would not avail & as for their parts could have nothing more to say to them as officers but to advise each of them to do the best they could for themselves—Upon this the meeting broke up, but it was generally rumored about, that a commissioner was sent to Lord Rawdon then in the Waxaw, so it was that a man of a respectable character that had represented the District in the Genl Assembly (did go) but whether employed by the officers or not, the author cannot say—The anxiety of the citizens to know the result of this mission was great & they met at the Iron works, at which place the person from Lord Rawdon met them & exhibited his commission from under the great seal of Lord Rawdon that he was empowered to take their submissions & give paroles & protections to all that choose to become British Subjects—he, the said commisr. took his stand & proceeded to read a proclamation of his Lordships that begun by asserting that Congress has given up the two Southern states. & would not contend further for them that as Genl. Washington's army was reduced to a small number of men. & that he, with that small army had fled to the mountains—Yr. author then stopped the commissr. from reading more of the proclamation and took the stand himself, & addressed the citizens in the following language

That he was happy to have it in his power to inform them that both the facts stated in the sd. proclamation was false and that it was in order to intimidate & deceive the citizens, so far from being a fact that Congress had come to a resolution not to give up any of the States, and that Genl. Washington was in a more prosperous way than he had been in for some time, that he had actually appointed an officer with a considerable army. and was then on their march to the relief of the Southern States, and that we had all taken an oath to defend & maintain the Independence of the state to the utmost of our power and that if we could not raise a force to meet the foe, we had one open side, we cd. keep in a body, go into No. Ca. meet our friends & return with them to recover our State—

After saying this and much more not necessary to relate, there was a visible animation in the countenances of the citizens and their former state of despondency visibly reversed, and the poor commisr. was obliged to disappear with his proclamation & protections for fear of the resentment of the audience

And here your Author wishes to remark that he by no means wishes to arrogate any thing to himself or to have it be supposed that he had or possessed more public virtue or firmness than other men who acted differently. And after these things took place the men appeared very anxious to keep in a body but they had no officers.—I then advised them to Ballot for two Colonels and they did so and it appeared their choice fell upon a young man by the name of Neel and your Author we then proceeded to further arrangements and that was for the men to choose all other of their officers to form into companies &c—we then formed a camp and erected the American Standard. And as soon as this was known there were men both of the states of Georgia and South Carolina adding daily to our numbers that we soon became a respectable body and a few days after these things happened we received information that there was a tory colonel by the name of Floyd in the western part of the District who much distressed the Inhabitants and was collecting men to go to the British post at Rocky Mount, upon this Col- Neel with all the men but about 12 or 15- that was left to keep the camp went in persuit of that party of Tories but unfortunately before he got to their settlement they had marched to Rocky Mount.—And from there a certain captain Hook with a company of Horse and about 500 Tories came to the Iron works, destroyed all the property they could not carry away. Burned the forge furnace, grist and saw mills together with all other buildings even to the negro huts, & bore away about 90 negroes all which was done before Col. Niel returned with the army to camp—About this time I was informed that Col. Sumter was then in Salisbury with a few men waiting for a reinforcement—I then wrote to him, informing him of our situation & that there was a probability of our making a handsome stand—and that we were about to form a junction with Genl. Rutherfd. in N. Cara. that we were going to attack a large body of Tories that had collected at a place called Ramsour's Mill — But so it was that a detached party of about 300 horse from Genl Ruthd. attacked the Tory camp said to be upwards of a 1000 men, killed & dispersd. the whole—and then it was that Col. Sumter met with us from So. Ca. He then got authority from the civil & military authority of that State to impress or take waggons horses, provisions of all kinds, from the enemy that was in that action—& to give a receipt to that state for the same—This being done we returned to So. Ca. & formed a camp on the East side of Catawba River at the place called Clem's Branch—from this out all our proceedings of importance, was done by a convention of the whole—a commission of captains appointed to take notice of all the property taken either from the enemy or friends. & a commissioner to supply us With provisions &c.

After we had been some time at this camp as before mentioned. in order to prepare for actual service a number of men together with yr. author. being desirous to go into their own settlements on the west side of the River, in order to get a reinforce as well as other necessaries to enable us to keep the field—shortly after we crossed the River we were informed by our friends. That Capt. Hook the same that had a few weeks before destroyed the Iron works had sent to most of the houses in the settlement. to notify the aged men, the young being in Camp, to meet him at a certain place, that he desired to make terms with them, & that he would put them in the King's peace accordingly they met him, he undertook to harrangue them, on the certainty of his majestys. reducing all the Colonies. to obedience, and he far exceeded the Assyrian Genls who we read of in ancient writ in blasphemy by saying that God almighty had become a Rebel, but if there were 20 Gods on that side, they would all be conquered, was his expression—Whilst he was employed in this impious blasphemy he had his officers & men taking all the horses fit for his purpose, so that many of the aged men had to walk many miles home afoot—This ill behaviour of the enemy made an impression on the minds of the most serious men in this little band and raised their courage under the belief that they would be made instruments in the hand of Heaven to punish this enemy for his wickedness and blasphemy— and no doubt the recent injuries that many of their families received from the said Hook and his party had an effect to stimulate this little band to a proper courage—The number of the Americans was 133, and many of them without arms Capn. Hook had about 100 horse & Col. Forguson, at this time commander of the Tory Militia, had about 300 men: they were encampd. in a Lane—a strong fence on each side—the Horse picketed in the inside of a field next to the lane, with their furniture on the officers in a mansion house in the field, in which was a number of women, which the said Hook had brought there. and at the moment the action commenced, be was then flourishing his sword over the head of these unfortunate women. & threatening them with death if they would not get their husbands & sons to come in—and marching all night, we made the attack about the break of day—The plan was to attack both ends of the Lane at the same time, but unfortunately the party sent to make the attack on the east end of the lane met with some embarrassments, by fences, brush, briars &c. that they could not get to the end of the lane until the firing commenced at the west end—The probability is that if that party had made good their march in time very few of them wd. have escaped— However Cap. Hook was killed, and also Col. Ferguson of the Tory Militia—Hook's Luitt. was wounded & died afterwards; considerable number of privates the number not known, as there were many of their carcasses found in the woods some days after— This happened about the. 10th of July 1780 at Williamsons Plantation in Yk. Dt, and it was the first check the enemy had received after the fall of Charleston; and was of greater consequence to the American cause than can be well supposed from an affair of small a magnitude—as it had the tendency to inspire the Americans with courage & fortitude & to teach them that the enemy was not invincible—And here in order to shew the present generation, what a set of unprincipled officers, with a few exceptions, their fathers had to deal with—Two very valuable young negroes, belonging to yr. author were taken by the wounded Leut. already mentioned, and were kept to wait upon him. He requested of me to grant him a guard & a waggon to take him to the post at Rocky Mount—Which request was granted to him. & while I was making arrangements to send the guard the two negroes disappeard. I then told the Liut. that I knew that they were gone to Rocky Mount. & that I sd. should expect him to send them back with the guard, he appeared to be very warm that I should have any doubt of his doing so, and said, that he would be a D—n scoundrel to keep my property, after receiving such human treatment from me—But so it was, it turned out that he shewed himself to be the person he mentioned: for the Capt. of the guard, knew the negroes, & found that he the said Liut. had them again in his service, and when he was ready to leave the place applied to him for the negroes: but he threatened him and the rest of the guard with confinement, if he would say any thing about them, & it was with a great difficulty he obtained a pass to return back to me—These two negroes have never been recovered by me by any other for me

Shortly after this, being the 13th. July 1780. Genl. Sumter made an unsuccessful attempt to reduce the British post at Rocky Mt. This was made under the impression that the Enemy was in a large framed house: the walls of which were only thin clap boards, and we supposed that our balls wd. have the desired effect by shooting through the wall. but so it was, that from the time we recd. this information until the time the attack was made the Enemy had wrought day & night and had placed small logs about a foot from the inside of the wall and rammed the cavity with clay, and under this delusion we made the attack—; but soon found that we cd. injure them no way, but by shooting, in their port-holes And here the brave Col. Neil was killed & 7 privates; upon this we were forced to retreat behind a ledge of Rocks about a hundred yds. from the house—Here the officers held a council & it was discovered that there was a large rock, and between this rock and the fort, stood a small house which might be fired by throwing fire brands over the rock, & that this house wd. communicate the fire to the house the Enemy was in and as we had the command of the water they could not possibly extinguish the flames—From this ledge of Rocks where the army lay, to the rock near the house was about 100 yds. free of any obstructions; & it is well known that when any object is going from or coming to a marksman, the marksman had near as good a chance as if the object was stationary it was then proposed by the Genl. & other officers for 2 men to endeavor to fire that small house. but the undertaking appeared so hazardous, that no two men of the army could be found to undertake it—After some considerable time was spent, yr. author proposed that if any other man wd. go with him he wd.: make the attempt, at length a young man, brother to the Johnsons now living in Fairfield Dt. proposed to undertake with me—and we had every assistance that cd. be obtained—Rich lightwood split & bound with cords to cover the most vital parts of our bodies, as well as a large bundle of the same wood to carry in our arms, being thus equiped we run the 100 yds. to the rock; Mr. Johnson was to manage the fire & yr. author was to watch the enemys sallying out of the house—but before the fire was sufficiently kindled the enemy did sally out with fixed bayonets; the same race was run again, to where the army lay, & under a heavy fire, not only from those who had sallied out, but like wise from a large number of Port holes in that end of the house—It was then proposed that the whole of our rifle-men shd. direct their fire to that space between the small & great house, which was about 15 ft.; we being equipt as before mentioned, made the 2d. attempt. & the plan already mentioned, prevented the Enemy from sallying a 2d. time We then had an opportunity of making a large fire behind the rock, & throwing fire brands on the roof of the little house & we staid until that roof was in flames. & the heat of it had caused the wall of the great house to smoke— We then concluded the work, was done, & undertook the 4th. race, which was much more hazardous than the former ones, as the Enemy during the interval, had opened a great many more port-holes in that end of the building—And here I beg leave to remark that Providence so protected us both, that neither of us lost a drop of blood, altho' locks of hair was cut from our heads and our garments riddled with balls—& Scarcily had we time to look back from behind the rock where our men lay, in hopes to see the fire progressing, but to our great mortification, when the great house was beginning to flame—as heavy a storm of rain fell, as hath fallen from that time to the present, & which extinguished the flames—We were then forced to retreat under as great mortification, as ever any number of men endured

About the 21st of July 1780, Genl. Sumter made a

successful attack on the British post at the Hanging Rock at which place were about 500 Regulars & about 800 Tories from N. Ca. commanded by Col. Bryan—Genl. Sumter had about 600 So Carolinians—Genl. Sumter's men were so short of ammunition, that when they began this attack generally, no one of them had more than 5 bullets — In the latter part of the action the arms & ammunition, which were taken from the British & Tories, who fell in the commencement of it, were turned against their associates. In this attack there was a number of men from Mecklenburg County in No. Ca. commanded by Col. Ervin; the number not known; & likewise about 80 horse commanded by Col. Davie—these men behaved well, and are entitled to equal merit with the So. Car.s.. This action commenced under many very unfavorable circumstances to the Americans, as they had to march across a water course & climb a steep cliff, being all this time under the enemys fire & could not injure them until they got around the side of their camp—But as soon as they got to their ground they instantly drove them out of their camp & pursued them a considerable distance—In the mean time the British camp being about one quarter of a mile from this Tory camp, advanced firing in platoons before the one half of the Americans cd.. be brought off from the pursuit of the Tories; these few took to trees & rocks; whilst the British were advancing firing in platoons, and they fell so fast by their unseen enemy that their officers were obliged to push them forward by their sabers—The loss of the British in the action, was great in killed & wounded—The Prince of Wales' Regiment was almost annihilated—The Tories lost & killed was considerable The Americans had about 40 killed, & two Captains and your author wounded

Here is a great _____ [text missing] from
the Battle of Camden on the 16th of Aug
was lost by Gl. Gates, & the battle
of Fishing Creek was lost by Gl Sumter
About the 12th November following Major Weymis was sent by Earl Cornwallis to surprise Genl. Sumter who was

encamped near Broad River—The detachment by Weymis consisted of dragoons & infantry, the whole about three times the number that were with Genl. Sumter —The attack was made in the night when most of the men were asleep; and two of the dragoons entered the Genls. markey, while he made his escape out of the back of the markey & got under the bank of the River—The Americans retreated in the dark to a commanding ground, (within Shot of their fires) where they waited until the enemy collected in great numbers around their fires, & began to plunder, not supposing that they would meet with any interruption, & while they were in this position around the fires, the Americans, having the advantage of the light, poured on them such a fire that they killed & wounded a great many—they then made a very rapid retreat & were pursued by the Americans some distance— Major Weymis wounded & taken prisoner, altho' he had in his pocket, the evidence of his having in cold blood hanged several of the Americans, likewise a list of a number of a number of the houses he had burned on Black River

On the 20th—of the same month a battle was fought—at Blackstocks on Tiger River, and here let me remark that there was no battle fought during the revolutionary war where was so much disparity between the two different combatants. The number of Americans did not exceed 600 and many of that number very indifferently armed. Col Tarlton who made this attack on Genl Sumter had 1200 horse and Infantry together with a field piece. The Americans were encamped on the bank of Tiger River. There were a number of houses between the River and a large open field from the American Camp, about a quarter of a mile there was a very large and strong fence not made with common rails but with small trees notched one on the other. On the west side of this Lane was a thick wood and at the mouth of this Lane was placed a strong Picket. The Americans having been pursued for 2 days and nights took this ground under the firm determination to defend it & not to retreat further—The action commenced by an attack on our Picket at the end of the Lane, they having the advantage of this strong fence above mentioned. They kept the Cavalry from entering the Lane the number in the houses mentioned joining the clear field kept the Infantry from advancing and those men from the houses were still dropping some of them though at the distance of 200 yards. The enemy being thus kept back gave time for as many men who had horses and accoutrements fit for action to advance to the West side of the Lane through the thick wood these men were headed by Col. Lacy, he very judiciously advanced within fire of them undiscovered, as they were then on horse back near the end of the Lane, he then gave them a fire so well directed that upwards of 20 of them fell from their horses as well as a number of their horses killed, the woods being so thick that the regular horse dare not penetrate it—and a number of the men dismounted occasionally crept up so as to kill many of them in their ranks—the action commenced at one o'clock and neither horse nor foot advanced to our camp between the Lane & the River until the going down of the Sun their horse then advanced in the Lane to attack our body of reserve that stood between the Lane & the River where the charge was made by their horse The Americans having the advantage of the before mentioned fence together with the thick wood just by the fence that before they got through the Lane their front both men & horse fell so fast that the way was nearly stopt up—a retreat was then ordered which was a pleasing sight for the Americans to behold—so many falling either by wounds or stumbling over the dead horses or men. They were pursued by the Americans with loud shouts of victory—at the time this happened to the horse the Infantry advanced to the houses before mentioned and there they received such a heavy fire from those in the houses as well as from a number of the reserve that had got round to that quarter they then made their retreat in as great confusion as the horse—and were pursued a considerable way and many of them suffered in their retreat.

The British had three officers killed *(viz)* Majr Money—Lieuts—Gibson & Cope their loss of privates very considerable the number not exactly known but supposed not short of 100—The Americans had but two killed

General Sumter severely wounded which for several months interrupted his gallant Enterprise in behalf of the State, his zeal and activity in animating the American Militia when they were discouraged by repeated defeats and the bravery & good conduct he displayed in sundry attacks on the British Detachments procured him the applause of his countrymen & the thanks of congress—And here I must break through the order of time by relating some circumstances that happened some months before the battle at Kings Mountain by which the reader will see the reason why Genl-Sumter was not at that action & likewise the reason why the chief command devolved on another—He will likewise see that the Historians who have heretofore written on that brilliant action have been very badly informed. In there omitting the names of the Officers that deserved the greatest merit & was instrumental by the aid of Providence to bring about that memorable event. & likewise giving merit to those that had laid a wicked & treacherous plan to prevent it, which they had nearly accomplished A short time after Genl. Sumter had formed his camp in South Carolina as before mentioned, a Colonel Williams of ninety six District with a few of his friends. or neighbours had been Northwardly securing some of the most valuable property—came to camp & being better acquainted with your Author than any other officer, he informed me that as he had no men he could not expect any command, but that he wished to do something to serve his country—I Informed him that a person was wanted to act as commisary to supply the army with provisions— Upon this I informed Genl Sumter—a convention was immediately called & a commission made out & given to the said Williams to act as commisary to supply the Army— And under his command was put a Majr Miles with 25 men & Horses—together with 4 wagons & teams, he continued to act in this capacity for some time & until after the battle at the hanging rock when our camp was at a place called Cane Creek, and on a certain morning it was discovered that our commisary & a col Brannon had eloped & had taken a great number of the public horses a considerable quantity

of provisions with the camp equipage & a number of men—
Upon this Genl. Sumter sent Col Lacy with a small guard after
them with a view at least to recover the public property—he
overtook them encamped on the west side of the Cattawba
River & finding their number too great for him to do any
thing by coercive measures he then got the said Williams to
walk with him out of the camp, he then presented a pistol to
his breast & informed him that if he made any noise to call
for assistance he was then a dead man, & after exposturating
with him on the baseness of his conduct he the said Williams
gave his word of honor that he would take back all the public
property & as many of the men as he could persuade to go
back—Upon this Col Lacy not confiding in his word exacted
an oath to the same purpose.

But so it was that neither the one or the other had the
desired effect, as he took the public property & the men to a
place called the Cherokee ford where there were a number
of North Carolinians encamped commanded by Maj
McDowel—Shortly after they were joined by Col Clark & Col
Shellby—this army made an attack on a British post at
Muskgrove's mill South Carolina this post was reduced & a
number of British prisoners taken. Shortly after this news of
Genl-Gates' defeat near Camden induced Col Clark & Col
Shelby to retreat to the Mountains leaving the prisoners in
the hands of the said Williams to take on to Hillsborough
which he did, who arrogated the whole honour to himself of
commanding the action in which they were captured Genl-
Gates after his defeat being at Hillsborough collecting his
men. Governor Rutledge of South Carolina also was there on
his return from Congress soliciting aid in behalf of the
Southern States—Upon his showing his prisoners to the
Governor & deceiving him by taking the whole merit to
himself as before mentioned and likewise the governor not
knowing that Genl-Sumter had the command of all the South
Carolinians then in arms in defence of their country under
this delution he gave the said Williams a General's
Commission, he had the assurance to march into Sumter's
Camp which was then on the Indian Land on the East side of

the Catawba River, he had his commission publicly read & required all the officers & men to fall under his immediate command, but much to his well deserved mortification they all to a man knowing his recent conduct in deserting his post & embezzeling the public property as before mentioned refused to have any thing to do with him or his commission & if he had not immediately left the camp he would have been stoned out of it — he then went up to the settlement in North Carolina on the Yadkin River where he engaged about 70 men—such as did not choose to do duty under their own officers by promising them that if they would go with him to South Carolina they could get as many negroes & horses as they chose to take from the Tories—This happened a short time before Earl Cornwallis took post at Charlotte North Carolina & that he the said Cornwallis detached Rawdon & Tarlton with a number of horse & foot to five times the number that Genl-Sumter had then in camp in order to surprise him but fortunately he got news of their intentions & crossed the River to the west side at Bigers' (now called Masons ferry) & there encamped. Your author then as chairman of the Convention called it together in order to deliberate on some plan respecting Genl-Sumter's commission as it was protested by Williams, but before any progress was made in the business the firing commenced across the River between our guard & Rawdon's men this soon broke up the convention & the army marched up the River & encamped that night in an uncommon thick wood, where we supposed we were safe from the horse of the enemy. In this place the convention again was called & five men chosen to go to governor Rutledge whose names were Genl-Richard Winn, Col Henry Hampton, Col Thomas, and Col Middleton, was four of those chosen the other name not recollected, these commissioners was to go to Hillsborough to the governor and Genl-Sumter was not to make his appearance until the business was decided—the command of the troops then devolved on Col Lacy & your Author—We then marched up the River & crossed it at the Tuckasegee ford our Intention being to form a junction with Genl-

Davidson the same that was killed when the British crossed the River at Cowan's ford after sending an express to the said Davidson of our intentions he informed us that there was a considerable number of men from the west as well as from the East side of the mountain—Marching with an intention to fight Col Ferguson & upon receiving this information we again crossed the River at Baty's ford, the evening after crossing the River. Williams & Brannon with their men engaged in the manner already mentioned came into our camp & Williams with an air of authority read his commission & required us to submit to his authority, your Author then informed him that there was not an officer or man in the whole army that would submit to his command as his recent conduct was such that no officer or sett of men would submit to such an officer & that we had sent commissioners to governor Rutledge that would soon return with full proof of the baseness of his conduct—upon this for fear of being worse treated by our men he thought fit to make good his retreat & formed his camp at a distance from ours—the night following I had a conversation with Col Lacy stating that there was a probability of our having to fight a superior force in a short time—though notwithstanding Williams' number was but small we would endeavour to bring them in to an action as it was probable by this measure that some of them would meet a fate they so well merited—Col Lacy approving my sentiments if any way could be devised without paying respect to Williams' commission. I then proposed as Cols Grimes & Hamright had that day joined us with a small party of North Carolinians, we would suppose the army to be in three divisions, the North Carolinians one, Williams' & Brannon's men one, & the South Carolinians the third & that we would choose a Majr-Genl- over the whole & that all orders should be assigned by all the Officers the following morning those propositions were offered to Williams but he spurned them & intimated that by virtue of his commission he would command the whole—upon this he was told to absent himself & not attempt to march with us or the North Carolinians, as the consequences would be serious, he then agreed to the proposition, accordingly we elected the officer that was to act as before mentioned, that day our spies came in & informed us that the mountain men were marching in a valley between a large & smaller Mountain—The next day in the morning an old gentleman well known to many of us to be a man of veracity gave us the following information—that he had been some days with Col Ferguson & that he had the address to make him believe that he was a great friend to the Royal cause that Ferguson the evening before had sent an express to Cornwallis then camped in Charlotte Noth- Cana- that he had pitched his camp on the top of a mountain & that he was so well pleased with the goodness of his position as well as the courage & skill of his men, that he had been training for some time with great success & that he defied God Almighty & all the rebels that could be collected to drive him from that camp—However as he had nearly compleated the business of collecting & training all the friends to the Royal government that could be collected in that part of the country, & that he could then add to the Royal army upwards of 1000 men but as he had to march upwards of 40 miles through a D—rebel settlement though he was not afraid of any serious loss happening in his forming the junction with his Lordship—but as the Rebels were such Dam—d cowardly rascals that they would ambuscade him & he would not have it in his power to retaliate for those reasons he requested his Lordship to send Tarlton with his horse & Infantry to escort him to his Lordship—But strange to relate, that the very same day on the morning of which we had this information, your author missed Williams & Brannon out of the line of march & being informed that they had taken a pathway that led to the mountain—Nothing more was heard of them until evening after sunset—your Author being on the water we then discovered them coming to the camp—he then enquired of them which way they had been as they had not been with the army the greater part of the day—They appeared unwilling to give the Information I desired however upon insisting further Williams replied that they had been with the mountain men & that they were a set of fine men &

well armed, upon being questioned where we were to form a junction with them, the answer was at Lawsons fork at the old Iron works, I then remarked that would be marching directly from Ferguson & that undoubtedly the design of these men was to fight Ferguson, that he had sent to Cornwallis at Charlotte for Tarleton with his horse and infantry and that this reinforcement might be expected in a day or two which would enable him to form a junction with the grand Army and that if this battle was not fought before the reinforcement came the certain probability was that it never would be fought—and that he was now in So Ca. & had been a bitter & cruel enemy, that it appeared as if Heaven had sent those men from the mountains to punish so great & cruel Enemy; & he the said Williams, appeared by these remarks to be for some moments embarrassed, but when he came to his speech, he acknowledged, that He had made use of deception to get them to go to Ninety Six —I inquired of him if they had any cannon with them—his answer was in the negative. & added that such men with their Rifles would soon reduce that Post—I then used the freedom to tell him that I plainly saw his design was to get that Army in his own settlement as well as to get some of his property (and plunder the Tories) from thence. In the course of the conversation he said with a considerable degree of warmth, that the No. Cans. might fight Ferguson or let it alone, & that our business was to fight for our own country—I then informed him that notwithstanding he had used such unwarrantable means to avoid an action that I hoped under Providence that I would prevent his design—I then left him & informed Col. Lacey what Williams had done, that to use the huntsman's phrase he had put our friends on the wrong scent, & that if they did not get better information before the next day, that Forguson would undoubtedly escape—As I was unable to ride without my arm in a sling, being not recovered from the wound I recd. at the Hanging Rock, I immediately procured a pilot, gave him my own horse he being better to travel in the night than his, he started with this pilot about 8 o'clock — & in crossing the spur of the mountain they lost the path, and he

Col. Lacey was so suspicious that he was taking him to the enemy, which was so very strong that he cocked his gun twice to kill him; but Providence prevented it. They then found their way & got to the camp of the mountain men before day—he Lacy then enquired of the officers if two men the day preceeding from So. Ca. had not visited them—they answered him in the affirmative—& further said that they had informed them that Forgsn had gone to Ninety Six, & that they the mountaineers were to form a junction with the So. Cas at Lawsons fork, at the old iron works. the evening following—Col. Lacey then gave our friends information that Forguson was encamped on Kings Mn. & that he had sent to Earl Cornwallis for the reinforcement as already mentioned, & he Col Lacy with the Officers of the mountain men agreed to march to a place called the Cowpens where the So- Carolinians were to form a junction with them—And here let me remark that when the officers found themselves thus deceived by Williams in the manner already mentioned they expressed the Highest degree of Indignation, as they had come so far with an intention to fight Ferguson & that they were so near being prevented of their intention by this supposed friend—The next morning before Col Lacy returned to Camp there was a likelyhood of there being a mutiny in the army for Col Williams went the rounds & ordered the Officers & men to march his way. Your author went the same rounds & informed those Officers & men of his wicked designs & requested them to wait Col Lacy' return, as until then we did not know where we were to form a junction with our friends. In this state of business my Officers & men appeared determined to bide by my advice & directions, & thus began to threaten the others, & I at this stage of the business had the presence of mind to parade the army in such a position as more fully to inform them of the base & injudicious design of Williams, & that it was very impolitic to march into So- Carolina leaving the enemy behind, & load themselves with plunder, & that Ferguson without doubt was a man of military talents & that he would embrace such a favorable opportunity to attack them on their return, & that the greatest part of the Tories with him were well acquainted with every gap of the mountain, every ford of the rivers or creeks, & many of them would lose their lives or plunder. After mentioning, these things & much more to work on their patriotism or fears I made the following proclamation—

All of you that love your Country & wish to fight for your country, your friends & posterity, & not to plunder your country in a day of distress, you will parade to the right; And all you that are of a different disposition & intend to plunder—not to fight you will parade to the left—

I am happy to say that to my great surprise the greatest part of the army paraded to the right—leaving but a very small number to the left—Upon this I ordered them to repair to their camp & make preparations for a march, which would commence as soon as Col. Lacey returned which he did about 10 oclock & informed us that we were to march to a place called the Cowpens; where we were to form a junction with these mountaineers, when we took the line of march & placed our front & rear guards we discovered that Col Williams having so few men that adhered to him, that he thought it rather hazardous to March by himself but hung in our rear, he was thus obliged to keep at such a distance as required by our rear guard, who held him & his men in such unfavorable light that they were throwing stones & otherwise offronting them the whole day—We arrived at the Cowpens at about sun sett & in a few moments our friends arrived also—The Officers of each army then convened together, the proceedings that took place was to give Col Campbell a nominal command over the whole this was done in courtesy as he & his men had come the greatest distance & from over the mountains. It also being known that Col Tarlton with his reinforcement would in at least 2 days, join Col Ferguson. This induced the Officers to select 933 men & mounted them on their fleetest horses, leaving about an equal number of foot & horse in the camp, they began their march about 9 o'clock but it proved a very dark & raining night the path being small & the woods very thick, the troop got scattered

& dispersed through the woods thus wondering the whole night, that when morning appeared the rear of them was but 5 miles from the Cowpens, this caused them to march uncommonly hard which caused many of the horses to give out as but few of them were shod, a small halt was made near the mountain in which the Officers planned the manner of attack—The officers that conducted this entreprise was Cols- Campbell, Cleveland, Shelby, Lacy, Hamrite, & Hawthorne, he being my Lieutenant. myself being with the rear guard & not being well of my wounds as before mentioned; there was very little military subordination as all that was required or expected was that every Officer & man should ascend the mountain so as to surround the enemy on all quarters which was promptly executed, this being the 7th- day of October 1780 commencing at one Oclock — And here let me remark that notwithstanding Col Ferguson was a brave military character it appeared that he was infatuated & brought to his own ruin by chosing this spot of ground on which he had to fight under every disadvantage as it will appear from the following relation— (*viz*) there being a small flat of ground where he had pitched his camp on, the sides of the mountain being very Rocky & steep as well as a great number of fallen & standing trees so that the Americans could attack his camp on all quarters, & their shot went over the americans without effect, his infatuation would more fully appear when it is known that he trusted much to the bayonet, as a proof of this he had trained his men to that purpose & those which he could not furnish with this weapon he had contrived a substitute by getting the Blacksmiths to make long knives to answer this purpose with a tang put in a piece of wood to fit the calibre of the gun & a button to rest on the muzzle of the piece, In the commencement of the action he ordered a charge on the Americans, but the ground was so rough as before mentioned that they were not able to overtake the americans to injure them, in this way, & when they had went a certain distance they had orders to retreat to their camp. & then it was that the americans had every advantage required. In this manner four different charges was made & with the same success—By this time the Americans were within shot of the whole of their camp chiefly under cover of rocks & trees Col Ferguson being killed the second in command sued for peace. about this time Col Williams with his small party came up the side of the mountain, at which time a number of white handkerchiefs were seen holding up in the camp & yet a number of men not knowing the intention of this signal continued their fire & it was some time before the officers could get them to cease firing—At this moment this Col Williams was killed It is generally supposed & believed that it was done by some of the Americans, as many of them had been heard to promise on oath that they would do it when they had an opportunity which promises were made at the time the dispute took place before mentioned, so that the Historians that have hitherto written of these transactions must have had very incorrect information—as it is a fact that after the attempt to deceive Col Campbell & the other Officers he dare not appear before them neither at the council of Officers at the Cowpens nor at the other near the mountain. In this action the americans had but few killed or wounded the number not exactly ascertained—Though generally believed the few that were killed & wounded was by the Americans after they had enclosed the camp by firing across. The loss of the enemy in killed & taken was about 1200, about 100 of those was regulars. 9 of those who surrendered were hanged by their conquerors they were provoked to this by severity of the British who had lately hanged a great number of americans at Camden, Ninety six, Augusta & &— But a much better reason that each individual of them was guilty of crimes for which their lives were forfeited by the Laws of the State & one in particular had taken a number of Indians to a small fort on the frontiers & murdered a number of women & children the men being absent from the fort.

There was an action fought at Muskgroves Mill Enoree river on the 19th- of August 1780. which it appears that none of the Historians which have written on the revolution of the Southern States have noticed—It was fought by a number of brave Officers & men who had volunteered their services,

I think it proper that posterity should know something of it—I do not give the information of my own knowledge but give it from an Officer of high standing who was present at the action—Genl- McDowell continued to manœver on the North side of Broad river, not being in force to attempt an action with Ferguson until the 18th- of August 1780 at which time he received information that 500 Tories were encamped at Muskgroves mill on the bank of Enoree river —Col Shelby & Lieut Col- Clarke were selected by Genl- McDowell to head the detachment destined to cut up that party of Tories— McDowell's camp was then at smiths ford on Broad river 40 miles or upwards from the Tories Encamped at Muskgroves— Majr.. Ferguson lay about half way with all his force and only two or three miles from the route our party had to travel. They commenced their march from Smiths ford at sun about one hour high in the evening of the 18th of Augt. 1780 with 700 picked men well mounted, among whom were several of the field officers of Mc.Dowal's army who had volunteered their services. & they were joined by Col. Williams with a few of his followers the whole army amounting to between 700 & 800 men. They travelled through the woods until nearly dark then took the road, & traveled fast all the night, a great part of the way in a canter, never stopped even to let their horses drink, & arrived within ½ mile of the enemy camp just at break of day, when they were met by a strong patrole party of the enemy coming out to reconnoitre—A sharp fire commenced in which several of the enemy fell—and they gave back to their camp at this juncture, a countryman who lived in sight came up & informed Col Shelby that the enemy had been strongly reinforced the evening before with 600 regulars from Ninety Six & the Queen's American Regt. from N. York—commanded by Col. Innis. The Americans after a hard travel all night of 40 miles, or upwards were too much broke down to retreat—they prepared for action as fast as possible by making a breast work of logs and brush, which they completed in half an hour, when the enemys whole force appeared in full view, their lines lay across the road upwards of half a mile in length—a small party had been sent under

Capt. Shadrack Inman to scrimage with the enemy, as soon as they crossed the River, for their camp was on the south side of Muskgrove's plantation Capt. Inman had orders to give way as the enemy advanced When they came within 70 yards of our breastworks a heavy & destructive fire commenced on them—.

The action was bloody & obstinate for upwards of an hour & a half. The enemy had got within a few yards of our works; at that juncture Col- Innis who commanded the Enemy was badly wounded & carried back, & every other regular Officer except one Lieutenant of the British were either killed or wounded when the enemy began to give way just at that moment also Capt- Hawsey an Officer of considerable distinction among the Tories was shot down near our lines while making the greatest efforts to animate his men—The Tories upon the fall of Capt- Hawsey broke in great confusion, the slaughter from thence to the Enoree river about half a mile was very great, dead men lay thick on the ground over which our men pursued the enemy. In this pursuit Capt. Inman was killed while pressing the enemy close in his rear great merit was due to Capt- Inman for the manner in which he brought on the action & to which the success of the day was greatly to be attributed—This action was one of the hardest ever fought in the United States with small arms—the smoke was so thick as to hide a man at the distance of 20 yards—Our men took 200 prisoners during the action & could have improved the victory to great advantage—their object was to be in Ninety Six that night, distant 25 or 30 miles & weak & defenceless. But just after the close of the action an express arrived from Genl- McDowell with a letter to him from Governor Caswell, informing of the defeat on the 16th- of our grand army under Genl- Gates near Camden—In this situation to secure a safe retreat was a most difficult task—our small party broke down with fatigue, 200 British prisoners in charge upwards of 40 miles advance of Genl- McDowell who retreated immediately & dispersed upon the receipt of the news of Gates' defeat—Ferguson with 3000 men almost directly in their rear—It required all the vigilance & exertion which human nature was capable of, to avoid being cut to pieces by Ferguson's light parties—It was known to Col Shelby that he had a body of dragoons & mounted men that would endeavour to intercept them which caused him to bear up toward the mountains—the enemy pursued as was expected 50 or 60 miles until their horses broke down & could follow no further—It is to be remarked that during the advance of upwards of 40 miles, & the retreat of 50 or 60 miles, the Americans never stoped to eat but made use of peaches & green corn for their support the excessive fatigue to which they were subjected — two nights & two days effectually broke down every officer so that their faces & eyes swelled & became so bloated in appearance as scarcely to be able to see—This action happened at the most gloomy period of the revolution, just after the defeat & dispersion of. the American Army & is not known in the history of the revolution. After our party had retreated into No- Ca- clear of their pursuers Col Shelby crossed the mountains to his own country & left the prisoners taken in the action in the possession of Col Clarke to carry them on to the North until they could be safely secured he gave them up shortly afterwards to Col Williams to conduct them to Hillsborough No- Ca- at this period there was not the appearance of a corps of americans embodied any where to the Southward of Virginia—In this action the American loss was small in comparison with that of the enemy who over shot them as they lay concealed behind their breastworks—The loss of Capt- Inman was much regretted he fell gloriously fighting for his country, on the 19th- of August 1780 — with many other brave spirits who volunteered their services on that occasion & defeated an enemy far superior in force to their own—The defeat of Genl- Gates, the surprise & complete dispersion of Genl Sumter & dispersion of Genl- McDowell's army, no appearance of an american army existed to the Southward of Virginia, & many of the Whigs from the Carolinas & Georgia with Genl- McDowell at their head retreated to the west side of the Alleghany Mountains for refuge from a pursuing foe—It was at this gloomy period of the revolution that Cols

Shelby, Sevier, Campbell & Genl- McDowell who fled to their country began to concert plans for collecting a force & making a forced march to surprise Majr- Ferguson who had advanced up to the foot of the mountains on the East side & threatened to cross over & lay waste the country on that side for their opposition to his Majesty's Arms—

Although David Ramsey the historian has given a pretty full account of the affairs of South Carolina, of their first measures taken to oppose the arbitrary demands of Great Britain, yet there are a number of matters & things omitted, that may be useful to the present generation, & especially as it is probable that a number of new states will yet be formed in the great American empire—And as there is a number of the old that are looking for a reformation in their constitutions, more especially to their representative system—I have therefore thought proper to give a short history of the proceedings of the people of South Carolina in their first forming the constitution. The South Carolinians took a very determined stand to oppose the measures of Great Britain, for as soon as the Boston port bill, & the other oppressive acts of the British parliament were known to them, the people, of Charleston & its vicinity convened under the shade of a tree in the commons, & then & there they entered into several resolves to oppose the arbitrary measures of that government. & they elected & sent a delegation to the first Congress that met in Philadelphia in the years 1774-75 at the same time they formed what is called a provincial Congress & assumed all the powers of government by emmitting money or bills of credit, raising troops for the defence of the Province The Legislative power they held, but the executive was placed in what was called a council of safety & in committees in different parts—The resolutions of this Congress & the recommendations of the council of safety were generally complied with—as they had been laws enacted by all necessary power & authority. This first Congress as already mentioned was chiefly composed of citizens from the lower division of the province, but they found a very judicious plan to get all the people in the interior & upper parts of the province engaged with them, which was to deputise two very influential characters, one a clergyman the other a Lawyer, the name of the former Tennent the latter Drayton. They were to go to the interior & upper country & explain to the people the nature of the dispute between this country & Great Britain—& likewise to lay off the country into Districts as places of general musters & to hold Elections The commissioners merit much for the care & pains they took in the discharge of their commission, they had the whole of the State laid off in elective districts not by surveyors who could not be had at that time but by such natural lines as rivers, creeks, roads &c—for under the old government there was not a county or district for the whole of the province was purchased from the Ocean to the mountains. by this arrangement the three districts (Richland-Fairfield & Chester) were called the districts between Broad & Cattawba Rivers, their place of meeting at Winnsborough —the district then called the new acquisition (now York) was left by itself the other parts of the State was laid out in a similar way as most agreeable to the people—Each of the districts were to send members to the provincial Congress, but no limit as to numbers, many or few, the constitution formed by the provincials was nearly such as before under the old government—The first magistrate was stiled President & commander in chief he was to have a privy council—the general assembly was to elect out of its own body 13 members 7 of whom should be a quorum, the members were called a Legislative council these were as a house of Lords. The President or commander was to have his veto or negative on all bills — Under these arrangements the State progressed in making many defensive arrangements still looking forward with a sincere hope that a reconciliation with great Britain would be effected—For at that time there was very few if any of the citizens who had any wish for independence But when the Continental Congress declared the 13 states Independent of great Britain & recommended to the different states to form State constitutions agreeable to free & independent States, then it was this Provincial congress invited the different

Districts to send members to that convention; and it was left to the People the number to be sent—About this time the citizens of the new acquisition met & sent five men to the convention, but these men were not chosen by Ballot, as but very few of the citizens had any knowledge of that mode of proceding, but they were named by such as pleased to give their assent—A short time after they had gone to Charleston & had taken their seats, a number of the citizens came to the Iron works of the Author and expressed great disapprobation at the course which had been taken, notwithstanding they seemed to have a wish to preserve both Church & State, as one of the men sent was a ruling Elder of the church another a Dutchman, he was to take care of money matters; the other being lately from Pensylvania where the mode of choosing their Representatives was by ballot—His advice was to convene the Citizens, on a certain day & elect them by Ballot—They accordingly met & elected five other men—they immediately set out for Charleston, & were allowed their seats with the other five—This will account for the new Acquisition having 10 members for a number of years when the three districts between Broad & Catawba River had only the same number—Previous to the meeting of this convention that was to form a constitution upon the principles of Independence, the public mind was much agitated upon the grand question, whether there was to be any Religious establishment of one denomination of Christians over the other & as most of the southern provinces had been under the church of England there was fear that if any denomination had any preference over the other it would in a great measure prevent that Harmony amongst the Citizens which was necessary to oppose the measures of the British government— About this time a number of the principle citizens of Charleston had a number of memorials or petitions printed & distributed through the different parts of the State—the memorial stated the bad policy either in a Religious or political point of view in establishing any one religious denomination over another. One of these memorials was sent to the Author & he in order to get as many names as possible—(& not believing in the doctrine of the turks that women have no souls) he got the women to sign their names with the men—this memorial when presented was a novelty & matter of surprise but when the principle was properly examined it was declared to be correct—happily for the state when the business was brought forward in the Convention even those who had been brought up adherents of the established church of England voted & spoke in favour of the memorial so that there was a very small minority thus happily that business which had for a length of time filled the minds of the Citizens with fearful forebodings was settled—In this place I shall observe, that Being who created all things He who hath the hearts of the human under his control & that it was owing to His agency that this matter terminated so happily—By the constitution established by the convention, the Legislative Power was vested in a Senate & House of Representatives—The Executive power was vested in a Governor & Commander in chief. he had no Legislative power—The judiciary with the other officers were elected by the Genl. Assembly—When that part of the Constitution Which respects the Representation (was debated?) a proposition was made by one of the most influential members, that Charleston should have 30 members, in the H. of Reps. & two in the Senate The other districts in the State might choose as many as they thought proper—The proposition was agreed to by a very large majority—and the members at a given time were to give in the numbers they wished, & this was done without adopting any principle of population wealth, or any thing else—Whilst this business was pending your Author took great pains, to induce the members to send such a number as would, be a proper balance to the great number from Charleston — And amongst a number of things, the following ideas

That the 32 members from Charleston would have a great advantage over the other from their local situation, having it in their power to arrange all the plans they wished for: that in a short time we would find we lived under an aristocratical

& not a free representative government—that as we had the loaf to cut, we should take such a cut as wd. prevent the evils to be feared—

But as if some fate had attended the business, not one of them would be brought to see as I did, although numbers of them were far superior in abilities to myself—By this contracted policy, the now three districts of Richland, Fairfield & Chester were content to send one senator & 10 Representatives; the most of the upper districts adopted a similar policy, but the most of the lower districts had 6 Representatives and one Senator, until some time after the peace—No great evil was felt, but in a few years the great emigration from the other States, and the other districts remaining stationary caused the inequality to be felt—

A large tract of country was purchased of the Cherokee Indians & was soon thick settled so the inequality became in time between the upper & lower divisions of the State as 16 to one & although the defect in the constitution was evident to every impartial eye yet so is power that however improper they are not for giving it up—& so it happened—in this case for notwithstanding the most vigorous efforts every meeting of the Legislature—the system still remained for about 20 years & then it was granted [only when] until the members of the upper division came to a determination no longer to submit but to apply to the general assembly that had promised to guarantee to each State a republican form of government. About 6 years past a reform took place & now each district has one Senator & representatives in proportion to the population & the amount of taxes paid to the support of government. I now go back breaking the order of time to relate that some time after the peace took place the meeting & sitting of the Legislature was in Charleston it being in the corner of the State & a commercial city these & [other] reasons induced the Legislature to purchase a tract a land now Columbia & to build a state house but this arrangement not being fixed by the constitution a convention was called to have it fixed when this convetion [met] at Columbia there was much of what may be called parliamentary jokeying—

there was a large number of members from Charleston & its vicinity who were for keeping it in Chaton—& in order to divide the votes three places were proposed (*viz*) at the High Hills, one near Col Thompson, & one at Columbia. but the sagacity of the country members prevented the fate of the plan that was laid for [them], notwithstanding the members from Charleston & all the lower members who voted for it with the exception of a few men—yet the votes were for Columbia & only by one—this trial of strength gave encouragement for the members of Charton—to threathen its removal at a future period—this threath induced the country members to have in the constitution another clause (*viz*) that no alteration should take place but by two thirds of both the branches of the Legislature at one meeting and then after a new election by the same vote — this had the good effect to prevent any further attempt to remove the government to Charleston. But as most good things have their alloy of evil this was a great bar in the way of having the representation fixed upon a proper principle, let it be observed there is a power who governs the fate of nations as that of individuals & this power often makes use of means that may be thought by the human eye to be weak & contemptible weak instrument as I was had I acted upon the policy which other men of superior abilities did as has been already stated & had I been content with two or three representatives instead of ten & a Senator—when the votes were taken as before said that instead of one in favour there would have been five or six against it—Upon this the most probable result would have been that the great & essential benefits of having the State government permanently fixed would not have been as early by many years & most probably not before the Reform which took place about six years ago.——

23 of January 1835

This is a true copy, including corrections, of a manuscript which I received from my father written in the year 1815 by Col-Wm. Hill and which never has been out of his possession or mine since it was received from the author except in that of Mr. J. W. Brownfield who made this copy & of Thos. D. Sumter who assisted me in examining & correcting the same from the original which I this day deliver to Francis B Sumter by the desire of Col Hill son of the author to be delivered into his bands—taking a receipt therefore—

S/ Tho. Sumter

(Taken from William Hill, *Col. William Hill's Memoirs of the Revolution*, A. S. Salley, Jr., ed. (Columbia, SC: The Historical Commission of South Carolina, 1921, 2nd printing, 1958).

Appendix 17
What Did McJunkin Really Saye?

Joseph McJunkin (1755-1846) was an officer in the South Carolina Whig militia from the Snow Campaign in late 1775 until the end of the American Revolutionary War in 1783. He took an active role in a number of the skirmishes and battles that occurred in the Carolina backcountry during that war, and he left accounts of his activities and observations as a participant in those events. The exact form of the accounts he left, however, has been obscured by two publications that have been mistakenly labeled as his memoirs, when in fact they were not written by him. In this appendix, the intent is to present annotated versions of the accounts that can be reasonably relied upon as having come solely from McJunkin and which therefore constitute primary sources.

The first of the articles to be mislabeled as McJunkin's memoirs appeared under the title "REVOLUTIONARY INCIDENTS: Memoir of Joseph M'Junkin, of Union." It was published in *The Magnolia or Southern Apalachian*, January, 1843, New Series-Vol. II. No author is listed in this publication itself. A review of the correspondence between Lyman C.

Draper[355] and McJunkin's grandson-in-law, the Reverend James H. Saye[356] reveals that this article was written by J.B. O'Neall.[357] Judge O'Neall used a narrative (the "Narrative") dated July 17, 1837, that Saye took down during interviews with McJunkin. In a letter to Draper dated January 5, 1870, Saye states that the Narrative was written down by him at the request of others and that in the Narrative he recorded statements made by McJunkin. McJunkin kept the Narrative until he gave it to Saye shortly after Saye moved to South Carolina in 1840. In June 1842 O'Neall applied to Saye for a copy of the Narrative and O'Neall used it in preparing his article for *The Magnolia*. Even O'Neall's labeling of his article as a "memoir," however, should not have misled any reader of that article as to its true nature since O'Neall liberally scattered statements in it that, on their face, could not have originated with McJunkin.[358]

The second article that has been mistakenly labeled as a memoir from McJunkin was published by Saye himself in serial form in the *Watchman and Observer*, Richmond, Virginia, during the years 1847 and 1848. Saye published this article under the title "Major McJunkin or An Original Sketch of the Revolutionary History of South Carolina." Saye did not offer this as a memoir of McJunkin. In fact, in his correspondence with Draper, Saye clearly states:

---

[355] Lyman C. Draper (1815-1891) for a fifty-year period, beginning in about 1836, traveled through the central, eastern and southern parts of the United States gathering information about the Revolutionary War and frontier life in the United States during the late 1700s. The materials he collected and copied were acquired by the Wisconsin Historical Society which has made the Draper materials widely available by putting them on microfilm. Lyman C. Draper Manuscript Collection, State Historical Society of Wisconsin, Microfilm at the South Carolina Department of Archives and History, Columbia, SC (hereinafter cited as Draper, MSS)

[356] Rev. James H. Saye (1808-1892) was an ordained Presbyterian minister and the grandson-in-law of McJunkin. Saye was married to Rebecca McJunkin (1818-1904), the daughter of McJunkin's third eldest son, Abram (1787-1859) and his wife, Margaret Savage (1789-1845).

[357] Judge John Belton O'Neall (1793-1863) was a noted jurist, legislator and militia officer born in Newberry County, SC. http://law.sc.edu/memory/1964/onealljb.shtml (viewed 9/12/12)

[358] The letter from Saye to Draper is dated January 5, 1870, and appears in Draper MSS: Sumter Papers, 22VV 1-6.

Appendix 17

After the death of Major Joseph McJunkin, which occurred May 31st, 1846, I began the preparation of a sketch of his life & service. I had the original manuscript [the Narrative prepared by Saye based on his interviews with McJunkin and used by O'Neall] but it suggested many things about which I wished to inquire. I found the histories in my reach faulty & defective as regards details. I visited many of the old men of the country & took down their recollections of the main things of the revolution. [I] [w]rote some letters to friends at a distance. The result of my investigations were published in the "Watchman & Observer," Richmond, Va. in 1847 & 1848.[359]

The indefatigable Reverend Saye did in fact do a great deal of research by interviewing the living Patriots who had participated in the important battles and skirmishes that occurred in the Carolina backcountry. Saye used the insights and facts gleaned from those interviews to expand the accounts left by McJunkin into a much fuller treatment of the backcountry war than was provided by McJunkin's accounts alone.

After Saye's death, his article was republished in 1898 in the *Piedmont Headlight*, a Spartanburg newspaper, under the misleading title "The Memoirs of Major Joseph McJunkin, Revolutionary Patriot." A pamphlet edition of the newspaper version under this same title was published by A Press, Inc., in 1977[360] and is widely available today. Because of the mislabeling of Saye's articles as a "memoir," some historians have mistakenly used it, along with Judge O'Neall's article, as primary sources.

This appendix contains annotated transcriptions of the three documents that can be directly attributed to McJunkin with reasonable certainty. Those documents are as follows:

1. his pension application (the "Pension Application") taken from the National Archives;

2. an undated statement (the "Statement") copied by Draper from the original which Draper notes was in McJunkin's

[359] *Ibid.*

[360] The Saye version is also available on the Internet. Phil Norfleet has posted it at http://www.sc_tories.tripod.com/sketch_of_josephmcjunkin.htm (viewed 9/9/12)

own handwriting. As to this Statement, Draper notes that Saye supposed McJunkin wrote at the request of Professor H. J. Nott who contemplated writing a biography of McJunkin;[361] and

    3. the Narrative.[362]

Unfortunately, the only versions of the Statement and the Narrative known to exist are the transcriptions made by Draper. The whereabouts of the originals of these documents are currently unknown. It may be that the originals were among the documents that Saye's widow gave to the Rev. J. D. Bailey [363] who wrote and published biographical notes on a number of the backcountry Whig leaders of the Revolution.

    By way of explanation of the transcriptions, the following is noted:

    1. As noted above, the transcriptions of the Statement and the Narrative are from Draper's transcription of the documents found in Saye's personal files. Ideally, of course, transcripts should have been made from the originals, but since the whereabouts of those originals are currently unknown, transcripts from Draper's versions will have to do. However, from experience with the numerous transcriptions Draper made of similar documents for which the originals are available for comparison, it can be stated that Draper was a meticulous scribe of unique documents then in private or semi-private collections such as McJunkin's accounts.[364]

    2. The latter portion of the Narrative has been italicized. The italics are intended to highlight the fact that this portion of the Narrative was noted by Draper as

---

[361] Draper, *MSS:* Sumter Papers, 23VV203-212. The lead-in to this statement in the Draper Manuscripts reads as follows: "A Ms. [manuscript] Statement of Maj. McJunkin as noted in his own handwriting without date or address, but which Mr. Saye supposes was written for Prof. Nott—as he furnished him a statement—also got his Diary or Journal kept in the war." Henry Junius Nott (1797-1837) was an 1814 graduate of South Carolina College (now the University of South Carolina), editor of the South Carolina Law Reports, professor of Logic, the Elements of Criticism, & Philosophy of Languages from 1824 until his death at sea off the coast of North Carolina, and chairman of the faculty in 1834-35.

[362] Draper, *MSS:* Sumter Papers, 23VV154-203.

[363] Bailey, *Commanders at Kings Mountain,* and *Heroes.*

[364] For documents such as pension applications that were in public repositories, Draper's transcriptions were often somewhat haphazard and he tended to omit the "boilerplate" portions of such documents.

being in handwriting different from the preceding portion of the Narrative. Saye believed the italicized portion of the Narrative was in the handwriting of one of McJunkin's sons. Because the italicized portion of the Narrative is in handwriting other than Saye's and Saye could not vouchsafe its having originated with McJunkin as he could and did the portion of the Narrative in Saye's handwriting, caution should be exercised in using it as a primary resource. The provenance of the italicized portion is uncertain, although it seems likely that McJunkin dictated it to one of his sons just as he dictated the preceding portion to Saye.

3. Because each of the three documents stands alone as a primary source, each has been annotated in full. Consequently, there is much duplication of the footnotes among the three documents.

1. *McJunkin's Pension Application*[365]

State of South Carolina: Union District

On the 25th day of December 1833 personally appeared in Open Court before John I. Pratt Esqr. Judge of the Court of Ordinary for Union District Maj. Joseph McJunkin a resident of the District of Union in the Seventy ninth year of his age Since 22nd June last who first being duly Sworn according to law doth on his oath make the following declaration in order to obtain the benefit of the Act of Congress the 7th June 1832.

Saith that he entered the Service of the United States as a volunteer the first of October 1775, against the Tories and Indians as a private Soldier under the Command of Capt. Thomas Brandon in Col. Thomas'[366] Spartan Regiment and

---

[365] National Archives, Revolutionary War Pension Records, S18118.

[366] John Thomas, Sr. (1720-1811) was the commander in 1775-1776 of the Spartan Regiment of SC Whig militia. He was taken prisoner at Charleston in 1780 and held for 14 months. Moss, *SC Patriots*, 925.

known by the name of the Snow Camps.[367] Much snow fell
on the 24th of December a short time before the attack,
Governor Martin[368] of North Carolina formed a Junction
with Genl. Richardson and part of each of their forces were
in the engagement. I continued until the last of January
1776. I again on the first of May 1776 entered the Service
under Capt. Jolly[369] in Col. Thomas' Regiment In the Indian
Expedition. The Indians States being hostile on the 28th of
June 1776, Broke into the White Settlements and did great
mischief. We Buried the dead that the Indians had kill'd;
and at a place Called Princes Fort[370] We Celebrated the first
American Jubilee. We then Pursued the Indians & retook
some Prisoners; and destroyed those Towns as with the
Enemy. We then marched to the Middle Settlement Towns,
where We had another engagement at a place called the
Horse Shoe or Black hole,[371] where we defeated the Indians,
& the next day we marched for the Valley Towns, on High &
Low Wassa Rivers.[372] We there Found the army under Genl.
Rutherford about the first of October, a detachment of which
forces was Commanded by Col. Thomas Sumpter was Sent to
a place Called Frog Town where we burned & destroyed the
Indian Towns; returned to the army at Chota then took up
our march to Keowee old Towns on Torgalow [*sic,* Tugalo]

[367] Traditionally referred to as the "Snow Campaign."

[368] Alexander Martin (ca.1740- ca.1807) was elected as governor of North
Carolina twice. He served first from 1782-1784 and then again from 1789-1792. During the Revolution, he was a Continental Line officer. Charles D. Rodenbough,
Governor Alexander Martin: Biography of a North Carolina Revolutionary War Statesman
(Jefferson, NC: McFarland & Company, Inc., 2004).

[369] Joseph Jolly (ca. 1718-1788) was a captain in the militia under Col.
John Thomas in the Spartan Regiment. Moss, *SC Patriots*, p. 508. *See also* http://www.
oursouthernancestors.com/jolly-001.htm (viewed 9/1/12).

[370] Prince's Fort was erected near the property of John Prince 2 1/2miles
northeast of the present village of Fair Forest on a commanding height of land
beside Gray's Creek, a branch of the Tyger River. J. B. O. Landrum, *Colonial and
Revolutionary History of Upper South Carolina*, (Greenville, SC: Shannon & Co., 1897;
reprinted Spartanburg, SC: Reprint Company, 1959), 31, 124.

[371] O'Kelley, *Slaughter* 1: 165-167. O'Kelley states that the Battle of Black
Hole of the Coweecho River, NC, occurred on September 19, 1776.

[372] Presumably the reference to the "High Wassa" is to the Hiwassee River
in North Carolina. No reference to a river named the Lowassee has been found.

River;[373] thence to the Seneca Towns on Seneca River and was discharged the first of November 1776.

I again went into Service the first of May 1777 as a Captain under Col. Thomas and by him ordered to the Indian line and performed a Tour of four months duty at a post Called Motley's on South Packollete (sic, Pacolet) River, this Tour of duty was done in conjunction with Capt. Bullock[374] & about this time the Spartan Regiment was divided and the Regiment under the Command of Col. Thos. Brandon was called the Second Spartan Regiment to which I was attached.

I again was out under the command of Col. Thos. Brandon on a Tour of Two Months & was ordered to Stono[375] & marched as far as Bacon's Bridge[376] & was dismissed the last of June 1778.

I again in November 1778 was ordered to the time to a place Called Thomason Fort and performed another Tour of duty of four months Status as Capt. ending Feby. 1779.

Again in Nov. 1779 was ordered to Charleston & was placed at Ten Mile Spring by Gov. Rutledge under the Command of Co. Jas. Steen, and continued until Feby 1780, when we were dismissed having Served Four months as a Captain at this time.

And when Charleston fell on the 8th of May, 1780, shortly afterwards the Whigs Collected together under the Command of Col. Thos. Brandon was on the 8th or Tenth of June 1780, Surprised & defeated by the Tories.[377]

---

[373] The Tugaloo River is now part of Lake Hartwell in Georgia.

[374] This may be a reference to Capt. Zachariah Bullock who served in the militia. Moss, *SC Patriots*, p. 121.

[375] The Stono River lies south of Charleston.

[376] Bacon's Bridge was located on the upper Ashley River, just upstream from Fort Dorchester, now a state park near Summerville, SC, where SC Highway 165 crosses the Ashley River.

[377] This skirmish known as Brandon's Defeat occurred on June 8, 1780. At the time, Col. Thomas Brandon was in command of the 2nd Spartan Regiment. The Tory forces were commanded by Capt. William Cunningham. O'Kelley, *Slaughter* 2: 163-165.

The British and Tories having now over run the Country, and from this date we were what we Call Refugees not Taking protection as many did but retreated from place to place and was continually on the Alert and having retreated over the Catawba River there meeting Genl. Rutherford[378] and being determined to defend our Country, there We Elected Col. Thomas Sumpter our General he taking the Command led us to Ramsours at which I did not get up until the close of the Battle in 20 June 1780, where he defeated the Tories.[379] We then collected some Military Stores & marched again for So. Carolina & marched to Clems Branch, from there to Rocky Mount[380] and then having no heavy artillery we were repulsed & marched to Hanging Rock[381] at which place there were 400 British regulars & 1400 Tories which we attacked & defeated after marching all night when we were about 540 Strong. I then fell under the Command of Col. Williams & hearing at Smith's ford that the British & Tories were encamped at Musgrove Mill on Enoree River marched 40 miles that night & attacked the Tories as day broke and defeated them on 20th August 1780, and at the Close of this action we received Word that both Sumpter & Gates were defeated, which Caused us to abandon the Idea of Crossing the River to attack the British; having passed Ferguson's on our right we retreated towards the mountains.

Soon after this Genl. Sumpter having recovered his forces & crossing Broad River, I fell in with

---

[378] Griffith Rutherford (1731-c1800) was a NC Patriot militia commander. He played a significant role in the Cherokee War of 1776; he commanded the troops (but not himself present) that defeated the Tories at Ramsour's Mill in June 1780. He commanded a NC militia brigade at the Battle of Camden on August 16, 1780, where he was captured and held as a prisoner of war until he was exchanged in June 1781. Boatner, *Encyclopedia*, 953.

[379] Actually, Sumter was not present at Ramsour's Mill until after the battle concluded. The Whig forces there were commanded by Col. Francis Locke of the North Carolina militia. The Battle of Ramsour's Mill occurred on June 20, 1780. O'Kelley, *Slaughter* 2: 180-187.

[380] An engagement at Rocky Mount occurred on July 30, 1780. The Whigs were commanded by Col. Thomas Sumter and the Tories by Lt. Col. George Turnbull. O'Kelley, *Slaughter* 2: 211-216.

[381] The second Battle at Hanging Rock occurred on August 6, 1780. The Whigs commanded by Sumter soundly defeated the Tories commanded by Major John Carden. O'Kelley, *Slaughter* 2: 221-233.

my command under him & In November 1780, I accepted a Majors Commission; from May 1777 to this time I was a captain. We then marched to the Battle of Blackstock's & being officer of this day, was attacked by the British Col. Tarleton, who was repulsed & defeated.[382] We then retreated to York district. Then Genl. Morgan came with his forces to the Grindal Shoals on Pacolet River, where we Joined him under the Command of Col. Brandon. Soon after, I was nominated & appointed to pilot Col. Wm. Washington[383] with his Troop of horse to attack a body of Tories at Hammonds Old Store, who was defeated.[384]

At this time Genl. Pickens was encamped between Fairforest & Tyger to watch the movements of Tarleton & give information to Genl. Morgan. I was sent as an express to Gen. Morgan. Morgan then sent an Express to Col. Washington who marched to Wofford's Iron Works[385] & inform

[382] The Battle of Blackstock's Plantation occurred on November 20, 1780. As McJunkin states, the Whigs were commanded by now General Thomas Sumter and the British by Lt. Col. Banastre Tarleton. O'Kelley, *Slaughter* 2: 365-373.

[383] William Washington (1752-1810) was a Continental Line cavalry officer. He was a cousin of George Washington. Stephen E. Haller, *William Washington: Cavalryman of the Revolution*, (Bowie, MD: Heritage Books, Inc., 2001).

[384] The skirmish at Hammond's Old Store occurred on December 30, 1780. Hammond's old store was located in present day Laurens County, South Carolina. William Washington commanded the Continentals and Col. Thomas Waters of the Savannah militia commanded the Tories. O'Kelley, *Slaughter* 2: 393-394. Interestingly, Col. James Williams, who resided in the portion of Ninety Six District that later became Laurens and Newberry Counties, refers in his will to an old store located on a 150-acre tract he purchased from Col. Hammond. Is it possible that Williams' heirs owned the site on which this skirmish was fought? The skirmish continued the next day when forces detached by Washington under the command of Col. Joseph Hayes, Williams' successor as commander of the Little River Regiment of Whig militia, attacked fortifications on Williams' plantation. The Tory militia had occupied these fortifications on at least three occasions during the summer, fall and winter of 1780 and, on the day of the skirmish, they were occupied by forces commanded by Williams' old nemesis, Gen. Robert Cunningham. *See* Lee F. McGee, "...The better order of men..." Hammond's Store and Fort Williams, Southern Campaigns of the American Revolution, Vol. 2, No. 12, (December 2005), 14, online at http://www.southerncampaign.org (viewed 9/9/12).

[385] Wofford's Iron Works was located just upstream of where road S-42-30 crosses Lawson's Fork Creek in the modern-day community of Glendale, South Carolina. Phil Norfleet has posted several photographs of the area on his website as well as given a general description of the events that occurred there. http://www.angelfire.com/folk/scsites/wofford's_iron_works.htm (viewed 9/9/12).

him of Tarleton's approach & to meet him at Gentleman Thomasons. The next morning (the 19th of January 1781), Tarleton attacked Morgan at the Cowpens where Tarleton was defeated.[386] We then marched to the Island ford on Broad River. Lord Corn Waslace (sic, Cornwallis) pursuing to retake the prisoners. Morgan Marched instead to the Catawba. We then directed our Caisson for the South Yadkin & crossed both Yadkins. Morgan directed the So. Carolina troops to return and defend their own State which we done & formed a Camp near Union Court House under Col. Brandon. It was at this time Genl Sumpter was making war down at his Country & ordered Col. Brandon to meet him on the East side of Congaree River, which Brandon attempted, I being one of his Majors. We marched to Granby[387] & finding a Superior force there, Col. Brandon thought proper to retreat. We then marched to assist Col. Roebuck[388] on which Command I got my Right arm Brokin by a ball on the 3rd day of March 1781.[389] (See my vouchers now filed in the War office). While lying with my wound & having the Small pox [I] was taken prisoner on the 9th of May 1781 by a party of the Bloody Scout[390] & carried to Wofford's Iron Works & condemned to be hanged for being a rebel in fifteen minutes,

[386] The Battle of Cowpens was one of the most important battles of the Revolution. The battle was fought on January 17, 1781, between Continental and militia forces commanded by Genl. Daniel Morgan and British troops commanded by Lt. Col. Banastre Tarleton. An excellent history of this battle has been written by Babits, *Devil of a Whippin.*

[387] Following the fall of Charleston in May 1780, one of the enclaves fortified by the British was Fort Granby located in present day Cayce, SC.

[388] Benjamin Roebuck (ca. 1755-1788) was a SC militia Whig officer under Sumter. He commanded one of the units at King's Mountain. Moss, *SC Patriots,* p. 827. He had at least two brothers who fought in the Revolution and claimed pensions for their services: George Roebuck (S9467) and John Roebuck (R8917), Moss, *SC Patriots,* 825.

[389] Moss states that McJunkin was wounded at the battle at Fletcher's Mill. Moss, *SC Patriots,* 631.

[390] This was one of the nicknames of William Cunningham. Cunningham (1756-1787) was an ardent of the backcountry Tory militiamen. He and the men under his command committed some of the most egregious acts of retribution perpetrated by either side during the bloody civil war that took place in the South Carolina backcountry from May 1780 until the British evacuated Charleston in December 1782. Lambert, *SC Loyalists,* 207-209, 219. Moss, *Chesney,* 133-135.

was respited in consequence of pursuers—was carried to 96 & put in Jail with prisoners of War. I was confined until a few days before Genl. Greene[391] besieged that place; was paroled—but meeting Greene near 96 & being anxious that he should capture that place returned with him to give my assistance as far as I was able in my crippled State, after the siege was raised I returned home and as Soon as I was able from my wounds I was out again and continued until peace was made and until the British left Charleston in December 1782 & after the British did leave Charleston The Tories at repeated times committed great depredations & I was out repeatedly.

I served as a private Soldier up to May 1777 and as a Capt. Up to Nov. 1780 & from then to the Close of the War as a Major.

I do hereby relinquish every Claim to a pension or annuity, except the present and declare that my name is not on the pension Role of any State, except that of So. Carolina at the rate of $18.00/month; from the United States, & which I also relinquish on Condition that I obtain a pension by this application to the level of Capt's pay.

In answer to the Interrogatories propounded by the Court, I answer as follows:

1st The 22nd June 1755

2nd None but one left by my Father

3rd Removed to So. Carolina & resided in Union District ever since.

4th I was a Volunteer

I have set out in my declaration

I never rec'd any written discharge. I have my Captain's Commission now in possession. My Major's Commission I have lost or mislaid. My Captain Commission is by Col. John Thomas. My Major Commission was signed by Govr. John Rutledge & countersigned by Col. Ths. Brandon.

---

[391] Nathanael Greene (1742-1786) was the commander of the Southern Department of the Continental Army from December 2, 1780 when he relieved Horatio Gates of that command in Charlotte until the end of the war. Golway, *Greene*.

I Refer to the Rev'd John Jennings & Major Thomas Young[392] to prove my Character for truth & moral deportment. I also refer to Maj. Thomas Young for the proof of my Services.

Sworn to this day & year aforesaid S/ Joseph McJunkin before me.

J. I Pratt, Judge of the Court of Ordy

Mr. John Jennings a clergyman residing in Union District & Maj. Thomas Young, Resident in the same, do hereby certify that we are well acquainted with Maj. Joseph McJunkin who has Subscribed & sworn to the foregoing declaration, that we believe him to be Seventy Nine years of age that he is reputed & believed in the neighborhood where he resides to have been a Soldier of the Revolution & we concur in that Opinion.

Sworn & Subscribed

S/ John Jennings

the day & year aforesaid

S/ Thomas Young

J. I. Pratt, Judge

And the said Court does hereby declare its opinion after the investigation of the matters & after putting the interrogatories prescribed by the War department that the above named applicant was a revolutionary Soldier, and served as he States, the Court further certifies that John Jennings who has Signed the foregoing Certificate is a clergyman residing in Union District & that Majr. Thomas Young who has also Signed the same is a creditable person and entitled to every credit.

S/ J. I. Pratt, Judge

Of The Court of Ordy.

---

[392] Thomas Young (1764-1848) was a teenaged militiaman who served under Col. James Williams, Col. Thomas Brandon (his uncle), General Andrew Pickens and others. Moss, *SC Patriots*, 1021. Young wrote a memoir covering his Revolutionary War experiences. This memoir was printed in Johnson, *Traditions*. Phil Norfleet also has posted the memoir in full at http://sc_tories.tripod.com/thomas_young.htm (viewed 9/9/12).

State of South Carolina
Union District
I John Rogers Clerk of the Court hereby Certify that the foregoing contains the original proceedings of the Said Court in the matter of the application of Maj. Joseph McJunkin for a pension.

In Testimony Whereof I have hereunto set my hand & Seal of Office this 7th day of June 1834.

S/ J. Rogers Clk

State of South Carolina
Union District

I Joseph Hughs Colonel of the Thirteenth Regiment of the Militia of South Carolina do hereby Certify that Major Joseph McJunkin was wounded on the second day of March 1781 under the Command of Colonel Thomas Brandon in the Arm (which has rendered it almost useless) in defense of his Country.

Given under my hand this 18th day of February 1807.

S/ Joseph Hughes, Lt. Colo.

Increase of Pension

It is hereby certified that Maj. Joseph McJunkin formerly an officer in the United States service and who, it appears by the accompanying certificate was placed on the pension roll at the rate of twelve dollars per month, on account, as he states, of having received a wound in the right arm by a ball fracturing the candyles (?) of the humeral bone which has left the Elbow in a state of anchylosis while in the line of his duty, and in the said service, on or about the 2nd day of March in the year 1781 at a place called Fletchers Mills in the state or territory of South Carolina, is not only still disabled in consequence of the said injury, but, in our opinions is entitled to Four dollars Sixty six & two thirds more than he already receives as a pensioner, being disabled to a degree amounting to Two Thirds of a total disability.

Appendix 17

South Carolina
Union District

Personally came Dr. Saml. Otterson[393] & Dr.
E. M. Bobo before Mr. L. B. Askers, J.P., who being sworn say
the above is correct to the best of their knowledge—that the
above named Physicians are creditable. . S/Saml. Otterson
S/ Edwd. M. Bobo

South Carolina
Union District

I Richard Gantt, one of the Judges of the
Court of general Sessions and Common Pleas , being a court
of record and unlimited jurisdiction, do hereby certify that
I have been satisfied that Dr. Saml. Otterson and Dr. E. M.
Bobo who Signatures appear within are respectable in their
profession and that their certificates are entitled to credit.
Given under my hand and Seal at Union C.
H. this seventh day of March 1828.
S/ Richard Gantt, LS

Increase in Pension

It is hereby certified that Joseph McJunkin
formerly a Major in the second Spartan Regiment of Col.
Thos. Brandon, who, it appears by the accompanying
certificate, was placed on the pension roll at the rate of
Sixteen 66 2/3 dollars per month, on account, as he states,
of having received a wound in the right arm by a Ball passing
through the elbow joint & thereby producing a partial
Anchylosis while in the line of duty, and in the said service,
on or about the Second day of March in the year 1781 at a
place called now Union District in the state or territory of

[393] It is probable that Dr. Samuel Otterson was a descendant (perhaps
the son of that name born circa 1793) of Major Samuel Otterson. Major Otterson
was born April 1, 1754 in what was then Berkeley County, SC, and died September
11, 1837, in Greene County, Alabama. He enlisted as a lieutenant in the Spartan
Regiment of militia under Capt. Daniel McKee and Col. John Thomas, Sr. in June
1776. Thereafter he participated in the Cherokee Campaign of 1776. In 1780,
he served as a captain under Col. Thomas Brandon and fought at Rocky Mount,
Hanging Rock and Blackstock's Plantation. Moss, *SC Patriots*, 744.

South Carolina, is not only still disabled in consequence of the said injury, but, in our opinion, is entitled to two 8 1/3 /100 dollars more than he already receives as a pensioner, being disabled to a degree amounting to three fourths of a total disability.
S/ Joseph H. Dagan
S/ E. M. Bobo
I certify that I am acquainted with the Physicians who have signed the above certificate and they are reputable in their profession.
S/ Wm Skelton, J. P.

State of South Carolina
Union District
I John Rogers Clerk of the Court of Sessions & Common Pleas for Said District do certify that William Skelton Esq. whose Signature is Signed on the within Certificate is an acting Justice of the Peace & properly authorized to administer Oaths and his official acts as Such are entitled to full faith.
Given under my hand & Seal of Office at Union Court House this 11th Feby 1832.
S/ J. Rogers, Clk.

State of South Carolina
Union District
Personally appeared Maj. Thomas Young before me and deposeth that he was before & during the Revolution & ever since well acquainted with Maj. Joseph McJunkin, who was an active enterprising soldier that this deponent was in the Service of his Country while Maj. Joseph McJunkin held the Commissions of Capt. and that of Maj. That Said McJunkin did Serve (as this deponent believes) as Set out in his declaration as the deponent was at repeated times in Company together in the Service of their Country during the Revolutionary War and that Said McJunkin is and was during

the war a respected and fine Soldier and has the esteem of his Country Since.

S/ Thos. Young
Sworn & Subscribed before me this 8th day of Jany. 1834.
S/ J. Rogers, Clk

State of South Carolina
Union District

Personally came Meshick Chandler Before me D. Wallace a Justice of the Peace in & for the Said District who being duly sworn on his Oath declares That He knew Samuel McJunkin, the Father of Maj. Joseph McJunkin, during the Revolutionary war. That he the Said Deponent was well acquainted with the said Samuel McJunkin until the End or Termination of the said War & that he the said Samuel McJunkin never did Bear any Military commission in the Said Revolutionary War.

S/ Meshick "M" Chandler, his mark
Sworn To & Subscribed Before me at Union Ct. House the 15th July 1834.
S/ D. Wallace, J. P.

State of So. Carolina
Union District

Personally came Major Thomas Young Before me D. Wallace, a Justice of the Peace in & for the Said District, who being duly sworn on his Oath Saith. That he knew Samuel McJunkin, the Father of Major Joseph McJunkin, during the Revolutionary War. That He also knew Samuel McJunkin Jnr., the Brother of Major Joseph McJunkin during the Revolutionary War & That neither of Them ever did bear a military commission during the Said War.

This Deponent also on oath states That the present Major Joseph McJunkin did Bear first the commission of Captain & then of Major during the said Revolutionary War

& That no man by the name of Saml McJunkin did bear any military commission during the said War To the Knowledge of this deponent.

This deponent also positively swears That he Served under Major Joseph McJunkin after the fall of Charleston, & That he commanded as & held the Commission of Major in the United States Service at the Battle of Cowpens.

S/ Thomas Young

Sworn To & Subscribed Before me the 19th July 1834.

S/ D. Wallace, JP

So. Carolina
Union Dist.

Maj. Joseph McJunkin Personally appeared before me & deposeth That he was a Major in the Revolutionary war from Novr. 1780 to Decr. 1782 the time the British left Charleston at least two years—and long after until the Tories were entirely Subdued—& Claims 10 months as a private at the Commencement of the Revolutionary War. This deponent further States that his commission as Maj. under which he Served during the Revolutionary War is either lost or mislaid but the facts of the Cause is Set out in my declaration for a pension under Act of June 1832.

S/ Joseph McJunkin

Sworn to & Subscribed before me this 16th June 1834.

S/ Hiram Gibbs, Q.M.

State of South Carolina
Union District

Drury Harrington[394] came personally before me John Rogers Clerk of the Court of Sessions & Common Pleas for Said District and deposeth that he [was] well acquainted with Maj. Joseph McJunkin during the

---

[394] Drury Harrington served under Col. Thomas Brandon. Moss, *SC Patriots*, 418.

Revolutionary War & ever Since, and During his Services in the Revolutionary War he the Said Joseph McJunkin did hold the office of Major for a considerable time & I did Service under him While he held the Said office of Major. I have heard the Declaration of Maj. Joseph McJunkin Read and believe the same to Contain facts great deal of which Service I Knew of my own knowledge.

S/ Drury Harrington

Sworn to & Subscribed before me this 15th June 1834.

S/ J. Rogers, Clk.

State of So. Carolina
Union District

Personally appeared before me Sarah A. O'Keefe who being duly sworn saith that sometime during the year 1833 she saw among her father, Major Joseph McJunkin's papers a Majors Commission authorizing her father to act as Major in the Revolutionary War and that the said Commission was directed to her father granted by John Rutledge Governor of South Carolina and countersigned by Col. Thomas Brandon and that she does not recollect the date of said Commission and that it is lost or mislaid as she supposed to that it cannot be come at.

S/ Sarah A. O'Keefe

Sworn to and subscribed before me this 16th day of June 1833.

S/ Stephen Johnson, J. P.

2. McJunkin's Narrative: Draper MSS, Sumter Papers 23VV153-203

Copy of a notable dream, dreamed 3rd April 1775. I saw a great collection of people approaching much agitated, they were at a house & in the yard was a beautiful tree with many branches. A great storm arose with the appearance of the blackness of darkness and raged so that everything appeared likely to be torn to pieces. Finally, the tree was split to pieces, which greatly distressed the people, who, after the storm had abated, raised the pieces from the ground, and fastened them together again and flourished. At the same time there was this uncommon appearance. A sun arose in the West at the clearing up of the storm—the common Sun shining at the same time; but the little sun which arose in the West shone with such brilliancy as to obscure the common luminary of days.

About Sept. 1775, the Provincial Congress had some dealing with the Cherokee Indians so as to quiet them & gave them ammunition, which the Tories supposed had been given to accomplish their destruction, & they raised a party, took the ammunition from the Indians, which so exasperated them that they immediately attacked the white settlements. The Tories were headed in this enterprise by one Cunningham.

About this time the Provincial Congress appointed the Rev. Josiah [*sic*, Oliver] Hart,[395] of the Baptist

---

[395] Reverend Oliver Hart (1723-1795) was a Baptist minister originally from Pennsylvania. He came to South Carolina in 1749 in response to a call from Charleston Baptists. In 1751, he organized the first Baptist Association in the South and initiated a program for the education of Baptist ministers. He was the third member of the team appointed in 1775 by the First Council of Safety to travel into the South Carolina backcountry in an effort to win support of the residents there for the "Association" recently promulgated by the First Provincial Congress in reaction to the resolutions of the Continental Congress of 1774. The other two members of the team, William Henry Drayton and the Reverend William Tennent, both left extensive records of their mission into the backcountry. Drayton's notes detailing his involvement in the backcountry mission were published by his son in 1821 and are still available in print. John Drayton, *Memoirs of the American Revolution, From its Commencement to the Year 1776, Inclusive: As Relating to the State of South-Carolina: and Occasionally Refering to the States of North-Carolina and Georgia* (n.p.: Reprinted by Arno Press, Inc., 1969). Tennent's diary was published in 1894 in *Yearbook, City of Charleston, South Carolina* (Charleston, 1894), 295-312. Until his diary was donated by his family in 1956 to the South Caroliniana Library at the University of South Carolina, it was thought that Hart left no record of his efforts. Hart, however, was a life-long diarist and, fortunately, his record is now safely preserved. An annotated transcription of Hart's diary appears in Southern Campaigns of the American Revolution, Vol. 2, No. 4 (April 2005), 26-31, http://www.southerncampaign.org (viewed 9/9/12).

order, Rev. Wm. Tennent,[396] a Presbyterian, & John [*sic,* William Henry] Drayton, a private gentleman, to visit various parts of the State for the purpose of imparting information to the people in general as to the principles involved in the controversy, and the Evils of non-resistance.

The writer of this accompanied them through various parts of Ninety Six, now called Union, Laurens, Spartanburg, Chester, &c. They called public meetings & addressed the people principally upon the following topics: 1. the constitution of a Roman Catholic Colony in Canada by the British Government;[397] 2. The Tax on tea; 3. The Stamp Act; 4. Church rates with Bish. [Bishop] of Lecker. All without the consent of the people or allowing them the right of representation. They explained the principles upon which the rights of man are based, and made particular allusions to the circumstances which brought our forefathers to seek a home in an inhospitable wilderness, and the criminality which wd. [would] result from indecision at the present crisis. Their manner of address was calm, Christian-like & persuasive.

At this time, as is well known, the people were greatly divided in sentiment. One Col. Thomas Fletcher [Fletchall], a man of note, who resided on Fairforest Creek not far from the present site of Unionville, was strenuously opposed to the principles and measures of the Liberty party & took the most efficient plan to counteract the influence of Hart, Tennent &c., and all others who thought with them. He

---

[396] Reverend William Tennent (1740-1777) was the minister at the Circular Church in Charleston from 1772 until his death in 1777. Undoubtedly trained as a Presbyterian (his grandfather by the same name founded the "Log College" in New Jersey and that institution is considered by some as being the germ that ultimately evolved into Princeton University), the Circular Church served both Congregationalists and Presbyterians.

[397] This is probably a reference to the Quebec Act which Parliament passed in 1774, and which, among other provisions, gave Quebec control of all the North American Indian territory including the land west of the 1763 Proclamation line. This act enraged the American colonies that viewed the land west of the Proclamation line as their territory for future expansion. The Quebec Act was repealed in 1775.

picked up one Joseph Robinson,[398] a runaway from Virginia, a man of some talent, but utterly void of correct principles. This Robinson was sent by Col. Fletcher to Charleston to confer with the British Governor,[399] who gave him a parcel of pamphlets called cutters, the scope of which was to show the criminality of resisting the laws and policy of the Lord's anointed; the Evils which would result, and to offer encouragements to support the claims of royalty.

On his return Fletcher called a meeting at Dining Creek meeting house, and appointed Robinson as orator to address the people, and read one of the pamphlets. The concourse of people was so great, that the house would not hold them, and Fletcher mounted Robinson upon a stone. He read a pamphlet, and commented upon it. He alluded to the case of David and Saul in proof of his positions. He abused the Continental Congress, Geo. Washington, and the principles they adopted. He stated that when they had involved the people in inextricable Difficulties, the dammed rascals would run away to the Indians, Islands, Spaniards, &c. When these last expressions were uttered, an old gentleman, Samuel McJunkin,[400] remarked: "I wonder where Preachers Joe Robinson and Cotton will be?" This was spoken in allusion to a dishonorable affair in which Robinson had been engaged. He was overwhelmed with a sense of shame, descended abruptly from his rostrum, and went off. As he was going he was heard to say, "I would have carried my point if it had not been for that d___d old Irish Presbyterian, but he has defeated me."

[398] Major Joseph Robinson (1748-1807) was a Tory militia officer serving under Col. Thomas Fletchall. Robinson authored the so-called "counter association" approved by most of the members of Fletchall's regiment. He was the commander of the Tory militia unit that laid siege to the Fort at Ninety Six and forced the surrender of that garrison by the Whig militia under the command of then Maj. Andrew Williamson.

[399] Lord William Campbell (17??-1778) was the last of the Royal Governors of South Carolina. He took an active role in trying to foment support for the crown among backcountry Loyalists and Native Americans and was forced by the Whigs to seek refuge on board a British man of war in Charleston harbor.

[400] Joseph McJunkin's father.

In November, 1775, the Provincial Congress took measures to raise an army in Ninety Six under the command of Gen. Richardson, to quell the Tories and Indians, who were making depredations. Col. John Thomas, who resided on Fairforest Creek, in the upper part of the present congregation of the same name, received orders from Richardson to raise a regiment to aid in the Expedition. Thomas raised a regiment as required, without the necessity of drafting a man. He proceeded to Granby[401] to meet Richardson, where Richardson presently arrived. The army then proceeded to Weaver's Ferry, on the Saluda, & whilst there encamped, there came in two persons, viz. Benj. Wofford & Betty Scrugg, emissaries of Col. Fletcher, to the British Governor in Charleston, and were on their return to the Tory's camp. They appeared to be exceedingly merry, & took notice of things without seeming to do so. Some of the soldiers Knew them, and reported them to Col. Thomas, who had them arrested. The man was first searched and nothing discovered. Betty was then taken into a camp, and her outer garment, called a Joseph, taken off; the Captain succeeded in finding a bundle of papers on her person (under her shirt in a bag) which fully apprized the General of the intended movements of the Tories, & the plan of union, &c &c with the British Governor.

The army proceeded through what is now Lexington District, to Casey's on Duncan's Creek, now in Laurens District. Thence to the Big Survey & awaited a while the co-operation of Gov. Martin of N.C. Thence to Liberty Hill, Laurens District, where Gov. Martin joined us. Thence the two armies marched to a place on Rabun's Creek called Hollingsworth's Mills, where they arrived on the 24th of Dec. 1775—at which place there was a noted Snow, which gave the

[401] Fort Granby was a two-story home, storehouse and trading post, built by Kershaw & Co., in 1765 and fortified by the British as a square redoubt with bastions, a ditch, and an abatis. It was located near the Congaree River and was captured by the Patriots after a short siege on May 15, 1781. The property was later acquired by James Cayce and a replica of it serves today as the Cayce Historical Museum in Cayce, SC, although the original site has been consumed by a gravel mine.

campaign the name of the Snow Campaign.[402] The place was within 12 miles of where the Tories were said to be.

While lying at Liberty Hill, Gen. Richardson being informed of Col. Fletcher's measures to sustain his cause, Gen. Richardson sent out a party of horse to apprehend Fletcher. They found him on his own plantation, with two of his captains viz. John Mayfield,[403] and James_____ [blank appears in the original], in a hollow Sycamore. They were brought to camp, and after Examination were sent prisoners to Charleston.

On Christmas morning a party was dispatched to the Tories, 12 miles Distant. The Tories and Indians race off without making much resistance. One of our Majors was wounded. On the return of the party, the campaign broke up.

About March, 1776, Col. Fletcher by some means was released from his imprisonment in Charleston and returned to the backcountry.

A combination was entered into by the British, Tories & Indians. The Tories erected what were called passovers at their houses—viz. peeled poles with white cloths wrapped around them.

The Indians on the 28th of June, in accordance with previous arrangements commenced the work of death among the Whig families along the frontiers from North Carolina through Georgia. All who erected the flags & sat under them were passed unhurt, except in one instance—viz. Capt. James Ford, who lived on the Enoree, at a place called the Cane-brake. He and his wife were killed under their passover, and his daughters were taken captive by the Indians.

In May, a party of Whigs was encamped on Fairforest under apprehension of a rise among the Indians.

[402] McJunkin is in error in attributing command to Alexander Martin. Martin was actually under the command of Col. Thomas Polk of the Mecklenburg County, NC, Whig militia.
[403] John Mayfield (1738-1782) was a Tory militia leader. Phil Norfleet has an excellent biographical sketch on Mayfield posted at http://sc_tories.tripod.com/john_mayfield.htm. (viewed 9/9/12).

Messengers were sent to find out the intentions of the Indians. The messengers were killed by the Indians. The party encamped in the neighborhood of Col. Thomas; was under Gen. Williamson. When the Indians were found to be killing the Whites, the party turned out in pursuit; the Indians were over taken at Paris's (an Indian agent)[404] at the present site of Greenville C. H., where the Indians fled with a few Tories. A number of prisoners were re-taken, among whom were the daughters of the Capt. Ford above mentioned. The party remained a few days at Paris's & recruited; afterwards we pursued to the nearest towns on Seneca and Tugalo.[405] The result of this campaign: we had sundry battles and skirmishes in the environs of the towns—at one of which we came up with a party which had an old lady prisoner; her name was Hite.[406] She was killed by the Indians when they found they would be compelled to give way. She was left naked. Her nephew, Mr. Edward Hampton,[407] was of our party, and supposing when he first saw the body of the old lady that she was his aunt, he took off his hunting shirt, & went backwards & covered the body, & afterwards buried it with as much of decency as circumstances would admit.

After this we rendezvoused at a place called Seneca Town upon Seneca River, and some of us were permitted to go home for clothing &c. After being refitted,

[404] Captain Richard Pearis (c 1725-1794), an ardent Tory militia leader and friend of the Cherokee Indians whose house on Reedy River in South Carolina was burned by Whig militia in 1776. The Greenville, SC, landmark, "Paris Mountain," is named for him.

[405] For more on the Cherokee Campaign of 1776, *See* Southern Campaigns of the American Revolution, Vol. 2, No. 9 (September, 2005), http://www.southerncampaign.org (viewed 9/9/12).

[406] This is the widow of Jacob Hite. The killing of Hite and other members of his family along with the kidnapping of his wife and two daughters by the Cherokees was used by the Whigs to justify their attack on the Cherokees. Moss, *SC Patriots*, 408. As noted by McJunkin, Mrs. Hite was subsequently killed by the Cherokees. The fate of Hite's daughters in unknown to me.

[407] Edward Hampton, (?-1780) South Carolina militia officer who served under Genl. Andrew Williamson. Following Williamson's withdrawal from service, Hampton served as a lieutenant colonel under General Thomas Sumter. Hampton was killed at Fairforest Creek in October 1780 by William "Bloody Bill" Cunningham. Moss, *SC Patriots*, 408.

we started to the Middle Settlements on the French Broad. After passing through several towns we went by a part of the No. Carolina army, whose main body, as they supposed, had gone to attack the Indians in the Valley Towns.

On the 22nd of September, just after passing this body of soldiers, the Indians had laid an ambuscade for the main No. Carolina army,[408] as they supposed. The mountain was in the form of a horseshoe; they lay upon the heights as we marched in at what might be called the heel of the shoe, when our advance had approached near the toe, the Indians in that part commenced the attack and were immediately followed by those along the sides. At which battle were Cols. Thomas Neel,[409] of York, John Thomas, of Spartanburg, Major A. Pickens of Abbeville, Col. John Lyles[410] of Newberry. In this battle Gen. Richardson [sic, Williamson] was enraged at a fifer, and would have put him to death, although the poor man was so exhausted as to be utterly unable to obey orders. (The General from the time we left Seneca—we had two swivels which he had fired at night and in the morning, at which the Colonels were exceedingly vexed). We drove the Indians from the heights, and sometimes came to close quarters. Major Ross,[411] of York, had a hard scuffle with one Indian, &c.

Col. Sumter was also in this battle with a few regulars, conducted himself with great bravery and much credit was given him for his conduct. Some Creek Indians were found among the slain. A large quantity of parched

[408] The provinces of Virginia, South Carolina and North Carolina all sent forces against the Cherokee in a coordinated attempt to negate any threat the Indians might align with the British causing the Whigs to have to fight a two-front war, one on the coast versus the British and the other in the mountains versus the Indians. The North Carolina forces were led by NC Patriot militia General Griffith Rutherford.

[409] Thomas Neel (1730-1779) was the commanding officer of a regiment of South Carolina militia formed in the "New Acquisition" (the area acquired from North Carolina just below Charlotte). Moss, *SC Patriots,* 719.

[410] John Lisle (also spelled Liles, Lyles) was a lieutenant colonel in the militia in 1775. Moss, *SC Patriots,* 572.

[411] This is possibly a reference to Francis Ross who is known to have served as a captain under Col. Neel on the Cherokee Expedition. Moss, *SC Patriots,* 831.

corn and moccasins, and dressed deer skins, were left on the ground by the Indians.

The next day we started to the Valley Towns, Hiwassee and Lowassee. There we destroyed corn in the fields and in the cribs—considerable corn was thrown into the river and floated down and lodged in fish traps, which was afterwards found & preserved by the Indians, & saved many of their lives. (In the first towns we burnt much corn and meat, destroyed much in the roasting ear, &c.)

After staying a few days in the Hiwassee towns, we started with the expectation of meeting the North Carolina army. We crossed the Hiwassee River, and afterwards a stream called the Lowassee. On this river were towns beautifully situated. We turned up the Lowassee nearly a South course; a considerable distance up this river we met the No. Carolina army. We staid all night near this army. We then came upon the Southern waters, & found a handsome town, I think called Chota, a fenced town.

Our leaders obtained information that a party of Indians was encamped at a town called Frog Town, twenty miles from Chota. An order was given that Col. Sumter should head a party and go and beset said town; and in obedience to which he set out and passed over a fearful precipice—the pass not over fourteen inches in breadth. We found nobody at the town but a set of miserable old squaws; we returned in darkness without seeing the narrowness of our passage as when we went out.

Thence we returned to the Keowee towns on the Tugalo River. Thence to Seneca Towns. At Seneca Towns no further expedition was planned.

The army was disbanded with the requisition that the forts on the frontiers should be guarded in a certain order by the soldiers, &c. In this campaign a number of Loyalists served in our army in consequence of the treachery of the Indians in the affair of Capt. Ford. The Loyalists remained with us in our defense of the frontier until the fall of Charleston, when they registered themselves subjects of his Britannic Majesty &c.

In 1777, the Florida Expedition took place. I was not in it. In May of this year I was commissioned a Captain. I first commanded at Jamieson's fort, on South Pacolet in the neighborhood of Hogback Mountain. Served three months by order of Col. John Thomas. The rest of the year taken up in scouting in various directions.

1778—In the month of June, a party of us was commanded to go to Bacon's Bridge upon Ashley River. In a few days after our arrival orders were received to disband the army. After my return I was sent to the frontier—date not recollected. I commanded at Wood's or Thompson's Station—it bore other names. Here I continued until February 1779.

In November of the year 1779, I went to Charleston, and staid till Feb. 1780. My company was discharged, & another came and [took our place] before Charleston fell.

On June 10th 1780, Brandon's defeat took place on Fairforest by Bloody Bill Cunningham, a Tory Colonel.[412] I was not in this battle.

Before Brandon's defeat, when we heard of the fall of Charleston, a number of us collected to save a parcel of powder which had been brought down from Col. Thomas', & deposited under the care of Col. Brandon. We held a consultation what should be done with it, and we determined to hide it, which was done with some difficulty in hollow logs. Some of this powder was afterwards used in the Battle of Hanging Rock.[413] Some of those Engaged in this business were Col. Brandon, Captn. Samuel Otterson,[414]

---

[412] Brandon's Defeat occurred on June 8, 1780. At the time, Brandon was in command of the 2nd Spartan Regiment. The Tory forces were commanded by Capt. William Cunningham. O'Kelley, Slaughter 2: 163-165.

[413] The second Battle at Hanging Rock occurred on August 6, 1780. The Whigs were commanded by Sumter and the Tories by Major John Carden. O'Kelley, *Slaughter* 2: 221-233.

[414] Samuel Otterson was born April 1, 1754 in what was then Berkeley County, South Carolina and died September 11, 1837, in Greene County, Alabama. He enlisted as a lieutenant in the Spartan Regiment of militia under Capt. Daniel McKee and Col. John Thomas, Sr. in June 1776. Thereafter he participated in the Cherokee Campaign of 1776. In 1780, he served as a captain under Col. Thomas Brandon and fought at Rocky Mount, Hanging Rock and Blackstock's Plantation. Moss, *SC Patriots*, 744.

Lieut. Benjn. Jolly,[415] Joseph Hughes,[416] Wm. Sharp[417] and myself.

After Brandon's defeat, we fled to the East side of Broad River to Bullock's Creek Meeting House, of which Dr. Alexander was then pastor, but he had been previously driven into North Carolina. Here we were in a sad case. Charleston was in the hands of the British and Tories; Brandon recently defeated; the Enemy in force were spreading over the country, & we like a flock of sheep, without a leader, we assembled, plus a few refugees from Georgia. Here after enumerating our dangers and trials past, & thinking of future dangers and hardships, with the offers of British protection before us—the question came up, what shall be done? Col. John Thomas, Jr.[418] addressed the meeting. He asked shall we join the British, or strive like men to gain the noble end for which we have striven for years past? Shall we declare ourselves cowards and traitors, or shall we pursue the prize, Liberty, as long as life continues? He advised the latter course. After he had finished, I addressed the people to the same effect—shall we pursue Liberty, or give up? The question was put—all who were in favor of fighting the matter out, were to clap their hands & throw up their hats. The question came. The hats flew upwards, and the air resounded with the clapping of hands & shouts of defiance to the armies of Britain and the foes of Liberty.

[415] Benjamin Jolly served as a lieutenant and captain under Capt. Palmer and Col. Thomas Brandon in 1779-1781. Promoted to major in early 1781, he fought under Col. William Farr at Cowpens. Moss, *SC Patriots*, 508.

[416] Joseph Hughes (ca. 1760-1834) was a nephew of Capt. Joseph Jolly and served under his uncle and Thomas Brandon following the fall of Charleston. He claimed to have participated in the battles at Rocky Mount, Hanging Rock, Musgrove Mill, King's Mountain, Hammond's Old Store and Cowpens. Moss, *SC Patriots*, 472.

[417] Moss, *SC Patriots*, 857.

[418] According to Dr. Moss, John Thomas, Jr., was the son of Col. John Thomas, Sr. and assumed command of the Spartan Regiment from his father on October 23, 1778. Following the fall of Charleston, he served under Col. Benjamin Roebuck and General Thomas Sumter. Moss, *SC Patriots*, 925.

We entered on this resolution—that he that through necessity of apparel, or a wish to see his family, desired to return home, was welcome to do so, if he would agree to meet us at Tuckaseegee Ford, on the Catawba River, East side, whither myself and others immediately proceeded, where we met Col. Thomas Sumter. After an interchange of views, we said to Col. Sumter, "if we choose you as our leader, will you direct our operations?" He replied, "I am under the same promise with you; our interests are identical—with me, it is Liberty or death." An election was held, and he was chosen the next day a report came that there was a collection of Tories at Ramsour's Mill.[419] We started before day, but did not reach the place until the battle is nearly over. Captains Armstrong [420] & Qualls[421] led the North Carolinians in this Spirited Engagement. Armstrong was killed, but the Whigs gained the day. There we staid a few days, & in that period a court martial was held to take measures of defense. Some said, "if we stick together, the Tories will fly before us." Sumter said: "They are backed by men accustomed to fighting; and if we would gain Liberty, we must contend like men, & now is the time to strive like soldiers."

We now pressed some wagons, & hitched our horses to them, & some of us acted the part of wagoners. We went into the Catawba Nation, and encamped on a hill which we called Poor Hill as a memorial of our fare in that region—when we went over into North Carolina to half buy & half beg provisions, the inhabitants asked us, why we didn't stay at home, & defend ourselves there? We got some barley,

---

[419] The Battle of Ramsour's (also Ramsauer's and Ramseur's) Mill was fought of June 20, 1780 and resulted in a Whig victory over the Tories gathered there. Ramsour's Mill was on Clark Creek in Lincolnton, NC. Boatner, *Encyclopedia*, 913-914. William A. Graham, *The Battle of Ramsour's Mill* (Raleigh, NC: E. M. Uzzell & Co., 1904).

[420] William Armstrong was a captain in the 1st Rowan (North Carolina) Militia Regiment and died from wounds suffered at Ramsour's Mill. O'Kelley, *Slaughter* 2: 181—187 and fns. 304, 309.

[421] This is probably an erroneous reference to Captain Galbraith Falls who commanded the 40-member North Carolina Partisan Rangers at the Battle of Ramsour's Mill. Falls was mortally wounded at the battle.

meal, & made batter—we put it into a kind of crock—dug a hole in the ground, set the crock in it, and covered it over with hot ashes and embers—cooked it without salt, beef, or bacon, and it tasted mighty sweet.

From this place some of Sumter's men came over into York to attack a Capt. Hook,[422] of the British Army, who said "if the rebels were as thick as the trees, and Jesus Christ would come down and hear them, he could defeat them." The Presbyterian Irish could not stand this; they must come over and try his metal.

Just before the attack commenced, a parcel of women were at Col. Bratton's,[423] & an old man—they had just read a Chapter, & the old man was praying for the destruction of that vile man, Capt. Hook, when the attack was made. Hook was killed, and the party under his command defeated & taken up. Several men claimed the honor of killing him, but one John Carroll's claim seemed to be best sustained by the circumstances.[424]

Preparations were making at the same time by Sumter to assault Rocky Mount.[425] The attack was made and proved unsuccessful. At which place young Col. Thomas [Draper has interlined "Andrew"?] Neal[426] of York District was Killed. He was a young man of great worth. Thence Sumter stole a march to Hanging Rock. We marched all night the 6th August—the battle commenced on the 7th. It was found

---

[422] Christian Huck (ca. 1748-1780) was an American Tory officer in the British Legion under Lt. Col. Banastre Tarleton. Huck was from Philadelphia and a lawyer by profession. For an excellent treatment of the Battle of Huck's Defeat (a/k/a, Williamson's Plantation and the Battle of Brattonsville), *See* Scoggins, *Huck's Defeat.*

[423] William Bratton (1743-1815), a South Carolina militia colonel and the commander of the forces in the engagement at Huck's Defeat. Moss, *SC Patriots,* 96.

[424] This is probably the man identified as John Carroll in Moss, *SC Patriots,* 150. However, Moss does not credit him with killing Huck or even with participating in the Battle of Huck's Defeat. Moss credits Joseph Carroll with serving at Huck's Defeat. *Ibid.*

[425] The Battle of Rocky Mount occurred on July 30, 1780. The Whigs were commanded by Sumter and the Tories by Lt. Col. George Turnbull. Sumter's attempt to take the British works was unsuccessful. Kelley, *Slaughter* 2: 211-216.

[426] Andrew Neel was a militia colonel and was killed at the Battle of Rocky Mount. Moss, *SC Patriots,* 719.

by the guides that we were close by the place an hour or two before day. A whispering order came along the line that any might sit down with arms in hand to be ready. I and a fellow soldier sat down by a pine and both slept a little, & when we awoke he said to me in a confident tone—"This day I shall die." When orders were given to march, he went cheerfully, but fell—the first fire of the Enemy. His name was Mitchell High of Fairforest.

The battle commenced at nearly sunrise. The Tory line was said to be 1,400 strong commanded by Col. Bryan,[427] while we were not five hundred strong, & some of our men were left to take care [of] our horses. And the British were about 400 strong encamped in Camden road, about 200 yards from the Troy camp, who were to the South of Hanging Rock creek, on a hill forming something like a half moon or a workman's square. Our line was divided into three divisions, right, center and left. The left was commanded by Col. Steen, who went up between the Tory and British lines. The other two divisions were commanded by Col. James Lisles,[428] Samuel Wilson [Draper has interlined "Watson"][429]

[427] Col. Samuel Bryan from Rowan County, North Carolina, received a lieutenant colonelcy in the Royal North Carolina Regiment. After Moore's defeat at Ramsour's Mill, Bryan retreated with his 800-man militia unit to Cornwallis' camp. There his force was reorganized into the North Carolina Volunteers, nominally a Provincial Regiment, but in terms of training and discipline, actually only a militia unit. The unit served at Hanging Rock, Camden (Gates' Defeat), Wahab's (Walkup's) Plantation, and the Guilford Court House campaign, finally ending up in Wilmington when Cornwallis came there in April 1781. After the war, Bryan was initially arrested and sentenced to death, but he was pardoned and returned to the Yadkin River area and lived out his life in peace with his neighbors. William Thomas Sherman, *Calendar and Record of the Revolutionary War in the South: 1780-1781*, 2003-2009, http://www.angelfire.com/d20/htfh (viewed 9/9/12), 55.

[428] James Liles was a SC Patriot militia colonel under Thomas Sumter. Moss, *SC Patriots*, 569.

[429] Samuel Watson (1731-1810) was a SC Patriot militia lieutenant colonel in the New Acquisition District Regiment of Horsemen. He assumed command of the unit upon the death of Col. Thomas Neel at Stono Ferry. After the fall of Charleston, he served under Sumter and fought at Hanging Rock. Moss, *SC Patriots*, 971.

& Irwin[430] of No. Caro., who was before this called Granny Irwin, & who afterwards was spoken very highly of on account of his good conduct that day—all led by Gen. Sumter, who had given orders not to fire a gun until we passed between the British and Tory lines to the extremities. The battle being thus commenced, the British sent out a party commanded by one McCollough,[431] commenced that was, then called on it firing upon Steen's command. Genl. Sumter with the center and 3rd divisions coming around at the same time—began to cut off their flank so, that of that detachment not one got back, but were all killed or taken—their commander McCullough falling near the Tory camp, surrendered, & begging for water, one of Steen's captains (myself) got a canteen out of the Tory camp (who were all by this time fled) and gave him to drink. Then turning our whole force upon the British line, forced them off the ground, when some of the prisoners informed us that Col. Turnbull[432] with 400 British soldiers lay last night four miles off, which caused our General (Sumter) on seeing a troop of British horse come in Light to say, "Boys, it is not good to pursue a victory too far," & returned to the Tory camp when the British line rallied & raised a whoop and Gen. Sumter in hearing said "Boys, cant you raise a whoop of victory?" Then the air was rent with the cry of victory. Then taking up the line of march, and having gone about a mile, the British sent a flag to get leave to bury their dead, which was granted. One of Col. Steen's captains (myself) being the rear having charge of the prisoners, said to General Sumter—"You have through the Divine hand of

[430] Col. Robert Irwin (also Irvin, Irvine), from Mecklenburg County, North Carolina, commanded a relatively large proportion of the Patriot militia troops at Sumter's battles of Rocky Mount and Hanging Rock. At the time of the offensive against the Loyalists operating out of Wilmington in the Fall of 1781, he commanded a militia regiment under General Rutherford. Sherman, *Calendar*, 32.

[431] Capt. Kenneth McCulloch commanded about 160 members of the British Legion infantry at the second Battle of Hanging Rock. *Ibid.*, 149-150.

[432] Lt. Col. George Turnbull was a Tory militia officer who commanded a battalion of DeLancey's New York Volunteers. Turnbull was in command of the forces which defended Rocky Mount from the attack mounted by Thomas Sumter in July 1780. Boatner, *Encyclopedia*, 1129.

Providence, achieved a great victory today." And he answered that we had got a great victory, but it will scarcely ever be heard of, because we are nothing but a handful of raw militia, but if we had been commanded by a Continental officer, it would have sounded loud to our honor.

After marching till about 2 o'clock, halted to take some refreshment, having marched all night, & had a hard fight this morning, & having taken none for 24 hours, you may be sure we felt somewhat in need of refreshment. Then took up our march till night, & took up camp. On the [next] morning we began to march again towards Charlotte in Nor. Carolina.

About this time we got very scarce of lead, and the ladies (or heroic females) being stimulated by the barbarous conduct of the Tories and two British officers, Hook & Tarleton, gave us their dishes, spoons, tankards, &c which we cast into balls, and used instead of lead.

About this time Col James Williams joined Sumter—the latter having a disposition to go Southward, & the former towards the West. Disagreeing in their notions, the troops joined with Sumter or Williams just as their own inclinations led them.

Gen. Sumter as well as all of us knew of Gen. Gates coming toward the South, went on towards Camden, & by written communication Sumter was directed to go down on the Wateree, to prevent, as much as possible, the British from sending provisions &c. to Camden, in which he was successful, for he captured a great many wagons, boats, military stores, and men. Then hearing of the defeat of Genl. Gates at Camden, began to march up the country to make his spoils as safe as possible, & having got up the Fishing Creek, on the west side of the Catawba river, was pursued by Col. Tarleton, when he lost all he had taken, & a number of valuable soldiers.[433]

---

[433] The Battle of Fishing Creek was fought in the afternoon of August 18, 1780, and resulting in the defeat of Sumter and his forces. The battle is also referred to as Sumter's Defeat or Catawba Fords. O'Kelley, *Slaughter* 2: 177-286.

Col. Williams, Col. Steen and myself one of his captains, with those who had a disposition to annoy the British and Tories at Ninety Six, by various marches went up to Smith's Ford on Broad river, & lay one day & on the evening of the 18th of August, took up our line of march for Musgrove Mill. On our march we were overtaken by Francis Jones, who informed us of the defeat of Gen. Gates & Sumter's defeat [Draper Note: "mistake as to the latter, which occurred on the 18th LCD"]. Continuing our march, & leaving Col. Ferguson a little to our right, reaching the Tory camp, 300 strong, forty miles from Smith's Ford, at the dawn of day, & commenced the fight; killed a great many, took many prisoners, & marched forty miles to North Tiger. The reason of our rapid march to North Tiger was this: The Tory prisoners told us, that there 400 British soldiers under the command of Col. Innis,[434] encamped just over the river; and Knowing that Col. Ferguson whom we had just passed a little on our right, must also have heard our firing, & not knowing but that they would break in upon us (who were only about 150 strong), & serve us worse than we did the Tories. We got our water as we passed the brooks, & hunger was so great that we pulled green corn and ate it as we marched.[435]

About this time Col. John Thomas and his two sons, Abram & William, being prisoners with the British at Ninety Six, Mrs. Thomas, the Colonel's wife; who lived on Fairforest in the Irish settlement, went on a visit to Ninety Six, & whilst there overheard a woman tell some others that the royalists, the Tories intended to surprise the Rebels at Cedar Spring the next night, & she, Mrs. Thomas, determined if possible to appraise them of it, having two sons and a number of relatives with the Rebel party at that place, & rode that day

---

[434] Alexander Innes was an officer and official of the British provincial forces in North America. Given the rank of lieutenant colonel, he commanded the South Carolina Royalists when that unit of provincials was formed in February 1779. *See* Moss, *Chesney*, 109-110.

[435] Although accounts differ on the exact date, the Battle of Musgrove Mill probably occurred on August 19, 1780. The Whig forces were commanded by Williams, Isaac Shelby and Elijah Clarke. The Tories were commanded by Lt. Col. Alexander Innes. O'Kelley, *Slaughter* 2: 286-292.

fifty miles and acquainted them with the intended scheme and the Rebels, after consulting, agreed to go a little off from their camp, & wait their approach, & letting them come full into the light of their fires when they let in upon them & completely defeated them. Among the Tory party that were defeated was one John White whom I called my Tory from the fact of his refusing to go against the Indians when they were butchering & cutting up our people. I commanded the company in which he lived, & when I called on him he was non-resistant. But when Charleston fell, he soon joined them, and in this action he got shot in the hinder parts. The information as above given by Mrs. Thomas was always regarded as Providential, for had the Tories have come upon them, they would have cut them to pieces, for there were not more than fifty or sixty of the Rebels, & it was said there was not less than 150 Tories.[436]

Now, in Sept. 1780, the British having possession of Charleston, Georgetown, & Camden, Lord Cornwallis lying at Winnsborough, having a strong hold at Orangeburg, Ninety Six, and various other places, Ferguson having been commissioned to secure the up country, & having done so, took his stand on King's Mountain. Cols. Campbell, Sevier, Williams, Brandon, having been watching the movements of Ferguson, gathered their little forces together, & determined to give him a fight. And on the 7th Oct. early in the morning commenced the battle, Ferguson having the advantage of the ground determined to stand it out, and did so till he fell, when all were taken that were not killed. The British strength was vastly greater than ours. There we lost our brave Col. Williams, and a number of privates. Col. Williams just before he breathed his last, & when the firing and clank of guns ceased asked Thos. Young [Draper Note: "now Maj.

---

[436] The events McJunkin describes here are clearly part of the story of the first Battle of Cedar Spring which occurred on July 12, 1780. For an excellent discussion of Cedar Spring and other engagements in the Spartanburg area of South Carolina, *See* Wes Hope, *The Spartanburg Area in the American Revolution* (Spartanburg, SC: Altman Printing Company, Inc., 2003, 2nd Edition). The story of Mrs. Thomas' heroism is also well told by Elizabeth F. Ellet, *The Women of the American Revolution*, 3 vols. (New York: Charles Scribner's Sons, 1853-1854).

Young"] holding him in an easy position, who had got the victory, answered "We have"—said "well, now I die satisfied." The much lamented Williams with all who fell of the Whig party that day, were buried with the honors of war. He was a member of the Presbyterian Church of Little River.

Sometime in November, Gen. Sumter having recruited his command a little, marched to the East side of Broad river at Fish Dam with a view to draw Col. Tarleton to battle; but was attacked by Col. Wemyss,[437] & after being wounded and worsted in the fight retreated to Winnsboro from whence he came.[438]

On the next day Sumter crossed to the west side of the river. I having recovered of a spell of fever with the few men that had not turned Tory in our neighborhood & some few refugee Georgians about Puget's Creek, in Union District, when we marched to Blackstock's with about 300 men, followed by Tarleton with his troops of horse & infantry mounted.

Sumter having stopped to take some refreshment, & the troops having made up fires, prepared the dough & rolled it around sticks, & sat it before the fire in order to bake. I being officer of the day was informed of Tarleton's near approach and immediately sent word to Sumter, who ordered that we should come up to the building where he was, which we did leaving our dough on the sticks for the British got it. Then Sumter said, "Boys, who will

---

[437] Major James Wemyss (pronounced "Weems") was the acting commander of the 63rd Regiment since its lieutenant colonel, James Patterson, was serving as a general officer in America. Wemyss led the mounted 63rd on raids burning homes and confiscating munitions and other property from suspected rebels in the Williamsburg area of South Carolina (i.e., north of the Santee) in late August and early September 1780. In November, he mounted an abortive attack on Sumter at Fishdam Ford of the Broad River on November 9, 1780. Badly wounded in his arm and knee in the encounter, Wemyss was taken prisoner, but was paroled in a few days. He retired to Charlestown, his injuries preventing him from serving further in the southern campaign. Sherman, *Calendar*, 53. *See* John Robertson, Global Gazetteer of the American Revolution, at http://gaz.jrshelby.com/wemyssgrave.htm (viewed 9/18/12) for the location of Wemyess' grave.
[438] The Battle of Fishdam Ford was fought on November 9, 1780. O'Kelley, *Slaughter* 2: 355-360.

bring on the action?" & Col. Farr[439] and myself stepped out
& said—who will go with us? When our heroes stepped out
till Sumter said there were enough. Then Sumter said "Go
on, and if you are not strong Enough, retreat & fight as you
retreat." In going we were met by a party intending to flank
us, when we Exchanged shots & retreated, & kept up the fire
until they made a charge on Sumter—then had it back & fore
till we beat them off the ground about sun down. Sumter
being wounded, we thought it most prudent to take him to
some place of safety, if possible, & carried him between two
horses to the other side of the river, when some of the British
whom we had taken prisoners, on hearing the sound of their
bugles, &c said they were worsted indeed for it was for the
purpose of collecting those who were missing. We lost a few
of our brave fellows, among whom was ____ [blank in the
original] Brown. But our loss was comparatively few to that
of our enemy—perhaps not more than one to five or six.[440]

On the next day the British came on the
battle-ground having taken one of our bravest fellows, John
Johnson, Esqr., a day or two before, who was coming on to
join Sumter, & who in an Evil hour had, when it appeared
that the British had completely over run South Carolina, &
his wife being in a state not to be left alone) taken British
protection, which he thought (unfortunately) preferable to
being carried off prisoner, and that day hanged him without
judge or jury.

Now notwithstanding Sumter had been
somewhat victorious in the two last engagements, the
prospect of successful resistance still appeared gloomy
indeed, for we had but just lost one of our braves Colonels,
Williams; our Gamecock Genl. Sumter, now wounded; and

---

[439] William Farr (1729-1794) served as a captain under Col. John
Thomas, Sr. in the Spartan Regiment in 1776. He later served as an adjutant, major
and lieutenant colonel under Cols. Andrew Pickens, Thomas Brandon and General
Thomas Sumter. He participated in the battles at Stono Ferry, Hanging Rock,
Blackstock's Plantation and Cowpens. Moss, *SC Patriots*, 304.

[440] The Battle of Blackstock's Plantation occurred on November 20,
1780. As McJunkin states, the Whigs were commanded by Genl. Thomas Sumter
and the British by Lt. Col. Banastre Tarleton. O'Kelley, *Slaughter* 2: 365-373.

the Tories prowling about robbing and burning our very few brave fellows' houses and hunting them like partridges, and murdering & hanging them wherever they could catch them. Yet notwithstanding all this gloom we did not entirely despair of success at last, for we had been victorious at Musgrove, King's Mountain, Fish Dam & Blackstock's—& even the fair sex, our mothers, our wives & our sweethearts stimulating us to persevere; and above all we had reason to believe that the Great Ruler of all Events was on our side.

Note: A Tory Col. of North Carolina whose name was Moore,[441] having heard of Sumter being wounded, came on with a band of Tories to my father's house, Samuel McJunkin, Esqr., there being none but females at home, and staid all night, was joined by some of the South Carolina Tories, among whom was one Bill Hanesworth, and on going off in the morning, began to pillage & take all they could of provisions, bed clothes, wearing clothes, &c. and after they got nearly all as they thought, this Bill Hanesworth, seeing a bed-quilt took & started to put it on his horse, when one of my sisters, Jane, seized it, & they began to pull (& she, no doubt, pulling with all her might for they had left nothing to cover the family from the cold of night) some of the Tories crying "well done, woman," & some "well done, Bill" till he slipping up in some of the filth by the garden, where they the Tories had beastly went the night before, when she putting one foot on him, pulled it away from him. Their Colonel having sworn during the scuffle that if she could get it from him, she should have it—then seeing her take it, & [Bill's] back well [?], told her to take it into the house—she sat down on it.

Now, in the month of December, 1780, Genl. Daniel Morgan (& Col. Washington's troop of horse) who was sent from Genl. Greene's army, with a few Continental troops, came & encamped near the Grindal Shoals on Pacolet river—Lord Cornwallis being still at Winnsboro.

---

[441] This probably is a reference to Lieutenant Colonel John Moore, the North Carolina Tory militia leader, whose forces were defeated at Ramsour's Mill.

Before Genl. Morgan came to Pacolet, what few Whigs I could command went under command of Col. Brandon to guard Love's Ford on Broad river, in order to prevent their intercourse with Lord Cornwallis; & while there a scout commanded by Capt. John McCool,[442] went to attack a party of Tories on Sandy river which was noted for Toryism, when Capt. McCool got worsted, and my brother Daniel who was along, was taken prisoner, & sent to Lord Cornwallis's at Winnsboro—when a flag was sent by Col Brandon, at my request, to exchange a Tory Colonel (Fanning)[443] whom we had prisoner, which Cornwallis would not do, but sent him to Camden, where he lay in jail till some that were in broke a hole in the grate big enough to let him and another little man out, thus made his escape, nearly perished to Death about the last of April, 1781.

Gen. Morgan while encamped at Grindal Shoals, hearing of a band of Tories under the command of Col. Cunningham, sent Col. Washington to Hammond's Old Store in the neighborhood of Little River appointing myself & Thos. Young as pilots—& charging them, surprised and stopped the wind of a few of them. (Note) An unfortunate occurrence took place in the charge on the Tories—one of Washington's troop on a very fine charger, while in the charge, aiming to go on one side of a tree which stood in the way & his rider the other, was received so that the horse struck the tree which Killed him instantly. The rider, I believe, was a soldier, for he took off his pistols &c & followed on in the charge, & I could not help being sorry, hearing his companions saying: "D_m you, Irish, it should have been you instead of the horse."

---

[442] John McCool served as a captain under Col. Thomas Brandon in 1780. Moss, *SC Patriots,* 606.

[443] David Fanning (1755-1825), from Randolph County, North Carolina, was a notorious Tory militia leader and renegade earning in North Carolina a reputation for brutality on a par with that of William ("Bloody Bill") Cunningham in South Carolina. After the Revolution, Fanning relocated to Nova Scotia, became a local politician and wrote a fascinating (and probably exaggerated) account of his exploits. Butler, *Fanning. See* also Hairr, *Fanning.*

We encamped near that place & returned on the next day to Gen. Morgan, myself to Gen. Pickens, who was encamped in the Plummer Settlement between Fairforest & Tyger Rivers. Gen. Pickens having just heard of Tarleton's intention to fall upon Gen. Morgan at Grindal's Shoals, & thinking it unsafe to send in writing, choose Majr. McJunkin to carry a verbal message to Gen. Morgan, & on being chosen, asked leave to choose a man to go with me, when I chose James Park,[444] & accordingly started about dusk, & the waters being very high, from excessive rains that had just fallen, & very dark, had to swim Fairforest Mill Creek & Pacolet, & on arriving at the northern bank was hailed by one of Morgan's sentinels, & kept in the edge of the river till the Capt. of the Guard should come, when I was conducted to Genl. Morgan's tent, when I informed him that Benny (Tarleton) was approaching to give him (Morgan) a blast, for Tarleton had said that the two Lords at Winnsboro (Rawdon[445] and Cornwallis) that he would have the old wagoner (Morgan) as he was pleased to call him, to dinner with them in a few days. Morgan on hearing the message said to Barron, a little Frenchman whom he had with him, & who was asleep, "Barron, get up & go back to the Iron Works & tell Billy (meaning Col. Washington, who was there getting his horses shod, & Barron had just come from there) that Benny is approaching & tell him to meet me tomorrow evening at Gentleman Thomason's" on the East side of Thicketty Creek. Accordingly Gen. Morgan & Col. Washington met on the evening appointed, 15th January, 1781, & marched on the 16th towards the Cowpens. Gen Pickens falling in with him

---

[444] Moss, *SC Patriots*, 752. It is likely that both the entries in Moss for "James Parh" and for "James Park" apply to the individual named by McJunkin.

[445] Francis Lord Rawdon-Hastings (1754-1826) was a British army officer and Irish nobleman. Boatner, *Encyclopedia*, 918-921. Paul David Nelson, *Francis Rawdon-Hastings, Marquess of Hastings: Soldier, Peer of the Realm, Governor-General of India*. (Hamilton, NY: Fairleigh Dickinson University Press, 2005).

on the way with Cols. Thomas, Casey,[446] Lyles & Brandon, who had all been out at different posts, & forming a junction encamped on the ground where the battle took place on the morning of the 17th.

Tarleton with a view to surprise Morgan at his camp had marched all night with his troop of cavalry & infantry mounted about 1000 men beside the Tories that were with him. Gen. Morgan being apprised of the approach of Tarleton by faithful spies, began before day to go from mess to mess with Gen. Pickens, saying "Boys, get up, Benny's coming; & you that have sweethearts or wives or children or parents, must fight for them and above all you must fight for liberty and for your country," which appeared to have the ears of Every true friend of this country, & were alive to action, but a few "pet Tories" whom it seemed like poison to. After speaking to the militia in this way, he went to his regulars, & the tattoo being sounded, the line was formed commanded by Col. Howard. Then Morgan addressed them –"My friends in arms, my dear boys, I request you to remember Saratoga, Monmouth, Paoli & Brandywine, & this day you must play your parts for your honor & liberty's cause."

The line being formed with the regulars in the center, commanded by Col. Howard,[447] the militia on the right and left—the right commanded by Gen. Pickens, the left by __(blank in the original). Col. Washington in the rear with his troop of cavalry. The line being thus formed in battle assay, & the Enemy in sight between day light and sun-up, Gen. Morgan addressed the Sovereign of the Universe

---

[446] Levi Casey served as lieutenant colonel of the Little River Regiment from area that would later become Laurens and Newberry after the death of Col. Joseph Hayes. Hayes had assumed command of the Little River Regiment after its original commander, Col. James Williams, died from wounds suffered at King's Mountain on October 8, 1780. It was Hayes, not Casey, who commanded the Little River Regiment at Cowpens. *See* Babits, *Devil of a Whipping.* Casey assumed command of the regiment after Hayes was hanged by William Cunningham at the Battle of Hayes Station.

[447] John Eager Howard (1752-1827) was a lieutenant colonel of the 2nd Maryland Line. Boatner, *Encyclopedia*, 519-520. Jim Piecuch and John H. Beakes, Jr., *"Cool Deliberate Courage" John Eager Howard in the American Revolution*, (Charleston, SC: Nautical & Aviation Publishing Co. of America, 2009).

in the following words, saying—"O thou Great Disposer of all Events, the battle is not to the strong, nor the race to the swift: Our domineering Enemy now being in sight, Oh, leave us not nor forsake us!" At this time Tarleton marching up and filing to the right and left, formed in battle assay, when Gen. Morgan said "Boys, who will bring on the battle?" When Col. Farr & Major McJunkin stepped out & said, "Boys, who will go with us" when others stepped out until Morgan said there were enough, & said "Go & bring on the action & if you are pressed, retreat, & come in on our flank." which we did. And soon the firing commenced & there was almost one continued roar & crash of arms, each striving for victory. Tarleton then made a charge on the right & left wings, treading & cutting till he got in the rear of Howard's command, when Col. Washington made a charge upon him, cutting and hewing (when Washington cut off some of Tarleton's fingers) when Tarleton began to retreat, which gave as it were, additional strength to both regulars & militia—Washington pursuing Tarleton to Gondelock's.[448]

Tarleton being gone, the red coats began to beg for quarters, & having been taught by Tarleton that Morgan would give no quarters, were hard to believe even when they were told that quarters would be given if they would lay down their arms: and when they were convinced that quarters would be given, they as it were rent the very air with thanks that their lives would be spared. These were called the Scots regiment.

The number of the slain on the side of the Americans was inconsiderable compared with that of the Enemy, Tarleton being completely discomfited, and driven from the ground. He with the remainder of his cavalry attempting to make his escape to Lord Cornwallis, who was at that juncture of time on the East side of Broad river, opposite Hamilton's Ford, with the view of intercepting Gen. Morgan—as they said, the old wagoner, & marching with

---

[448] For an excellent treatment of the Battle of Cowpens, *See* Babits, *Devil.* Adam Goudelock owned two plantations, one on Thicketty Creek and the other near Grindal Shoals on the Pacolet River.

rapid strides to gain this object. Gen. Morgan, who having taken the Scotch regiment, being 700 in number—marched towards the North Carolina line to Broad river to a place called the Island Ford—crossing the same on the East side, there encamping all night—next morning after the battle was over (the people of the neighborhood having gathered in) our officers requested them to bury the dead, & take care of the wounded on both sides, & ordered a march & reached the Island Ford on Broad river, & crossed where the baggage was sent to in the morning previous to the battle, and encamped for the night. Our poor Scot's prisoners almost perished to death having eat nothing for 24 hours. Now when Tarleton got to Lord Cornwallis, encamped near Bethel Creek Church (as I was afterwards told by my father, Samuel McJunkin, Esqr.—who was a prisoner, together with Col. Hopkins & Capt. Jamieson) with his Lordship at that time. After Tarleton had related his defeat, with the loss of one whole regiment, and a great many of his cavalry, his Lordship was so enraged that he swore he would retake them at all hazards—at the same time leaning so hard on his sword that he broke it.

[Note by James H. Saye: "End of Maj. McJunkin's Narrative—that part commencing with the retreat of Morgan through North Carolina at Burke Court House was written down by some other person—a son of Maj. McJunkin, I believe."]

Now, not knowing well what course to take for safety, thought sometimes of marching towards the Mountains, but knowing that they were filled with none by Tories determined to strike for Virginia, & on the 18th took up our line of march, recrossed the Island Ford—Reversed his march on towards Virginia with all [194] Scotch prisoners that he had taken thru North Carolina, passing by Burke Court House. Thence on to Catawba River, crossing at Beatties' Ford in the evening with his army and prisoners. The same night on which he crossed, Lord Cornwallis hotly pursuing, with sanguine expectation of gaining his object in intercepting the old wagoner, the river, with a most tremendous rain that fell at that juncture of time, almost instantaneously was swollen to such a degree that completely frustrated his hopes, for he could not cross—which the Americans attributed to an immediate interposition of Divine Providence in their favor. Tarleton forming a juncture with Lord Cornwallis and marching on with him from Broad river at Hamilton's Ford to the aforesaid ford at Catawba. On their way, now being on the East side of Catawba river, in full pursuit of Gen. Morgan, in the settlement of the Widow Torrance, used the most profane language, & renting out the most abusive expressions, & boasting in the name of his Maker he would in a very few days deliver his Scotch prisoners, and have the old Wagoner drive with him, swearing at the same time he had slain a considerable number of rebels. Well, says Lord Cornwallis, who was a gentleman of considerable wit, asked Tarleton jocosely if he had buried them? He said yes. Well, his Lordship further observed, "Colonel, if you have not buried them face downwards, they will all spring up & give you fresh battle." He still pursuing Gen. Morgan with great fury towards the Yadkin rivers, a rain providentially falling, both streams which he must have passed, suddenly were swollen to such a degree that the was discomfited as he had been previously at the Catawba—by which remarkable Providence Morgan with his troops completely escaped falling into the hands of the merciless enemy, or contending against them to great disadvantage.

Gen. Morgan dismissed the South Carolina troops who had been a faithful band as auxiliaries to his army, advising them to return home, & grant aid according to their power in protecting their own State, in this critical juncture, under the command of their worthy and energetic Gen. Sumter, which accordingly they accepted, being faint and weary, having passed through many fatiguing and dangerous scenes.

Having accomplished their march back, they found their beloved commander, Gen. Sumter so much indisposed with the wound he had received from the Enemy, that he was lying by, though with great impatience, as he was fired with true heroic ambition to be actively engaged in the field in his country's cause. However, they on their return, according to regular appointment, were under the present command of Col. Brandon. The troops were ordered by Sumter to meet him at a time designated at Congaree River. Brandon with the troops directly commenced his march towards the designated place; but finding that a superior force of the Enemy were hovering over the way which we must have passed, were impelled to take a retrograde march to Union District, then called part of Ninety Six.

Then hearing Col. Roebuck fired with the same patriotic zeal to lessen the power of the rapacious Enemy, was marching with hasty strides towards Saluda River, in Laurens District, then Ninety Six, the Enemy being near Little River, Col. Brandon deemed it expedient to order Maj. McJunkin, who was possessed of the greatest patriotic zeal, to take a part of the troops under his command, and march to the relief of Roebuck; and in going on to the destined place, Maj. McJunkin hearing that Col. Roebuck had had an engagement with a party of Tories that morning, being the 2nd of March, 1781, he deemed it expedient to return with the troops again, which he accordingly did. At the same time, Col. Roebuck wishing to take proper care of the sick and wounded of his troops, among whom was Robert Thomas[449] and Wm. Thomas,[450] the brothers-in-laws of Maj. McJunkin, the latter of whom was but slightly wounded, while the former was mortally wounded.[451]

---

[449] Moss, *SC Patriots*, 926.

[450] *Ibid.*

[451] The battle at Williams Fort (or Roebuck's Defeat or the Battle of Mudlick Creek) occurred on March 2, 1781. Roebuck attacked the Tory force stationed at the re-built fortifications on Mudlick Creek on Col. James Williams' plantation. The Tories suffered casualties but wounded Roebuck and several of his men, including Captain Robert Thomas who was mortally wounded. Patrick O'Kelley, *Nothing but Blood and Slaughter: The Revolutionary War in the Carolinas, Volume Three: 1781.* (Lillington, NC: Blue House Tavern Press, Booklocker.com, Inc., 2005), 105-106.

Major McJunkin in marching back came in contact with a posse of Tories, & in having a conflict with them was very seriously wounded in his right arm. Still the patriotic troops under the present command of Maj. McJunkin gained a complete victory over the bloodthirsty Tories, & continued to march to the camp of Gen. *(sic)* Brandon at night. Major McJunkin experienced the most excruciating distress from the wound in his arm, there being no surgical aid to be obtained. Some of the troops whose hearts were warmed with pure patriotic zeal exclaimed that their good commander should be relieved, & accordingly set about & cut out the bullet with a dull razor instead of a surgical instrument.[452]

The camp of Col. Brandon being a flying camp, Maj. McJunkin and his troops had to subsist in the best manner they could. Major McJunkin was by his patriotic troops borne into a far distant grove; if possible, to be out of the reach of the Enemy—especially to be concealed from the bloodthirsty Tories, more to be dreaded than the British, who were without principle, roaming about like roaming lions. Being in this situation the friends of the Major were apprehensive that amputation was necessary to save his life, for his arm turning green & black was indicative of an approaching inflammation in his arm. They apprised the Major of what they believed to be his case; he replied to them he should not submit to part with his arm. If his arm must go, "I will go with it," he said. A certain Irishman, at this juncture, of the name of David Brown, who always appeared to have great friendship for the Major, voluntarily offered his services to go immediately in quest of Dr. Ross,[453] &, if possible bring him to the Major's assistance. Accordingly he started, & brought on the Doctor, & by his aid he providentially saved his life & arm too. The Major always considers this to be a kind interposition of heaven, & has accordingly noted it as one of the great epochs of his life in which God in his Providence appeared in his favor. But how wonderful and intricate are the ways of Providence. A Dark scene is soon after this juncture,

---

[452] *See* O'Kelley, *Slaughter* 3: 106-107.
[453] George Ross served as a doctor in the SC Patriot militia from 1778 to 1782. Moss, *SC Patriots*, 831.

to be presented to Major McJunkin. The bloodthirsty Tories finding out where he was with his few patriotic troops in the woods were about to march right upon them; the Major being apprised of it, they immediately removed from the thicket near Brown's Creek, & crossed over to the East side of Broad river in the neighborhood of the Revd. Dr. Alexander in York District, whose house had been a real Lagoretta,[454] where the Patriot troops who were in distress, found the kindest relief—so kind & charitable was this worthy clergyman. Here Maj. McJunkin found the most friendly attention, but he having taken the Smallpox in the natural way, was soon in need of that assistance peculiar to such a malignant disorder, which he could not have received but by the kind Dr. Alexander & his friends. Here he passed many a wearisome day & night, while the disorder passed through its several stages experiencing the most extreme distress. The Major's Mother in the most affectionate manner attending him through his whole sickness, granting all the assistance in her power; but in performing the tender offices of a kind maternal friend, she took the contagious disorder herself & soon fell a victim. Thus the Major found himself introduced into a gloomy scene of sorrow. Notwithstanding he was tolerably well to a state of health with a heart burning with zeal to be engaged in active service in his country's cause.

On the 8th day of May, 1781, before the Major was fairly recovered from the disorder, lying at the house of his father where Widow Beatty now lives & having arrived the evening before to see his father was there next morning taken prisoner by a villainous pack of Tories, a branch of the bloody Scout,[455] commanded by one Bud Anderson (a gentleman in principle) & carried him on to the Iron Works on Lawson's Fork.[456] On their way there,

[454] According to the Random House Unabridged Dictionary, Second Edition, (New York: Random House, 1993), "lazaretto" means "1. a hospital for those affected with contagious diseases, esp., leprosy;" or "2. a building or ship set apart for quarantine purposes."

[455] This is a reference to William Cunningham, aka, "Bloody Bill" and/or "Bloody Scout."

[456] This reference is to Wofford's Iron Works on Lawson's Creek near present day Glendale, South Carolina.

these same bloody Tories took several prisoners, some of whom they killed while on their knees begging for mercy. At the Iron Works the other parties of the Bloody Scout rendezvoused. On the 9th of May, morning, they held a mock trial, & condemned the Major to be hung in a few minutes; while standing under the limb of a tree awaiting his awful doom, just at this moment a man was seen coming in full speed—rode up & communicated some secret intelligence. It then was determined to postpone the execution. The cause of this sudden change was understood afterwards that a party of Whigs was at hand. Meeting many insults & called hard names, he was finally carried to the British garrison at Ninety Six, commanded by Col. Cruger[457]—was laid down on the ground, with one more prisoner, a lad, the son of a Whig—one mile from Ninety Six, before they arrived at that slaughter ground. Here the Major again made a providential escape. A company of Tories came up at full speed—one of whom came up with a drawn sword, & said "its not the man I thought it was," & turned away.

That day another court martial was held— somewhat honorable—in which he was sentenced to remain a prisoner at Ninety Six from 12th May till last of June— receiving many insults from the Tories, continually from day to day. On the last day of May, was paroled, with Several others, & marched on home, by Saluda ferry—when they came to the ferry, got an account of a skirmish up the river, & shortly after met with a part of Gen. Greene's advance guard, by whom these paroled prisoners were carried to the General's camp, with whom the Major had a consultation.

[457] John Harris Cruger (1738-1807) was a Tory officer from New York who accompanied Lt. Col. Archibald Campbell in his successful expedition to capture Georgia in late 1778 and early 1779. He participated in the successful defense of Savannah in October 1779. He succeeded Nisbet Balfour as commander of the Tory forces at Ninety Six. He defended that location against the siege mounted by Nathanael Greene in the late spring of 1781. He was at the Battle of Eutaw Springs on September 8, 1781. He participated in the defense of Charleston for the remainder of the war. At the conclusion of peace, his New York properties having been confiscated, he removed to London where he lived out his life. Lorenzo Sabine, *Biographical Sketches of Loyalists of the American Revolution, with an Historical Essay*, 2 vols. (Boston: Little, Brown and Company, 1864).

The Major went with Greene to the siege of Ninety Six[458]—
the other prisoners went on home. He remained until the
siege was raised, when the Major returned home: was beat
about with his crippled arm, with scouting party in the day, &
hiding at night—The Tories now having over-run the upper
part of South Carolina—meeting with many scenes of heart-
rending sorrow—continuing to do occasional service until
the close of the struggle. There was a block-house kept about
this time on Fairforest Creek, which was rendezvous for the
Whigs until peace was made in 1783, two years afterwards.

As the Major passed the Starry Redoubt [at
Ninety Six siege] a Quaker Tory rose up & reproached him.
Not long afterwards, this same Tory met his fate—was killed
by Greene's six-pounder.

3. McJunkin's Statement: Draper MSS, Sumter Papers 23VV203-212

Sir: In order to have some connection—on the
4th June, 1780, Col. Brandon, Col. Thomas & Col. Liles made
a secret appointment to concentrate their force on Fairforest
Creek, about six miles below where Union Court House now
stands—in order to defend the country against the Tories as well
as they could. Brandon being the nearest, he got to the place the
first. The Little River Tories getting information by Col. Fletcher
[*sic*, Fletchall], collected in force under William Cunningham,
made a forced march, & Brandon having taken a pet Tory by
the name of Adam Stidam, who made his escape from Brandon's
camp on the night of the 9th & met his friends & informed them
where & how Brandon was camped, & surprised him killing some
& dispersing some, & wounding others—amongst the last, one of
my brothers [thought to be mortally], & killing one of my cousins.

---

[458] The siege of Ninety Six occurred from May 22, 1781 through June 19,
1781, and was led by Nathanael Greene against Provincial Tory forces commanded
by John Harris Cruger. The siege was lifted upon the approach of reinforcements
under Col. Francis Lord Rawdon. O'Kelley, *Slaughter* 3: 245-258.

Amongst the missing was Robert Lusk,[459] whom the Tories threatened to Kill if he would not disclose where the magazine was that Col. Brandon had. The old man to save his life, disclosed where it was, but Providence who superintends the affairs of men had ordered matters so that the Enemy was disappointed— which thing fell thus: Col. Brandon had selected Jos. Hughes,[460] William Sharp,[461] John Savage,[462] Aquilla Hollingsworth,[463] Samuel Otterson, Benj. Jolly, & Joseph McJunkin to secrete the powder & ball, which they did by carrying it to some distance & hiding it, a cask in a place, in hollow logs—which powder & lead were of great service to us afterwards through the summer of 1780. Col. Thomas & Col. Liles being informed of Col. Brandon's disaster, provided for the safety of their men as well as the nature of circumstances permitted. Us powder men not being in the defeat, & getting timely notice fell in with our scattered friends & my father, & passed over Broad River on the said 11th day, & on the 12th passed on the Bullock's Creek Meeting House, & there rendezvoused a few hours to give time to collect some of our own regiment, & there fell in with some of Liles' men, & Capt. John Thomas with some of Col. Thomas' men. There it was put to vote whether should we go back & take protection, or go on towards North Carolina to seek shelter there—for it was a stubborn fact that wherever a Presbyterian settlement was, the people were Whigs. The matter was decided by cheers, shouts & a cry by every man— that surrender they would not; but that they would see their country free or die—death or liberty. Some having parents, some loving wife & children, our State being then over-run by the British & Tories, save York District—then according to our declaration we made the best of our way to the Tuckaseegee

---

[459] Robert Lusk, Sr. is listed in Moss, *SC Patriots*, 587, as having served under Thomas Brandon following the fall of Charleston.

[460] Joseph Hughes (ca. 1760-1834) was a nephew of Capt. Joseph Jolly and served under his uncle and Thomas Brandon following the fall of Charleston. He claimed to have participated in the battles at Rocky Mount, Hanging Rock, Musgrove Mill, King's Mountain, Hammond's Old Store and Cowpens. Moss, *SC Patriots*, 472.

[461] Moss, *SC Patriots*, 857.

[462] Moss, *SC Patriots*, 846.

[463] Moss, *SC Patriots*, 456.

Ford on the Catawba river, & crossed over, & beat about on the East side of the river for sometime, & fell in with Sundry with [of] our vanquished friends from the South, & a few from Georgia—& amongst them our much beloved Col. Thomas Sumter. Just at that time we were informed that the Tories were collecting in a large body at Ramsour's Mill, in North Carolina, & also that Genl. Rutherford was collecting a force to disperse them. We being all in fire for the cause of our beloved country, we unanimously chose Col. Thos. Sumter to be our leader or General, to lead us to face the Enemy, & the first was Sumter joined Rutherford that day, & Sumter & us, & some of the men & officers of Rutherford, could hardly be constrained from proceeding that evening to attack the above Tories; but Rutherford would not consent for him to start until next morning, him & men, all anxious to meet the Enemy, started by time, & posted on with all possible speed, but the distance being too great, our hero & his party did not get to the place of action until it was over. That battle fought by Capt. Qualls[464] & Capt. Armstrong & that neighborhood who totally defeated those loyal Tories, but Quall fell & Capt. Armstrong was mortally wounded. General Sumter encamped there that night & the next day, & procured some provisions & some wagons & horses, aided & assisted by Genl. Rutherford. He then entered on his expedition—the plan of which was to aid his own State; he therefore marched from Ramsour's towards the nearest post of the Enemy, which post was at Rocky Mount, & on his march, where camped one night, he summoned all of his commissioners to attend at his markee, which was composed of a wagon cloth & the broad canopy of heaven—under whose auspices we were certainly then, to hold a court martial—the subject of which was to fall on a method of the then opening campaign, the General being president. One of the officers allowed that as soon as we got in proper order of defense, that the Enemy would fly away;

[464] This is probably an erroneous reference to Captain Galbraith Falls who commanded the 40-member North Carolina Partisan Rangers at the Battle of Ramsour's Mill. Falls was mortally wounded at the battle. O'Kelley, *Slaughter* 2: 181-187 and fns. 304, 309.

other officers held that as the British backed the Tories, that they would fight hard. Gen. Sumter said—"Gentlemen: You may depend upon it, that in order to regain our country, we must expect to fight hard, & that force must repel force, or otherwise we need not attempt to regain our beloved country." The conclusion was to gain our point, or die in the attempt. The next day we marched towards the Catawba old Town,[465] the place designed to concentrate his force, & to collect some provisions, which place we got to, & on or about the first of July. The great difficulty to obtain provision, & the meanness of it, caused the men to give it the name of Starved Valley or Poor Hill, it being one of the Catawba Indian old fields where we camped—at which we were—or at Clem's Branch,[466] all July—poor, moneyless, or at least money that would do us nay good. It must be remembered that Sumter & party frequently crossing & recrossing the Catawba, that there were frequent skirmishes between his men & the Enemy.

A Capt. Hook, of the British, who had the command of a troop of horse was sent by Col. Turnbull from Rocky Mount up into York District, to punish the Presbyterian inhabitants of that place, which he did with a barbarous hand, by killing men, burning churches, & driving off the ministers of the gospel to seek shelter amongst strangers. And his intention was to collect the dirty Tories. He, this mighty Hook, defied all the rebels (as he called the Americans) saying that if they were as numerous as the trees of the forest, & if Jesus Christ was to come down & head them, that he could destroy them, which so angered the inhabitants, & God being on their side, that they watched his movements surprised him—& a

[465] This is probably a reference to the Catawba Indian town shown as being located near Kings Creek on the 1764 map of the Catawba Indian Reservation made by Samuel Wyly. Archaeological excavation of the possible site of the town is currently being conducted by the University of North Carolina, Charlotte. *See* http://rla.unc.edu/Catawba (viewed 9/9/12).

[466] Mills depicts Clem's Branch as being a tributary of Big Sugar Creek, itself a tributary of the Catawba River. Big Sugar Creek marks the dividing line between York and Lancaster Counties, South Carolina. Mills, *Atlas*.

little David by the name of John Carroll,[467] of York, slew him by drawing a bow at a venture, while he was harassing his men, & placed two leaden arrows in his head so fatal that this mighty man fell with his face across the threshold of liberty, & like Dagon broke in pieces.

About this time, or a little after in July, some of us refugees as we were of South Carolina & Georgia were called, went from Sumter's to attack a collection of Tories that had made a stand at a man's by the name of Stallion,[468] of York, together with some of the neighbors. The attack was made, & the Tory party defeated & dispersed, with some being Killed & wounded on both sides. Old Squire Kennedy's son[469] of our District was wounded here. Stallion being a Tory, but his wife a Whig, when the house was laid beset, & being afraid her husband would be slain, she to save him placed herself in the door as being generally known, she supposed there, by her friends, would desist or cease from the attack, but unfortunately a ball struck her, & ended her days. It was a pity. She was of a respectable family—the Love's.[470]

About this time, or in this month, the Enemy had burned Hill's Iron Works.[471] About this period there were

---

[467] This is probably the man identified as John Carroll in Moss, *SC Patriots*, 150. However, Moss does not credit him with killing Huck or even with participating in the Battle of Huck's Defeat. Moss does credit Joseph Carroll with serving at Huck's Defeat. *Ibid.*

[468] For a discussion of the skirmish at Stallion's Plantation, *See* O'Kelley, *Slaughter* 2: 198-199.

[469] Thomas Young in his memoir states that William Kennedy was wounded at Stallion's Plantation. Young's memoir was printed in Joseph Johnson, *Traditions and Reminiscences Chiefly of the American Revolution in the South*, (Spartanburg, SC: Walker & James, 1851 Charleston: The Reprint Company, 1972). Phil Norfleet also has posted the memoir in full at http://sc_tories.tripod.com/thomas_young.htm (viewed 9/9/12). Moss, *SC Patriots*, 529, does not mention Kennedy's sustaining a wound at Stallion's.

[470] Mrs. Stallion's brother, Captain Andrew Love, was a Whig and was part of Brandon's force at the skirmish at Stallion's Plantation. O'Kelley, *Slaughter* 2: 198.

[471] Col. William Hill, in partnership with Isaac Hayne, owned and operated an important ironworks on Allison Creek in what is today York County, South Carolina. Until its destruction by Tory Capt. Christian Huck, the ironworks cast artillery and shot for the Whigs. The site of the ironworks is probably covered by Lake Wylie now.

some doubts respecting the soundness of the principles of Col. Edward Lacey's,[472] fearing he would join the Enemy; but Sumter sent an armed party & brought him into camp—he was detained some time a prisoner in camp; & then declared himself on the side of the American cause, & he was set at liberty & joined Sumter, & proved ever after a good soldier & a good officer & was reinstated in his command.

At this time there were still some of our friends coming in & joined camp, & General Sumter was all this time very busy both in collecting his friends gathering thereby all possible intelligence of the State & standing of the Enemy who at this time had over-run South Carolina & Georgia, & also trying to gain assistance from the head officers of South Carolina,[473] which object in some degree he obtained. He then was acting in concert with Genl. Marion, who did all he could with his band of veterans in the lower part of the State to disturb & annoy the Enemy in that quarter—while he, General Sumter, was in this situation doing all he could to annoy this strong & intrepid foe the British approaching in all their great, grand & martial appearance—their captains great of flash—their soldiers lusting for blood & straining to overcome virtue. The faithless & treacherous Tories flocking to the British daily, Killing the rebels as they called the friends of America—burning, plundering & distressing women & children. The State being thus over-run, now nothing but military law or the oppressive deeds of rapine & destruction, but at this time the head of innocence droops its head & hand—it must arise in triumph.

[472] Edward Lacey (1742-1813) was a South Carolina militia officer under the command of Thomas Sumter. M. A. Moore, Sr., *Life of General Edward Lacey* (Greenville, SC: A Press, Inc., 1981, reprint from 1859 edition).

[473] After the fall of Charleston, Governor John Rutledge was forced to flee the state. He took refuge in Hillsborough, NC, where he exercised the almost dictatorial powers granted him by the state legislature in Charleston immediately before its fall. Rutledge was vested by the legislature with the power to conduct all legislative and executive business for the state, excluding only the power to impose the death penalty in enforce of his decrees.

Appendix 18

Petition by Williams' heirs for his services during the Revolutionary War and Actions of South Carolina Legislative Committees

The State of South Carolina

To the Honorable the Speaker and other Members of the House of Representatives of this State

The petition of Col. James Williams of the Newberry Dist. For himself and the other heirs of Col. James Williams Decd.

Showeth:

That his father James Williams in the year 1776 was elected Colonel and served in the Cherokee expedition, that from that time untill his death at the Battle of Kings Mountain he continued in the active service of the state. That he was in the Battle of Stono, at the siege of Savannah, in the battles of Musgrove's Mill, and that of Kings Mountain in which he was shott in one of the advancing parties ascending the mountain and fell near to Col. Ferguson.

That for the whole of his services he never rec'd any compensation (so far as your petitioner is informed).

That your Petitioner for himself and the other heirs of Col. James Williams, is desirous that these facts should be inquired into and if found to be true that then that such compensation may be rendered as the state in its wisdom may think proper.

Wherefore your Petitioner prays that this claim may be investigated and that payment for the same may be made to your Petitioner and the other heirs of Col. James Williams Dec'd.

And your Petitioner will pray.

S/ James Williams

I Hugh Oneall [*sic*] do hereby certify that I knew Col. James Williams, that I recollect distinctly his service as Colonel in the Cherokee expedition in 1776, that from that time to his death at Kings Mountain he was constantly engaged as a Colonel in the service of this State, that he commanded the troops who went from the section of country in which I was raised to the Battle of Stono, the siege of Savannah, the battles of Musgroves Mills and of Kings Mountain.

Novr. 3rd 1829

S/ Hugh O'Neill

Robert Stark Esq., Col. Samuel Hammond & Thomas Taylor are referred to by the Petitioner for the proof of Col. James Williams Revolutionary Services.

Resolved—that the Heirs of Col. James Williams who was killed at the Battle of Kings Mountain have leave to take the examination in writing of Col. Thomas Taylor, Robert Stark, Esq., Col. Samuel Hammond and Hugh Oneal aged & infirm persons to be read in evidence before this House or its committee in any future investigation of their claims against the State and that Col. James [looks like "Grady"] Col. Wm Preston and Col John G. Brown or either of them be appointed commissioners to take said examinations

S/ W Caldwell

In the House of Representatives

Resolution appointing Commissioners to take the examination of certain witnesses. Dec. 18, 1829

Resolved that the House do agree to the Resolution—to Senate for consideration

By action of the House.

S/ R. Anderson, CHR Senate Dec. 18, 1829

The Joint Committee of both branches of this Legislature to whom was referred the examination of the Claims of Col. James Williams for Revolutionary services [illegible] that they have considered the same and beg leave to recommend that a joint committee be appointed from both branches of the Legislature to examine into the details on which the Claims have been predicated and to [illegible] the [illegible] of their investigations at the next Session of this Legislature.

S/ Richard Gillaming [?]
Acting Chairman of the Joint
Committee

No. 33 Treasury Office
(Duplicate)
Columbia 29 May 1833
Received of Tandy Walker, Treasurer of the Upper Division
Four Thousand Dollars on account of Claims for the Revolutionary Services of Col. James Williams, appropriated at December Session 1832 for James Williams and others heirs of said Col. James Williams.

$4,000   S/ Abra. P. Pool

(Transcribed from the original by the author. SC Archives, Columbia, SC: Series Number: S108092; Reel: 0158; Frame: 00389)

Appendix 19

A Concurrent Resolution passed by the South Carolina Senate and concurred in by the House

S. 269
Introduced by Senator Virden

A CONCURRENT RESOLUTION

TO REQUEST THE GOVERNOR BY PROCLAMATION TO CONFIRM THE RANK OF BRIGADIER GENERAL

JAMES WILLIAMS BESTOWED UPON HIM BY ACT OF THE SOUTH CAROLINA PROVINCIAL CONGRESS DURING THE AMERICAN REVOLUTION AND TO REQUEST THE DEPARTMENT OF TRANSPORTATION TO NAME THE LITTLE RIVER BRIDGE ON SOUTH CAROLINA HIGHWAY 560 IN LAURENS COUNTY AS THE "JAMES WILLIAMS MEMORIAL BRIDGE" TO HONOR THIS REVOLUTIONARY WAR HERO.

Whereas, there is not and has not been a South Carolina state monument to Laurens County's Brigadier General James Williams; and

Whereas, his family cemetery and his plantation known as "Mount Pleasant" are located at the southwest corner of the Little River Bridge on South Carolina Highway 560 in Laurens County. This sizeable parcel was also his home and the site of two Revolutionary battles, the Battles of Fort Williams and Mud Lick Creek; and

Whereas, General Williams was a Revolutionary War hero who gave his life to ensure the liberty and freedom of the United States of America. He led the victorious forces from North Carolina, South Carolina, and Georgia at the Battle of Musgrove Mill; and

Whereas, he was promoted by act of the South Carolina Provincial Congress, which was signed by Governor Rutledge and South Carolina Chief Justice Drayton, to the rank of Brigadier General but died of battle wounds just hours before the orders and commission arrived. Some observers maintain that the promotion was not official because he never received it; and

Whereas, during the course of the American Revolution, he gave to South Carolina:

(1) the equipment and supplies for a regiment of the Little River Mounted Rifles Regiment, which he also commanded until his heroic death; and

(2) two month's pay for his regiment, food supplies, generous amounts of shot and powder, plus one hundred fifty gallons of whiskey for the foragers to use to pay for hams, chickens, and fodder from local farmers; and

(3) his life, having been mortally wounded leading the local men up the seemingly impossible sides of King's Mountain, in the movement that ultimately won the battle for both Carolinas and indeed for all thirteen of the original colonies; and

Whereas, after his death, local Tories, before departing for the Caribbean, also killed his two older sons, ages fourteen and seventeen, and burned his plantation house, leaving his wife and small children to live in the barns and cribs of the farmyard; and

Whereas, this brave and courageous hero of the American Revolution deserves to be honored by his beloved South Carolina in order to recognize and remember his contributions to and sacrifices for his State and country. **Now, therefore,**

Be it resolved by the Senate, the House of Representatives concurring:

That the members of the General Assembly, by this resolution, request the Governor by proclamation to confirm the rank of Brigadier General James Williams bestowed upon him by act of the South Carolina Provincial Congress during the American Revolution.

Be it further resolved that the members of the General Assembly further request the Department of Transportation to name the Little River Bridge on South Carolina Highway 560 in Laurens County as the "James Williams Memorial Bridge" in his honor and bestow appropriate markers to reflect this name.

Be it further resolved that the Department of Transportation is requested to plan and conduct an appropriate ceremony to celebrate the naming of this bridge for Brigadier General Williams and to coordinate the ceremony with members of the Henry Laurens Chapter of the Daughters of the American Revolution, the Clinton High School JROTC, and local clergy and civic leaders.

Be it further resolved that a copy of this resolution be forwarded to the South Carolina Department of Transportation and Governor Mark Sanford._____

In the Senate
Columbia, South Carolina
February 24, 2005
I hereby certify that the foregoing is a true and correct
copy of a resolution passed by the Senate and concurred in
by the House.
[State Official Seal]
S/ Jeffrey S. Gossett
Clerk of the Senate

Appendix 20

Account of re-burial of Col. Williams' body

THE SPARTANBURG HERALD, SPARTANBURG, S.C.,
SUNDAY MORNING, AUGUST 26, 1928

Williams' Grave Recalls Mysterious Death in the Battle of
Kings Mountain
Some Believe American and Ferguson Killed in Pistol
Duel as the Battle Ended
Grave Located and Marked by the Late Rev. J. C. Bailey:
BONES MOVED TO GAFFNEY

By Jonathan C. Bailey
Next to his profound love for the searching of the Holy
Scriptures, nothing gave my father, the late Rev. J. D. Bailey,
more pleasure and delight than the seeking out and the
recording of some bit of local history or tradition.

In the foreword to his book, "Some Heroes
of the American Revolution," he says, "But few, if any sections
in the Southland are richer in Revolutionary history than that
of upper South Carolina. Yonder in the extreme northern
part of the State stands Kings Mountain like a mighty sentinel,
rearing its head heavenward, forming the pivot on which the
tide turned in favor of the liberty of the American Colonies. A
few miles to the westward, near the base of Thicketty Mountain,
lies the elevated plain of The Cowpens, where the "Bloody" and

seemingly unconquerable Tarleton met his Waterloo. These two mighty victories, won in the darkest days of the war, did more to hearten the lovers of freedom and hasten the culmination of full liberty than any other. Then, there was Musgrove Mill, Blackstock's, Fishdam, Thicketty Fort, Prince's Fort, First and Second Cedar Spring, to say nothing of the many daring and heroic achievements of a lesser nature. There are but few square acres together in all our territory that did not at some time drink the blood of friend or foe and witnessed more or less suffering endured by the heroes and heroines of Independence.

"From early life, having the most profound admiration and veneration for those who participated in the mighty struggle for independence, during the past forty years as we have itinerated among the Baptist churches in Union, Spartanburg and Cherokee counties, we have left no stone unturned, as far as we were able, to secure any and everything bearing on local Revolutionary history."

At King's Mountain.

To father, one of the outstanding leaders of the American Revolution in the South was Colonel James Williams, who fell mortally wounded at King's Mountain on October 7, 1780. Feeling that the daring achievements of this noble Patriot had been too much neglected by the early writers, he has devoted much space in his historical works to eulogize the memory of the hero of King's Mountain. I am giving here various accounts of Colonel Williams' fall as father has gathered them from different writers, and father's personal account of his relocating the grave of the hero.

The Fall of Colonel Williams

After the battle had raged for some 40 or 50 minutes, Ferguson, the British leader, realizing that all was lost, attempted to break through the Whig lines and escape; but in so doing he was shot from his horse, and a few minutes later his whole force surrendered.

"But," says Draper, "an occurrence now transpired that for a few moments changed the whole scene in that quarter and threatened for a brief period the most traffic consequences. It is known as a British account relates it, that a small party of the Loyal militia, returning from foraging, unacquainted with the surrender, happened to fire on the Rebels. The prisoners were threatened with death if the firing should be repeated. Whether it was the volley from this party, who probably scampered off, or whether from some Tories in the general huddle, exasperated, perhaps, that proper respect was not instantly paid to their flag, now fired upon and mortally wounded Colonel Williams, who was riding back towards the British encampment, and, wheeling back, said to William Moore, one of Campbell's men: 'I'm a gone man.' Colonel Campbell was close at hand when this unhappy event transpired; and doubtless reasoned that if the fatal firing proceeded from an outside party, it was the precursor of Tarleton's expected relief: if from the surrendered Tories, at least some considerable portion were inclined to spring a fresh on the Whigs, shoot down their leaders, and make a bold attempt to escape when the Patriots were measurably off their guard, and least prepared for it; and acting on the spur of the moment, he [resorted] to strong military tactics to quell the intended mutiny by immediately ordering the men near [him]—those of Williams' and Brandon's command—to fire upon the enemy. The order was quickly obeyed by the soldiers who had been so treacherously deprived of their intrepid leader; 'and,' said Lieut. Joseph Hughes, one of Brandon's party, 'we killed near a hundred of them.' But the probabilities are that those who fired and those who suffered from it were not so very numerous. It was, however, a sad affair; and in the confusion of the moment its origin and its immediate effects were probably little understood by either party; and doubtless Colonel Campbell himself deeply regretted the order that he had given to fire upon an unresisting foe."

According to the above, Colonel Williams was not wounded until the enemy had surrendered and the firing ceased; but during an unexpected outbreak, while the surrounding hills and valleys were yet filled with reverberations of the shouts of victory. The whole scene changed in a moment, the twinkling of an eye. The expressions of joy and gladness instantly gave way to the sounds of rifle volleys as they were again brought to bear on the Tories by the maddened followers of Colonel Williams.

Joseph Hughes, an officer of Williams' corps, in his pension application, says, "Was at King's Mountain where General Williams was mortally wounded after the British had raised their flag to surrender, by some Tories." Dr. John Welchel, another of Williams' command, a man of such intelligence and most probable an eye-witness, says: "Colonel Williams received his fatal shot after the enemy had hoisted a flag to surrender."

Major Young's Account

Major Thomas Young, one of Brandon's men, gives this graphic account: "On the top of the mountain, in the thickest of the fight, I saw Colonel Williams fall, and a braver man never died upon the field of battle. I had seen him but once before on that day: it was in the beginning of the action as he charged by me at full speed around the mountain. Toward the summit, a ball struck his horse's under jaw. Colonel Williams threw the reins over the animal's neck, sprang to the ground an dashed onward. The moment I heard the cry that Colonel Williams was shot, I ran to his assistance—for I loved him as a brother—he had been ever so kind to me, almost always carrying a cake in his pocket for me and his little son, Joseph. They carried him into a tent and sprinkled some water in his face. As he revived his first words were: 'For God's sake, boys, don't give up the hill!' I remember it as well as if it had occurred yesterday. I left him in the arms of his son, Daniel, and returned to the field to avenge his fall."

Williams and Ferguson

On the numerous accounts given of Colonel Williams' fall, probably the most romantic of all is that of Sims in his History of South Carolina: "Tradition reports that Williams and Ferguson perished by each other's hands; that after

Ferguson had fallen by the pistol of Williams, and lay wounded on the ground, the latter approached and offered him mercy; and that his answer was a fatal bullet from the dying man."

A similar statement was made by Col. Samuel Hammond in a Private letter written to a friend in 1823: "Sir, I feel much mortified at the manner in which Colonel Williams and his family have been neglected by all the writers, as well as those who ought to have written on the subject of the celebrated and fortunate Battle of King's Mountain. The patriotic officer died in personal combat with the British commanding officer: both fell at the same moment, and their bones are bleaching together on the brow of that hill."

The Battle Ends

The battle ended about 4 o'clock, and as soon as possible thereafter such attention was given to the wounded as circumstances would permit. The Americans possessed neither baggage nor camp equipage. Colonel Williams was taken into a British tent and it appears that he received some attention from Doctor Johnson, of Ferguson's corps, as there was not a single surgeon in the Whig ranks. There was none killed in Williams' command except himself and one unknown man.

On the March

The next morning, which was Sunday, October 8, the sun shone brightly for the first time in several days. About 10 o'clock the army took up its line of march, and though encumbered by a large number of prisoners, they were strongly guarded; and, at the same time, the tenderest possible care was bestowed upon the wounded. None received more careful attention than the heroic Colonel Williams; for, notwithstanding several reports to the contrary, he did not die on the battle hill. The army moved in the direction of what was then called Beer's Ferry on Broad river—this ferry was near the present Dravo power dam—and for several miles traveled over the same road upon which they had journeyed the day before. Early in the afternoon they again reached Jacob Randall's place, where they had made a brief halt on the previous Friday evening. At this place on the roadside stood a large chestnut tree with wide, spreading branches, which produced a most inviting shade. Reaching that spot the little party having Colonel Williams in charge, seeing that he was rapidly sinking, halted under this tree, where he quietly breathed his last. As a writer has expressed it, "The spirit of the gallant Williams quit forever the fields of carnage and blood below for realms of peace and life above." Such was the earthly end of this brave, unflinching and "martyr hero" of the Revolution.

Spot Marked

More than twenty-five years ago, the late Ira Hardin, of Blacksburg, informed father that this tree stood near the edge of his father's yard; and, though it was dead at that time, when a boy he had often shot birds which perched upon it. The tree has long since disappeared, but Mr. Hardin kindly located the spot, and upon father's request, Mr. F. H. Dover, who at that time owned the place, set up a large rough stone, with these words chiseled upon it, "Where Colonel Williams Died."

Williams' Death Mourned

The death of Colonel Williams was a matter of sincere regret to the whole army. His friends resolved at first to convey the body to his home at Mt. Pleasant, in Laurens district; so carrying his remains with them, the army resumed its march towards Beer's Ferry. Passing over, or near the site of the present town of Blacksburg, they proceeded until they came to—according to Benjamin Sharp—"a large deserted Tory plantation," about twelve miles from the battleground. Here they found a good camping ground with plenty of dry rails and poles for making fires and luckily a sweet potato patch sufficiently large to supply the whole army. "This," says Sharp, "was most fortunate for not one in fifty of us had tasted food for the last two days and nights."

Body Interred

The next morning for want of suitable conveyance and not thinking it wise to go in the direction of Colonel Williams' home, it was decided to bury his remains without further delay. "They were," says Draper, "accordingly interred with the honors of war between the camp and the river, a little above the mouth of Buffalo creek—on what was long known as the Fondren, then the old Carruth place, now belonging to Capt. J. B. Mintz. After having performed this touching service, and then firing a parting volley over the newly-made grave of one of the noted heroes of the War of Independence, the army late in the day renewed the line of march apparently up Broad River."

Grave Neglected

In a foot-note, Draper further says, "Col. John R. Logan adds that he learned from Captain Mintz that a tradition had been handed down that Colonel Williams was buried in that neighborhood, and no little pains had been taken to identify the grave by various people, and even by some of Colonel Williams' descendants; but without success. At length Captain Mintz employed some men to shrub off a field, long overgrown, and requested them to watch for the long forgotten grave, and sure enough they found a grave, with a headstone and footstone composed of a different kind of rock from those abounding there, and well overgrown with grapevines. There was no inscription on the headstone, but there is no doubt that it is the grave of 'Old King's Mountain Jim.'

Letter in *Yorkville Enquirer*

The following letter, originally published in the *Yorkville Enquirer* many years ago, throws additional light on, and corroborates quite a number of the foregoing statements:

Thursday, Nov. 19, 1857

"It is well known that Colonel Williams— the hero of King's Mountain—fell mortally wounded in the moment of victory. With a vow that he would silence the whistle of Ferguson, whose shrill, clarion notes rang out above the din of battle, and brought again the wavering Red Coats to the charge, he rushed upon the foe, and fell just as the enemy was giving away—just as the shouts of the victors were going up from the 'Grand Old Mountain.' It was a fit requiem for the gallant soldier, the music which sounded so sweetly in the ear of Wolfe on the plains of Abraham. But it is not generally known that the spot of earth where sleeps the hero can be distinctly located. The tread of pilgrim feet have echoed through the [valleys] of the mountain baptized in the blood of heroes; but patriotism has never sought out, nor love and [admiration] consecrated that [hollowed] ground—the narrow house of the big hearted Williams. Two rude stones mark that sacred spot, and oral and traditional evidences have lone given it a 'local habitation and a name.'"

Further Testimony

"But the chain of testimony by which it is identified has recently been traced out, link by link, by William C. Black, Esq. From him we gather the following evidence, which he has taken the trouble to collect: 'Williams Camp, Esq., a highly respectable citizen of this district, now upwards of seventy years of age, who has resided in the immediate neighborhood for the last fifty-eight years, says that tradition, and the oldest contemporaries of the Battle of King's Mountain, have uniformly designated a grave on the plantation of Mr. John B. Mintz as the final resting place of Colonel Williams. The plantation of Mr. Mintz lies between Buffalo and Broad rivers, and was pointed out to him forty-odd years ago by Mrs. David Quinn, the daughter of Anthony Morgan, who resided within forty rods of the grave where Colonel Williams was buried. She was a full grown woman at the time. The American army, on the night after the battle, camped near her father's spring and early next morning their dead commander was interred.' This evidence accords with the well known facts that the army retreated immediately after the battle, for fear of Cornwallis; that Colonel Williams died under a chestnut tree, which we have seen often, which until recently stood near the residence of A. Hardin, Esq., and that the army, then in full retreat, did not stop to bury him, but carried him along with them.

"This statement of Mrs. Quinn was confirmed by Peter Morgan, her brother, Mr. Collins, who lived within a mile of the encampment at the time, likewise attested the same.

"Silas Randall, who recently died at the age of ninety, gave Mr. Camp the following information: He was with Colonel Williams at A. Hardin's; raised his head and gave a drink, when he immediately went to sleep—his soul passed quietly away, so that it scarcely seemed like death. Mr. Randall also asserted that Colonel Williams was carried on to the camp and buried as above stated. No man ever possessed a fairer character than the last witness, and therefore his evidence is conclusive.

Fitting Abode

"The grave itself appears to be a fitting abode for the hero of King's Mountain, it is situated on the side of a hill, in full view of the blue mountain tip, so that at the resurrection morn his eye will rest first on the scene of his glory and earthly immortality. Was it the native taste of the rude mountaineers or the directing hand of that Providence which shapes our ends—which we call chance—that selected this site and this position, ere in the haste of retreat, they left the hero alone in his glory?"

Rediscovered

I am giving here father's personal account, word by word, as recorded in his historical works, of his rediscovery of Colonel Williams' grave:

"Feeling that the grave of such a noted hero should be definitely located, if possible, this writer set about more than a quarter of a century ago to make some investigations. Accordingly, on the morning of April 25th, 1898, in company with some friends, we visited the supposed place of Colonel Williams' sepulcher. It answered Draper's description exactly. He says that on leaving the battleground, the army marched 'on the route towards Deer's Ferry on Broad River, and marching some twelve miles from the battleground, they encamped that night near the eastern bank of Broad River, and a little north of Buffalo Creek.' At this point a large hill rises toward the west, and about midway between its bottom and tip, on the eastern slope, is where the grave was found. A little higher up, running almost exactly east and west, the road to Deer's Ferry passed, signs of that road were than visible. The grave was just ninety yards to the south of that ancient highway. From that spot to the southeast, the river is about a quarter of a mile to the right, and Buffalo Creek about a half-mile directly in front— both river and creek being in plain view. We have seen that tradition also pointed to that locality as the burial place of Colonel Williams, though the exact spot was long lost sight of; that when Captain Mintz cleared a particular field, command was given that search be made, the result of which was the finding of a lone grave.

"Mr. D. D. Gaston, a son-in-law of Captain Mintz, informed the writer that he had often heard his father-in-law say that when he first came to the place an old Negro woman told him (Mr. Mintz) that Colonel Williams was buried on the him—the one where the grave was found—for she, when a girl, went with her mistress to the newly-made grave. Hence search was made in that particular place, with the results already mentioned, so history and tradition agree exactly and both point to the single grave on the hill as that of Col. James Williams—'Old King's Mountain Jim.'

"As we went up the hill from the river toward the grave, one of the party picked up a large round leaden ball, just such as have been found on the King's Mountain and Cowpens battlegrounds. We were informed that balls of that kind had been picked up there, occasionally, for thirty years previous. No doubt but that they were discharged when the parting volley was fired by the Patriots over the grave of their beloved, but fallen leader.

Bones Disinterred

"Arriving at the spot, we found a black-oak growing on, or near the grave. Captain Mintz had this tree left when the field was cleared for the purpose of marking it. Armed with axe, pick and shovel, we began the work of excavation on the south side of the tree, but without success. Beginning on the north side, we soon had reason to believe that we had struck the grave, and sure enough we had. Going down about three feet, we found a rib bone, and then the entire skeleton, which was in a fair state of preservation.

The skull was perfect from the base to the eye-sockets. All the bones removed were put back at once, except the skull, which was kept out long enough to be photographed; then it, too, was replaced. No military relic was found; but when we reached the skeleton, the dirt contained a great deal of short hair; and we believe that it was indicative of the shroud in which he was buried—a cow hide. With this vast array of acts, we have no doubt about finding the grave of, and handling the bones of James Williams—a martyr hero of the Revolution.

Moved to Gaffney

"Having located the grave of Colonel Williams beyond dispute, we set about to enlist his descendants, and any others who would, in the erection of a suitable monument to mark his grave and perpetuate his memory; but did not succeed. A few years ago the Daughters of the American Revolution, of Gaffney, had the bones disinterred, placed in an iron chest, removed to that place, and deposited in the front yard of the Gaffney Carnegie Library. A granite marker was placed over the deposit, which is surmounted by two small cannon balls."

Bibliography

Anthony Allaire, "The Diary of Lieut. Anthony Allaire of Ferguson's Corps." In Lyman C. Draper. *King's Mountain and its Heroes: History of the Battle of King's Mountain October 7th, 1780 and the Events Which Led to It.* Cincinnati: Peter G. Thomson, 1881; reprint, Johnson City, TN: The Overmountain Press, 1996. 484-515

Lawrence E. Babits. *A Devil of a Whipping: The Battle of Cowpens.* Chapel Hill: The University of North Carolina Press, 1998

Lawrence E. Babits & Joshua B. Howard. *Long, Obstinate, and Bloody: The Battle of Guilford Courthouse.* Chapel Hill: The University of North Carolina Press, 2009

J. D. Bailey. *Commanders at King Mountain.* Gaffney, SC: Ed. H. DeCamp, 1925; reprint with index added Greenville, SC: A Press, 1980

—*Some Heroes of the American Revolution.* Spartanburg, SC: Band & White, 1924; reprint Greenville, SC: Southern Historical Press, 1976

N. Louise Bailey and Elizabeth Ivey Cooper, eds. *Biographical Directory of the South Carolina House of Representatives, Volume III: 1775 - 1790*, 5 vols. Columbia: University of South Carolina Press, 1974-1992

N. Louise Bailey, Mary L. Morgan, and Carolyn R. Taylor, eds. *Biographical Directory of the South Carolina Senate 1776 - 1985.* Columbia: University of South Carolina Press, 1986

Robert Bain, Joseph M. Flora, Louis D. Rubin, eds., *Southern Writers: A Biographical Dictionary.* Baton Rouge, Louisiana State University Press, 1979

George Bancroft. *History of the United States,* 10 vols. New York: Little, Brown, 1875

Richard Barry, *Mr. Rutledge of South Carolina.* New York: Duell, Sloan and Pearce, 1942

Robert D. Bass. *Gamecock: The Life and Campaigns of General Thomas Sumter.* New York: Holt, Rinehart and Winston, 1961

—*Ninety Six: The Struggle for the South Carolina Backcountry.* Lexington, SC: The Sandlapper Store, Inc., 1978

–*Swamp Fox: The Life and Campaigns of General Francis Marion.* Orangeburg, SC: Sandlapper Publishing Co., Inc., 1959

Mark M. Boatner, III. *Encyclopedia of the American Revolution.* Mechanicsburg, PA: Stackpole Books, 3rd ed., 1994

John Buchanan. *The Road to Guilford Courthouse: The American Revolution in the Carolinas.* New York: John Wiley & Sons, Inc., 1995

James Leland Bolt and Margaret Eltinge Bolt. *Family Cemeteries Laurens County, S.C.,* 2 vols. Greenville, SC: A Press, 1983

Lewis Shore Brumfield. *The Williamses and The Hendersons¬ Descendants of John "The Wealthy Welshman" Williams.* Yadkinville, NC: N. p., 1991

Lindley S. Butler, ed. *The Narrative of Col. David Fanning.* Davidson, NC: Briarpatch Press, 1981

Marvin L. Cann. "Prelude to War: The First Battle of Ninety Six: November 19-21, 1775." *South Carolina Historical Magazine,* 76 (1975)

Jimmy Carter. *The Hornet's Nest: A Novel of the Revolutionary War.* New York: Simon & Schuster, 2003

David R. Chesnutt, *et al.,* eds. *The Papers of Henry Laurens,* 15 vols. Columbia: University of South Carolina Press, 1968-1999

Walter Clark, ed. *The State Records of North Carolina, Vol. XV: 1780 - 1781.* Goldsboro, NC: Nash Brothers Book and Job Printers, 1898

–*The State Records of North Carolina, Vol. XXI-1788 - 1790.* Goldsboro, NC: Nash Brothers Book and Job Printers, 1903

–*The State Records of North Carolina Vol. XVI: 1782-1783.* New York: AMS Press, 1968-1972

Dennis M. Conrad, ed. *The Papers of General Nathanael Greene, Volume VIII 30 March-10 July 1781.* Chapel Hill: The University of North Carolina Press, 1995

David L. Corbett. *The Formation of The North Carolina Counties 1663-1943.* Raleigh: State Department of Archives and History, 1950

Alexander Craighead, *Renewal of the Covenants, National and Solemn League; A Confession of Sins; An Engagement to Duties;*

and a Testimony; as They Were Carried on at Middle Octorara in Pennsylvania, November 11, 1743, 1748 [a collection of sermons] Philadelphia: 2nd ed., 1748, 1743: Cerlox Bound Photocopy Series. Edmonton, AB, Canada: Still Waters Revival Books, N. D.

David Colin Crass, Steven D. Smith, Martha A. Zierden, and Richard D. Brooks, eds. *The Southern Colonial Backcountry: Interdisciplinary Perspectives on Frontier Communities.* Knoxville: The University of Tennessee Press, 1998

Arnold A. Dallimore, *George Whitefield: The Life and Times of the Great Evangelist of the 18th Century Revival.* 2 vols. Edinburgh: The Banner of Truth Trust, 1970

Lyman C. Draper. *King's Mountain and its Heroes: History of the Battle of King's Mountain October 7th, 1780, and the Events Which Led to It.* Cincinnati: Peter G. Thomson, 1881; reprint, Johnson City, TN: The Overmountain Press, 1996

–Lyman C. Draper Manuscript Collection, State Historical Society of Wisconsin, Microfilm

Walter Bellingrath Edgar. *Partisans & Redcoats: The Southern Conflict That Turned the Tide of the American Revolution.* New York: William Morrow, 2001

–*The Libraries of Colonial South Carolina*, PhD dissertation, 1969, University of South Carolina

Elizabeth F. Ellet, *The Women of the American Revolution.* 3 vols. New York: Charles Scribner's Sons, 1853-1854

Jean Martin Flynn. *The Militia in Antebellum South Carolina Society.* Spartanburg, SC: The Reprint Company, 1991

William Henry Foote. *Sketches of North Carolina: Historical and Biographical, Illustrative of the Principles of a Portion of Her Early Settlers.* New York: Robert Carter, 1846

H. Ronald Freeman. *Savannah Under Siege.* Savannah: Freeport Publishing, 2002

R. W. Gibbes, ed. *Documentary History of the American Revolution: Consisting of Letters and Papers Relating to the Contest for Liberty, Chiefly in South Carolina, From Originals in the Possession of the Editor, and Other Sources.* 2 vols. New York: D. Appleton & Co., 1857; reprint, Spartanburg, SC: The Reprint Company, 1972

M. M. Gilchrist. *Patrick Ferguson: "A Man of Some Genius."* Edinburgh: National Museums of Scotland, 2002

Joseph C. M. Goldsmith. *The Official Comprehensive Cambridge Compilation: Including A Colony by Colony Comparison of Revolutionary Battles and All of South Carolina's known "Official" Battles, and Major Events of the American Revolution, with modern Locations.* Third Edition. N.P.: Cambridge Chapter SC Society of the Sons of the American Revolution, 2007

Terry Golway, *Washington's General: Nathanael Greene and the Triumph of the American Revolution.* New York: Henry Holt and Company, 2005

Christopher Gould. "The South Carolina and Continental Associations: Prelude to Revolution." *South Carolina Historical Magazine,* 87 (1986)

William A. Graham, *The Battle of Ramsour's Mill.* Raleigh, NC: E. M. Uzzell & Co., 1904

William T. Graves. *James Williams: An American Patriot in the Carolina Backcountry.* San Jose: Writers Club Press, 2002

– *"Pension Application of Col. Samuel Hammond,"* Transcribed and Annotated, *Southern Campaign of the American Revolution,* Vol. 2, No. 1, (January 2005)

– *"Reverend Oliver Hart's Diary of a Journey to the Backcountry,"* Transcribed and Annotated, *Southern Campaign of the American Revolution,* Vol. 2, No. 4, (April 2005)

– *"Journal of the 1776 Cherokee Indian Campaign in South Carolina, Georgia and North Carolina,"* Transcribed and Annotated, *Southern Campaign of the American Revolution,* Vol. 2, No. 10, (October 2005)

– *"What Did McJunkin Really Saye,"* *Southern Campaign of the American Revolution,* Vol. 2, No. 11, (November 2005)

Anne King Gregorie. *Thomas Sumter.* Columbia, S.C.: The R. L. Bryan Company, 1931

Francis Vinton Greene, *Nathanael Greene.* New York: The Confucian Press, Inc., 1981

Zae Hargett Gwynn, comp. *Estate Abstracts of The Wills and Records of Granville County, NC 1746-1808.* Rocky Mount, NC: Joseph W. Watson, 1973

Bibliography

John Hairr, *Colonel David Fanning: The Adventures of a Carolina Loyalist.* Erwin, NC: Averasboro Press, 2000

Stephen E. Haller, *William Washington: Cavalryman of the Revolution.* Bowie, MD: Heritage Books, Inc., 2001

James Haw. *John & Edward Rutledge of South Carolina.* Athens, GA: The University of Georgia Press, 1997

William E. Hemphill, ed. *The State Records of South Carolina: Extracts from the Journals of the Provincial Congresses of South Carolina, 1775-1776.* Columbia: South Carolina Archives Department, 1960

–*The State Records of South Carolina: Extracts from the Journals of the Provincial Congresses of South Carolina, 1776-1780.* Columbia: South Carolina Archives Department, 1960

William Hill. *Col. William Hill's Memoirs of the Revolution.* Columbia: The Historical Commission of South Carolina, 1921, 2nd printing, 1958, ed. A. S. Salley, Jr.

Ronald Hoffman, Thad W. Tate and Peter J. Albert, eds. *An Uncivil War: The Southern Backcountry During the American Revolution.* Charlottesville, VA: United States Capitol Historical Society by The University Press of Virginia, 1985

Brent H. Holcomb, abstractor. *South Carolina Deed Abstracts 1773-1778.* Columbia, SC: CMAR, 1993

Wes Hope. *The Spartanburg Area in the American Revolution.* Spartanburg, SC: Altman Printing Company, Inc., 2003, 2nd Edition

George Howe. *History of the Presbyterian Church in South Carolina,* 2 vols. Columbia, SC: Duffie & Chapman, 1870

George Lloyd Johnson, Jr. *The Frontier in the Colonial South: South Carolina Backcountry, 1736-1800.* Westport, CN, Greenwood Press, 1997

Joseph Johnson. *Traditions and Reminiscences Chiefly of the American Revolution in the South: Including Biographical Sketches, Incidents and Anecdotes.* Charleston, SC: Walker & James, 1851

William Johnson, *The Life and Correspondence of Nathanael Greene.* 2 vols. Charleston, SC: A. E. Miller, 1822, reprinted New York: De Capo Press 1973

E. Alfred Jones, ed. *"The Journal of Alexander Chesney, a South Carolina Loyalist in the Revolution and After,"* The Ohio State University Bulletin, Vol. XXVI, No.4, (October 30, 1921)

Lewis Pinckney Jones, *The South Carolina Civil War of 1775.* Lexington, SC: The Sandlapper Store, Inc., 1975

S. Roger Keller. *Isaac Shelby: A Driving Force in America's Struggle for Independence.* Shippensburg, PA: Burd Street Press, 2000

Cynthia A. Kierner, *Southern Women in Revolution, 1776-1800: Personal and Political Narratives.* Columbia, S.C.: The University of South Carolina Press, 1998

Thomas Kirkland and Robert M. Kennedy. *Historic Camden, Colonial and Revolutionary, Vol. 1.* Columbia, SC: The State Company, 1905; reprint Kershaw County Historical Society, 1994

Rachel N. Klein. *Unification of a Slave State: The Rise of the Planter Class in the South Carolina Backcountry, 1760-1808.* Chapel Hill: The University of North Carolina Press, 1990

Keith Krawczynski, *William Henry Drayton: South Carolina Revolutionary Patriot.* Baton Rouge: Louisiana State University Press, 2001

Robert Stansbury Lambert. *South Carolina Loyalists in the American Revolution.* Columbia: University of South Carolina Press, 1987

J. B. O. Landrum. *History of Spartanburg County.* Spartanburg, SC: The Spartanburg Journal, 1954, reprint edition

Robert Lathan. H*istorical Sketches of the Revolutionary War in the Upcountry of South Carolina,* Robert Jerald L. West, transcriber, from "The Yorkville Enquirer." N.P.: Broad River Basin Historical Society, 1998

Alexander A. Lawrence. *Storm Over Savannah.* Savannah: Tara Press, 1979

Scott Liell. *46 Pages: Thomas Paine, Common Sense, and the Turning Point to Independence.* Philadelphia, PA: Running Press, 2003

Roderick Mackenzie, *Strictures on Lt. Col. Banastre Tarleton's History*. London: R. Faulder, 1787

David J. McCord, ed. *The Statutes at Large of South Carolina: Edited, Under Authority of the Legislature*, 9th Vol. Columbia, SC: A. S. Johnston, 1841

Robert L. Meriwether. *The Expansion of South Carolina: 1729-1765*. Kingsport, TN: Southern Publishers, Inc., 1940

H. Roy Merrens, ed. *The Colonial South Carolina Scene: Contemporary Views, 1697-1770*. Columbia, SC: University of South Carolina Press, 1977

[Robert Mills]. *Mills' Atlas: Atlas of the State of South Carolina: 1825*. Greenville, SC: 1825; reprint: Southern Historical Press, Inc., 1980

M. A. Moore, Sr. *Life of General Edward Lacey*. Spartanburg, SC: Douglass, Evins, 1859; reprint, Greenville, SC: A Press, 1981

Bobby Gilmer Moss. *Journal of Capt. Alexander Chesney: Adjutant to Maj. Patrick Ferguson*. Blacksburg, SC: Scotia-Hibernia Press, 2002

—*Roster of the Loyalists in the Battle of Kings Mountain*. Blacksburg, SC: Scotia-Hibernia Press, 1998

—*The Loyalists in the Siege of Fort Ninety Six*. Blacksburg, SC: Scotia-Hibernia Press, 1999

—*Roster of South Carolina Patriots in the American Revolution*. Baltimore: Genealogical Publishing Co., Inc., 1983

—*The Patriots at King's Mountain*. Blacksburg, SC: Scotia-Hibernia Press, 1990

—*Uzal Johnson, Loyalist Surgeon: A Revolutionary War Diary*. Blacksburg, SC: Scotia-Hibernia Press, 2000

—and Michael C. Scoggins. *African-American Patriots in the Southern Campaign of the American Revolution*. Blacksburg, SC: Scotia-Hibernia Press, 2004

Jesse Hogan Motes III and Margaret Peckham Motes. *Laurens and Newberry Counties South Carolina: Saluda and Little River Settlements 1749-1775: Neighborhood Maps, and Abstracts of Colonial Surveys and Memorials of Land Titles Including a Case Study Jonathan Mote 1727-1763 Migration to Little River*. Greenville, SC: Southern Historical Press, 1994

William Moultrie. *Memoirs of the American Revolution, so Far as it Related to the States of North and South Carolina, and Georgia*, 2 vols. New York: David Longworth, 1802

Paul David Nelson, *Francis Rawdon-Hastings, Marquess of Hastings: Soldier, Peer of the Realm, Governor-General of India*. Hamilton, NY: Fairleigh Dickinson University Press, 2005

Thomas McAdory Owen. *History and Genealogies of Old Granville County, North Carolina 1746-1800*. Greenville, SC: Southern Historical Press, 1993

Patrick O'Kelley. *Nothing but Blood and Slaughter: The Revolutionary War in the Carolinas, Volume One: 1771-1779*. Lillington, NC: Blue House Tavern Press, Booklocker.com, Inc., 2004

–*Nothing but Blood and Slaughter: The Revolutionary War in the Carolinas, Volume Two: 1780*. Lillington, NC: Blue House Tavern Press, Booklocker.com, Inc., 2004

–*Nothing but Blood and Slaughter: The Revolutionary War in the Carolinas, Volume Three: 1781*. Lillington, NC: Blue House Tavern Press, Booklocker.com, Inc., 2005

–*Nothing but Blood and Slaughter: The Revolutionary War in the Carolinas, Volume Four: 1782*. Lillington, NC: Blue House Tavern Press, Booklocker.com, Inc., 2005

John Belton O'Neall. *The Annuals of Newberry, Historical, Biographical and Anecdotal*. Charleston, SC: S. G. Courtenay & Co., 1859

–"Random Recollections of Revolutionary Characters and Incidents;" *Southern Journal and Magazine of Arts*, Vol. 4, No.1, (July 1838), 40-45

John S. Pancake. *This Destructive War: The British Campaign in the Carolinas, 1780-1782*. Tuscaloosa: The University of Alabama Press, 1985; reprinted Fire Ant Books, 2003

John C. Parker, Jr., *Parker's Guide to the Revolutionary War in South Carolina: Battles, Skirmishes and Murders*. Patrick, SC: Hem Branch Publishing Company, 2009

Jim Piecuch. *Three People One King: Loyalists, Indians and Slaves in the Revolutionary South, 1775-1782*. Columbia: University of South Carolina Press, 2008

—Blood Be Upon Your Head: Tarleton and the Myth of Buford's Massacre: The Battle of the Waxhaws May 29, 1780. Lugoff, SC: Southern Campaigns of the American Revolution Press, 2010

Jim Piecuch and John Beakes. *"Cool Deliberate Courage" John Eager Howard in The American Revolution.* Mount Pleasant, SC: Nautical & Aviation Publishing Company of America, 2009

William S. Powell, ed. *Dictionary of North Carolina Biography,* 6 vols. Chapel Hill: The University of North Carolina Press, 1979-1996

David Ramsay. *History of the Revolution of South Carolina from a British Province to an Independent State,* 2 vols. Trenton, NJ: Isaac Collins, 1785

George H. Reese, compiler. *The Cornwallis Papers: Abstracts of Americana.* Charlottesville, VA: The University Press of Virginia for the Virginia Independence Bicentennial Commission, 1970

Charles D. Rodenbough. *Governor Alexander Martin: Biography of a North Carolina Revolutionary War Statesman.* Jefferson, NC: McFarland & Company, Inc., 2004

Ian Saberton, Arranger and Editor, *The Cornwallis Papers: the Campaigns of 1780 and 1781 in the Southern Theater of the American Revolutionary War* 6 vols. Uckfield, East Sussex, England: The Naval & Military Press Ltd., 2010

Lorenzo Sabine, *Biographical Sketches of Loyalists of the American Revolution, with an Historical Essay* 2 vols. Boston: Little, Brown and Company, 1864

James Hodge Saye. *Memoirs of Major Joseph McJunkin: Revolutionary Patriot.* Spartanburg, SC: A Press, 1981

Michael C. Scoggins. *The Day it Rained Militia: Huck's Defeat and the Revolution in the South Carolina Backcountry: May-July 1780.* Charleston, SC: History Press, 2005

Martha Condray Searcy. *The Georgia-Florida Contest in the American Revolution, 1776-1778.* Tuscaloosa: University of Alabama Press, 1985

William Thomas Sherman. *Calendar and Record of the Revolutionary War in the South: 1780-1781,* (n.p., Sixth Edition, 2009), http://www.angelfire.com/d20/htfh (viewed 9/12/12)

345

C. Gregg Singer, *Theological Interpretation of American History.* Philadelphia, PA: The Presbyterian and Reformed Publishing Co., 1981

M. Eugene Sirmans. *Colonial South Carolina: A Political History: 1663-1763.* Chapel Hill: The University of North Carolina Press for the Institute of Early American History and Culture at Williamsburg, Virginia, 1966

Gordon Burns Smith. *Morningstars of Liberty: The Revolutionary War in Georgia 1775-1783.* Milledgeville, GA: Boyd Publishing, 2006

Michael E. Stauffer. *South Carolina's Antebellum Militia.* Columbia: South Carolina Department of Archives & History, 1991

Banastre Tarleton. *A History of the Campaigns of 1780-1781 in the Southern America.* London: T. Cadell, 1787; reprint, North Stratford, NH: Ayer Company Publishers, 1999

Theodore Thayer, *Nathanael Greene: Strategist of the American Revolution.* New York: Twayne Publishers, 1960

The Papers of the Continental Congress, National Archives, Washington, DC, Microfilm 247, roll 174, item 154

Larry Vehorn, compiler, *Laurens County South Carolina Deed Abstracts: Books A-D: 1785-1793 (1769-1793)* Greenville, SC: Southern Historical Press, Inc., 2004

Alice Waring. *The Fighting Elder: Andrew Pickens, 1739-1817.* Columbia: University of South Carolina Press, 1962

David K. Wilson. *The Southern Strategy: Britain's Conquest of South Carolina and Georgia, 1775-1780.* Columbia: University of South Carolina Press, 2005

Charles Woodmason, (Richard Hooker, ed.), *The Carolina Backcountry on the Eve of the Revolution: The Journal and Other Writings of Charles Woodmason, Anglican Itinerant.* Chapel Hill: University of North Carolina Press, 1953

Thomas Young, "Memoir of Major Thomas Young, A Revolutionary Patriot of South Carolina." *Orion* (October 1843), also published in Joseph Johnson. *Traditions and Reminiscences Chiefly of the American Revolution in the South: Including Biographical Sketches, Incidents and Anecdotes.* Charleston, SC: Walker & James, 1851: 446-454

Index

A

Absom, James 188
Abston, John 210
Adair, Benjamin 187
Adair, Isaac 187
Adair, James 187
Adair, James Jr. 187
Adair, James Sr. 187
Adair, John 187, 210
Adair, John Sr. 187
Adair, Joseph 187
Adair, Joseph Jr. 187
Adair, Joseph Sr. 187
Adair, William 70, 183, 184, 187
Adams, John 210
Adams, John C. 210
Addison, Joseph 206
Aiken, Alexander 210
Ainsworth Dictionary 199
Ainsworth, Robert 199
Akins, George 187
Akins, John 187
Alamance County, North Carolina 10
Alexander, ____ Rev. Dr. 313
Alexander, James 210
Alexander, Joseph 210
Alexander, Travice 210
Allaire, Anthony 97, 119, 139, 227, 229
Alleghany Mountains 231, 260
Allen, David 210
Allison, Hugh 210
Allison, John xiv
Altamaha River 65, 175
Amburgay, John 210
American Revolution Association the magazine of xiv
Anderson, Bud 313
Anderson, George 202
Anderson, Jacob 187

Anderson, John 210
Anderson, R. 322
Anderson, Robert 135, 210
Anderson, William 16, 210
Angel, Lawrence 210
Anglican Church 163, 164
Anthony, Philip 210
Anticosti 174, 175
Apalachicola River 174, 175
Appendix 1 155, 174
Appendix 2 27
Appendix 3 xi, 13, 18, 71, 182
Appendix 4 18, 27, 65
Appendix 5 75, 188
Appendix 6 76
Appendix 7 viii, 27, 29, 191
Appendix 8 18, 78, 95, 96, 194
Appendix 9 195
Appendix 10 102
Appendix 11 37, 41, 146, 199
Appendix 12 86, 132, 207
Appendix 13 xix, 96, 210
Appendix 14 86, 102, 223
Appendix 15 102, 123, 224
Appendix 16 235
Appendix 17 94, 267
Appendix 18 91
Appendix 19 322
Appendix 20 325
Archbishop of Canterbury 163
Arinton, Drury 17
Armstrong, ____ Capt. at Ramsour's Mill 317
Armstrong, Matthew 210
Armstrong, William 210, 295
artesian wells on James Williams' estate 15
Arthur, William 187
Ashe, John 68, 90
Ashley River 273, 293
Askers, L. B. 280

347

Hiwassee 272, 292
Hiwassee River 272
Hodge, George 216
Hoffman, Ronald 43
Hofstalar, George 216
Hogan, David 216
Hogback Mountain 293
hogshead 34, 35
Holcomb, Brent H. 14
Holland, Charles 216
Hollingsworth, Aquilla 316
Hollingsworth, Benjamin 214
Hollingsworth's Mills 288
Hollis, John 212
Holyoake, Francis 200
Holyork's Dictionary 199
Hood, Thomas 216
Hook, Jacob Van 219
Hooker, William 210
Hope, Wes 301
Hopkins, ___ Col. 309
Horace, Watson's 201
Horn Book 203
Hornet's Nest, The
    novel by President Jimmy
    Carter 2
Horry, Daniel 25
Horse Shoe, Battle of 272
Horton, Abrah 211
Horton, Daniel 212
Horton, John 216
Houser, John 217
Houston, James 216
Houston, John 216
Houston, Samuel 214
Houstoun, John 65
Howard, John Eager 307
Howe, ___, Mr. 72
Howe, David 212
Howe, George 15
Howe, Robert 65, 66
Howerton, James 187
Huck, Christian 43, 116, 135, 240,
    241, 242, 296, 299, 318, 319
Huddleston, James 187
Huddleston, William 187
Hudgens, Ambrose 214

Hudgins, John 217
Hudson, Hall 211
Hudson's Streights 175
Hughes, Francis 212
Hughes, Joseph 94, 96, 138, 139,
    214, 279, 294, 316, 328, 329
Hughes, William 187
Hughey, George 213
Hughlett, William Thrift 217
Hughs, Peter 216
Hume, David 202
Humphreys, William 214
Hunter, Dempsey 212
Hunt, Esli 212
Hunt, Howell 216

I

indents
    filed by Williams family 30
Indians xxi, 9, 44, 51, 62, 63, 64,
    67, 155, 156, 160, 161, 178,
    179, 180, 204, 257, 265, 271,
    272, 285, 287, 288, 289, 290,
    291, 292, 301
Ingram, John 214
Inman, Shadrach 103, 104, 113,
    114, 115, 116, 228, 229, 231,
    259, 260
Innes, Alexander 103, 104, 106,
    107, 110, 111, 112, 114, 115,
    118, 197, 228, 229, 258, 259,
    300
Irby, Greaf
    Hayes Station monument 154
Irby, Joseph Jr
    Haynes Station monument 154
Irby, Joseph Sr.
    Haynes Station monument 154
Irby, William
    Hayes Station monument 154
Irvine, John 69
Irwin, Robert 298
Isbell, James 216
Isbell, Pendleton 217
Island Ford 276, 309
Island of Anticosti 174

Index

Island of Dominico 175
Island of St. John's 175
Isle Royale 175

J

Jackson, William 216
Jacob, Giles 200
Jacob's Law Dictionary 200
James, Joseph 211
Jamieson, ___ Captain 309
Jamieson's fort 293
Jefferies, John 214
Jeffers, Berry 212
Jefferson Davis Road (State Road S-30-38) 30
Jefferson, Thomas 40
Jennings, John 278
Jewell, William 213
Johnson, ___ Dr. 330
Johnson, Alexander 216
Johnson, Arthur 217
Johnson, James 212, 217
Johnson, John 188, 303
Johnson, John Moses 212
Johnson, Joseph 24, 59, 102, 108, 150, 278, 319
Johnson, Robert 187
Johnson, Samuel 41, 200, 216
Johnson, Stephen 284
Johnson, Uzal 97, 111
Johnson, William 80
Johnson's Dictionary 41, 200
Johnston, James 188, 193
Johnston, John 217
Johnston, Martin 217
Johnston, Robert 188
Johnston, William 192, 193, 217
Jolly, Benjamin 94, 96, 215, 294, 316
Jolly, Joseph 272, 294, 316
Jones, ___, Captain 72
Jones, Alfred E. 61
Jones, Benjamin 210, 215
Jones, Francis 106, 300
Jones, Freeman 217
Jones, Gabriel 217

Jones, John 188, 212, 213, 215
Jones, Joseph 213
Jones, Lewis Pinckney 50
Jones, Thomas 218
Jonston, Robin 192
Jordan, James 215
Joseph McDowell 122, 136, 226
Judd, John 216
Judd, Rowland 216
Justice, Burn's 201

K

Kanselar, John 218
Karpinski, L. C. 204
Kars, Marjoleine 158
Keele, Richard 212
Kell, Robert 215
Keller, Devault 218
Kelly, John 212
Kelso, Alexander 218
Kelso, Samuel 215
Kenedy, William 215
Kennedy, Robert 218
Kennedy, Robert M. 70
Kennedy, Thomas 217
Kennedy, William 319
Kennedy, William Sr. 215
Kentucky 86, 102, 224
Keowee 272, 292
Kerby, Christopher 216
Kerr, David 218
Kerr, James 229
Kerr, Joseph 133, 134, 135, 215
Kerr, William 114
Kershaw & Co. 288
Kershaw County, South Carolina 70
Kershaw, Joseph 21, 23, 25
Kettle Creek 68, 108
Keys, James 217
Kilgore, Charles 217
Killpatrick, Hugh 188
Kincaid, John 212
Kincannon, Andrew 218
Kincannon, George 217
King Charles I 163

361

363

Index

Made in the USA
Columbia, SC
12 July 2023

20306912R00243